THE JOSSEY-BASS READER ON TECHNOLOGY AND LEARNING

Introduction by

Roy D. Pea

JOSSEY-BASS
A Wiley Company
San Francisco

Jossey-Bass books and products are available through most bookstores. To contact Jossey-Bass directly, call (888) 378-2537, fax to (800) 605-2665, or visit our website at www.josseybass.com.

Substantial discounts on bulk quantities of Jossey-Bass books are available to corporations, professional associations, and other organizations. For details and discount information, contact the special sales department at Jossey-Bass.

Manufactured in the United States of America.

Credits are on pp. 339–341.

Library of Congress Cataloging-in-Publication Data

The Jossey-Bass reader on technology and learning.
    p.   cm. — (The Jossey-Bass education series)
Includes bibliographical references.
   ISBN 0-7879-5282-6
   1. Educational technology—United States.   2. Computer-assisted instruction—United States.   3. Education—United States—Data processing.   I. Jossey-Bass Inc.
II. Series.
   LB1028.3 .J66 2000
   371.33'4—dc21

                                               99-050968

FIRST EDITION

PB Printing 10 9 8 7 6 5 4 3 2 1

CONTENTS

Source Texts   vii

About the Authors   xi

Introduction   xv
Roy D. Pea

PART ONE
Reports and Standards

1. Summary of Findings and Recommendations from
   *Report to the President on the Use of Technology to
   Strengthen K–12 Education in the United States*   3
   *President's Committee of Advisors on Science and Technology,
   Panel on Educational Technology*
2. National Educational Technology Standards for Students   20
   International Society for Technology in Education
3. New Technology Standards for Teachers   33
   California Commission on Teacher Credentialing
4. Excerpts from *Long-Range Plan for Technology,
   1996–2010*   38
   State Board of Education, Texas
5. Challenges of Creating a Nation of Technology-
   Enabled Schools   48
   Thomas K. Glennan, Arthur Melmed
6. Internet Use by Teachers   80
   Henry Jay Becker
7. The Link to Higher Scores   112
   Jeff Archer

PART TWO
Equity, Access, and Literacy

8. The Digital Divide   127
   Don Tapscott

9. Should We Be Worried? What the Research Says
   About Gender Differences in Access, Use, Attitudes,
   and Achievement with Computers   155
   Heather Kirkpatrick, Larry Cuban

10. Girl Games and Technological Desire   168
   Cornelia Brunner, Dorothy T. Bennett, Margaret Honey

11. Rethinking How to Invest in Technology   184
   Chris Dede

12. The World's the Limit in the Virtual High School   192
   Sheldon Berman, Robert Tinker

13. Computer Technology, Science Education, and Students
   with Learning Disabilities   197
   David Kumar, Cynthia L. Wilson

14. The Computer Doesn't Embarrass Me   209
   Ted S. Hasselbring, Laura Goin, Rose Taylor,
   Brian Bottge, Patrick Daley

15. Digital Literacy   215
   Paul Gilster

PART THREE

Technology and School Change

16. Computers and Computer Cultures   229
   Seymour Papert

17. Teaching by Machine   247
   David Tyack, Larry Cuban

18. The Evolution of Instruction in
   Technology-Rich Classrooms   255
   Judith Haymore Sandholtz, Cathy Ringstaff, David C. Dwyer

19. Redefining Computer Appropriation:
   A Five-Year Study of ACOT Students   277
   Robert J. Tierney

20. Some New Gods That Fail   289
   Neil Postman

21. Computer Mini-School: Technology Builds Community   299
   Andrea R. Gooden

22. Engaging Students in a Knowledge Society   312
   Marlene Scardamalia, Carl Bereiter

23. Using Technology to Support Innovative Assessment   320
   Karen Sheingold, John Frederiksen

SOURCE TEXTS

CHAPTER ONE
President's Committee of Advisors on Science and Technology, Panel on Educational Technology. *Report to the President on the Use of Technology to Strengthen K–12 Education in the United States.* March 1997. http://www.whitehouse.gov/WH/EOP/OSTP/NSTC/PCAST/k–12ed.html

CHAPTER TWO
International Society for Technology in Education. *National Educational Technology Standards for Students.* http://cnets.iste.org

CHAPTER THREE
California Commission on Teacher Credentialing. *New Technology Standards for Teachers.* http://www.ctc.ca.gov

CHAPTER FOUR
State Board of Education, Texas. *Long-Range Plan for Technology, 1996–2010.* http://www.tea.state.tx.us

CHAPTER FIVE
Thomas K. Glennan and Arthur Melmed. *Fostering the Use of Educational Technology: Elements of a National Strategy.* Santa Monica, CA: RAND, 1996. http://www.rand.org

CHAPTER SIX
Henry Jay Becker. "Internet Use by Teachers." http://www.crito.uci.edu/TLC

CHAPTER SEVEN
Education Week, October 1998, Vol. 18, No. 5, pp. 10–19.

CHAPTER EIGHT
Don Tapscott. *Growing Up Digital: The Rise of the Net Generation.* New York: McGraw-Hill, 1998.

CHAPTER NINE
Educational Technology, July-August 1998, Vol. 38, No. 4, pp. 56–61.

CHAPTER TEN
From Barbie to Mortal Kombat: Gender and Computer. Cambridge: MIT Press, 1998.

CHAPTER ELEVEN
Educational Leadership, 1997, Vol. 55, No. 3, pp. 12–16.

CHAPTER TWELVE
*Educational Leadership,*1997, Vol. 55, No. 3, pp. 52–54.

CHAPTER THIRTEEN
Journal of Science Education and Technology, 1997, Vol. 6, No. 2, pp. 155–160.

CHAPTER FOURTEEN
Educational Leadership, 1997, Vol. 55, No. 3. pp. 30–33.

CHAPTER FIFTEEN
Paul Gilster. *Digital Literacy.* New York: John Wiley & Sons, 1997.

CHAPTER SIXTEEN
Seymour Papert. *Mindstorms: Children, Computers and Powerful Ideas.* New York: Basic Books, 1993.

CHAPTER SEVENTEEN
David Tyack and Larry Cuban. *Tinkering Toward Utopia.* Cambridge: Harvard University Press, 1995.

CHAPTER EIGHTEEN
Judith Haymore Sandholtz, Cathy Ringstaff, David C. Dwyer. *Teaching with Technology: Creating Student-Centered Classrooms.* New York: Teachers College Press, 1997.

CHAPTER NINETEEN
Charles Fisher, David C. Dwyer, and Keith Yocam, editors. *Education and Technology: Reflections on Computing in Classrooms.* San Francisco: Jossey-Bass and Apple Press, 1996.

CHAPTER TWENTY
Neil Postman. *The End of Education*. New York: Random House, 1996.

CHAPTER TWENTY-ONE
Andrea R. Gooden. *Computers in the Classroom: How Teachers and Students Are Using Technology to Transform Learning*. San Francisco: Jossey-Bass and Apple Press, 1996.

CHAPTER TWENTY-TWO
Educational Leadership, 1997, Vol. 54, No. 3, pp. 6–11.

CHAPTER TWENTY-THREE
Barbara Means, editor. *Technology and Education Reform*. San Francisco: Jossey-Bass, 1994.

ABOUT THE AUTHORS

Jeff Archer is a staff writer for *Education Week.*

Henry Jay Becker is professor of education at the University of California, Irvine.

Dorothy T. Bennett is senior project director and senior research associate at Education Development Corporation, Center for Children and Technology, New York City.

Carl Bereiter is a professor at the Center for Applied Cognitive Science, Ontario Institute for Studies in Education at the University of Toronto.

Sheldon Berman is superintendent of the Hudson Public Schools in Hudson, Massachusetts.

Brian Bottge is assistant professor, Department of Rehabilitation Psychology and Special Education, University of Wisconsin–Madison.

Cornelia Brunner is a researcher, teacher, and consultant on educational technology. She has taught courses at Bank Street College and the Media Workshop in New York City.

The California Commission on Teacher Credentialing, and a list of its commissioners, can be found at [http://www.ctc.ca.gov/].

Larry Cuban is professor of education at Stanford University.

Patrick Daley is director and publisher, Intervention Curriculum, Scholastic, Inc.

Chris Dede is professor of education and information technology in the Graduate School of Education at George Mason University.

David C. Dwyer, an award-winning teacher, was a distinguished scientist with Apple Computer in the Advanced Technology Group. He is currently president and CEO of Edpoint, Inc.

John Frederiksen directs the Bay Area Cognitive Science Research Group for the Educational Testing Service. Dr. Frederiksen is also an adjunct professor at the University of California, Berkeley.

Paul Gilster is a professional writer and speaker on technology.

Thomas K. Glennan is a senior advisor for education policy at RAND.

Laura Goin is instructional design consultant at Designs for Learning, Franklin, Tennessee.

Andrea R. Gooden is program manager for education and community development in worldwide corporate affairs at Sun Microsystems, Inc.

Ted S. Hasselbring is the William T. Bryant Professor of Special Education at the University of Kentucky.

Margaret Honey is associate director of the Center for Children and Technology and served as associate director for the national Center for Technology in Education, funded by the Office of Educational Research and Improvement (OERI).

The International Society for Technology in Education, and detailed information on the Technology Standards for Students, can be found online at [www.iste.org].

Heather Kirkpatrick is a doctoral student at the Stanford University School of Education and a former high school teacher.

David Kumar is professor of science education in the College of Education at Florida Atlantic University

Arthur Melmed is a research professor at the Institute for Public Policy at George Mason University.

Seymour Papert holds the Lego Chair for Learning Research at the Massachusetts Institute of Technology.

Neil Postman is chair of the Department of Culture and Communication at New York University.

The President's Committee of Advisors on Science and Technology, including the Panel on Educational Technology and a list of its members, can be found at [http://www.whitehouse.gov/WH/EOP/OSTP/NSTC/PCAST/k–12ed.html].

Cathy Ringstaff is an independent educational research consultant.

Judith Haymore Sandholtz is director of the Comprehensive Teacher Education Institute at the University of California, Riverside.

Marlene Scardamalia is a professor at the Center for Applied Cognitive Science, Ontario Institute for Studies in Education, at the University of Toronto.

Karen Sheingold, who served as director of the Center for Performance Assessment at Educational Testing Service and as director of the Center for Children and Technology at Bank Street College, is an independent consultant and a member of the National Advisory Board of the George Lucas Foundation and of the OERI Expert Technology Panel.

The State Board of Education and Texas Education Agency can be found at [http://www.tea.state.texas.gov].

Don Tapscott is chairman of the Alliance for Converging Technologies and president of New Paradigm Learning Corporation.

Rose Taylor is director of professional development for Scholastic, Inc.

Robert J. Tierney is a professor at the School of Teaching and Learning at Ohio State University.

Robert Tinker is founder and president of the Concord Consortium, Concord, Massachusetts.

David Tyack is Vida Jacks Professor of Education and professor of history at Stanford University.

Cynthia L. Wilson is an associate professor in the College of Education at Florida Atlantic University, where she chairs the Department of Exceptional Student Education.

INTRODUCTION

Beginnings

WHY DOES TECHNOLOGY MATTER for learning? It is worth reflecting on this topic as the reader prepares to launch into a hefty group of chapters on theory and practice concerning key educational issues that relate to learning technologies. In this book, "technologies" refer typically to uses of computing but also Internet telecommunications, in applications as diverse as programming, word processing, games, simulations, multimedia composition, performance assessment, and distance education. But "technologies for learning" has a deeper meaning upon which these more recent historical developments depend.

We may distinguish two senses in which technology and learning are intertwined. The first is thinking *with* technology, the second is thinking *about* technology. The second twist of phrase is crucial for technological literacy and technical education and is the topic of recent standards for student learning. But thinking *with* technology is far more important historically and substantively, for it is in this sense that technology is an instrument of knowing, reason, culture, and humanity itself.

Technologies as instruments of thinking, *cognitive technologies,* are at the heart of the human condition. Before the cognitive revolution in the last half of the 20th century, Ernst Cassirer (1944, 1953–1957) and Kenneth Burke (1966), among others, highlighted in influential writings during the first half of the 20th century that humans are fundamentally and distinctively symbol-making and symbol-using animals. Fluencies with expressing and interpreting symbolic representations are at the core of what it means to understand subject matter domains, to put knowledge to use in activities. The philosopher Nelson Goodman (1978) talks of humans as "world-making" with their symbol systems, as they create fictional and possible worlds in literature, science, mathematics, and the arts. For example, long before computing, written language and number systems have served as technologies of thinking. By making explicit with inscriptions the traces of verbal and mathematical thinking, written words and numbers preserved cognition for the ages and led to new forms of activity (such as publishing and commentary) that have had remarkable consequences. The philosopher Ludwig Wittgenstein captured this power of representation aphoristically when he asked, "How do I know what I think until I see what I say?" As Jack Goody (1987), Walter Ong (1982), and David Olson (1996) have highlighted in their accounts of the historical importance of writing systems, an oral argument on paper provides the literate reader with the opportunity to better judge the coherence of that argument than listening to an oration, in which the speaker's emotive powers may hold sway. Similar arguments apply to the uses of mathematical and logical notation in the formulation and testing of scientific theory. Such systematicity has been taken to new levels by the rigor required in programming computers to execute extraordinarily complex actions, like the tens of millions of lines of code that define today's computer operating systems, or the circuitry that enables a billion instructions per second in the newest computer chips.

Early in the days of computing, President Roosevelt's science advisor Vannevar Bush (1945) wrote a seminal essay on imagined future uses of computing to amplify and extend human thinking with new digital renderings of diverse symbolic forms from text to graphics and other media, anticipating the interlinked and globally accessible data records we now know as the World Wide Web. He emphasized how computers could serve to simplify processes for creating documents and other representational forms, invent new means for sharing them with others, and enable powerful search activities. Howard Rheingold's (1985) book *Tools for Thought* provides an excellent introduction to how computers evolved as cognitive technologies based on the visions of Bush and others, particularly at Douglas Engelbart's Augmentation Research Center at SRI International in the 1960s with the invention of personal computing, hypermedia, the mouse, real-time text editing, and collaborative computing (Engelbart, 1963; http://www.bootstrap.org).

Unlike other waves of technology that were predicted to have important implications for learning and education, such as the radio, the filmstrip, and television, computing provides a *meta-medium*—a representational substrate—in which these previous media forms may be readily assimilated and elaborated in their potential uses and interrelationships (Pea & Gomez, 1992). For example, a digital videoclip of an African savannah can have "hot spots" at key features of interest that, when clicked with a mouse input device, will open up footnote-like expositions of related information. The interactive capabilities of computing make it possible to transform the nature of the relationship between media author and media user in fundamental ways, as interactivity becomes the rule rather than the typical "information delivery" metaphor of previous media. And beyond simply accommodating and extending these previous media, computers have been used to provide fundamentally new representational forms for thinking, including dynamic visualization of large geo-gridded global datasets in the environmental sciences (Edelson, Gordin, & Pea, 1999) and virtual realities for exploring phenomena at nano-level or cosmology-level scales. Children today using LEGO Mindstorm "toys" can program the actions of robots with sensors, which, when first invented in the 1960s, cost millions of dollars, filled a large room, and engaged some of the best minds in artificial intelligence programming.

In short, while cognitive technologies such as writing and mathematical notation have long been influential for thinking and learning and education, computer technologies have *accelerated* this cultural process of invention and the societal appropriation of new representational tools for thinking. Due to the large and growing installed base of multimedia networked computers and the World Wide Web, the time course of these changes continues to contract as new software programs propagate over the Web in a matter of weeks for use by tens of millions of users through web portals like Yahoo and AOL.

New technological systems of representation and communication make possible new forms of activity, discourse, and reflection. The co-evolution of technology systems and social functions thus has an essential relevance to education and learning. If one takes seriously the reasonable conjecture from sociocultural theory that changing what one does changes what one becomes (Pea, 1985), access to and facility with such new representational tools is not only vital in society, but their universal accessibility becomes an issue of empowerment and identity.

With this preamble, and seeing the large issues at stake, we may now turn to how the chapters of this volume provide a window into contemporary issues in technologies, education, and learning.

Contents

The Jossey-Bass Reader on Technology and Learning is made up of twenty-three chapters on a broad range of topics that are intended to provide useful knowledge about theory and practice of key educational issues involving technologies and learning. The focus is very much on K–12 education, with a repeated and appropriate emphasis on the role of teachers and teacher professional development. The chapters are arrayed in three parts: Reports and Standards; Equity, Access, and Literacy; and

Technology and School Change. Many of the chapters contain classics that are repeatedly cited and debated nationally.

Reports and Standards

During the last half of the 1990s, numerous national commissions were convened and reports were developed on information technologies and education. Chapter One, an excerpt from the 1997 PCAST report to the President on using technology to strengthen K–12 education, is a comprehensive, insightful, and influential document in this vein. The wisdom of the recommendations of the PCAST Panel on Educational Technology has been echoed in many federal programs and state initiatives since that time: (1) focus on learning with technology, not about technology; (2) emphasize content and pedagogy, not just hardware; (3) give special attention to professional development; (4) engage in realistic budgeting; (5) ensure equitable, universal access; and (6) initiate a major program of experimental research.

Parallel with this development was a movement toward greater accountability in K–12 educational systems, which sought to find ways to establish standards for learning and teaching. These trends converged in technology-related standard-setting, with several instructive examples provided by ISTE's creation of technology standards for student learning (Chapter Two) and California's new technology standards for teacher credential candidates (Chapter Three). Chapter Four provides insight into how Texas has grappled with developing a long-range plan for technology in education through the year 2010. A RAND Institute report explores the challenges of financing, teacher professional development, and educational software development that accompany learner-centered, technology-intensive schools (Chapter Five). Hank Becker's comprehensive empirical report on Internet use and valuation by 2,250 teachers (Chapter Six) is my favorite research study in this volume, and bears close scrutiny by educators and policymakers for its many lessons. Chapter Seven provides an accessible report on a complex study by ETS on the conditions under which educational technology is effective for learning mathematics.

Equity, Access, and Literacy

Since computers were first broadly introduced into U.S. schools in the early 1980s, policy issues of equity and access have been fundamental concerns. The development and implementation of state and district technology plans, as well as the allocation of billions of dollars of Title I funding and E-Rate funding, have turned on policy positions and legislation concerning these issues. These are extraordinarily important, highly charged, and analytically nuanced issues worth careful study, dialogue, and reflection.

Many comparative topics come together in this complex array: socioeconomic level, race, ethnicity, gender, disabilities of different types, geographical region. Furthermore, different assumptions about what specifically is at issue come into play that keep changing the nature of the discourse on these topics. For example, numbers of computers and Internet connections are more readily measurable than equitable access to integral, ongoing, quality uses of computing and telecommunications to improve learning and teaching for all. And yet the effectiveness with which educators use "access" (in the readily measurable sense) turns on the specific conditions of the learning environments—including teacher preparedness, curriculum, assessment, and school climate—in which the technology is available. Even if two schools have equal computer access, they may dramatically vary in the specific applications used (for example, drill-and-practice CAI versus tool use) and in the social context in which they are used (such as labs versus classrooms or solo versus small groups). New measures of "Internet connectivity access" are playing out similarly, with the percentage of schools and classrooms connected as the new quantitative variables of concern. Now more nuanced questions are arising about what activities teachers and students are engaged in once they have such Internet access (Chapter Six). Not all access is created equal for learning.

The chapters in this part of the reader explore these issues in some detail. Tapscott writes that "the most widely feared prediction surrounding the digital revolution is that it will splinter society into a race of information haves and have-nots, knowers and know-nots, doers and do-nots— a digital divide" (Chapter Eight). Tapscott broadens the dialogue beyond access per se to the consequences of inequitable availability of services, technology fluency, and opportunities to learn. Nonetheless, I recommend Cisler's essay (2000) on the many problems of the phrase "digital divide" for those whose experience is "on the other side" and for whom other issues may be more critical (such as health care, education, and quality of life).

Will there always be computers and connectivity of diverse capabilities, where more money will buy enhanced features, speed, and other perks? Of course, and business or other sectors will be able to afford to pay for it in ways that schools and homes inevitably will not. Will this fact preserve existing inequities? Or amplify existing inequities? Or create new inequities? These empirical and policy issues deserve ongoing scrutiny and principled action.

Other chapters in this section ask whether there are gender differences in patterns of K–12 technology use (Chapter Nine), and in what ways girl games could more suitably reflect their "technological desires," which differ from those of boys (Chapter Ten). Several chapters tackle the opportunities of supporting students with learning disabilities in learning science (Chapter Thirteen) and literacy skills (Chapter Fourteen) with computers.

Highlighting the Union City, New Jersey, model of distributed learning, Chris Dede (Chapter Eleven) challenges school administrators to think differently about how to invest in technology-based systemic reform in ways that are affordable, generalizable, and sustainable. Berman and Tinker describe the benefits for hundreds of students from dozens of high schools taking netcourses in a cooperatively organized Virtual High School, such as significant expansion of curricular offerings (Chapter Twelve).

This section closes with Gilster's helpful portrayal of "digital literacy" (Chapter Fifteen), his account of the new aspects of literacy in an Internet age, including search skills, critical thinking about on-line information sources, and mastery of the rhetoric of hyperlinking in making or critically evaluating an argument.

Technology and School Change

Whenever I have taught courses on learning and technology, I have found it effective to organize readings around controversies. Controversies engage and motivate students, and can help them to understand the sources and consequences of different perspectives on key issues. Controversies also often bring out the best writing from authors. On the topic of technology and school change, I have found that utopian and dystopian writings on the promises (or perils) of technology use for learning provoke the kind of critical reading and reflection I seek in such controversy-centered discussions. And several of the selections in this section light up the extremes of the utopian continuum in my experience: Seymour Papert's *Mindstorms* chapter on "Computers and Computer Cultures" (Chapter Sixteen) and dystopian selections from Neil Postman's *End of Education* (Chapter Twenty) and Tyack and Cuban's *Tinkering Toward Utopia* (Chapter Seventeen). Mapping the claims, counterclaims, and assumptions of these works can provide a powerful exercise for thinking deeply about these subjects.

Somewhere in the middle of this utopian continuum are several chapters from the broadly researched Apple Classroom of Tomorrow (ACOT) Project, a ten-year effort that led to many insights about stages relating instruction to technology in technology-rich classrooms (Chapters Eighteen and Nineteen). There will be findings here to delight the utopian, feed the dystopian, and serve the practical reader as ACOT's critical "technoromanticism"—hopeful of powerful results, open to seeing challenges and problems, but empowered to seek improvements through new iterations on design and support—becomes apparent. In a rich description of another technology-intensive school, Gooden's profile of P.S. 125, Ralph Bunche School, in Central Harlem (Chapter Twenty-One) helps us understand why many visitors have been compelled to learn from their experience as a "computer mini-school" integrating technology across the grade-school curriculum.

The two remaining chapters depict some important developments from the learning sciences research community on how school change for deeper learning can build on appropriate uses of technology. Scardamalia and Bereiter (Chapter Twenty-Two) convey a vision of a knowledge-building society comprising interlinked networks from different communities, including schools, universities, businesses, and cultural institutions. They seek to involve "people in the actual work of a society engaged in constructing, using, and improving knowledge." As part of Canada's Tele-Learning Research Network, they are pursuing this dream using their Computer Supported Intentional Learning Environment (CSILE) software, and they distinguish the Knowledge Society model from other models for educational networking.

Finally, Sheingold and Frederiksen (Chapter Twenty-Three) describe how technology is being used to support innovative performance assessments that model challenging learning activities for students instead of the traditional closed-response or short-answer paper-and-pencil test. Such assessments employ student work portfolios, can require collaborative work among students, and seek to provide what they call "transparency" in making clear what good work looks like and by what criteria it will be judged. Technologies can serve the multiple roles in this vision of supporting students' project work, creating replayable copies of their performances, providing libraries of examples and interpretive tools, expanding the community of judges, and publishing best works for recognizing learner accomplishments.

Looking to the Future

As one of the primary generative functions of a society, education is an exceptionally vital enterprise. The goals of education—what a society seeks to achieve through its activities—essentially involve *renewal*. In this sense, education is both a conserving enterprise, looking to the past and learning from it, and a futuristic enterprise, second-guessing the needs of the possible worlds ahead and readying learners to adapt to them creatively and successfully. No wonder the issues around technology and education evoke such vital passions in advocates and detractors, educators and policymakers.

Defined by both Moore's Law on processor speed and cost and Metcalfe's Law on the power of network effects, technology change is proceeding at an exponential pace, and outstripping the capacity of society and social institutions, including schools, to deal with its ramifications. What is education to make of these transformations under way? How should educators, education policymakers, parents, and the related marketplace of publishers engage with these changes?

This volume provides an indispensable resource for learning about many of the key issues, lively concerns, and recurrent controversies in K–12 education using learning technologies. These readings are fertile with materials for making sense of these changes, in providing "concepts and controversies to think with." Nonetheless, this volume provides a snapshot of learning technologies and education that is inevitably several years old.

But beyond this book, and on the World Wide Web itself, educators, policymakers, researchers, parents, and others need to become more connected in an ongoing way with the pulse of transformations in technologies as they bear on learning and education. How is this achievable? There is unfortunately no good central resource today for keeping apace of developments. A reasonable place to begin is the regularly updated Web site of the U.S. Department of Education, which seeks to provide a service to these audiences with regular analyses of new developments in learning and technology. But for imagining the future of education, nothing substitutes for personal experience and observations of new learning environments in action, so when you have the opportunity to see something new, take advantage of it. Seek out vivid examples that are held up as models of innovation, and ask hard questions about the issues this book has helped you think about.

What will we be looking back to when the next volume like this appears? I see several likely new dimensions of major change. One is toward ubiquitous or pervasive access to Web-based computing. For many global citizens, their first access to the Internet will be via smart cell phones, information appliances like e-books, and interactive cable television services. The growing convergence of the industries of computing, telecommunications, publishing, video, and entertainment will assure new opportunities for learning and education, and new dilemmas and challenges around equity, access, and digital literacies. Another issue will be the dot.com'ing of education, as virtual universities and virtual schools take shape and new public-private partnerships are tried out and found to be working or wanting.

I also expect a next edition will document a real and growing erosion of boundaries in the contexts for learning with computer and communications technologies. Schools are changing too, but the nodes of distributed learning networks are lighting up throughout other settings and institutions. Over half of U.S. homes have multimedia computers that are connected to the Internet, and nearly all public libraries are now connected. TV time is being supplanted by Internet use time among our youth. Community centers, clubhouses, and churches are also increasingly common places of computer-based learning, and as computers like the Palm Pilot become more commonplace, children are learning with computers in the streets and neighborhoods, in cars and buses. What we do not know is whether and how these pervasive technologies for learning will make new forms of education, and what new problems they will raise. But the adventures are in the making. Participate!

ROY D. PEA
SRI International
Director, Center for Technology in Learning

REFERENCES

Burke, K. (1966). *Language as symbolic action: Essays on life, literature, and method.* Berkeley, CA: University of California Press.

Bush, V. (1945). As we may think. *Atlantic Monthly.*

Cassirer, E. (1944). *An essay on man.* New Haven, CT: Yale University.

Cassirer, E. (1953–1957). *Philosophy of symbolic forms.* (Ralph Manheim, trans., 3 vols.) New Haven, CT: Yale University. (Originally published 1923–1929.)

Cisler, S. (2000, January 16). Subtract the "digital divide." *San Jose Mercury News,* Business section, p. 2D.

Edelson, D. C., Gordin, D. N., & Pea, R. D. (1999). Addressing the challenges of inquiry-based learning through technology and curriculum design. *Journal of the Learning Sciences, 8*(3&4), 391–450.

Engelbart, D. C. (1963). A conceptual framework for the augmentation of man's intellect. In P. W. Howerton and D. C. Weeks (Eds.), *Vistas in information handling* (Vol. 1, pp. 1–29). Washington, D.C.: Spartan Books.

Gilder, G. (1990). *Microcosm.* New York: Touchstone Books.

Goodman, N. (1978). *Ways of worldmaking.* Indianapolis, IN: Hackett.

Goody, J. (1987). *The logic of writing and the organization of society (studies in literacy, family, culture and the state).* New York: Cambridge University Press.

Olson, D. R. (1996). *The world on paper: The conceptual and cognitive implications of writing and reading.* New York: Cambridge University Press.

Ong, W. J. (1982). *Orality and literacy: Technologizing the word.* New York: Methuen.

Pea, R. D. (1985). Beyond amplification: Using computers to reorganize human mental functioning. *Educational Psychologist, 20,* 167–182.

Pea, R. D., & Gomez, L. (1992). Distributed multimedia learning environments: Why and how? *Interactive Learning Environments, 2*(2), 73–109.

Rheingold, H. (1985). *Tools for thought.* New York: Simon & Schuster.

WELCOME to *The Jossey-Bass Reader on Technology and Learning*. With the Jossey-Bass education readers we hope to provide a clear, concise overview of important topics in education and to give our audience a useful knowledge of the theory and practice of key educational issues. Each reader in this series is designed to be informative, comprehensive, and portable.

Your feedback is important. If you are familiar with articles, books, or reports that have a national sustained audience and address the topic of this reader, please send us an e-mail at readers@jbp.com.

*In the interest of readability, the editors
have slightly adapted the following selections
for this volume. For the complete text,
please refer to the original source.*

PART ONE

REPORTS AND STANDARDS

WE BEGIN WITH AN OVERVIEW of how top researchers and governmental commissions are approaching the myriad issues that arise when schools integrate technology into their curricula. While it is impossible to include every report, study, or standard, our intent in Part One is to give our reader a concise but thorough introduction to how researchers and political entities are defining the way technology is used in schools.

The report of the President's Committee of Advisors on Science and Technology presented in Chapter One is an example of the finest minds in the field coming together. The list of contributors to this project virtually defines the field. We have also included state documents. We chose works from California and Texas (Chapters Three and Four) not only because they are quality examples of how states are planning for and implementing the use of technology in schools, but also because these states are large and diverse, in terms of both geography and population. In addition, in Chapter Two we have included technology standards for students published by the International Society for Technology in Education, the leading independent organization in the field of education technology. These standards are similar to those currently being adopted at the state and federal levels in subject areas such as mathematics and language arts. These documents are excellent resources that outline what students need to know and when they need to know it. In Chapter Five, RAND, a leading education policy think tank, provides analysis of the challenges in creating a nation of technology-enabled schools.

In the field of education technology, much of the evidence, although compelling, has been provided anecdotally. We have included here two pieces that provide hard data. Henry Jay Becker, as a member of the Center for Research on Information Technology and Organizations (CRITO), released a study on how teachers use the Internet (Chapter Six); and *Education Week* published a study in their 1998 annual technology issue that provided hard data on student improvement linked to certain ways of using technology in the classroom (Chapter Seven).

These chapters create an initial understanding and appreciation for the breadth and depth of work that exists on this topic, and they create curiosity and an analytical foundation on which to judge the rest of the chapters.

I

REPORT TO THE PRESIDENT ON THE USE OF TECHNOLOGY TO STRENGTHEN K–12 EDUCATION IN THE UNITED STATES

MARCH 1997

President's Committee of Advisors on Science and Technology,
Panel on Educational Technology

10. Summary of Findings and Recommendations

THIS SECTION consists of a summary of the Panel's principal findings and an abbreviated list of general recommendations to the President. In the interest of brevity, however, and in order to highlight such information and advice as the Panel believes to be most important, this section does not include all of the detailed findings and recommendations incorporated within the full text of the Report.

10.1 Overview of the Panel's Findings

While information technologies have had an enormous impact within America's offices, factories and stores over the past several decades, our country's K–12 educational system has thus far been only minimally affected by the information revolution. Although it is not yet possible to fully characterize the optimal ways in which computing and networking technologies might be used, the Panel believes that such technologies have the potential to transform our schools in important ways, and finds ample (albeit partially anecdotal) justification for the immediate and widespread incorporation of such technologies within all of our nation's elementary and secondary schools.

HARDWARE AND INFRASTRUCTURE

Significant investments will be necessary in hardware and infrastructure if educational technology is to be effectively utilized on a nationwide basis. American schools are now purchasing hardware at a relatively rapid rate, but the ratio of computers to students remains suboptimal from an educational viewpoint, and those machines which are available are often obsolete, and thus incapable of executing contemporary applications software. In addition, the computers in many schools are centralized within a single laboratory rather than distributed among the various classrooms, making it difficult for teachers to integrate technology within the curriculum.

Used equipment donated by corporations may be of value under certain circumstances, and may have collateral benefit to the extent such involvement helps to draw the private sector into closer contact with our schools. It should be noted, however, that the value of such donations (particularly when measured net of public revenue reductions associated with the corresponding federal and state tax deductions) may in other cases be offset by the increased maintenance costs and decreased utility typically associated with older machines, and by the need to integrate and support multiple platforms. Hardware donations are thus unlikely to obviate the need for a significant federal, state, and/or local investment in new equipment, and in the personnel-related expenditures (for installation, training, systems administration, user support, and hardware and software maintenance) that in fact account for the majority of the life-cycle cost of a computer system.

The inadequate physical and telecommunications infrastructure of our nation's schools poses another challenge for the effective exploitation of educational technologies. The optimal use of such technologies will require that computers be distributed throughout each school and interconnected through both local- and wide-area networks. The wiring systems in many school buildings, however, are incapable of supporting the electric power and data communications requirements of a modern networked computing environment. In some cases, the cost of retrofitting our schools for technology will be further increased by a lack of adequate air conditioning, by the presence of asbestos, and by various other factors. Wiring efforts based on the conscription of volunteers may be productive under certain circumstances within certain geographic areas, but cannot realistically be expected to make more than a relatively modest overall contribution toward solving the infrastructure and networking problems of America's schools.

SOFTWARE, CONTENT AND PEDAGOGY

While a significant investment in hardware and infrastructure will be required if the promise of educational technology is to be realized, the Panel believes that the effective use of these resources to improve our nation's educational system poses an even greater challenge. Even the earliest computer-aided instruction systems (typically used in a "drill-and-practice" mode to teach isolated facts and basic skills) provided the benefits of self-pacing and individualized instruction, and a number of studies have found such systems to offer significant improvements in learning rate, particularly within low-achieving student populations. In recent years, however, attention has increasingly focused on the ways in which technology might help to achieve some of the central objectives of educational reform, providing students with the ability to acquire new knowledge, to solve "real-world" problems, and to execute novel and complex tasks requiring the effective integration of a wide range of basic skills.

Within the framework of this newer paradigm, technology is viewed not as a tool for improving the efficiency of traditional instructional methods based largely on the unidirectional transmission of isolated facts and skills from teacher to student, but as one element of a new constructivist approach in which teachers concentrate instead on helping their students to actively construct their own knowledge bases and skill sets. This approach is typically characterized by the independent exploration of a limited number of topics in unusual (relative to traditional instructional methods) depth, and often relies on the availability of extensive information resources that can be drawn upon by the student as and when needed. Students may also use the computer as a tool for various forms of simulation; for written, musical, or artistic composition; for mathematical manipulation and visualization; for the design of various devices, environments, and systems; for the acquisition of computer programming skills; for the collection and analysis of laboratory data; for many forms of problem-solving; and for various modes of group collaboration.

Neither the constructivist pedagogic model nor the proposed role of technology within a constructivist curriculum have yet been validated through a process of extensive, rigorous, large-scale experimentation, and it is quite possible that alternative approaches may ultimately be found useful as well. This caveat notwithstanding, a combination of theoretical considerations (based in part on research in cognitive psychology and other fields) and the observation of a limited number of apparent "success stories" suggest that computing and networking technologies could potentially find their most powerful application within the framework of the constructivist paradigm.

While the role of the teacher is likely to change within a technology-rich constructivist classroom, the Panel found no evidence to suggest a diminution of that role. Preliminary research suggests that the potential benefits of such an environment decline as class size increases, and that teachers will still be required to play an important role in helping students to assimilate abstract concepts and develop higher-order thinking skills. Teachers can be expected to spend a great deal of time monitoring, directing, and assisting in the (largely self-directed) learning process, and helping to "debug" faulty "mental models." There is some (again preliminary) evidence that students spend more time interacting with teachers and other students within the technology-rich classroom, calling into question the intuitively plausible notion that computers might interfere with the acquisition of valuable social and collaborative skills. Technology may also improve educational outcomes by supporting various forms of interaction with parents and the community. While the greatest promise of educational technology lies in the possibility of utilizing computers and networks as an integral part of virtually all aspects of the curriculum, most of the elementary and secondary schools that actually use such technologies today do so in far more limited ways. A large fraction of current usage especially at the high school level is accounted for by "computer education," which aims to teach students about computers (focusing, for example, on the acquisition of keyboarding skills; instruction in the use of word processing, database management, spreadsheet, and other software tools; and the study of computer programming) rather than using computers as a tool for learning in all subject areas. Educational games and instruction in isolated basic skills also account for a significant portion of current usage particularly within the elementary school, but few schools have integrated computing and networking technologies extensively and effectively into the learning process, or used it as a key element of educational reform.

One obstacle to the effective integration of information technology is a dearth of state-of-the-art software and digital content designed for the K–12 school environment. A plateau in the sales of traditional Integrated Learning Systems [ILS] has led to a precipitous decrease in R&D spending by ILS vendors at a time when education reform is placing new demands on such systems. Moreover, neither traditional vendors nor newly organized firms have thus far invested in the development of software suitable for use within a constructivist curriculum to the extent that will be required to effectively cover a wide range of content areas (especially at the secondary school level) and skill levels. Among the apparent reasons for these market problems are weak incentives for private sector R&D (resulting from inadequate software acquisition budgets and various forms of market fragmentation); lack of modern hardware within the schools; peculiarities in the procedures used for software procurement; and inadequate federal funding for innovative early-stage research whose benefits cannot be appropriated by any one company, and which is thus unlikely to be conducted without public sector involvement, an economic externality sometimes referred to as the "free rider" problem.

TEACHERS AND TECHNOLOGY
In order to effectively integrate new technologies into the curriculum, teachers will have to select appropriate software, construct new lesson plans, resolve a number of logistical problems, and develop appropriate methods of assessing student work. The Panel finds, however, that our nation's K–12 teachers currently receive little technical, pedagogic or administrative support for these activities, and that few colleges of education adequately prepare their graduates to use information technologies in their teaching.

Contributing to this problem is the fact that only about 15 percent of the typical computer budget is devoted to professional development, compared with the 30 percent or more that is generally believed to represent a more optimal allocation. Moreover, most of these expenditures are aimed at training teachers to operate a computer, rather than to use computers to enhance their teaching. In addition, many teachers do not have adequate access to technological and pedagogical support on an ongoing, "as-needed" basis. Fewer than five percent of all schools have full-time computer coordinators capable of providing such sustained assistance, and such coordinators as are available typically spend only 20 percent of their time helping teachers, selecting software, or formulating technology-oriented lesson plans.

Fortunately, technological progress may itself contribute toward the solution of some of the problems of professional development by making educational software easier for teachers to use; by helping teachers in various ways to recover some of the time invested in the introduction of technology; and by supporting online professional development seminars and remote mentoring and consulting activities, which the Panel believes are likely to prove significantly more cost-effective than conventional instruction under appropriate circumstances.

Perhaps the greatest single factor now holding back the adequate preparation of teachers is a lack of sufficient time in their work week to effectively incorporate technology into the curriculum. Unless additional time can be made available by eliminating or de-emphasizing other, less critical tasks, however, each hour set aside in the school week for technology-related curricular design and professional development can be expected to (directly or indirectly) add between $4 and $5 billion to our nation's yearly expenditures for K–12 education. Moreover, research reviewed by the Panel suggests that the typical teacher will require between three and six years to fully integrate technology into his or her teaching; in the presence of continued technological innovation, a teacher's learning curve is thus unlikely to ever level off entirely.

While America's colleges of education have the potential to play an invaluable role in preparing our teachers to use technology effectively in their professional activities, information gathered by the Panel suggests that most education schools are still far from realizing that potential. Although pre-service instruction in the use of technology is required by 22 states (in contrast with only two states that require in-service training), the courses used to satisfy such requirements typically provide no actual experience in using computers to teach, and impart little knowledge of available software and content.

In order to prepare our teachers for the effective use of technology, education schools will have to overcome some of the same problems now encountered by our nation's K–12 schools: inadequate funding for the acquisition of hardware and software; a paucity of programs aimed at providing education school faculty members with the background necessary to prepare future teachers in the use of technology; and the lack of sufficient time for professors of education to incorporate technology within both the content and methods of their courses.

ECONOMIC CONSIDERATIONS

Based on currently available data, the Panel estimates that public elementary and secondary schools in the United States spent between $3.5 and $4 billion on educational technology during the 1995–96 school year, including investments in hardware, wiring, infrastructural enhancements, software and digital information resources, systems support, and technology-related professional development. This figure, which represents about 1.3 percent of projected total spending in our schools, is extraordinarily low by comparison with most other information-based industries, and in the opinion of the Panel, will have to rise significantly if technology is to have a material impact on the quality of American education.

By way of contrast with these current expenditure figures, the seven studies reviewed by the Panel suggest that annual expenditures of between

$6 billion and $28 billion (or between 2.4 and 11.3 percent of total educational spending) will likely be required to adequately support various degrees of technology usage within the public schools, and that even those spending levels will be insufficient to support the sort of technology usage that might be considered optimal if cost were not an issue. Because computing and networking hardware will account for only a minority of this spending, educators and policy-makers will not be able to rely solely on one-time bond issues and private capital campaigns of the sort often used to finance the construction of school buildings, and will have to budget for substantial ongoing operating expenditures if they are to avoid a situation in which valuable hardware is left unused.

Based on models from other industries, it seems likely that further experience with the use of technology in our schools could ultimately result in significant improvements over time in the educational outcomes achievable at a given level of expenditure. Such improvements, however, are likely to be critically dependent on rigorous, large-scale programs of research and evaluation aimed at assessing the efficacy and cost-effectiveness of various approaches to the use of technology in actual K–12 classrooms.

Most importantly, educational technology expenditures are best analyzed not on the basis of cost alone, but in terms of return on investment. While it would be difficult to quantify all of the benefits that might be derived from the use of educational technology, the Panel believes that a substantial investment in technology may be justifiable even if no value is placed on the direct (economic and non-economic) benefits accruing to the American people, using return calculations based solely on projected marginal tax revenues associated with an increase in their expected lifetime taxable earnings.

EQUITABLE ACCESS

Educational technologies have the potential to either ameliorate or exacerbate the growing gulf between advantaged and disadvantaged Americans, depending on policy decisions involving the ways in which such technologies are deployed and utilized on behalf of various segments of our country's student population. Although federal programs have played a major role in limiting certain inequities, disparities in the access to and use of information technologies by students of different socioeconomic status (SES), race and ethnicity, gender, and geographical location, and by children with various types of special needs, remain a source of concern to the Panel.

Income-related inequities in the number of students per in-school computer have narrowed significantly over the past decade, largely as a result of Title I spending, which provided about $2 billion in federal funding over that period for the provision of educational technology within low-income schools. Low-SES students, however, still use computers less extensively in school, and are less likely to use computers for higher-order learning activities, than their higher-income peers. Such disparities may be accounted for in part by differences in the preparation and support available to teachers at more and less affluent schools.

The largest SES-related inequities, however, are found in the availability of computers within the home: Whereas computers were found in 73 percent of all homes with college-educated parents and more than $50,000 in annual household income in 1995, they were present in only 14 percent of all households headed by adults having no more than a high-school education and a combined income of less than $30,000. Since school-aged children in homes with computers frequently use these machines for schoolwork or other educational purposes, these SES-related disparities in home computer ownership materially limit the educational opportunities available to low-income students, and thus help to perpetuate familial patterns of socioeconomic disadvantage.

As in the case of socioeconomic status, Title I funding has helped to reduce, but not eliminate, racial and ethnic disparities in the access to computers within the school. Hispanic students, in particular, attend schools with an unusually low density of computers, especially at the elementary school level. Once again, however, the disparity is even greater within the home. As of 1993, for example, the rate of computer ownership was 57 percent lower in African-American homes, and 59 percent lower within Hispanic households, than in the homes of non-Hispanic whites. While a portion of this gap is accounted for by differences in socioeconomic status, differences of 36 percent and 39 percent, respectively, remain even after controlling for household income, educational attainment, age, gender, and location of residence (urban or rural). Race and ethnicity thus represent an independent source of inequity in children's access to educational technology, a source of additional concern to the Panel.

Although certain regional differences are apparent in the use of computers, in-school computer density is roughly comparable across the nation's Western, Midwestern, Northeastern and Southern regions. Rural schools enjoy a significantly higher density than their urban counterparts, but this difference would appear to be largely explained by the fact that rural schools are smaller on average, and smaller schools tend to have a higher computer density. While the available statistics do not support a definitive quantitative comparison of different types of urban environments, anecdotal evidence suggests that inner city schools may face special problems in making effective use of educational technology, as may rural schools in certain areas where wide area networking is rendered more expensive by a lack of economical telecommunications access.

Gender-specific variation in the extent of computer use is relatively small in magnitude, both in school and at home, but certain systematic differences are found in the ways in which boys and girls use computers. Although research has shown that high school girls make 50 percent greater use of the computer for word processing than their male classmates, for example, they have been found to account for only 26 percent of all elective computer use before and after school, and for only 20 percent of all in-school computer-based game-playing activities. There is also some evidence that girls and boys engaging in computer-related learning activities may differ in their relative responses to cooperative, competitive, or individualistic reward structures—a phenomenon which, if validated, could have implications for both the design of optimal pedagogical methods for and the provision of equitable access to male and female K–12 students.

One less obvious form of inequity involves the accessibility of educational technology to low-achieving students. The available data indicates that students with higher grades are allowed more in-school computer time than their underperforming peers, in spite of a substantial body of evidence suggesting that technology may in fact be of greater relative benefit to low-achieving than to high-achieving students. This disparity is compounded by the fact that when underperforming students do use computers, they are more likely than high achievers to engage in drill and practice on isolated basic skills, and less likely to use computers for tasks involving the acquisition and integration of a wide range of knowledge— a practice that runs counter to the recommendations of many educational technology researchers.

Technology also has the potential to significantly improve the educational opportunities available to many American students with learning disabilities, behavior disorders, emotional problems, or physical disabilities. The realization of this potential, however, will depend in part on the widespread availability of special input, output, and other devices, and on teachers and support personnel who have the training necessary to effectively deploy such technologies. The case for federal involvement in mobilizing technology on behalf of students with special needs rests in part on the observation that within a typical school district (and in the case of certain less common disabilities, even within a given state), the number of students with a given disability is likely to be too small to adequately amortize the cost of researching, developing, and effectively deploying the assistive technologies that would provide appropriate educational support for those students.

RESEARCH AND EVALUATION

Both the enormous importance and the enormous cost of K–12 education in the United States argue for careful research on the ways in which computing and networking technologies can be used to improve educational outcomes and the ratio of benefits to costs. The majority of the empirical research reported to date has focused on traditional, tutorial-based applications of computers. Several meta-analyses, each based on dozens of independent studies, have found that students using such technology significantly outperform those taught without the use of such systems, with the largest differences recorded for students of lower socioeconomic status, low-achievers, and those with certain special learning problems. While certain methodological and interpretive questions have been raised with respect to these results, the most significant issue may be the question of whether the variables being measured are in fact well correlated with the forms of learning many now feel are most important.

Although constructivist applications of technology are intended to more directly support the goals of the current educational reform movement, research on such applications is still at a relatively early stage. Most of the work in this area is formative in nature, intended more as a preliminary exploration of new intellectual territory than a definitive evaluation of any one possible solution. Although some interesting and potentially promising empirical results have been reported in the literature, a substantial amount of well-designed experimental research will ultimately be required to obtain definitive, widely replicated results that shed light on the underlying sources of any positive effects, and which are sufficiently general to permit straightforward application within a wide range of realistic school environments.

One important issue that arises in this context is the manner in which "favorable" educational outcomes are defined and measured for purposes of evaluating the relative effectiveness of alternative approaches to the use of technology. Conventional, standardized multiple-choice tests have certain advantages, but tend to emphasize the accumulation of isolated facts and basic skills, and not the acquisition of higher-order thinking and problem-solving competencies of the sorts that are central to both the constructivist paradigm and the goals of contemporary educational reform. Since researchers, educators and software developers can be expected to develop content and techniques that optimize student performance with respect to whatever criteria are employed to measure educational attainment, progress within the field of educational technology will depend critically on the development of metrics capable of serving as appropriate and reliable proxies for desired educational outcomes.

While research in a wide range of areas could directly or indirectly facilitate the effective utilization of educational technology within our nation's K–12 schools, much of the research that the Panel believes to be most important falls into one of the following three categories:

1. Basic research in various learning-related disciplines (including cognitive and developmental psychology, neuroscience, artificial intelligence, and the interdisciplinary field of cognitive science) and fundamental work on various educationally relevant technologies (encompassing in particular various subdisciplines of the field of computer science)

2. Early-stage research aimed at developing innovative approaches to the application of technology in education which are unlikely to originate from within the private sector, but which could result in the development of new forms of educational software, content, and technology-enabled pedagogy, not only in science and mathematics (which have thus far received the most attention), but also in the language arts, social studies, creative arts, and other content areas.

3. Rigorous, well-controlled, peer-reviewed, large-scale (and at least for some studies, long-term), broadly applicable empirical studies designed to determine not whether computers can be effectively used within the school, but rather which approaches to the use of technology are in fact most effective and cost-effective in practice.

To date, however, research on educational technology (and indeed, on education in general) has received minimal funding, particularly when measured relative to our nation's expenditures for K–12 education, which currently total more than a quarter trillion dollars per year. By way of comparison, whereas some 23 percent of all U.S. expenditures for prescription and non-prescription medications were applied toward pharmaceutical research in 1995, less than 0.1 percent of our nation's expenditures for elementary and secondary education in the same year were invested to determine what educational techniques actually work, and to find ways to improve them.

Research funded by the National Institute of Education dropped by a factor of five (in constant dollars) between 1973 and 1986, and although steps have recently been taken to ameliorate the severity of this decline, federal funding continues at a small fraction of the level that would seem appropriate even if our goal were solely to minimize ongoing expenditures by enhancing cost-effectiveness, without any attempt to improve educational outcomes. State, local, and industrial support for educational research has for the most part been limited to functions that are unlikely to significantly advance the general state of knowledge within the field, a reflection of intrinsic economic externalities that will not be overcome in the absence of funding at the highest level of taxing authority. Moreover, private foundations and corporate philanthropic programs have in recent years tended to favor "action-oriented" programs over research and evaluation, leaving no obvious alternative to pick up the slack left by inadequate federal funding.

Quality control problems affecting the administration of federal research programs in the field of education have historically presented another obstacle to progress in the field of educational technology. While certain programs (most notably, those overseen by the National Science Foundation) have generally adhered to high standards of excellence, independence, and scientific integrity, others (including the Office of Educational Research and Improvement and its institutional predecessors) have in the past been adversely affected by counterproductive political influence and other problems. Fortunately, considerable attention has been given over the past several years to the strengthening of OERI, which enjoys a broader mandate in some respects than the NSF, and could thus play an important role in advancing our nation's understanding of the potential applications of technology to K–12 education.

PROGRAMS AND POLICY

The President's Educational Technology Initiative, which was announced in President Clinton's January 1996 State of the Union address, was designed to achieve four goals which the Panel believes will indeed be central to realizing the promise of educational technology: providing our schools with the modern computer hardware, local- and wide-area connectivity, high-quality educational content, and appropriate teacher preparation that will be necessary if information technologies are to be effectively utilized to enhance learning. This initiative serves as an umbrella for a number of distinct but interrelated programs aimed at achieving these four goals within a relatively ambitious time frame.

One Administration program that has already shown considerable promise is the Technology Learning Challenge, which awards five-year matching grants averaging $1 million each to help local consortia (typically consisting of private and public sector partners) to apply technology within schools in their respective areas. Although the overall impact of this program will be limited by funding constraints, these grants would appear to represent an excellent example of the effective leveraging of federal dollars in support of high-quality, locally initiated efforts to improve education through the use of computing and communications technologies.

In February 1996, President Clinton also proposed a program called the Technology Literacy Challenge, which would create a $2 billion Technology Literacy Fund that would be used to "catalyze and leverage state, local, and private sector efforts" to meet the four goals outlined above. Federal funds would be allocated to the states (or under certain circumstances, local communities), which would be given considerable flexibility in deciding how to achieve the goals of the President's Educational Technology Initiative. If enabling legislation is in fact enacted, the Panel believes that this program is indeed likely to significantly advance the objectives outlined by the President, particularly during an initial period in which wide-ranging, exploratory experimentation with a number of different technological and pedagogic approaches is likely to prove most productive.

The Panel also believes, however, that a large-scale, rigorously controlled, federally sponsored program of research and evaluation will ultimately be necessary if the full potential of educational technology is to be realized in a cost-effective manner. Data gathered systematically by individual states, localities, school districts, and schools during an initial phase of federally supported educational technology efforts could prove invaluable in determining which approaches are in fact most effective and economically efficient, thus helping to maximize the ratio of benefits to costs in later phases. Federal funding will ultimately also be required for research aimed at analyzing and interpreting this data.

The effort to incorporate technology within America's K–12 schools has also been directly or indirectly advanced by a number of other programs that have been initiated, supported, or promoted by the White House, including the Commerce Department's Telecommunications and Information Infrastructure Assistance Program, which provides federal matching funds to develop the information infrastructure available to schools; the Telecommunications Act of 1996, which requires the Federal Communications Commission to revise the universal service system in such a way that elementary and secondary schools are provided with affordable access to advanced telecommunications services; and the Department of Education's Regional Technology Consortia Program, which was designed to help educators (among others) to utilize technology through various forms of professional development, technical assistance, and information dissemination.

Responding to current pressures for fiscal restraint, the Clinton Administration has also made effective use of extra-budgetary tools, relying on the purposeful coordination of already-funded programs, the encouragement of extra-governmental efforts based largely on voluntarism, and the personal persuasive powers of the President and Vice President to leverage as extensively as possible those aspects of the President's Educational Technology Initiative that will require the appropriation or redeployment of federal funding. One example in the first category is provided by the activities of the Committee on Education and Training of the National Science and Technology Council to promote the use of technology for education and training, and to coordinate the programs of the various federal agencies that currently engage in education-related research and development.

The second category of extra-budgetary leadership is exemplified by Presidential and Vice Presidential support for the Tech Corps, a private sector organization organized to coordinate the provision of volunteer technical assistance to the schools, and for NetDay96, a "high-tech barnraising" event in which private companies and individual volunteers helped to wire a significant fraction of California's elementary and secondary schools to the Internet. While the Panel believes that it would be unrealistic to expect such purely voluntary efforts to dramatically reduce the dollar cost of effectively utilizing educational technologies on an ongoing basis, it seems clear that such efforts can play an important supporting role, not only directly, but also by calling public attention to the pressing technological (and other) needs of our nation's K–12 schools.

Both President Clinton and Vice President Gore have assumed leadership roles in promoting the use of the Internet by educational institutions, calling for the connection of all American classrooms to the Internet by the year 2000, with special emphasis on economically distressed areas. The President and Vice President have also made effective use of their respective offices to acknowledge (and thus direct attention toward) the efforts of those who have made particularly effective use of educational technology. While some of the objectives outlined in this report cannot be achieved by the President alone, and will require the appropriation or redeployment by Congress of substantial funds, the Panel believes that the Clinton Administration has thus far done an excellent job of addressing such needs as can be satisfied in the absence of such funding.

10.2 *Principal Recommendations*

The body of this report includes a number of relatively specific recommendations related to various aspects of the use of technology within America's elementary and secondary schools. In order to focus attention on a limited number of high-level strategic (as opposed to tactical) issues which the Panel believes to be most important, however, much of this detail is omitted from the summary of selected recommendations that follows.

1. *Focus on learning with technology, not about technology.* Although both are worthy of attention, it is important to distinguish between technology as a subject area and the use of technology to facilitate learning about any subject area. While computer-related skills will unquestionably be quite important in the twenty-first century, and while such skills are clearly best taught through the actual use of computers, it is important that technology be integrated throughout the K–12 curriculum, and not simply used to impart technology-related knowledge and skills. Although universal technological literacy is a laudable national goal, the Panel believes the Administration should work toward the use of computing and networking technologies to improve the quality of education in all subject areas.

2. *Emphasize content and pedagogy, and not just hardware.* The widespread availability of modern computing and networking hardware will be necessary for technology to realize its promise, but will not be sufficient. Although the purchase of computers and the provision of Internet connectivity are perhaps the most visible and most easily understood manifestations of progress, a less obvious (and in some ways, more formidable) challenge will be the development and utilization of demonstrably useful educational software and information resources, and the adaptation of curricula to make effective use of technology. Particular attention should be given to exploring the potential role of technology in achieving the goals of current educational reform efforts through the use of new pedagogic methods based on a more active, student-centered approach to learning that emphasizes the development of higher-order reasoning and problem-solving skills. While obsolete and inaccessible computer systems, suboptimal student/computer ratios, and a lack of appropriate building infrastructure and network connectivity will all need to be addressed, it is important that we not allow these problems to divert attention from the ways in which technology will actually be used within an educational context.

3. *Give special attention to professional development.* The substantial investment in hardware, infrastructure, software and content that is recommended in this report will be largely wasted if K–12 teachers are not provided with the preparation and support they will need to effectively integrate information technologies into their teaching. At least 30 percent

of all federal expenditures for educational technology should be allocated to professional development and to ongoing mentoring and consultative support for teachers. Schools and school districts should be encouraged to provide time for teachers to familiarize themselves with available software and content, to incorporate technology into their lesson plans, and to discuss technology use with other teachers. Finally, both presidential leadership and federal funding should be mobilized to help our nation's schools of education to incorporate technology within their curricula so they are capable of preparing the next generation of American teachers to make effective use of technology.

4. *Engage in realistic budgeting.* The Panel believes that at least five percent of all K–12 educational spending in the United States, or approximately $13 billion annually (in constant 1996 dollars), should be earmarked for technology-related expenditures. Because the amortization of initial acquisition costs will account for only a minority of these recommended expenditures, schools should be encouraged to incorporate technology within their ongoing operating budgets rather than relying solely on one-time bond issues and capital campaigns. While voluntarism and corporate equipment donations may also be of both direct and indirect benefit under certain circumstances, White House policy should be based on a realistic assessment of the relatively limited direct economic contribution such efforts can be expected to make overall. The President should continue to make the case for educational technology as an investment in America's future, while seeking to enhance the return on that investment by promoting federally sponsored research aimed at improving the cost-effectiveness of technology usage within our nation's elementary and secondary schools.

5. *Ensure equitable, universal access.* The Panel feels strongly that access to knowledge-building and communication tools based on computing and networking technologies should be made available to all of the nation's students, regardless of socioeconomic status, race, ethnicity, gender, or geographical factors, and that special attention should be given to the use of technology by students with special needs. Equity should be a central consideration in all federal programs dealing with the use of technology in education. In particular, Title I spending for technology-related investments on behalf of economically disadvantaged students should be maintained at no less than its current level, with ongoing adjustments for inflation, expending U.S. school enrollment, and projected increases in overall national spending for K–12 educational technology. Because much of the educational use of computers now takes place within the home, and because the rate of home computer ownership diverges alarmingly for stu-

dents of different race, ethnicity, and socioeconomic status, consideration should also be given to public policy measures designed to reduce disparities in student access to information technologies outside of school.

6. *Initiate a major program of experimental research.* In view of both the critical importance of and massive expenditures associated with K–12 education in the United States, the Panel recommends that an amount equal to at least 0.5 percent of the nation's aggregate spending for elementary and secondary education (about $1.5 billion at current expenditure levels) be invested on an ongoing basis in federally sponsored research aimed at improving the efficacy and cost-effectiveness of K–12 education. Because no one state, municipality, or private firm could hope to capture more than a small fraction of the benefits associated with a significant advance in our understanding of how best to educate K–12 students, this funding will have to be provided largely at the federal level in order to avoid a systematic underinvestment (attributable to a classical form of economic externality) relative to the level that would be optimal for the nation as a whole.

To ensure high standards of scientific excellence, intellectual integrity, and independence from political influence, this research program should be planned and overseen by a distinguished independent board of outside experts appointed by the President, and should encompass (a) basic research in various learning-related disciplines and on various educationally relevant technologies; (b) early-stage research aimed at developing new forms of educational software, content, and technology-enabled pedagogy; and (c) rigorous, well-controlled, peer-reviewed, large-scale empirical studies designed to determine which educational approaches are in fact most effective in practice. The Panel does not, however, recommend that the deployment of technology within America's schools be deferred pending the completion of such research.

WEB SITE

http://www.whitehouse.gov/WH/EOP/OSTP/NSTC/PCAST/k–12ed.html

NATIONAL EDUCATIONAL TECHNOLOGY STANDARDS FOR STUDENTS

International Society for Technology in Education

THE TECHNOLOGY FOUNDATION standards for students are divided into six broad categories. Standards within each category are to be introduced, reinforced, and mastered by students. These categories provide a framework for linking performance indicators within the Profiles for Technology Literate Students to the standards. Teachers can use these standards and profiles as guidelines for planning technology-based activities in which students achieve success in learning, communication, and life skills.

TECHNOLOGY FOUNDATION STANDARDS FOR STUDENTS

1. Basic operations and concepts
   - Students demonstrate a sound understanding of the nature and operation of technology systems.
   - Students are proficient in the use of technology.
2. Social, ethical, and human issues
   - Students understand the ethical, cultural, and societal issues related to technology.
   - Students practice responsible use of technology systems, information, and software.

- Students develop positive attitudes toward technology uses that support lifelong learning, collaboration, personal pursuits, and productivity.

3. Technology productivity tools

- Students use technology tools to enhance learning, increase productivity, and promote creativity.
- Students use productivity tools to collaborate in constructing technology-enhanced models, preparing publications, and producing other creative works.

4. Technology communications tools

- Students use telecommunications to collaborate, publish, and interact with peers, experts, and other audiences.
- Students use a variety of media and formats to communicate information and ideas effectively to multiple audiences.

5. Technology research tools

- Students use technology to locate, evaluate, and collect information from a variety of sources.
- Students use technology tools to process data and report results.
- Students evaluate and select new information resources and technological innovations based on the appropriateness to specific tasks.

6. Technology problem-solving and decision-making tools

- Students use technology resources for solving problems and making informed decisions.
- Students employ technology in the development of strategies for solving problems in the real world.

Profiles for Technology-Literate Students

Performance Indicators, Curriculum Examples, and Scenarios

A major component of the NETS Project is the development of a general set of profiles describing technology-literate students at key developmental points in their precollege education. These profiles reflect the underlying assumption that all students should have the opportunity to develop technology skills that support learning, personal productivity, decision making, and daily life. These profiles and associated standards provide a framework for preparing students to be lifelong learners who make informed decisions about the role of technology in their lives.

The Profiles for Technology Literate Students provide performance indicators describing the technology competence students should exhibit upon completion of the following grade ranges:

- Grades PreK–2
- Grades 3–5
- Grades 6–8
- Grades 9–12

These profiles are indicators of achievement at certain stages in PreK–12 education. They assume that technology skills are developed by coordinated activities that support learning throughout a student's education. These skills are to be introduced, reinforced, and finally mastered, and thus integrated into an individual's personal learning and social framework. They represent essential, realistic, and attainable goals for lifelong learning and productive citizenry.

The standards and performance indicators are based on input and feedback from educational technology experts as well as parents, teachers, and curriculum experts. In addition, they reflect information collected from professional literature and local, state, and national documents.

Technology Integration—Examples and Scenarios

Linked to each profile is an example or scenario that exemplifies the use of technology by teachers and students to facilitate learning. The scenarios describe classroom practice that reflects not only the NETS standards and profiles, but also content standards from curriculum organizations such as the National Council of Teachers of Mathematics, International Reading Association, and National Council for the Social Studies. The scenarios provide a curricular context for the use of technology to create varied learning environments being established across the United States. It is not the purpose of this book to promote the use of technology in isolation, but rather for it to be an integral component or tool for learning and communications within the context of academic subject areas.

Performance Indicators for Technology-Literate Students

Grades PreK–2

All students should have opportunities to demonstrate the following performances. The numbers in parentheses following each performance indicator refer to the standards category to which the performance is linked. The categories are:

1. Basic operations and concepts
2. Social, ethical, and human issues
3. Technology productivity tools
4. Technology communications tools
5. Technology research tools
6. Technology problem-solving and decision-making tools

Prior to completion of Grade 2 students will:

1. Use input devices (e.g., mouse, keyboard, remote control) and output devices (e.g., monitor, printer) to successfully operate computers, VCRs, audiotapes, and other technologies. (1)
2. Use a variety of media and technology resources for directed and independent learning activities. (1, 3)
3. Communicate about technology using developmentally appropriate and accurate terminology. (1)
4. Use developmentally appropriate multimedia resources (e.g., interactive books, educational software, elementary multimedia encyclopedias) to support learning. (1)
5. Work cooperatively and collaboratively with peers, family members, and others when using technology in the classroom. (2)
6. Demonstrate positive social and ethical behaviors when using technology. (2)
7. Practice responsible use of technology systems and software. (2)
8. Create developmentally appropriate multimedia products with support from teachers, family members, or student partners. (3)
9. Use technology resources (e.g., puzzles, logical thinking programs, writing tools, digital cameras, drawing tools) for problem solving, communication, and illustration of thoughts, ideas, and stories. (3, 4, 5, 6)

10. Gather information and communicate with others using telecommunications, with support from teachers, family members, or student partners. (4)

Curriculum Examples and Scenarios

Grades PreK–2

SCENARIO 1: ANIMALS AND THEIR SOUNDS

Grade Levels: PreK–2

Technology Profile Performance Indicators: 1, 2, 3, 4, 8, 9

Subject Areas: Reading, Science

Source: Sharon Fontenot, Prien Lake Elementary. Lesson developed for Louisiana Challenge Grant Technology Leadership Program, Louisiana Tech University

While every child may not be able to see animals in the wild, every child can see, hear, and learn about wild animals through multimedia technology. In Sharon Fontenot's class at Prien Lake Elementary School, students learn to identify polar bears, lions, and other wild animals through images, video clips, and sounds on the Wide World of Animals CD-ROM. The teacher models the creative use of technology by making a tape recording based on information from the CD-ROM, incorporating her own voice to fit the group's needs.

Students practice reading and listening skills by answering questions that encourage them to think about both the science and social living issues related to these animals. Where do these animals live? What do they eat? Why do some have thick fur? How do they interact with each other?

Students then create their own stories about what they have learned using Kid Pix®, a software program that allows them to make their own pictures of the animals, assemble them into slide shows, and print out their own books to share with classmates and family. The teacher videotapes the students' activities as part of their assessment and to share with students and parents.

SCENARIO 2: I LOST MY TOOTH!

Grade Levels: PreK–2

Technology Profile Performance Indicators: 1, 2, 4, 5, 8, 9, 10

Subject Areas: Health, Language Arts, Social Studies

Source: Boehm, D. (1997, April). I Lost My Tooth! *Learning & Leading with Technology,* 24(7), 17–19.

A first-grade teacher can use this activity to introduce her class to Internet technology for the first time. Teachers worldwide use e-mail, once a month, to relate how many teeth their students lost, along with one special fact about their region or culture. Students share tooth fairy traditions and other stories from their region.

Using the information gathered from students around the world, teachers develop activities including creative writing, graphing, art, and social studies. Students use an interactive bulletin board where they post dates when teeth were lost, create a class letter about the project to post on the Internet, collect information from other children about tooth fairy stories, develop creative writing stories about their "tooth" experiences, and share them with other children via the Internet.

Students can initiate electronic conversations about where other children live, use maps to locate the countries/cities, and address topics with other children such as weather, politics, clothing, and local heroes. The students use electronic slide show/drawing software to illustrate the fairy stories and graph the tooth data. Then they write a letter explaining what the graph means and send it to keypals around the world.

Performance Indicators for Technology Literate Students

Grades 3–5

All students should have opportunities to demonstrate the following performances. Numbers in parentheses following each performance indicator refer to the standards category to which the performance is linked. The categories are:

1. Basic operations and concepts
2. Social, ethical, and human issues
3. Technology productivity tools
4. Technology communications tools
5. Technology research tools
6. Technology problem-solving and decision-making tools

Prior to completion of Grade 5 students will:

1. Apply strategies for identifying and solving routine hardware and software problems that occur during everyday use. (1)
2. Demonstrate knowledge of current changes in information technologies and the effect those changes have on the workplace and society. (2)

3. Exhibit legal and ethical behaviors when using information and technology, and discuss consequences of misuse. (2)

4. Use content-specific tools, software, and simulations (e.g., environmental probes, graphing calculators, exploratory environments, Web tools) to support learning and research. (3, 5)

5. Apply productivity/multimedia tools and peripherals to support personal productivity, group collaboration, and learning throughout the curriculum. (3, 6)

6. Design, develop, publish, and present products (e.g., Web pages, videotapes) using technology resources that demonstrate and communicate curriculum concepts to audiences inside and outside the classroom. (4, 5, 6)

7. Collaborate with peers, experts, and others using telecommunications and collaborative tools to investigate curriculum-related problems, issues, and information, and develop solutions or products for audiences inside and outside the classroom. (4, 5)

8. Select and use appropriate tools and technology resources to accomplish a variety of tasks and solve problems. (5, 6)

9. Demonstrate an understanding of concepts underlying hardware, software, and connectivity, and of practical applications to learning and problem solving. (1, 6)

10. Research and evaluate the accuracy, relevance, appropriateness, comprehensiveness, and bias of electronic information sources concerning real-world problems. (2, 5, 6)

Curriculum Examples and Scenarios

Grades 3–5

SCENARIO 1: GLOBAL LEARNING AND OBSERVATIONS
FOR A BETTER ENVIRONMENT (GLOBE)

Grade Levels: 3–5

Technology Profile Performance Indicators: 2, 3, 4, 5, 6

Subject Areas: Science, Social Studies

Source: NASA Classroom of the Future Program

Ms. Smith and her class have made extensive use of online resources, such as Exploring the Environment (ETE) found at http://www.cotf.edu/ete/ and Global Learning and Observations for a Better Environment (GLOBE) found at http://www.globe.gov/. She uses ETE to access classroom-tested problem-based learning modules that extend and sometimes replace her old paper-based activities. These self-contained resources have provided a new spark of vitality into her science and interdisciplinary classes, where students grapple with real-world issues and current data.

Using the GLOBE structure, Ms. Smith has students collect information from environmental observations around the school and vicinity, report the data to a processing facility through GLOBE, and use global images created from their data to study local environmental issues. The students have been contributing to an environmental database used by research scientists to improve our understanding of the global environment.

Recently, her students used GLOBE and other electronic resources to research a hot local issue. The community was debating whether to allow a biotechnology firm to locate nearby. Her students chose to analyze this issue very carefully. Students working in groups engaged in collecting and analyzing data about the proposed plant. Ms. Smith set forums in the class so that the students could present their findings and engage in debate. Then students created Web pages to present their findings and arguments to the community. She reports that because of the authenticity and relevance of the issue, her students were even more engaged as they used technology in researching the issues. Parents were pleased to see their children's work on the school's Web site, as viewing the materials at home helped parents feel closer to what the students did in school. Parents also reported subtle changes in their children's attitudes when they were immersed in this hands-on, minds-on, technology-infused classroom.

Performance Indicators for Technology-Literate Students

Grades 6–8

All students should have opportunities to demonstrate the following performances. Numbers in parentheses following each performance indicator refer to the standards category to which the performance is linked. The categories are:

1. Basic operations and concepts
2. Social, ethical, and human issues
3. Technology productivity tools
4. Technology communications tools
5. Technology research tools
6. Technology problem-solving and decision-making tools

Prior to completion of Grade 8 students will:

1. Apply strategies for identifying and solving routine hardware and software problems that occur during everyday use. (1)

2. Demonstrate knowledge of current changes in information technologies and the effect those changes have on the workplace and society. (2)

3. Exhibit legal and ethical behaviors when using information and technology, and discuss consequences of misuse. (2)

4. Use content-specific tools, software, and simulations (e.g., environmental probes, graphing calculators, exploratory environments, Web tools) to support learning and research. (3, 5)

5. Apply productivity/multimedia tools and peripherals to support personal productivity, group collaboration, and learning throughout the curriculum. (3, 6)

6. Design, develop, publish, and present products (e.g., Web pages, videotapes) using technology resources that demonstrate and communicate curriculum concepts to audiences inside and outside the classroom. (4, 5, 6)

7. Collaborate with peers, experts, and others using telecommunications and collaborative tools to investigate curriculum-related problems, issues, and information, and to develop solutions or products for audiences inside and outside the classroom. (4, 5)

8. Select and use appropriate tools and technology resources to accomplish a variety of tasks and solve problems. (5, 6)

9. Demonstrate an understanding of concepts underlying hardware, software, and connectivity, and of practical applications to learning and problem solving. (1, 6)

10. Research and evaluate the accuracy, relevance, appropriateness, comprehensiveness, and bias of electronic information sources concerning real-world problems. (2, 5, 6)

Curriculum Examples and Scenarios

Grades 6–8

SCENARIO 1: USING TECHNOLOGY TO LEARN ABOUT ROCKS AND MINERALS

Grade Levels: 8

Technology Profile Performance Indicators: 4, 5, 6, 7

Subject Areas: Science, Social Studies

Source: Hemmer, J. (1998, November/December). Lakeisha's year in eighth grade: Technology Integration Vignette, part 3. *Learning & Leading with Technology,* 25(7), 27–31.

Lakeisha's eighth-grade class began a unit on rocks and minerals. They explored topics using CD-ROM encyclopedias and stored the information they found and results from their laboratory sessions, including a weeklong rock simulation program, in their databases. When their studies were complete, Mrs. Perkins helped the students create HyperStudio® presentations to share with the class. She also found an Internet site called "Ask a Geologist." Lakeisha and her classmates were then able to e-mail questions about rocks and minerals to the geologists who were sponsoring the site. Lakeisha and her friends were fascinated with the information they received on rocks and minerals in their native area. Lakeisha's science teacher organized a local geologic dig to help students begin their own rock and mineral collections.

SCENARIO 2: THE LOUISIANA LABOR MARKET LESSON

Grade Levels: 8

Technology Profile Performance Indicators: 5, 6, 7, 8

Subject Areas: Mathematics, Social Studies

Source: Callaway, B. (1997). Teacher and students present Louisiana labor lesson at the BESE Meeting. *Louisiana Challenge Grant Newsletter,* 2(1), 9. [Full plan at: www.challenge.state.la.us/k12act/lp/index.html]

At Marthaville Elementary, a small rural K–8 school, Laura Strahan and her eighth-grade students studied the Louisiana labor market in their math class. Students used the Internet to access the Louisiana Department of Labor's Web site (www.ldol.state.la.us) and search for the top 20 projected occupations in the state. The U.S. Department of Labor receives and distributes labor information from each state and updates its statistics daily.

Students were divided into groups. Each group selected five occupations and developed a survey for them. Each survey was used to query other individuals regarding the estimated annual income for those occupations. The students then assisted in analyzing the survey results, comparing results to actual salaries as reported on the Department of Labor and other Internet sites, calculating averages of estimates, and displaying the information in appropriate graph format. Students from Ms. Strahan's class presented their results to the Board of Elementary and Secondary Education to illustrate the importance of providing technology resources to schools in Louisiana.

This lesson provides numerous opportunities for use of technology to access, analyze, and present information. Information is accessed using telecommunications, then analyzed and presented using word-processing, database, spreadsheet, graphing, and multimedia software. The Web is used to share findings with a larger audience.

Performance Indicators for Technology Literate Students

Grades 9–12

All students should have opportunities to demonstrate the following performances. Numbers in parentheses following each performance indicator refer to the standards category to which the performance is linked. The categories are:

1. Basic operations and concepts
2. Social, ethical, and human issues
3. Technology productivity tools
4. Technology communications tools
5. Technology research tools
6. Technology problem-solving and decision-making tools

Prior to completion of Grade 12 students will:

1. Identify capabilities and limitations of contemporary and emerging technology resources and assess the potential of these systems and services to address personal, lifelong learning, and workplace needs. (2)
2. Make informed choices among technology systems, resources, and services. (1, 2)
3. Analyze advantages and disadvantages of widespread use and reliance on technology in the workplace and in society as a whole. (2)
4. Demonstrate and advocate for legal and ethical behaviors among peers, family, and community regarding the use of technology and information. (2)

5. Use technology tools and resources for managing and communicating personal/professional information (e.g., finances, schedules, addresses, purchases, correspondence). (3, 4)

6. Evaluate technology-based options, including distance and distributed education, for lifelong learning. (5)

7. Routinely and efficiently use online information resources to meet needs for collaboration, research, publications, communications, and productivity. (4, 5, 6)

8. Select and apply technology tools for research, information analysis, problem-solving, and decision-making in content learning. (4, 5)

9. Investigate and apply expert systems, intelligent agents, and simulations in real-world situations. (3, 5, 6)

10. Collaborate with peers, experts, and others to contribute to a content-related knowledge base by using technology to compile, synthesize, produce, and disseminate information, models, and other creative works. (4, 5, 6)

Curriculum Examples and Scenarios

Grades 9–12

SCENARIO 1: PRESIDENTIAL ELECTIONS

Grade Levels: 9–12

Technology Profile Performance Indicators: 5, 7, 8

Subject Areas: Social Studies, Language Arts, Mathematics

Source: Based on a lesson created by a southern California teacher and presented in a class at California State University, Los Angeles.

The U.S. system of presidential elections can be a mystery for many citizens. Teaching middle school or high school students about the Electoral College can be quite a challenge. Mr. Sanchez, a high school social studies teacher in southern California, developed an activity for his students that involves election data from the closest presidential election in history—the 1960 election between John F. Kennedy and Richard M. Nixon. This activity helps students understand the Electoral College and some of the strategies used by presidential candidates. Complete, state-by-state election results can be found at the following Web site: www.geocities .com/CapitolHill/6228/.

Mr. Sanchez divides his students into groups and gives each a spreadsheet containing data from the 1960 presidential election. The spreadsheet contains the popular and Electoral College results from every state and territory. Formulas at the bottom of the columns calculate the total number of popular votes and Electoral votes for each candidate.

The groups are asked to conduct a series of investigations by manipulating the spreadsheet data. Students have printouts of the original data and the original data file on disk so that they can restore the spreadsheet after each manipulation. The questions they investigate are: "Can you change the data so that Mr. Nixon wins the election rather than Mr. Kennedy?" "Can you change the outcome of the election by changing the election results in only one state?" "Two states?" "Three states?" "Can you change the popular vote so that one candidate wins the popular election but loses the Electoral College results?" "Can you change the popular vote so that the same candidate loses the popular vote but wins the election (via the Electoral College results)?" "What is the fewest number of states you can change to have one candidate win the popular vote but lose the election?" These "What if?" activities help students gain an understanding of the Electoral College.

Finally, the groups prepare a multimedia report on the 1960 election using HyperStudio®. They can include pictures of the candidates, charts and graphs from the election (e.g., www.multied.com/elections), and a discussion of their spreadsheet manipulations.

WEB SITE

http://cnets.iste.org

3

NEW TECHNOLOGY STANDARDS FOR TEACHERS

STANDARD 20.5 (NEW—FOR THE MULTIPLE AND/OR

SINGLE SUBJECT TEACHING CREDENTIAL)

USE OF COMPUTER-BASED TECHNOLOGY

IN THE CLASSROOM

California Commission on Teacher Credentialing

CANDIDATES ARE ABLE to use appropriate computer-based technology to facilitate the teaching and learning process.

Rationale

The widespread reliance of contemporary society upon computer-based technologies reflects the increasing importance of electronic information management and communication tools. Technology, in its many forms, has become a powerful tool to enhance curriculum and instruction. Productivity, communication, research, and learning are dramatically enhanced through the appropriate use of technology, thereby allowing educators to accomplish tasks that were not previously possible.

The true power and potential of computer-based technologies lies not in the machine itself but in the prudent and appropriate use of software applications to gather, process, and communicate information. Teachers' integration of these tools into the educational experience of students, including those with special needs, is crucial to preparing them for lives of personal, academic, and professional growth and achievement.

Teachers must become fluent, critical users of technology to provide a relevant education and to prepare students to be lifelong learners in an information-based, interactive society. The appropriate and efficient use of software applications and related media to access and evaluate information, analyze and solve problems, and communicate ideas is essential to maximizing the instructional process. Such use of technology supports teaching and learning regardless of individual learning style, socioeconomic background, culture, ethnicity, or geographic location.

Factors to Consider

When an evaluation team judges whether or not a program meets this standard, the Commission expects the team to consider the extent to which:

Prior to Issuance of the Preliminary Credential (Level I)

GENERAL KNOWLEDGE AND SKILLS

- Each candidate demonstrates knowledge of current basic computer hardware and software terminology.

- Each candidate demonstrates competency in the operation and care of computer-related hardware (e.g., cleaning input devices, avoiding proximity to magnets, proper startup and shut down sequences, scanning for viruses, and formatting storage media).

- Each candidate implements basic troubleshooting techniques for computer systems and related peripheral devices (e.g., checking the connections, isolating the problem components, distinguishing between software and hardware problems) before accessing the appropriate avenue of technical support.

- Each candidate demonstrates knowledge and understanding of the appropriate use of computer-based technology in teaching and learning.

SPECIFIC KNOWLEDGE AND SKILLS

- Each candidate uses computer applications to manage records (e.g., gradebook, attendance, and assessment records).

- Each candidate uses computers to communicate through printed media (e.g., newsletters incorporating graphics and charts, course descriptions, and student reports).

- Each candidate interacts with others using e-mail.

- Each candidate is familiar with a variety of computer-based collaborative tools (e.g., threaded discussion groups, newsgroups, list servers, online chat, and audio-video conferences).

- Each candidate examines a variety of current educational digital media and uses established selection criteria to evaluate materials, for example, multimedia, Internet resources, telecommunications, computer-assisted instruction, and productivity and presentation tools. (See California State guidelines and evaluations.)

- Each candidate chooses software for its relevance, effectiveness, alignment with content standards, and value added to student learning.

- Each candidate demonstrates competence in the use of electronic research tools (e.g., access the Internet to search for and retrieve information).

- Each candidate demonstrates the ability to assess the authenticity, reliability, and bias of the data gathered.

- Each candidate identifies student learning styles and determines appropriate technological resources to improve learning.

- Each candidate considers the content to be taught and selects the best technological resources to support, manage, and enhance learning.

- Each candidate demonstrates an ability to create and maintain effective learning environments using computer-based technology.

- Each candidate analyzes best practices and research findings on the use of technology and designs lessons accordingly.

- Each candidate demonstrates knowledge of copyright issues (e.g., distribution of copyrighted materials and proper citing of sources).

- Each candidate demonstrates knowledge of privacy, security, and safety issues (e.g., appropriate use of chatrooms, confidentiality of records including graded student work, publishing names and pictures of minors, and Acceptable Use Policies).

- The program meets other factors related to this standard of quality brought to the attention of the team by the program.

Prior to Issuance of the Professional Credential (Level II)

- Each candidate uses a computer application to manipulate and analyze data (e.g., create, use, and report from a database; and create charts and reports from a spreadsheet).

- Each candidate communicates through a variety of electronic media (e.g., presentations incorporating images and sound, web pages, and portfolios).

- Each candidate interacts and collaborates with others using computer-based collaborative tools (e.g., threaded discussion groups, newsgroups, electronic list management applications, online chat, and audio/video conferences).

- Each candidate demonstrates competence in evaluating the authenticity, reliability; bias of the data gathered; determines outcomes and evaluates the success or effectiveness of the process used.

- Each candidate optimizes lessons based upon the technological resources available in the classroom, school library media centers, computer labs, district and county facilities, and other locations.

- Each candidate designs, adapts, and uses lessons which address the students' needs to develop information literacy and problem-solving skills as tools for lifelong learning.

- Each candidate creates or makes use of learning environments inside the classroom, as well as in library media centers or computer labs, that promote effective use of technology aligned with the curriculum.

- Each candidate uses technology in lessons to increase each student's ability to plan, locate, evaluate, select, and use information to solve problems and draw conclusions.

- Each candidate uses technology as a tool for assessing student learning and for providing feedback to students and their parents.

- Each candidate frequently monitors and reflects upon the results of using technology in instruction and adapts lessons accordingly.

- Each candidate collaborates with other teachers, mentors, librarians, resource specialists, and other experts to support technology-enhanced curriculum. For example, they may collaborate on interdisciplinary lessons or cross-grade-level projects.

- Each candidate contributes to site-based planning or local decision making regarding the use of technology and acquisition of technological resources.

- The program meets other factors related to this standard of quality brought to the attention of the team by the program.

WEB SITE

http://www.ctc.ca.gov

4

LONG-RANGE PLAN FOR TECHNOLOGY, 1996–2010

*A Report to the 75th Texas Legislature
from the State Board of Education*

Vision of Technology in Education, 2010

> *"We don't buy glasses; we buy vision. We don't buy awnings;
> we buy shade. We don't buy a newspaper; we buy information.
> It isn't the product we want. It's what the product will do for us.
> We buy something or pursue something, not because we want
> the thing itself, but because we want what that thing
> will give us or do for us."*

—Max Anders in *The Good Life: Living with Meaning
in a "Never Enough World"*

Imagine a home . . .

. . . where every parent—regardless of native language or socioeconomic background—can communicate readily with teachers about children's progress, improve parenting skills, and get a degree or job training without leaving home or work.

Imagine a school . . .

. . . where every student—regardless of zip code, economic level, age, race or ethnicity, or ability or disability—can be immersed in the sights, sounds, and languages of other countries; visit museums; research knowledge webs from the holdings of dispersed libraries; and explore the inner workings of cells from inside the cell or the cold distance of outer space from inside a virtual* spacesuit.

Imagine a district . . .

. . . where every educator—regardless of subject, experience, or district location, size or wealth—can get hands-on training instantaneously, when or where he or she needs it; interact with a virtual community of professional colleagues; and have access to financial data and student performance information as well as the analytical tools to use them effectively.

Imagine a state . . .

. . . where every community member can visit the doctor for an examination and needed laboratory tests while at home or the office; collaborate with work colleagues at distant sites about complex data sets or video graphics; search primary source materials on an event half-way around the world; and take a high school or college course with fellow students from Port Arthur to El Paso by communicating rather than commuting.

What needs to happen for these images to become a reality?

- A technology infrastructure connecting schools, colleges, medical facilities, libraries, businesses, and homes must be established.

- Successful partnerships must exist among industries, the educational system, and other public service providers so that the new technologies and their applications are available and appropriate for education—and not only for the business and entertainment markets.

- The educational system must consider extending the traditional boundaries of the school year, scholastic age, and geographic location.

---

*Virtual relationships or items are based on interactions or objects or representations that are in digital rather than in physical form.

- The teaching and learning process must be receptive to a wide variety of options, including expansion of learning into the home and into the broader community, development of virtual relationships among learners, and learning through distributed synthetic environments as well as on site.

- Educators must learn to access and incorporate a wide variety of resources for instructional support, research, and administration.

- Students of all ages and backgrounds must be active in the pursuit of resources to build individual and collaborative knowledge communities.

If the images become reality, who will benefit and what will the benefits be?

Students can expect higher performance and deeper engagement in academic endeavors by accessing resources available through a variety of modalities appropriate to individual learning styles.

Parents can expect not only to participate more directly in their children's education but also to improve their own knowledge as parents and citizens.

Teachers can expect to employ a wider variety of instructional approaches by having access to professional resources and by determining when and how to receive support, staff development, and classroom information.

Administrators can expect to be more fully informed and to manage more efficiently through timely access to and analysis of information, and to assist in direct operations of schools and administrative decision making.

Taxpayers and school board members can expect more efficient use of resources, both financial and human, and more equitable allocation of each.

Community members can be afforded the opportunity to participate in key educational and community decisions and to participate in the educational process.

Communities can maintain their integrity because of the ability to move information and not people.

Teaching and Learning: Executive Summary

The Teaching and Learning component of this document focuses on the instructional needs of teachers and the learning needs of students in meeting the vision of technology in education. Tools need to be appropriately acquired, accessed, and integrated to enhance academic achievement of all Texas students in all aspects of instruction.

This plan recognizes the need for graduates to demonstrate mastery of technology conveyed in the Texas Essential Knowledge and Skills (TEKS) as both a course of study and as applied in other content areas. Students today need appropriate technological skills and knowledge to achieve academic success and to become productive members of society.

Over the past decade, these skills have become more complex. Citizens must now have the expertise to interact with and to compete in a global society. This long-range plan directs the Texas Education Agency and provides recommendations for districts and campuses to help schools and communities meet these technology needs.

Technology for Teachers and Learners

The teacher-learner relationship in our schools is evolving and will remain important over the duration of this plan. Learners across the state gain access to learning opportunities when teachers have the incentives, expertise, resources, and human support to feel confident in their own technology skills and to provide opportunities to students.

The Texas long-range plan for technology embraces the belief that, before technology can significantly improve learning, teachers must first be competent with the technology applications that facilitate their work and support student learning.

Short-term (two-year) initiatives in Teaching and Learning focus on:

- meeting students' learning needs through distance learning and other technologies,
- clarifying the technology proficiencies expected of students and teachers,
- highlighting effective practices,
- establishing partnerships to provide tools and services, and
- encouraging effective planning.

These initiatives will build on the technology-based experiences begun under the previous long-range plan for technology and extend them into the mid-term (the following four years) and beyond.

The mid-term actions and recommendations strengthen teachers' and students' skills by:

- fostering the development and integration of rigorous TEKS into technology-related classroom activities and into electronic instructional materials,

- developing state accountability measures,
- encouraging regional service centers and state and local partnerships with commercial concerns to develop products appropriate for Texas schools, and
- continuing to encourage effective local planning.

Initiatives for the long term sustain and extend attention to teachers and students. At the same time, they define a new focus on parent involvement in planning for technology, using technology-based educational resources, and addressing the needs of the larger community.

Community Involvement

At each stage, actions are recommended to other state agencies, regional education service centers, schools, communities, institutions of higher education, and the private sector. Each has a role to play in building education and students' technology proficiencies and in fostering technology integration to meet the ultimate goal of increased student achievement.

Integration of Technology

The state's current initiative to redefine the curriculum by specifying essential knowledge and skills across all discipline areas offers a rare opportunity to position technology as it should be—integrated into all aspects of teaching and learning for all students and teachers. The Teaching and Learning Actions and Recommendations, along with the other three critical components, contribute toward meeting the vision for technology use in education by ensuring appropriate application of technology in the TEKS as well as TEKS-driven training, instructional materials, and assessment.

Educator Preparation and Development: Executive Summary

Research on successful professional development reveals that all members of an institution must share a common understanding of the goals and knowledge base in order for the institution to improve. As a result, the *Long-Range Plan for Technology, 1996–2010* addresses the staff development needs not only of teachers but of all the members of the professional education community.

At the public school level, these include teachers, administrators, curriculum coordinators, counselors, librarians, and other educational professionals. The plan also addresses the training needs of faculty at the university level, particularly those involved in pre-service educator preparation.

Retraining Is a Priority

To provide quality education to all learners, the training and retooling of the current educator workforce in using technology tools to teach and learn must be identified as a priority. In addition, technology can and should be used to provide equitable access to quality, standards-based professional development.

All pre- and post-service educator preparation personnel must possess and demonstrate the capacity to use technologies effectively in all facets of their professional duties. These include personnel at colleges and universities, at Centers for Professional Development and Technology, and at other organizations that offer training to teachers.

To use technologies effectively, pre-service and educator preparation personnel must continually:

- learn about current educational technologies and their applications,
- develop planning skills for and through technology use,
- integrate educational technologies throughout the entire teacher preparation program,
- model the best practices regarding the effective integration of educational technology throughout the curriculum,
- learn about new technologies,
- integrate technologies appropriately into their teaching, and
- use technology to increase their knowledge, to seek expert advice, and to collaborate.

Higher education faculty should be encouraged to expand their technology skills for instructional purposes. Thus, the State Board for Educator Certification is asked to establish requirements in technology proficiencies for both educator preparation and educator renewal.

Just-in-Time Professional Development

When they have a concern about instruction or management, educators need immediate access to relevant, high-quality professional development and technical support both during and outside the instructional day. This type of professional development is known as "just-in-time" rather than "just-in-case" assistance.

Just-in-time professional development rejects the standard of often irrelevant or ill-timed professional development presented just in case one ever needs it. It replaces this with a new standard for professional development, one that is on demand and just in time for effective use. All educators should have cost-effective access to high-quality information regardless of geographic location or time of day. Technology makes this feasible.

State, regional, and local institutions as well as the private sector all play a role in developing, facilitating, and providing this model of professional development. Significant coordination among these entities and allocation of resources will be necessary to train the educator workforce in integrating technologies into all facets of instruction, management, and planning. . . .

Administration and Support Services: Executive Summary

Technology systems provide tools for many purposes. The Actions and Recommendations for Teaching and Learning and those for Educator Preparation and Development focus on those purposes that are critical for learners—whether the learners are students, in a classroom or at a distant site, or teachers. In their roles as seekers and providers of knowledge, students and teachers alike rely on technologies for functions such as communications, research, analysis, and presentation.

Various Administrative Functions

Teachers also serve as managers of instruction. They can benefit from having access to nonsecure information, made readily available electronically, about their students' strengths and needs.

Administrative and support services staff in school districts require sophisticated technological tools to accomplish their functions. These staff include those responsible for keeping track of student attendance, participation in special programs, student performance, the educational progress of mobile students, expenditures from multiple sources of funds, and local accountability information. Also included are those responsible for making decisions about food, transportation, and other services critical to the comprehensive and efficient operations of a school district.

Sharing the Challenge of Technology

The requirements of the Public Education Information Management System (PEIMS) and of the Academic Excellence Indicator System (AEIS), in particular, challenge administrative staff to take full advantage of technology tools for data gathering, analysis, and distribution. It is imperative that administrative and support staff have access to both the tools and the professional development needed to effectively and efficiently learn to use these tools.

Furthermore, the rich information available through PEIMS can and should be shared, following decisions regarding security and confidentiality, with teachers, parents, and community members. . . .

As the technological infrastructure, described in the next section, is established, PEIMS could also be redesigned to reduce paperwork, replace some data items with sampling methods, and improve the quality and timeliness of data acquisition and transmittal. This redesign will, in turn, make the information available through PEIMS even more accessible to and useful for both instructional and non-instructional personnel.

Meeting the Challenge

To meet these needs, the state will:

- coordinate actions to standardize state information reports from districts and campuses,
- plan for and construct a revised PEIMS,
- seek ways to use technology for student assessment and record-keeping purposes, and
- provide leadership in the use of data for sound decision-making.

Regional education service centers will also play a key role. They can assist school districts with selection of and training on appropriate data systems, and with revising PEIMS.

Schools will be asked to use technology-based data systems in planning and decision making. They can use technology to offer parents and other community members access to nonsecured data.

Infrastructure for Technology: Executive Summary

The establishment of an infrastructure for technology is fundamental to undertaking many of the Actions and Recommendations that precede this section. In this plan for technology, the infrastructure consists of two complementary components.

The Components of an Infrastructure for Technology

One component focuses on technological aspects. Often called the "boxes and wires," these are the hardware and the connecting peripherals that cause the hardware to function properly, such as the network connections and the resulting communications capabilities. Also relevant are the software, including applications programs, such as graphics or spreadsheet, and the content, such as the TEKS.

The second—and equally important—component of the infrastructure for technology is the human infrastructure. This refers to the capabilities or proficiencies of those who use the technical components.

The two aspects work symbiotically to create communication and enhanced skills and knowledge among public education stakeholders. The ultimate result is networks of people and information made possible by networks of telecommunications.

Establishing a Comprehensive System

To achieve these networks, it is the responsibility of the Texas Education Agency to first take a leadership role in establishing the comprehensive state technology system that undergirds and makes possible the communications among students and educators, the data distribution and analysis, the just-in-time professional development, and the other key factors conveyed in this long-range plan for technology that are discussed in the previous sections.

Coordination with other state agencies, regional and local education agencies, and the private sector will be of paramount importance in determining connectivity and the technical, functional, and other standards for this system. Coordination will also be needed to ensure that access will be equitable statewide.

Concomitant with this effort will be the actions necessary to ensure that students and educators acquire the proficiencies they need to take advantage of the technology infrastructure. In the long term, the state will also need to develop policies regarding public access to the data and to the educational resources available through the infrastructure.

The Regional and Local Roles

Regional education service centers should take responsibility for participating in planning and supporting the technology infrastructure. Each center should also raise the level of expertise of educators and technical staff at the schools and districts in its use and maintenance.

It is at the local level where the greatest use and, perhaps, the greatest benefits will accrue. To reap these benefits, school districts will need to determine the funding mechanisms that best fit local conditions for acquiring, maintaining, and recycling workstations and other technologies.

They will also benefit most by implementing the ratios of workstations to students and educators introduced above and by determining how best to deploy the workstations to ensure universal accessibility.

Many Roles in Technology and Education

It will be incumbent on institutions of higher education to prepare pre-service educators with the skills they need to integrate the technology infrastructure into teaching and learning, instructional management, professional development, and administration.

The private sector—the developers and vendors of the technology systems, the instructional materials, and the training and other services—is asked to work closely with the public education system to provide products appropriate for students, educators, and managers at favorable prices.

Finally, as conveyed in the previous sections, entire communities will benefit by seeking access to the wealth of information and services that will be available on the networks.

WEB SITE

http://www.tea.state.tx.us

5

CHALLENGES OF CREATING A NATION OF TECHNOLOGY-ENABLED SCHOOLS

Thomas K. Glennan, Arthur Melmed

THERE ARE MANY CHALLENGES to making extensive use of technology for improving the performance of the education system in the United States. In this chapter, we want to deal with the three most important:

1. Financing the costs of creating and sustaining technology-rich schools.
2. Providing teachers with the skills and time needed to implement such schools.
3. Features of the educational software market that may restrict the supply of some important classes of software.

At the end of each subsection, we suggest possible actions that the public and private sectors can take to deal with these challenges.

Financing the Costs of Introducing and Using Technology in Schools

If policymakers want to significantly increase the level of technology in the schools, they face two key financial problems.

1. How does a school system obtain the resources for the initial investment necessary to transform a school into a technology-rich enterprise?

2. How does a school system obtain 3 to 5 percent (or more) of their budget per year to devote to technology and training on a continuous basis?

Past experience suggests that initial investment funding will be provided by a wide variety of means specific to the individual financial and political conditions of states and school districts. We believe that the continuing costs associated with extensive use of technology in all schools can only be achieved with significant restructuring of school budgets.

Front-End Investment

The schools examined in the Keltner and Ross (1996) cost study are representative of the current approach to investment for technology-rich schools. These schools have financed themselves with a combination of special grants, donations from business, fund-raising by parents, categorical funding from federal or state programs, and, occasionally, a little restructuring of a school's budget. Training has been supported by normal staff development funding as well as substantial "sweat equity" of committed teachers. Funding was pieced together by exceptional leaders, administrators, teachers, and parents who had unusual capabilities to identify and tap external sources of funds. Thus these schools are exceptions rather than the norm.[1]

This form of "expedient" financing is symptomatic of a deeply ingrained problem of social service providers in general and educational agencies in particular. Compared with the private sector, they lack an investment mentality.[2] School districts do not regularly set aside a specified

---

[1] The funding obtained by these schools was largely devoted to initial investments. Several of the schools reported that they were beginning to face problems with the sustained maintenance and updating of their capital stock. Many of the funding sources supported the investments but not the costs of long-term continuing operations.

[2] School systems do plan for building and renovating schools, but these activities are normally tied to specific bond issues and are not closely related to school programs. Requirements for networks and adequate power for technology are often part of these projects.

portion of their revenues for investing in activities to improve school performance. The reasons for this are found in the political nature of resource allocation in public education.

The allocation of resources in public school districts is a highly political process. The governance of school systems forces a superintendent and his or her staff to satisfy a large number of claimants. Teachers, other staff, advocates for students with special needs, schools with politically powerful parents, employers seeking a steady supply of job entrants, and government leaders seeking schools to enhance economic development all put pressures on the leaders of a school district. Funding restrictions may be imposed by state or federal governments in support of one or another interest that has made its needs known at higher levels of government.

To cope with these demands, many superintendents and their staffs adopt coping rather than strategic behaviors. The resulting budget is a product of political compromise intended to minimize political pain. Existing allocations of resources are the starting point and only marginal changes are made. Firm, long-term commitments of the type required to install technology throughout a system are seldom made. Such commitments restrict future capabilities to allocate funds, while key district actors prefer to keep their options open.

This behavior is reinforced by the difficulty of assessing the relative values of alternative investments. The sort of investment planning possible in the private sector is hampered by the lack of clear measures of outcome and an understanding of the link between investment actions and outcomes.

An example may illustrate this. Consider two quite different investment options. The first is an "academy" at which the district's staff can be trained or provided opportunities to plan with the assistance of specialized staff. Funds are required to build or renovate space, acquire necessary materials, and hire and train a staff. The returns are presumably improved programs in individual schools. The second option is investment in the technology infrastructure of a set of schools coupled with the training necessary to exploit that infrastructure.

Both of these alternatives are forms of investment. Both can plausibly be expected to yield a long-term return on the investment. However, generally agreed-to causal links between investment actions and learning outcomes are lacking, and the latter are difficult to measure. Under similar circumstances, private organizations might be able to use expert judgment in evaluating the alternatives, but for schools, this is complicated by the open nature of school decision-making.

Most decisions like these have to be made in public forums where virtually all decisions must be politically defensible. Aggregating resources for a strategic purpose inevitably means that resources must be taken from other activities. If widely agreed-to relations between investment acts and outcomes are not available, those losing resources will complain loudly and, if politically powerful, will be likely to prevail. It is easy to see why there is a tendency to spread resources among claimants rather than to mass resources for a strategic purpose.[3]

As with any broad generalization, there are important exceptions to this observation. Some districts have had a significant history of investing in technology for their schools. To develop a better understanding of how they operated, we interviewed administrators in 14 districts that have invested heavily in technology.[4] Several points stand out.

Taken as a whole, these districts relied heavily on their own local funding sources. Nearly half had made technology a part of one or more local bond issues that supported building expansion and renovation as well.[5] Many of the systems had moderately restructured their central office expenditures to free up funding. Several had strong support from the local business community; for example, Jefferson County, Kentucky, reported that 60 percent of the costs of acquiring computers were covered by the business community. Where state programs were available, schools took advantage of those funds. Only a few of the districts we surveyed reported making significant use of federal Title I or Title II funding.[6]

---

[3] This certainly should not be taken to say that such investment behaviors are impossible. For example, during the 1980s both superintendents Richard Wallace in Pittsburgh and Donald Ingwerson in Jefferson County, Kentucky, succeeded in introducing investment-like behaviors with the strong support of the business leaders in their communities.

[4] The work reported here was carried out by Karl Sun. The districts were chosen using QED's [Quality Education Data's] list of large districts rank-ordered by the number of students per computer. These districts had ratios of students to computers ranging from 4.1:1 to 7.5:1. QED, 1994, Appendix H.

[5] It appears that the payback periods for these bond issues were structured so that the part that supported the technology was paid in five to seven years, in keeping with the expected lifetime of the equipment.

[6] These were sections of the Elementary and Secondary Education Act that supported funding for schools with high proportions of students from disadvantaged backgrounds and school improvement. The act has been reauthorized as the Improving America's Schools Act, with a substantially different program structure.

As would be expected with efforts funded largely by local sources, the respondents reported that the investments in technology seemed to have strong public support. The public felt that widespread use of computers and other technology was important and that the educational system was doing an effective job of deploying technology in its schools. As with other school reforms, good strategies for engaging the public are important.

While the school districts that we surveyed provide some guidance concerning the manner in which investments in technology can be fostered and an investment mentality developed, it is important to note some important caveats concerning this sample of districts. Because of the source and nature of the data used to select them, the 14 districts are all large ones with substantial student populations. Most are in regions that are experiencing population and/or economic growth. The sample does not include either small, resource-poor districts or urban districts that have lost much of both their tax base and their middle-class families. For many schools that fall into these groups, it is probably unreasonable to expect that the districts and schools can finance substantial technology and reform efforts wholly on their own.

We believe that if schools are going to significantly restructure themselves and if technology is to be a major element of the restructuring, an investment mentality must be engendered in state and local districts. There are several possible ways to do this.

1. Districts could decide to set aside a portion of their total funding explicitly for investment and develop decision procedures governing the use of these funds.

2. Communities could establish and fund independent foundations intended to support the acquisition and deployment of technology.

3. Higher levels of government, more insulated from local politics, could establish special funds or programs that can be used to support technology investments.

Each of these approaches intended to create a pool of resources that can be allocated in a manner that differs from a school district's normal budget allocation process.

DISTRICT SET-ASIDE FUNDS. We are not aware of any district that formally allocates funds to an investment "account." However, funds are often allocated to staff and/or curriculum development activities. There are likely to be technology line items in some districts. There are funds for purchasing textbooks that may be allocated centrally. Each of these activities has an investment purpose although they may be treated as a current expense.

Funding for these activities (and others having an investment purpose) could be aggregated and an explicit investment planning process instituted. While these investments should not be restricted to technology, for districts that have decided that technology and its implementation should be a major investment activity, technology could constitute a major theme. Funds raised from the sale of bonds might also be allocated through the same investment planning process.

Decisions on the level of funding for investment should be a major concern of the school board, presumably based on the recommendation of the superintendent. A significant effort to engage the public in this activity would be necessary, with a major goal being to establish the legitimacy of this means of allocating funds.

COMMUNITY-BASED FUNDS. We noted above that in one of the districts we interviewed, Jefferson County, the business community had established a local foundation over a decade ago with the explicit goal of putting computers in schools.[7] While this is the most ambitious example of a community fund for technology we know of, there are many examples of less formal agreements between businesses or collections of businesses and schools.

Creating a community fund allows the allocation of investment resources to be separated somewhat from the normal budget allocation process of the school system. Moreover, the actions of the fund can be coordinated with related activities by the district such as the allocation of funds for the support of professional development. In communities where business and local foundations exist, this may be an attractive option for supporting initial investment in technology.

STATE AND FEDERAL FUNDING. Quite a number of states have provided funds for technology. Some have explicitly sought to create networks (e.g., Texas and North Carolina). Others have provided funds for equipping schools and training staff (e.g., Ohio and Florida). Several have provided funds for exemplary projects (e.g., California and Kentucky). As we noted, while most of the districts we surveyed relied largely on local funds, 8 of the 14 mentioned state funding (including lottery funding) as a source of some funding.

---

[7] See the Jefferson County case study in Beryl Buck Institute for Education, 1994.

Only 3 of the 14 districts surveyed mentioned federal funds as a primary funding source, but as we noted above, the districts we interviewed were generally ones for which federal funding was not very important. In fact, nationwide, perhaps 30 percent of the funding for technology in elementary and secondary education in 1994 came from federal sources.[8] Much of this was supported by Chapter I, the component of the Elementary and Secondary Education Act that provides resources to districts with high proportions of educationally disadvantaged students.[9]

Both the states and the federal government have the advantage that they are somewhat distant from the politics that focuses on district-level allocations. As a consequence, both have placed more emphasis on investment both in technology itself and in training. While all levels of government are under heavy political pressure to hold down overall spending, future initial investments in technology almost certainly will require additional funding from sources above the local district.

Whether the funds come from improved local allocations, community-level foundations, or state and federal sources, it is important that they be seen as initial investments. Planning surrounding their use should anticipate the need for continuing expenditures for operations, maintenance, and replacement.

Continuing Costs of Operating Technology-Rich Schools

The capability to devote a steady level of funding to maintaining and updating the stock of educational technology and the school staff seems to us to be a somewhat (although not wholly) separate issue from that of making initial investments. Continuing support for technology-rich learning environments requires a significant restructuring of school and district-level budgets to permit the reallocation of resources from existing to new uses. Such a reallocation seems unlikely unless schools are given substantial authority over their entire budget, and school personnel and par-

---

[8] It is estimated that the federal government provided about $850 million of the funds invested in educational technology and related training in 1994. Of this, more than half came from Chapter I. Interview with Charles Blaschke, Education Turnkey Systems, August 15, 1995.

[9] The changes incorporated in its recent reauthorization to expand the number of "whole school" Chapter I (now Title I) programs should make it an even more effective source of funds supporting technology for schools serving high proportions of economically and educationally disadvantaged children.

Figure 5.1. Allocation of School Expenditures, 1992–93.

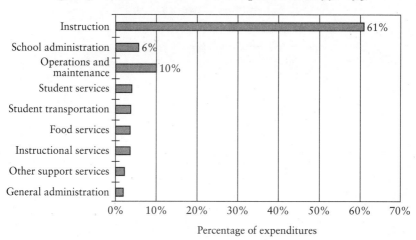

Source: *NCES, 1995b, Table 160.*

ents feel the reallocation will improve the education of their students. Obviously, decisions by individual schools to reallocate will depend upon solid information concerning the benefits associated with integrating technology into their educational program, strong support from the community, and the availability of the assistance that schools need to make the transformation from current programs to new ones.

Historically, there has been little inclination to make significant shifts in resources. Figure 5.1 shows the overall distribution of current expenses for K–12 education in the nation as a whole. About two-thirds of the resources are allocated either to instruction or to school administration at the school-building level. Instructional services include funding for curriculum development and staff training and are therefore a potential source for some of the resources needed to support a school in transition to a technology-enabled program.

The instructional budgets of the schools themselves are largely allocated to teaching staff. Figure 5.2 provides a further breakdown of the top bar (instruction) in Figure 5.1.

The most obvious source of funding for technology is the category "supplies," but, according to participants in our software workshop, at least half of those resources are devoted to textbooks and a quarter of the remainder goes to material such as pencils, paper, and other supplies. Much of the rest does currently support instructional software. The pur-

Figure 5.2. Distribution of Instructional Expenditures Among Expenditure Categories, 1991–92.

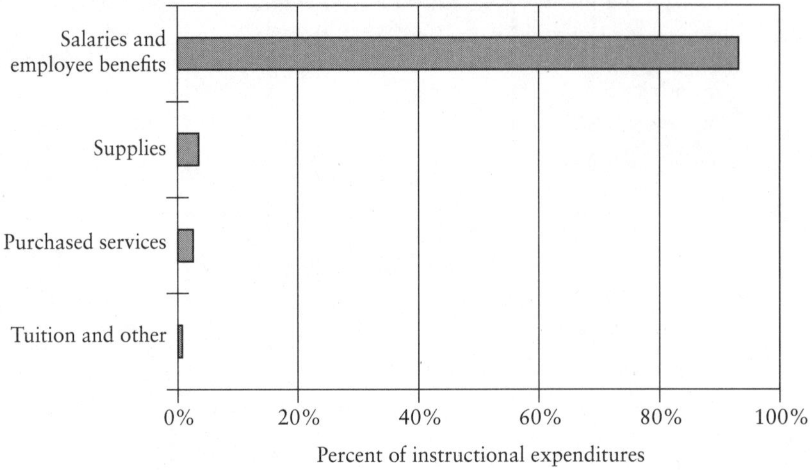

Percent of instructional expenditures

Source: *NCES, 1995b, Table 158.*

chased services and tuition-and-other categories may, in some instances, provide limited resources to support training and to purchase technical assistance.[10]

In short, the resource picture that is presented in Figures 5.1 and 5.2 suggests that the modest reallocations of existing budgets (possibly supplemented with some additional capital funds from state or local bond issues) could be used to promote the $180 per student that we recommend—always with the caveat that some schools and districts facing particularly difficult fiscal and student population challenges are exceptions to this generalization. Our assumed costs for technology in such schools was on the order of 3 percent of total educational costs (or 4.5 percent of expenditures at the school-building level).

---

[10] Our available study resources did not permit us to dig into any school budgets in detail. Our impression from discussions both at our workshops and with technology coordinators in schools is that the funds for technology at any particular site are likely to come from a wide variety of sources and that it would be quite impossible to track those costs back into the data underlying Figures 5.1 and 5.2. These charts simply provide a view of the relative magnitudes of classes of expenditures.

The situation is different, however, for schools that are truly technology intensive. If we assume that such schools might have a continuing annualized cost of $450 per student for hardware, additional personnel, software and materials, and training, this cost constitutes nearly 8 percent of the expected national average, current, per-student expenditure of $5,600—or about 12 percent of the resources allocated directly to the school building. Clearly, this poses a different magnitude of difficulty.

There are existing sources of funding to offset some of these costs. The most obvious are the resources currently available in the form of released time for teachers, pupil free days, or other time for teacher planning and professional development. In some states and school systems, up to 10 or more days per teacher can be assembled if the school and its teachers act to effectively marshal these resources. Funding, either at the school level or in the central office can also provide resources for outside expertise necessary to support the effective implementation of a technology-rich learning environment.[11]

Ross and others have also made proposals to use the incentives for professional development provided by the salary systems of many school districts. These systems make a significant part of a teacher's salary dependent on accumulated educational credits. Currently, there is little restriction on what additional training is sought, and many feel that much of the training is distinctly marginal in terms of teaching performance. Reforms that sharpened the incentives of teachers to develop the skills needed in technology-rich (and other learner-centered) schools could further support the needs for staff training.

Requirements for new staff positions, such as technology coordinators or lead teachers that work with classroom teachers, can, to some degree, be met by redefining existing staff positions. The schools represented at our workshop often operated in this fashion. A teacher was designated as a part-time technology coordinator. Teachers decided to accept slightly larger classes to free one person for the role of technology coordinator. Schools, given adequate levels of autonomy with the use of their staff, can make important reallocations of staff responsibilities.

However, the marginal tapping of all these sources will defray only a part of the total resource requirements for a technology-intensive school. Given that 93 percent of the resources at the school-building level are

---

[11] RAND has made a limited examination of these sources of funds in three districts in its work for the New American Schools Development Corporation. See Ross, unpublished.

Figure 5.3. Decline in Pupil-Teacher Ratios over Time.

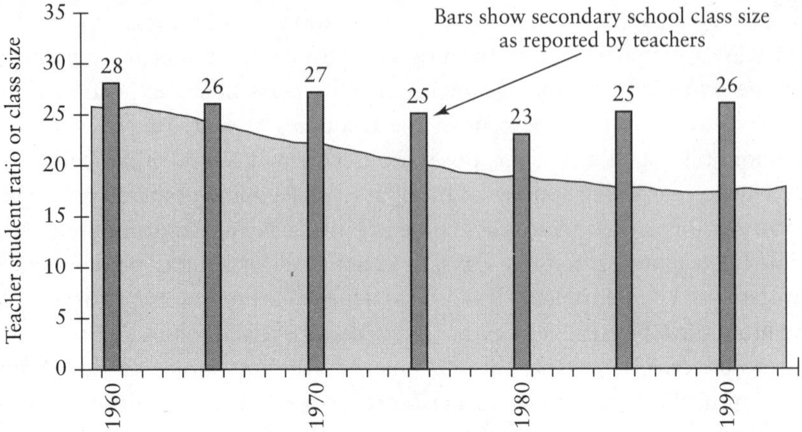

Source: *NCES, 1994a, Tables 64 and 69.*

devoted to salaries and benefits, assuming that there are limited opportunities for further pruning of noninstructional costs, and assuming that there will be little addition to overall revenues beyond that needed to accommodate additional students, some substitution of technology costs for personnel costs will be required.

Discussions of both the means and the probability of actually making such substitutions are beyond the scope of this report, but several "facts" are relevant. Over the past 25 years, the nation has steadily reduced the ratio of students to teachers from 25.8 to one to 17.6 to one. This is shown in Figure 5.3. This decline appears largely to be due to the addition of a significant number of teachers who serve special needs and populations, including students requiring special and remedial education or bilingual education.[12] These classes are often held in separate settings. Thus, the school class sizes reported by teachers have not declined significantly over the same period as shown by the bars in the figure.[13]

---

[12] Richard Rothstein and Karen Miles have recently examined differences in the allocation of resources for K–12 education between 1967 and 1991. Their analysis provides a consistent but more detailed confirmation that most of the increases in teachers have been devoted to special education, education of the disadvantaged, and other functions than decreasing the class size in general education. Rothstein and Miles, 1995.

[13] The sources of the data in Figure 5.3 are not comparable. The teacher-pupil ratios come from the Common Core Data Set, which is a census collection. The

As we have noted, technology provides the opportunity to significantly tailor instructional experiences to individual students. In the schools represented at the RAND workshop, teachers had regrouped themselves, and class periods had been changed. In such settings, the meaning of class size becomes blurred. Some activities may involve 40 students with one teacher in a group activity; others may involve three or four students working closely with a single teacher. Some will involve small groups of students working collaboratively with coaching from a single teacher; others will involve a student working intensively with a computer, largely on his or her own. It seems not only possible but desirable that schools integrating extensive technology into their programs review how personnel are used and even whether substituting technology or technical assistance for some personnel will lead to a more effective school.

Such changes are very difficult to make. They involve individual careers, the imperatives of the teachers' union, and beliefs of parents. Because the reallocations should occur at individual schools, it is important that those schools have substantial autonomy, either through explicit grants of authority or by the use of waivers to state and local regulations and rules. Successful budget reallocations require skillful and participatory management at the school-building level and a scope of interaction with parents at the school that has proven difficult to achieve in the past.[14]

Opportunities for Federal and State Action

The primary message of this chapter is that financing both the initial and continuing costs of incorporating technology into schools is a local and state responsibility. Decisions concerning how to use technology and obtain required resources must be made close to the schools if support for technology is to become accepted as a normal cost of operations. Continuing reliance on special, add-on funds will delay this acceptance.

Moreover, it is likely that substantially more ubiquitous use of technology will profoundly affect the roles and work of school staffs. Such use should involve trade-offs among expenditures for equipment, software,

---

class sizes are reported in a sample survey done by the National Education Association. The picture they paint, however, is consistent with that painted by long-term teachers with whom we have talked.

[14]Researchers associated with the Consortium for Policy Research in Education (CPRE) have discussed the prerequisites for the decentralization of authority in school systems that is needed to achieve effective, restructured technology-rich schools.

connections to data resources, and personnel. Consequently, success in making transitions to technology-rich learning environments will require active participation by local school staffs in deciding how to acquire and use that technology. State and federal agencies can help in a variety of ways, but the fundamental direction together with the engagement of the public must rest with schools and school districts.

While local schools and districts may have the most important long-term roles, state systems have accepted and continue to play important roles. Particularly for early adopters, risks for schools are high—risks to their reputations and to the careers of their staff and the welfare of the students. It is unlikely that many restructured schools can be created without states and localities aggregating resources and making them available for the effort, as many already have.

States and larger local jurisdictions should consider setting up investment funds to support the initial development of technology-rich schools. Continued funding for operations, maintenance, and replacement should be built into the individual school's budget. These schools should also be expected to use their staff development resources to support the development of teaching skills appropriate to technology-rich learning environments.

Many states have played and are likely to continue to play important roles in seeing that schools are connected to useful information infrastructures. Some have encouraged their public utility commissions to see that all schools can have access to the national information infrastructure at a reasonable cost.

Finally, if the federal government decides to provide categorical funding for the initial startup of technology-rich schools, it is critical that such funds be provided in ways that strongly encourage schools and school systems to incorporate the continuing costs of maintaining and replacing equipment in their budgets. Federal funding for demonstrations of school programs using advanced technology and funding to schools serving special populations to support the acquisition and use of technology should, in our view, receive the highest priority. The Department of Education's research and assistance arms should also collect and disseminate information on exemplary financing practices.

Providing Teachers with Skills Needed for Effective Technology-Rich Schools

Successful use of technology in schools depends upon the skills of the teachers and other staff in those schools. Unfortunately, as participants in the RAND/CTI workshop on technology and teacher professional development put it, "professional development as currently conceived and de-livered—one-shot seminars, an afternoon with an expert, or 200 teach-ers in a gymnasium—will not bring the profession up to speed with emerging school reforms." [15] Moreover, not only is teacher continuing professional development shallow, but there is broad consensus that the preparation of people to enter teaching is deficient as well. [16] Increasingly widespread use of technology in schools requires changes in both preser-vice and in-service training and, more generally, reform of policies that govern the professional development of teachers. In these changes, tech-nology has two roles: It is the object of skill development (teachers and staff must learn to apply technology effectively for teaching and learning) and it is a means of developing skills (technology can deliver information and training).

The Nature of the Current Teaching Force

In 1991, the nation had 2.6 million public school teachers. Over 64 per-cent of these teachers had 10 or more years of experience in teaching (Figure 5.4). About 20 percent of these teachers were 50 or older. [17]

The turnover in teachers is concentrated at the extremes of the experi-ence distribution. Some 17 percent of the teachers with less than one year of experience left teaching in or following the 1990–91 school year. [18] This figure fell to 2.4 percent for teachers with 10 to 19 years of experi-ence. The largest percentage of those that quickly leave the profession appear to do so because of family or personal moves, pregnancy or child-rearing, or health reasons. [19] This group forms a pool of potential teach-ers that often reenter teaching later in their professional lives.

Judging from the experience of the early 1990s, increasing proportions of the new hires in schools are first-time teachers. (See Table 5.1.) Of the new hires in 1990–91, nearly 42 percent were first-time teachers, while a

---

[15] Harvey and Purnell, 1995, p. 1.

[16] A brief review of the recent critiques of preservice education and of proposals for its reform is contained in OTA [U.S. Congress, Office of Technology Assess-ment], 1995, pp. 167–181.

[17] NCES, 1994a, Table 67.

[18] This may have been an unusually high figure; 11 percent of those with less than a year's teaching experience left teaching the year before.

[19] In 1988–89, 45 percent of teachers with three years of experience or less gave this as a reason. Only 6 percent said they were leaving because they were dis-satisfied with teaching, while about 15 percent said they left for other career opportunities. NCES, 1993, Table 3.18.

Figure 5.4. Teaching Experience of Public School Teachers, 1991.

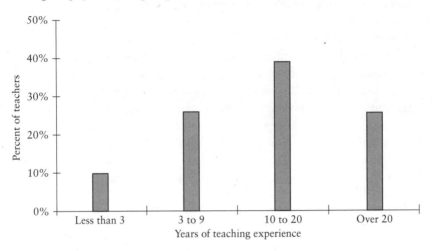

Source: *NCES, 1994a, Table 67.*

Table 5.1. Sources of Newly Hired Teachers in Public Schools,
1988 and 1991.

Source of Supply	1988	1991
First-time teachers	30.6	41.7
Transfers from other schools	36.6	34.3
Reentrants	32.8	24.0

Source: *NCES, 1994b, p. 158.*

third were transfers from other schools or school districts.[20] Twenty-four percent were reentrants to teaching. In contrast, in 1987–88, about a third of the new hires were transfers, while only 31 percent were first-time teachers. Most (about 60 percent) first-time teachers in 1991–92 were fresh out of college.

The number of public school teachers is expected to grow over the coming decade. The National Center for Education Statistics projects that there will be nearly 2.8 million public school teachers by 2000 and over

[20] NCES, 1994b, p. 158.

2.9 million five years later.[21] On the basis of data such as these, the Office of Technology Assessment suggests that two million teachers will need to be hired over the next decade and that a high proportion will be newly trained teachers.

It is difficult to pin down the level of computer literacy possessed by the current population of teachers. It has often been said to be low, but two years ago, a survey commissioned by the National Teachers Association found that 54 percent of teachers had access to computers in their home.[22] Moreover, according to the same National Education Association survey, 65 percent of the teachers rated their computer skills as good or excellent. No doubt the majority of the younger new entrants to teaching will have used computers in schools and colleges and feel reasonably comfortable with them.

However, many additional skills are required. In such environments, teachers would be expected to recurrently assess student progress, create learning opportunities appropriate to the student, access resources needed for projects, and relate diverse instructional activities to the school's educational goals. By the testimony of school reformers and the individuals who attended the RAND workshops, comparatively few teachers have been prepared to perform these functions. Successful implementation of technology-enabled schools depends upon the capability to help existing teachers, as well as new entrants to the profession, to develop the skills required to perform these functions effectively.

Support for Continuing Professional Development

The RAND/CTI workshops on professional development and technology-assisted effective schooling provided insights concerning the development of the skills teachers need to possess to carry out their functions in increasingly learner-centered schooling. The workshops seem to suggest at least three common requirements for successful support of teachers moving to create these new learning environments:

1. Adequate time (and organization of time) for teachers to acquire skills and to plan the school's program and activities.

2. Assistance that is keyed to the needs of the teachers and administrators and provided at the times when they need it.

---

[21] NCES, 1995c, Table 32. We have used the "middle alternative projection."
[22] Princeton Survey Research Associates, 1993.

3. A clear vision concerning the purposes and the educational goals that guide the program of the school and classroom.

In the following paragraphs we highlight each of the three requirements briefly.

ADEQUATE TIME. Teachers engaged in reform universally complain about the shortage of time in which to develop the plans and new skills needed. The problem is that many of those skills must be learned at the same time teachers are carrying out their teaching functions. Many of the reforms enabled by technology require collaboration among teachers rather than simply allowing teachers to make the changes in the isolation of their own classrooms. If ways cannot be found to provide collective time for such activities without it all being done on the teachers "own" time, it is unlikely that the reforms we are discussing can take place.

Blackstock Junior High School in Port Hueneme, California, took a quite unique approach to this issue. Eight years ago, a history teacher was given a year off from teaching and told to develop a year-long history program that made significant use of technology. He was given considerable freedom and resources to allow him to redesign his classroom into what the school now calls a "smart classroom." Later, several other teachers were given the same opportunity. The initial effort appears to have been program or class centered as opposed to emphasizing the entire school.

While this may be an exemplary way in which to provide teachers with the time to learn about and develop applications of technology, a look at the cost figures in the previous section suggests that this approach is almost certainly not feasible on a large scale. More cost-effective ways of providing teachers time and skills to innovate must be found.

Northbrook Middle School in Houston, Texas, provides a different example. In a newly opening school, the principal was chosen a year in advance and had considerable latitude in choosing staff that shared her vision. Two weeks were provided all teachers to prepare during the summer before school opened.[23] The school schedule was substantially restructured to provide planning periods for teams of teachers working closely together and for staff development days. The district does provide training and support, and teachers are encouraged to attend conferences. Teachers spend time on planning and learning skills before and after school.

---

[23] New teachers joining the school must agree to spend two days in training (without compensation) before they start at the school.

The Apple Classroom of Tomorrow Teacher Development Center project makes the provision of time for development of skills and plans a key requirement for participation. In addition to providing a teacher the time to attend week-long practicums and/or four-week summer institutes, a principal must agree to

- provide teachers with the authority and flexibility to adjust daily instructional schedules and to develop curriculum objectives that promote team teaching and interdisciplinary instruction

- allow time each day for teachers to meet and plan

- provide time for teachers to reflect on their practice

- acknowledge the importance of the team's efforts to the rest of the staff.[24]

Each of these three efforts is developmental, and thus it is obvious that teachers must have time during the development to acquire the new skills they need. However, workshop participants and others argue that this is not just a one-time requirement at the beginning of the implementation of a restructured school or program. The restructuring should provide continued time for teachers to plan and reflect and to develop professionally. Obviously, planning for professional development must also provide for new teachers at a school to develop the skills needed to function and succeed in that school.

RESPONSIVE ASSISTANCE. The attendees at the workshop on professional development emphasized the importance of assistance that is timely and keyed to the needs of teachers rather than the convenience of assistance-providing institutions or the central office. The same has been regularly emphasized by teachers implementing NASDC designs. Preparation of teachers in NASDC-related schools places a great deal of emphasis on the value of coaching—provision of assistance in situ so that teachers can relate lessons to their specific situations. (In some NASDC designs, this preparation is provided by a trained coordinator, who either is a part of the school's staff or is a frequent visitor to the school.)

Both workshop participants and teachers in the NASDC schools strongly emphasized the limitations of traditional approaches to in-service activities that do not effectively meet the needs of teachers and school staff in a timely way when those needs arise. Some believe that technology, in

---

[24]Ringstaff, Marsh, and Yocum, 1995, p. 6.

the form of interactive media or a network of practitioner experts, can be effective in providing timely and relevant assistance. However, aside from the numerous on-line networks that enable practitioners to ask for and provide advice, we have found no extensive examples of such activities. While wide-band communications and multimedia materials may be able to provide timely support to teachers at some time in the future, perhaps more practical approaches involve development of the capabilities and ethos to allow teachers to support one another in a school.[25]

Individuals filling the emerging role of technology coordinator may be able to play an important role in the development of their colleagues. We have heard from several school leaders that technology coordinators sometimes do play an important role in demonstrating effective technology-enabled pedagogical strategies and in coaching teachers in the effective use of technology. However, it appears that this is not a very common practice. Becker, in his analysis of the 1992 IEA data, reports on the distribution of effort of what he terms major coordinators.[26] His findings are shown in Table 5.2. Clearly, training and helping teachers is not a major function for most of the coordinators surveyed. Teaching and supervising students using computers occupies an average 54 percent of their time. Help to teachers averages 3.6 hours of effort per week.

PROFESSIONAL DEVELOPMENT RESPONDING TO EDUCATIONAL VISION AND GOALS. Perhaps the importance of a clear, school-level educational vision and goal seems peripheral to the issue of professional development, but it seemed very important to the school representatives attending the RAND workshop on technology-assisted effective schooling. Computers, communications, and video can make a day's experience in a classroom fun. Kids can be deeply engaged. The idea that teachers should be guides to or co-learners with students is appealing. Moreover, many implementations of technology in classrooms and schools have heavy leadership from technologists or developers who visualize exciting

---

[25] A study commissioned by the Office of Technology Assessment provides case studies of two districts that have technology programs fostering such activities. See the case studies on Bellevue, Washington, and Jefferson County, Kentucky, in Beryl Buck Institute for Education, 1994.

[26] "'Major coordinators' are those who either spent at least 20 hours per week in activities related to this position or for whom the position of computer coordinator constituted at least 50 percent of their responsibilities." Becker, 1994, Table 7.4.

Table 5.2. Activities of School-Level Technology Coordinators, 1992.

Activities	Hours	Mean Percentage of Effort
Teach, supervise students using computers	19.5	54
Train, help teachers to use computers	3.6	9
Select and acquire material, equipment	2.3	6
Maintain equipment and software	4.0	11
Self-development	4.0	11
Other (write software, lesson plans, all other)	4.1	11
Total number of hours per week	37.5	

Note: *Percentages in final column are means of the responses for the activity. Data are for those categorized as "major coordinators."*
Source: *Becker, 1994, Table 7.4.*

opportunities made possible by the infusion of new technologies, software, or communications.

The danger is that these exciting things will not add up to anything. The student may develop some deep knowledge about one subject area or an enthusiasm for a classroom activity that is exciting, but parents and the community are left with the uncomfortable feeling that the fundamental skills and knowledge that they believe kids should have are not being imparted.

Each of the schools that made presentations to the workshop appeared to have a clear educational sense of purpose. Technology served that purpose. The professional development of teachers served that purpose. The Christopher Columbus school derived its guidance from an extensive systemwide effort to create a curriculum framework emphasizing a "whole language philosophy of education." This starting point led to revamping the schedule of the school day, the introduction of more cross-curricular thematic units, support for professional development, and as a final step, the integration of technology into school activity. The district and school administration made it clear that this last step was a means to the curricular ends that they had established.

The Taylorsville school represented a distinctive, school-centered approach to the development of a technology-enabled school. It is an elementary school affiliated with the Modern Red School House (MRSH) design activity funded by NASDC. Its efforts to transform itself started with a set of standards for student learning that MRSH has developed that derive from the various national standards development efforts. These standards, which may be modified somewhat by the requirements of the district or state (Indiana), provide guidance to the curriculum development, the assessments, and the sequencing of activities in the school. The standards are built into a computer-based instructional management system that supports the refinement of the curriculum as well as student learning contracts that are intended to provide the individualization that is sought in the school design. The design implementation requires teachers to develop curriculum units as a means to professional development. The design also seeks to develop the skills of teachers as members of the governance structure of the schools. Altogether, the professional development activities of the school staff are guided by an overall vision and goals inherent in the MRSH design.

In sum, as illustrated by these two examples, a reformed and restructured school (whether or not it uses technology) must have a clear sense of its educational mission that is shared by its staff, its students, and its parents. The professional development required of its staff must, in turn, be guided by the functional needs associated with the vision, together with the existing capabilities of the teachers. An important implication is that the details of professional development activities should be shaped by individual schools rather than by a school system's central office.

Preservice Training for Teachers

The emphasis in our meetings was clearly on the continuing professional development of teachers who were already in schools. However, over the coming decade a significant number of newly trained teachers will enter the nation's schools. The training of these new teachers should impart skills and attitudes that will allow these teachers to function effectively in technology-enabled learning environments. This is far more than a matter of ensuring that they possess the skills needed to use computers and other equipment, and it requires fundamental changes in the curriculum of most colleges and changes in the accreditation requirements for teachers.

The recent OTA [Office of Technology Assessment] report on teachers and technology reviewed activities of colleges of education and painted a fairly discouraging picture of their capabilities to make such changes.[27] The difficulties faced by these schools are systemic and related to their place in higher education generally. OTA suggests that these difficulties

---

[27] OTA, 1995, Chapter 5 in general and pp. 187–191 in particular.

stem from a lack of access to resources, faculty attitudes and training, and lack of institutional support for work with technology. However, the reform and restructuring of these institutions is much broader than that required by the increasing importance of technology and beyond the scope of this report.

On the other hand, the OTA report does catalogue a number of experiments by schools of education using technology that provide a rather rich picture of the potential technology has as both a means for fulfilling traditional missions in more effective ways and as an agent for fostering college of education reforms. The examples, which have required substantial funding over sustained periods of time, suggest the potential fruitfulness of research and development expenditures in this area.

Opportunities for Federal, State, and Local Action[28]

The preceding discussion suggests that teachers' and administrators' greatest problems are not with learning to use technology but instead with learning to develop and manage the types of learning environments that are facilitated by these technologies. Judging from the experience of the schools that participated in our workshop, as well as explicit professional development activities such as the ACOT Teacher Development Centers, we believe that much of the best professional development occurs at work, doing work, and reflecting on the work that is done.

If this is the case, a principal task for local school districts is to make such activities possible and to provide assistance to school faculties in accordance with their needs. For many districts, this means a profound restructuring of the way in which they conduct staff development activities. It also requires a cultural change at the school-building level that leads the principal and the faculty to take greater responsibility for their professional development.

While we believe much of the action must be at the local level, there are important roles for state and federal actors as well. States play a major role shaping teacher certification requirements which, in turn, shape the programs of teacher training institutions. Working with organizations like the National Council for Accrediting of Teacher Education (NCATE),

---

[28] It should be noted that a number of national and local foundations are making important investments to help school districts develop improved professional development strategies. Among these are The Pew Charitable Trusts and The MacArthur Foundation.

they should seek to revise certification requirements to ensure that new teachers possess skills that allow them to enter and effectively work in technology-enabled schools.

The federal government supports many programs and institutions providing assistance to teachers, schools, and school districts.[29] It also supports R&D for improved methods for training teachers and supports programs to train teachers, primarily in math and science. These programs should be periodically reviewed and encouraged to address needs posed by technology-rich learning environments as well as to use technology to enhance the delivery of training and assistance relevant to those environments.

Ensuring That Needed Software Is Available

Educational technology without appropriate software is of little or no use. As we conducted this study, we repeatedly heard that despite the voluminous listings of educational software titles, there was a shortage of software that teachers and others viewed as needed in schools. As a consequence, RAND sponsored two workshops devoted to the issue of educational software. These, together with the experiences of the technology-rich schools surveyed, suggest the existing market for educational software does not appear to provide appropriate incentives to develop all the software that is needed.

Today's technology-rich schools rely on a spectrum of software. They use

1. drill-and-practice software developed in the past (frequently with partial federal support) and focused primarily on the needs of the elementary grades

2. curricular and pedagogical practices exploiting existing applications software (e.g., communications, word processing, or spreadsheets) coupled with access to computer-based and other content

3. reference materials that are now appearing in CD-ROM formats that are sold both to schools and homes

4. instructional management software that aids a school's staff to help all students acquire and demonstrate the skills and knowledge sought by the community

5. administrative support software such as programs supporting student grading or keeping attendance records.

---

[29] A list of such programs is contained in OTA, 1995, Tables 6-2 and 6-3.

In quite a few instances, individual teachers and schools have also acquired software originally developed for the home entertainment market (e.g., *Where in the World is Carmen San Diego* and *SimCity*) that they feel can help them in their classes.

The software underlying the above applications falls into three broad categories. Software "tools" are application packages similar or identical to those commonly used in offices and homes. The development of word processors and spreadsheets is driven by these larger markets, and schools use what is available. Content software incorporates information, curricular structure, and often, some form of specialized instructional management system. Common examples are the integrated learning systems (ILS) and less elaborate drill-and-practice programs. Instructional management systems are a newly emerging class of software that helps a school to relate its instructional program to the district's curriculum framework, supports the development of individual work plans for students, and tracks and displays indicators of the performance of students.

The tools software poses little problem because it relies on larger commercial markets. Some instructional management software is available and more is being developed. While school representatives at our workshop said the existing products were expensive and not yet fully suited to their needs, there was no general sense conveyed that there is a significant market problem. Workshop participants generally agreed, however, that there was a shortage of content software, particularly for middle and secondary school students.

Current technology-rich schools tend to place a good deal of emphasis on project-based learning using communications, word-processing, and spreadsheet software. As we noted earlier, this reflects the lessons of modern cognitive science concerning constructivist and situated learning as well as the long-espoused views of educational philosophers such as Dewey. In such schools (and in others sharing these views, if not the technology), individual teachers normally design the projects and must ensure that these projects produce the skills that students need to acquire. Such projects are found in virtually all subject areas, including science, math, history and social studies, and language arts—often in interdisciplinary activities.

While we are strong supporters of project-based learning, we believe that too extensive a reliance on such pedagogy may pose a significant risk for the current school reform movement. Much of the current development of such projects takes place in exceptional schools at the leading edge of school reform. The teachers involved are often among the most qualified in their schools and school systems. When expanded to many more schools, particularly to those with teachers less motivated or less well prepared, the educational benefits of this pedagogy may prove disappointing to policymakers and parents alike. Moreover, many teachers may come to resent the added burden of creating and recreating motivating projects for students. The result could be disillusionment similar to that which killed the progressive school movement in the 1930s.

A complement, and partial alternative to this use of technology, is content software that incorporates some of the structure of current textbooks but does so in a manner that engages students in a far more effective way. Such software would be sophisticated in pedagogy and rich in the imagery required to motivate the attention of today's adolescent student. Properly used, such software could help "demassify" current instruction and attend to the individual needs of each student. It can do this, in part, by freeing "learning time" from the restrictions of the rigid schedules of today's schools and extending it to other hours and places.

Market Supply and Demand for Educational Software

As we have noted, there is a general consensus that there is too little high-quality content software. This is particularly true for the upper grade levels. There are repeated rumors that major software firms intend to develop applications for the education market. The so-called home education market is growing rapidly. There is software to coach students in taking major examinations such as the Scholastic Achievement Test (SAT). But an abundance of high-quality content software, such as we described above, has yet to appear.

To investigate the nature of the education software market, RAND held two workshops (one in November 1993 and the other in February 1995[30]) at which representatives of textbook publishers, ILS vendors, educational software publishers, and multimedia developers were present. Both workshops explored the demand for and the supply of software, with emphasis on content software. Based on information provided by the participants, we estimate that the size of the school market for software was less than $750 million in 1994—about 0.3 percent of all K–12 educational expenditures. This figure can be compared with an estimate of nearly $400 million in expenditures by households for "edutainment" and reference CD-ROMs in the first year (1994) that "home" computers

---

[30]Harvey, 1995b.

were marketed with integrated CD-ROM drives. The largest fraction of sales was basic-skills software to elementary schools, often in the form of large-scale, integrated learning systems costing $30,000 or more per installation.

The attendees at the workshops clarified the disincentives they face in expanding the supply of software. Traditional school textbook publishers consider that they operate in a zero-sum game, that the school budget structure sharply limits what can be spent on instructional materials of all kinds, and that any software sales they make will simply cut into their volume of textbook sales. They note too that software development costs can be high, and that even such an unambiguous marketing success as selling one software copy to each and every one of the nation's schools need not guarantee a positive return on investment.

These factors do not appear to inhibit low-overhead educational software publishers, who can successfully find a market niche for education and training materials in schools, hospitals, and prisons. Such companies have found profitable markets for materials that supplement existing textbook and other materials. They do not, however, have the capital necessary to engage in major development efforts.

New multimedia developers, whether conglomerates like Paramount or more modest independent firms like Broderbund, find the home market with its nearly 100 million households a far more appealing target than the nation's 100 thousand schools. Even at $50 a copy, a single successful CD-ROM that sells to only 1 percent of U.S. households can produce revenues of $50 million in a relatively short time period. By contrast, if it developed a comparably priced CD-ROM for schools and sold it to *all* 100,000 of them, it would have revenues of $5 million. So while an industry is taking shape that is potentially capable[31] of meeting the school need for sophisticated content software, its output is presently directed to a more lucrative market segment.

The pioneer, technology-rich schools provide some additional hints on why the school software market is not now particularly attractive. In these schools, software expenditures ranged between 4 percent and 10 percent of total annualized technology implementation costs—about one-fifth of hardware costs. (By contrast, software costs tend to approach the value of hardware costs in typical enterprise computing.)

---

[31] That is, with a capability for the necessary rich imagery, and potentially able to acquire the capabilities for sophisticated pedagogy and course content.

In their report,[32] Keltner and Ross provide a partial explanation for the low proportion of technology expenditures devoted to software:

> The school environment is not one that puts sophisticated demands on the software component of a technology program. The number of basic software programs installed on individual student computers is typically limited. None of the schools in our survey purchased site licenses for more than five to six "tool-based" software products, e.g., Microsoft Word, Clarisworks, Hypertext or Hypercard, and the average figure was more like three. With a site license for 25 computers costing between $1000 and $1500, an expenditure of $3000 to $4000 typically proved enough to outfit an entire classroom of computers with basic software applications.

Continuing with their explanation, they write:

> Another explanation for the low level of software expenditure is the ability of schools to generate economies of scale in the use of expensive "content-based" software products. The Christopher Columbus, Corona and Elizabeth St. schools each spent $30,000 to $40,000 to set up large libraries of CD-ROM and laserdisk software products. While expensive, these software items do not increase software expenditures per student significantly, because their cost is distributed over a large number of classrooms. Blackstock and Taylorsville schools spent $43,000 and $70,000 respectively on network and instructional management software. Network and instructional management system software products too are also normally used on a school-wide or classroom-based LAN.

When these school-level perspectives are put together with the comparatively small number of schools and the complexity of selling to 15,000 school districts governed by all manner of adoption practices, it is easy to see why software firms that are not traditionally associated with formal education view this market with some skepticism.

To summarize, the traditional providers of instructional materials, the textbook manufacturers, are anxiously watching but apparently not ready to strike out in a big way for fear of jeopardizing current markets. The major providers of educational software, firms specializing in integrated learning systems, have developed a business based upon a low volume with high margins, which is not well adapted to developing and

---

[32] Keltner and Ross, 1996.

selling applications for individual use on large numbers of unintegrated computers. Small software firms have found profitable niches but lack the resources (and perhaps a taste for risk) needed to strike out into new developments. The new multimedia firms not only lack deep knowledge of educational needs in schools but have a production and distribution system keyed to high sales volumes with comparatively low margins. To date, the result is the "shortage" of content software reported by so many of the people with whom we have consulted.[33]

Opportunities for Federal, State, and Local Action

In a market as dynamic as educational technology, it is difficult to decide whether specific government actions will help or hinder the public interest. We have heard of potentially exciting product ideas from individual developers, but whether they can find the capital, produce a product, and overcome the marketing barriers that we have described is uncertain. Surely large firms like Microsoft, Apple, and IBM have plenty of resources and ideas; in both IBM and Apple's case they also have a substantial history of working in the K–12 education market. However, content software of the sort needed for middle and secondary schools has not been their priority.

Our discussion of financing earlier in this chapter did consider two approaches that would serve to increase demand for software and thus should promote improvements in the quantity and quality of supply. The first is the restructuring of traditional school budgets so as to raise the current proportion of the budget devoted to the acquisition of instructional materials. The second is state or public-private investment strategies for increasing the investment in technology generally and thus software expenditures as well. If such changes are made and the density of computers continues to increase significantly, the attractiveness of the market will increase correspondingly.

---

[33] We should note another problem with the educational technology market that has been important in the past. As we noted earlier, while there are many computers in the schools, they are of an immense variety of brands and vintages. Developing for multiple platforms increases costs substantially, and the fact that many of the computers lack hard drives and modern video displays limits the installed base available to a software developer. This problem is lessening with time, but as long as the Macintosh-PC distinction remains strong it will remain.

The major tool available to the federal government is its R&D program. As we have noted, federal R&D support was a major contributor to the early development, and hence the current availability, of drill-and-practice materials in the basic skills. Current NSF funding is providing support for potentially important content software, primarily in mathematics and science. The transfer of such developments to the private sector (where appropriate) has always been very difficult, but the magnitude of the investment suggests that explicit attention should continue to be given to the problem. It is possible too that a program of federal support for pre-competitive multimedia educational software R&D might also serve to counter market disincentives presently faced by software vendors.

Beyond this, the federal government should be looking for every chance it can to promote discussion and consultation among software developers, publishers, scholars, and educators concerning potential software applications. No one group can deal with this problem alone. At our first workshop, attendees suggested that a joint public-private institute be founded, one of whose major purposes would be to support just such discussions. Such an institution would hold regular symposia for developers and educators, maintain databases of exemplary technology applications, foster the development of technical standards, and generally serve as a clearinghouse and convener. Whether such an institution could capture the support of the members of a potentially highly competitive industry is a question that would have to be answered before serious consideration is devoted to its establishment.

BIBLIOGRAPHY

Anderson, Robert H., Tora K. Bikson, Sally Ann Law, and Bridger M. Mitchell, Christopher R. Kedzie, Brent Keltner, Constantijn W. Panis, Joel Pliskin, and Padmanabhan Srinagesh, *Universal Access to E-Mail: Feasibility and Societal Implications,* MR–650–MF, RAND, Santa Monica, CA, 1995.

Apple Computer, Inc., *Changing the Conversation about Teaching, Learning, and Technology: A Report on 10 Years of ACOT Research,* Cupertino, CA: Apple Computer, Inc., 1995.

Becker, H. J., *Analysis of Trends of School Use of New Information Technology,* Prepared for the Office of Technology Assessment, University of California, Irvine, CA, March 1994.

Beryl Buck Institute for Education, *Exemplary Approaches to Training Teachers to Use Technology,* Vol. 1, prepared for the Office of Technology Assessment, Washington, D.C., 1994.

Committee on Education and Training, *Strategic/Implementation Plan, FY 1995–1999,* January 24, 1995, pp. 8–9.

Cuban, Larry, *Teachers and Machines: The Classroom Use of Technology Since 1920,* Teachers College, Columbia University, NY: Teachers College Press, 1986.

Fletcher, J. D., D. E. Hawley, and P. K. Piele, "Costs, Effects and Utility of Microcomputer Assisted Instruction in the Classroom," *American Educational Research Journal,* 27, 1990, pp. 783–806.

Gerstner, Jr., Louis V., Chairman and CEO-IBM Corporation, Remarks at the National Governors' Association Annual Meeting, Burlington, Vermont, July 30, 1995.

Harvey, James (ed.), *Planning and Financing Educational Technology,* DRU–1042–CTI, RAND, Santa Monica, CA, March 1995a.

Harvey, James (ed.), *The Market for Educational Software,* DRU–1041–CTI, RAND, Santa Monica, CA, May 1995b.

Harvey, James, and Susanna Purnell (eds.), *Technology and Teacher Professional Development,* DRU–1045–CTI, RAND, Santa Monica, CA, March 1995.

Hayes, Jeanne, and Dennis L. Bybee, "Greatest Need for Educational Technology," paper prepared to support congressional testimony in March 1995, Quality Education Data, Inc., undated.

Keltner, Brent, and Randy Ross, *The Cost of School-Based Educational Technology Programs,* MR–634–CTI/DoED, RAND, Santa Monica, CA, 1996.

Kulik, James A., "Meta-Analytic Studies of Findings on Computer-based Instruction," in E. L. Baker, and H. F. O'Neil, Jr. (eds.), *Technology Assessment in Education and Training,* Hillsdale, NJ: Lawrence, Erlbaum, 1994.

Means, Barbara, and Kerry Olson, *Technology's Role in Education: Reform, Findings from a National Study of Innovating Schools,* Menlo Park, CA: SRI, September 1995.

Melmed, Arthur (ed.), *The Costs and Effectiveness of Educational Technology: Proceedings of a Workshop,* DRU–1205–CTI, RAND, Santa Monica, CA, November 1995.

National Center for Education Statistics (NCES), *America's Teachers: Profile of a Profession,* U.S. Department of Education, Washington, D.C., May 1993.

National Center for Education Statistics (NCES), *Digest of Educational Statistics,* U.S. Department of Education, Washington, D.C., 1994a.

National Center for Education Statistics (NCES), *The Condition of Education 1994,* U.S. Department of Education, Washington, D.C., 1994b.

National Center for Education Statistics (NCES), *Advanced Telecommunications in U.S. Public Schools, K–12,* U.S. Department of Education, Washington, D.C., January 1995a, p. 3.

National Center for Education Statistics (NCES), *Digest of Educational Statistics,* U.S. Department of Education, Washington, D.C., 1995b.

National Center for Education Statistics (NCES), *Projections of Education Statistics to 2005,* U.S. Department of Education, Washington, D.C., January 1995c.

National Commission on Excellence in Education, *A Nation At Risk,* Washington, D.C.: National Commission on Excellence in Education, 1983.

Newman, Dennis, "Computer Networks: Opportunities or Obstacles?", in Barbara Means (ed.), *Technology and Educational Reform,* San Francisco, CA: Jossey-Bass Publishers, 1994, pp. 57–80.

New York Times, "Apple Holds School Market, Despite Decline," September 11, 1995.

Princeton Survey Research Associates, *National Education Associations Communications Survey: Report of Findings,* Princeton, NJ, June 2, 1993.

Quality Education Data, Inc. (QED), *Technology in Public Schools, QED's 13th Annual Census Study of Public School Technology Use,* Denver, CO, 1994.

Raizen, Senta A., *Reforming Education for Work: A Cognitive Science Perspective,* Berkeley, CA: National Center for Research in Vocational Education, 1989.

Resnick, Lauren, "The 1987 AERA Presidential Address: Learning in School and Out," *Educational Researcher,* 16 (9), 1987a, pp. 13–20.

Resnick, Lauren, *Education and Learning to Think,* Washington, D.C.: National Academy Press, 1987b.

Ringstaff, Cathy, Jean Marsh, and Keith Yocum, ACOT *Teacher Development Center Annual Report: Year Two,* ACOT, Cupertino, CA, January 1995.

Ross, Randy, unpublished RAND research on the cost of implementing new American schools.

Rothstein, Randy, and Karen Miles, *Where's the Money Gone? Changes in the Level and Composition of Education Spending,* Economic Policy Institute, Washington, D.C., 1995.

Secretary's Commission on Achieving Necessary Skills, *What Work Requires of Schools: A SCANS Report for America 2000,* Washington, D.C.: U.S. Department of Labor, June 1991.

Software Publishers Association, *Report on the Effectiveness of Technology in Schools, 1990–1994,* Washington, D.C.: Software Publishers Assn., 1995.

Software Publishers Association, *SPA K–12 Education Market Report,* Washington, D.C., July 1994, p. 61.

Special Issue on Educational Technologies: Current Trends and Future Directions, *Machine-Mediated Learning,* Vol. 4 (2&3), 1994.

Tyack, David, and Larry Cuban, *Tinkering Toward Utopia,* Cambridge, MA: Harvard University Press, 1995.

U.S. Congress, Office of Technology Assessment (OTA), *Teachers and Technology: Making the Connection,* OTA-EHR–616, U.S. Government Printing Office, Washington, D.C., April 1995.

WEB SITE

http://www.rand.org

6

INTERNET USE BY TEACHERS

Henry Jay Becker

Introduction

ALTHOUGH THE POTENTIAL impact of computer technologies on teaching and learning goes far beyond the Internet, the Internet's rapid growth in the last two to three years suggested that we devote our first presentation of findings from the TLC [Teaching, Learning and Computing] survey to Internet use by teachers and their students. This paper includes information about

- How frequently teachers and students use the Internet and in what ways
- To what extent teachers value having the Internet in their own classroom
- How much access teachers have to the Internet
- Variations in Internet use and perceived value by the teachers' level of Internet access
- Variations in Internet use and value by teaching responsibility
- Internet use and value by professional experience and technology expertise
- Internet use and value by whether teachers participated in staff development
- Internet use and value by the school professional climate

- Internet use and value by the teacher's pedagogical approach
- Combined effects on Internet use of all predicting factors

Study Sample

The information presented here derives from the national probability sample of teachers of 4th through 12th grade classes in U.S. public and private schools conducted in the Spring of 1998. Approximately 2,250 teachers in the probability sample responded to the survey (69.4 percent of the teachers identified and sampled) and are included in the charts below. Statistics presented are weighted to constitute a nationally representative sample of teachers.

Part I. Teachers' Access to the Internet

Over the past five years, schools have been rapidly acquiring access to Internet telecommunications. This has been shown through information provided by the National Center for Education Statistics, as well as our own 1998 data on school-level Internet connectivity. Over 90 percent of schools now have some sort of access to the Internet, someplace in their building.

Until very recently, though, the *type* of Internet access that schools had was limited to individual telephone modems connected to single computers, sometimes in a teacher's classroom but more often in an office or computer lab. It is quite remarkable, then, that more than one-third of U.S. teachers (39 percent, among 4th–12th grade teachers) now have some kind of Internet access in their own classroom. Moreover, nearly as many teachers have high-speed direct Internet connection routed through a local area network to their classroom as have the older, and slower, "dial-up" modem connection.[1, 2]

In addition to the 39 percent of teachers who have Internet access in their classrooms, another 25–30 percent teach at schools where at least

---

[1] The percentage of teachers with direct (non-modem) Internet connections (and the particular teachers so ascribed) had to be imputed from survey data, since the question about direct access itself proved to be ambiguous. The question had been phrased in terms of "high speed access," which was contrasted to "modern access," but apparently many teachers regarded their modem access as "high-speed."

[2] Note that this result, though tentative because of the problem just cited, occurred well in advance of schools receiving funds through federal e-rate programs.

Figure 6.1. Public Schools with Any Internet Access, 1994–1998.

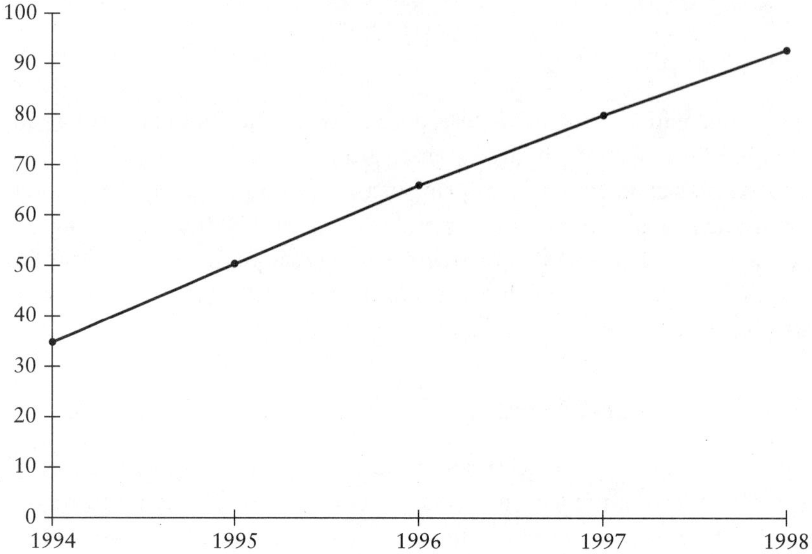

Sources: *Data for 1994–1997 from NCES Issue Brief 98–031. Data for 1998 from Teaching, Learning and Computing—1998, "Internet Use by Teachers," http://www.crito.uci.edu/TLC.*

some instructional rooms in their building have LAN-based Internet connectivity. Moreover, a majority of teachers (59 percent) have Internet access at home and only one-quarter (27 percent) have no access either at home or in their classroom.

These statistics suggest that, as with other knowledge-oriented professionals, the Internet has begun to be established as an information and communications resource in the working and home environments of most teachers. The next question is whether and to what extent teachers have begun using this resource in their professional lives.

Part II. Frequency of Different Internet Uses

A. Teachers' Uses

1. USE IN LESSON PREPARATION

Most teachers report making some use of the Internet in their professional activities. Our survey asked about three professional uses in particular:

finding information and other resources on the Internet; e-mailing with teachers at other schools; and posting information, suggestions, opinions, or student work on the World Wide Web.

A majority of teachers (68 percent) use the Internet in their effort to find information resources for use in their lessons, and more than one-quarter of all teachers report doing this on a weekly basis or more often (28 percent). Teachers who use the Internet in this way typically have either home or classroom access. Both home and classroom access are about equally related to use, and teachers who have the combination of both home and classroom access report the most frequent use, with 46 percent of such teachers reporting weekly or more frequent use. Of course, it is also likely that teachers who want to use the Internet may go to some effort to acquire either home or classroom access, but it also may be that the presence of the technology increases utilization. Despite these findings, it is also true that even among teachers with both home and classroom Internet access, more teachers report only "occasional" use of the Internet for lesson preparation than report use on at least a weekly basis.

2. TEACHER PROFESSIONAL COMMUNICATIONS

The survey asked about two additional areas of professional use of the Internet by teachers—e-mail with teachers from other schools and publishing on the World Wide Web. Far fewer teachers engage in these types of communications than use Internet as an information-gathering tool to obtain resources for lesson preparation. Only 16 percent of teachers communicated by e-mail with teachers from other schools as often as five times during the school year. However, classroom access to the Internet may make a difference in whether they use e-mail for professional purposes: Teachers with Internet access both at home and in their classroom were more than three times as likely to e-mail teachers at other schools than teachers who had only home Internet access (33 percent vs. 9 percent).

Also, relatively few teachers have begun posting information, suggestions, opinions, or student work on the World Wide Web. Only 18 percent of teachers did this at all last year. While this is a relatively small percentage of teachers, publishing information on the Web is a substantially new activity, not within the experience of teachers as much as electronic mail or Web browsing might be. To have even that many teachers involved in some way suggests that more growth in this area should be expected, as teachers' experience with using the Internet develops their interest and confidence in being information producers as well as consumers.

Figure 6.2. Percent of All Teachers Having Their Students Use Different Types of Software.

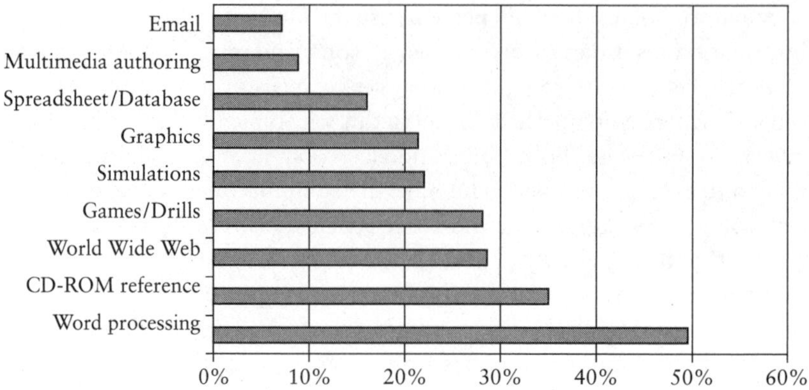

Source: *Teaching, Learning and Computing—1998, "Internet Use by Teachers,"*
http://www.crito.uci.edu/TLC.

B. *Teacher-Directed Student Use*

1. STUDENT INFORMATION-GATHERING (STUDENT RESEARCH)

Just as information-gathering for lesson preparation is the most common use of the Internet by teachers, teachers have students use the Internet for "research," or information-gathering, more than for any other purpose. In fact, in the past two years, Web searching has become the third most common use of computers by students at school, after word processing and use of CD-ROMs. Web searching even slightly surpasses skills practice by computer drills and learning games in terms of how frequently teachers have students use computers in that way.

Although only a minority of teachers had students use Web browsers during the last school year, the effects of having classroom-located Internet connectivity seems to have been large, at least in terms of baseline levels of use. Among teachers with modems in their classroom, nearly half had students use Web browsers on at least 3 occasions. What might be called "regular" use—using the World Wide Web to do research on at least 10 occasions—was a practice of nearly one-quarter of all teachers with a modem in their classroom and 30 percent of those with direct high-speed connections. Of course, with a limited number of computer stations in the classroom, the amount of experience that any one student may have had with Web-based research could be quite limited.

2. STUDENT PROJECTS AND PUBLISHING

Beyond the traditional activity of using information sources to write reports, some teachers have had students use the Internet to contact other individuals, to collaborate with classes in other schools in joint projects, and to become experts on a topic and publish their findings on the World Wide Web. As of 1997–98, however, very few teachers have had their students involved in those Internet-based activities. Overall, 7 percent of teachers had students e-mail at least 3 times during the school year, and even fewer involved students in cross-classroom collaborative projects on in Web publishing.

Among teachers whose primary teaching responsibility concerned the subject of computers (as opposed to other subject-matter areas), use of the Internet for these purposes was somewhat more common. Between 12 and 17 percent of computer-subject teachers had students use the Internet for each of those three purposes—e-mail, cross-classroom collaborations, and Web publishing. In some cases, it may be that student project work in a computer class is linked to instruction occurring in their subject-matter classes. But this is probably not true most of the time.

Part III. The Internet's Perceived Value for Teachers

Even though a majority of teachers have still not used the Internet in their teaching, and even fewer have used it in a major way, there may be many reasons for this—the recent development of Internet tools and resources, the rapidity with which technologies are changing, the limited opportunity that teachers have had to see how the Internet can be used in their practice, and the rarity of fast and convenient Internet access. Some teachers who have not used the Internet may be looking forward to a day when they might. How do teachers see the Internet's potential value for them in the near future? Do most teachers see the Internet as a valuable or an essential resource in their teaching, as something of limited value, or perhaps something that is not even needed?

We asked teachers about the value of the Internet in two respects: the value of a teacher's computer station with electronic mail access; and the value of having World Wide Web access in their classroom. In each case, almost one-half of all teachers saw these resources as "essential" for their teaching (49 percent and 47 percent respectively) and nearly 90 percent reported that they would consider these resources either valuable or essential. Even among teachers who did not have access to the Internet either at home or in their own classroom, one-third regarded the Internet as an essential teaching resource.

Part IV. Correlates of Internet Use and Perceived Value

Clearly, the access that teachers have to the Internet as well as their teaching responsibilities affects the likelihood that they will use the Internet themselves or with their students and, to some extent, whether they have come to value this resource in their teaching. This section reports our analysis of the degree to which different factors are correlated with teachers' Internet use and perceived value.

A. Measures of Use Employed

Three measures of Internet use are employed, and each measure is based on two or three dichotomous criteria (i.e., meeting or not meeting a given standard). Thus, each teacher received a score of 0, 1, 2, or 3 in each of these categories.

A teacher's TEACHER USE score is the number of the following three criteria met:

- Did they get information from the Internet on a weekly basis?
- Did they send e-mails to teachers at other schools at least 5 times during the year?
- Did they ever post information or student work to the World Wide Web during the year?

A teacher's STUDENT RESEARCH USE score is the number of these three criteria met:

- Did they have students use the World Wide Web in at least 3 lessons during the year?
- Did they have students use the Web at least 10 times?
- Did they choose an Internet browser software as one of the three most valuable pieces of software used in their teaching?

A teacher's STUDENT PROJECTS AND PUBLISHING score comes from three criteria as well:

- Did they have students do e-mail in at least 3 lessons?
- Did they have a class participate in a cross-school collaborative project?
- Did they do a lesson where students became expert in a topic and put their information on the Web?

Finally, a teacher's PERCEIVED VALUE score is the combination of whether they believed desktop e-mail for themselves was essential and whether they believed classroom Web access was essential.

Each of these numerical scores can also be converted to a fraction of the maximum possible score, for individual teachers or for groups of teachers. In other words, if, on average, a group of teachers met 1.5 of the 3 criteria for Student Research Use, then that group of teachers would have an average score of 2 (1.5 divided by 3) for Student Research Use. Here we convert these fractions to decimals and would report that average score as .50. (These decimals are essentially an average of the percentage of teachers who met a typical criterion in the set.)

Across all teachers, the mean scores for the four measures of Internet use and perceived value are shown below (standard deviations in parenthesis):

.48 (.44) Perceived Value

.21 (.28) Teacher Use

.20 (.34) Student Research

.05 (.15) Student Projects and Publishing

B. Association Between Internet Access and Use

Certainly teachers have to have access to the Internet in order to use it. But what kind of access makes the biggest difference in use and perceived value—whether the teacher has access at home or somewhere in school; whether the school access is in her own classroom; or whether her classroom access is through a modem or through high-speed/LAN-based direct access? Our data provides some evidence on this issue.

In terms of a teacher's own professional Internet use, having a modem at home may be almost as important for teachers as having one in their classroom. Teachers with a home modem but no access at school at all have nearly the same Teacher Use score as teachers with an Internet connection in their classroom but no modem at home (.23 vs. .20). Moreover, teachers with a home modem but working in a school without Internet connectivity still have an average Internet Use score that is twice what teachers have who have Internet access somewhere in their school but not at home and not in their own classroom. Teachers with home Internet access also have stronger beliefs about the need for Internet in their teaching.

For student use, teachers with Internet access in their own classroom are much more likely to assign students to do work on the Internet than where access is limited to locations outside of their own classroom. It does look from these data that home Internet access is an advantage for teachers even for stimulating teacher-directed student use. For example, the average Student Research score for teachers with both home and classroom access is .41 and for those with only classroom access it is .32. However, teachers who have a home modem may be initially different from non-modem owning teachers in terms of other factors that make them more likely to assign students Internet-based work. They may perceive the Internet to be more relevant to their teaching responsibilities (so that is why they have a modem), or they may have greater computer expertise. Multivariate analysis shown later in this paper suggests that such an explanation may be true. Controlling on other factors, having a home modem only affects Teacher Professional Use, not teacher-directed Student Use.

There are also differences in Internet use and perceived value between teachers with LAN-based direct high-speed Internet connections in their classroom compared to teachers with simple dial-up modem access. These differences are probably understated by our data as indicated in the note above. Teacher Use and Student Research percentages are both somewhat higher for classrooms with LAN-based-direct connectivity than in classrooms with modem connections.

It is not, however, just the speed and ease-of-use factors that may be responsible for these differences. Classrooms with LAN-based-direct connections are more likely to have at least several computers with simultaneous Internet connections than classrooms where each connection requires a separate modem. *We find the greatest levels of student use,* both for Student Research and for Student Projects and Publication, *in classrooms with LAN-based Internet connections where at least 4 computers are present* as well. (The accompanying figure shows this for teachers with home modem access as well, but this is true overall, too.) Among those teachers who have 4 or more computers in classrooms with LAN-based connections (and home modems as well), the average Student Research score is .66, and the average Projects & Publication score is .17, substantially higher than in classrooms with fewer directly connected computers or where Internet connection is by modem.

C. Teaching Responsibilities and Internet Use

1. SUBJECT-MATTER AND GRADE LEVEL RESPONSIBILITIES

The fact that student Internet use is higher in classrooms with LAN-based direct Internet connections feeding multiple numbers of computers could be partly due to different subjects being taught in classrooms with more

Figure 6.3. Internet Use/Value and Levels of Classroom Connectivity, for Teachers with Home Access.

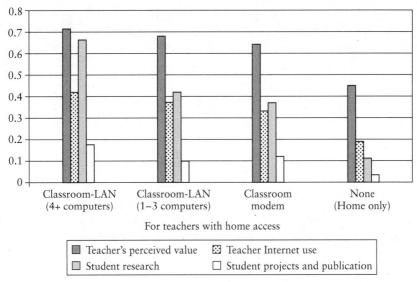

Sources: *Teaching, Learning and Computing—1998, "Internet Use by Teachers," http://www.crito.uci.edu/TLC.*

Internet connectivity. To a large degree, teaching students to use computer resources such as the Internet remains a specialized province of the "computer teacher" rather than having been integrated into the instructional repertoire of teachers across all subjects. Thus, computer teachers would be expected both to have greater connectivity and to report greater amounts of use.

Our analysis of differences in teachers' Internet use based on their teaching responsibilities employs a typology of six categories (plus "other") that is partly based on subjects taught and partly based on school level (grade levels taught). In this typology, teachers of science, social studies, English, and other humanities subjects are grouped together under the label "academic subjects" because their basic patterns of Internet use were not noticeably different from one another. Math teachers were separated out from these other academic subjects because they showed very different patterns of Internet use.[3]

---

[3] Teachers whose responsibilities place them into more than one of the six categories (i.e., math-science teachers) were placed into the residual ("other") category unless more than 50 percent of their classes reflected a single category.

Figure 6.4. Internet Use/Value by School Level Taught.

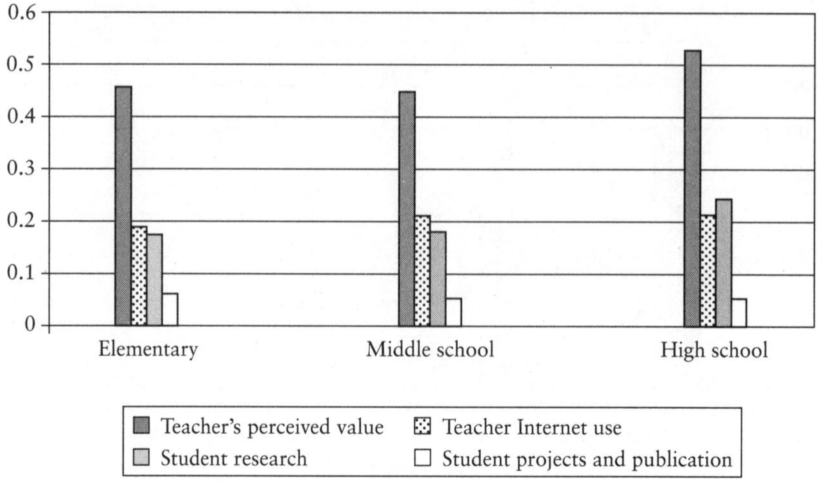

Legend:
- ■ Teacher's perceived value
- ▨ Teacher Internet use
- ▨ Student research
- □ Student projects and publication

Sources: *Teaching, Learning and Computing—1998, "Internet Use by Teachers," http://www.crito.uci.edu/TLC.*

Subject-matter comparisons reveal some consistent patterns with respect to the three types of Internet use and value that were examined. Computer class teachers in secondary school reported the highest scores on all four measures, particularly on the student use measures. Next to computer teachers, high school teachers of "academic" subjects (mainly science, social studies, and English) had slightly higher use and value scores than other teachers. By far the lowest scores on all four measures including teacher Internet use, student use, and perceived value were those of mathematics teachers. Overall, high school teachers had somewhat higher perceived value scores and higher Student Research Use scores than other levels.

Perhaps the most interesting finding in this section is *the sharply lower measures of Internet use and perceived value held by math teachers compared to every other group.* Only 12 percent use the Internet themselves (using the mean value for the three Teacher Use criteria) compared to more than 20 percent for every other teacher category. Only 9 percent of math teachers have students use the Internet for gathering information, compared to 17 percent of elementary mixed-subject teachers and 19 percent or more for every other group of teachers. And use of Internet-based student cross-school project and publication work rarely exists among math teachers, being only one-third as frequent as with other teacher populations. Clearly, math teachers have not figured out how to use the Internet in their curriculum, nor do as many see it as essential as do other teachers.

2. CHARACTERISTICS OF STUDENTS TAUGHT: PRIOR ACHIEVEMENT LEVELS

A rough measure of prior academic performance was provided by teachers about the students in each of the classes which they taught. Teachers were divided into three groups according to the average achievement levels across classes that they reported—low, average, and high. This procedure identified 19 percent of teachers as generally teaching high-performing students and 14 percent teaching primarily low-performing students. Teachers assigned to "high-achieving" classes were slightly more likely to use the Internet and to find it essential in their teaching than teachers with "average" classes, and the teachers of "average" classes were slightly more likely than teachers with "low" classes to use it as well.

D. Experience and Expertise

The value of teaching resources depends to some extent on teachers' having pre-requisite skills that enable them to exploit resources to their full potential. We examined several aspects of the teachers' backgrounds to see whether these were correlated with Internet use and perceived value— their technology experience and expertise, their own education and their teaching experience and professional leadership activities.

1. TECHNOLOGY BACKGROUND
(a) How Long Have They Had a Home Computer and Modem?
We earlier presented the not-unexpected finding that teachers with Internet access at home were more likely to use the Internet in their teaching. Here we look at the issue of whether how long teachers have had a modem is associated with their valuation and use of the Internet. Our data show that teachers with a home modem, even those who have had one for a brief time, are more likely to make professional use of the Internet. On the other hand, only teachers with at least 3 years of home modem use are more likely to have students use the Internet and more likely to believe classroom Internet access is essential to their teaching.

(b) Self-Reported Computer Competencies
Teachers were asked to assess their own current skills related to using computers. Six of the items were not specific to the Internet itself—simply questions about computer file handling, setting up database files, and using word-processors, presentation software, and hypermedia authoring programs. The seventh item asked about their ability to use a Web search engine. Teachers who reported they could use a search engine (62 percent of all teachers) were compared with those who said they could not or could only use it "somewhat." Similarly, teachers with relatively high scores on an index combining the other six items (35 percent of all teachers) were compared with all other teachers.

Both general computer skills and the specific skill of being able to use a Web search engine are correlated with both teacher and student use of the Internet and with greater perceived value. Teachers with high computer skills or who said they could use an Internet search engine had an average Teacher Use and Student Research Use score of nearly .30, while those with average or low computer skills overall had scores averaging .16 and those who reported not having the ability to use an Internet search engine had scores averaging under .10.

(c) Duration of Computer Use with Students
Most teachers now use computers in some way with their students. However, some have been doing so for many years. It is reasonable to think that teachers who have been having their students use computers for several years would be more likely to use the Internet and to value its use than those with less experience with using computers in the classroom. However, our data show that the major difference in teachers' professional use and valuation of the Internet is between teachers who have never assigned computer work to students and those who have—regardless of how long they have been using computers with students. The duration of a teacher's use of computers with students makes almost no difference in average scores on teacher use, student research use or student use for projects and publication.

2. PROFESSIONAL BACKGROUND

(a) Years of Teaching Experience and Age
Compared to most of the other predictors we have been examining, duration of teaching experience has a relatively small relationship to Internet use and valuation by teachers. However, those teachers in their first few years of teaching *are* somewhat different from other teachers. Even though they are younger and possibly more computer-savvy in general,

the teachers with less than four years of teaching experience are slightly less likely than other teachers to use the Internet with students. However, their younger age makes them more comfortable with the Internet in terms of their own use. *Teachers under age 30 in their first few years of teaching are the ones most likely to use the Internet professionally,* and, overall, teachers under 30 are also more likely than older teachers to consider the Internet to be essential in their classroom. The teachers who are most likely to use projects and student Web publishing are those who have 4 to 7 years of teaching experience behind them.

(b) Educational Background—GPA, College Attended, Advanced Coursework

Several measures of educational background were examined to see how much of a difference they made, in combination, in predicting teacher Internet use and valuation. The background measures were (1) the teacher's undergraduate grade-point average (GPA), (2) the "selectivity" of the college the teacher attended as an undergraduate, (3) an index of units and degrees obtained beyond a BA, and (4) the number of courses outside of education taken since college.[4]

Our analysis of the relation between educational background and Internet use employed the statistical procedure of multiple linear regression. We summarize that analysis here in terms of two "typical" teachers representing differing educational backgrounds: Hypothetical Teacher A had an undergraduate GPA of 3.1 or lower, attended a college whose entering students scored an average of about 850 on the SATs (colleges such as Middle Tennessee State, Western Illinois University, or Bridgewater State College), and has not taken any courses outside of education since receiving the BA degree nor accumulated as much as 30 units of any university credit since the BA. Teacher B had a grade average 3.5 or higher, attended a school whose students averaged about 1100 on the SAT (such as U.C. San Diego, Villanova University, or New York University), has an MA degree plus 30 units beyond the MA, and has taken 10 courses outside of education since the BA. These two teachers, based on the linear prediction model used, show distinct differences in Internet use and valuation.

---

[4] Selectivity was measured by an index of test scores of entering freshmen in 1983, close to the median year for college entry for the teaching population as a whole. Scores were provided by the Higher Education Research Institute at UCLA.

In general, Teacher A, suggesting *a teacher with relatively limited educational experiences, is less sure of the need for the Internet in her classroom and is perhaps half as likely to use it herself or with students as* Teacher B, who represents *a teacher with extensive educational experiences.* All four of the educational background measures contributed to the differences between Teacher A and Teacher B, but generally only one measure made a sizable difference for each outcome. The largest effect on predicting use of the Internet with students comes from selectivity of the college attended. The teacher's own success in school (i.e., GPA) made the biggest difference in predicting their own use of the Internet. Advanced degrees and coursework contributed the most of any measure for predicting the teacher's judgment of the value of the Internet for classroom teaching.

(c) Professional Leadership Activities

The teaching profession is generally regarded as having a very flat hierarchy. Each teacher works independently to plan and direct the learning of their own class. This planning occurs with only occasional input from supervisors or colleagues. However, the profession is increasingly recognizing that teachers can become better at their craft when many in their profession engage in peer leadership activities—for example, by mentoring less experienced teachers, leading workshops for disseminating new ideas, or writing and publishing for other teachers. Do teachers who become involved in leadership activities of this sort also use the Internet more in their professional work? Do they necessarily use the Internet more with students in their teaching? Are they more likely to regard it as an essential part of an effective classroom?

We measured a teacher's involvement in leadership activities by asking respondents to report which of six types of activities they had engaged in during the previous three years, if any: informally mentoring a teacher for most of a year, having a formal mentoring relationship with a teacher, giving a workshop or conference talk for at least 25 teachers, giving workshops on at least five occasions, teaching a college-level course for credit, or publishing an article in a magazine or journal for professional educators. Although 60 percent of teachers have done one or more of these things in the past three years, only 20 percent have engaged in at least three of these six leadership activities.

These *teacher leaders are much more likely to use the Internet than other teachers, both in their own professional activities* (mean scores of .29 vs. .19) *and in terms of using them with students* (for example, in research activities, the differences are .30 vs. .18).

E. School Support for Teaching Using Technology

Even though software developers have been conscious of the need to make their programs easy for teachers to learn and to use, the power and flexibility of most computer applications inevitably requires [that] teachers master new skills before they can become expert users of computer resources. The new understandings required of teachers include not only technical skills but an understanding of the relevance of the various features and information provided by the software to their own instructional and curricular priorities, as well as pedagogical strategies for using the software in the context of other constraints, such as time limitations and prerequisite student skills. To accomplish those understandings, many schools provide formal staff development for teachers on computer skills; and some facilitate informal contact among teachers so that the understandings may spread in the normal course of their professional interactions. Our data explored the relationship of both of these processes to teacher Internet use and related beliefs.

I. FORMAL STAFF DEVELOPMENT

Three out of ten teachers report having attended a workshop or other formal staff development activity in the past year in which "how to use the Internet" or other on-line activities was a central topic of discussion. Teachers who attended such staff development activities were more likely to believe the Internet to be an essential classroom resource and more likely to use the Internet than other teachers, by a fairly large degree.

Nevertheless, one could argue that teachers who were more interested in using the Internet participated in this staff development in the first place. To partly control for prior interest and motivation to attend, we looked only among teachers who had the same level of Internet access (for example, they had it at home but not in their classroom). Even among teachers with the same access at home and in their classroom, teachers who attended staff development on the Internet were somewhat more likely to use it in their teaching and for professional work. The "staff development effect," at least as modeled so far, seems to be most clearly present for teachers who have access both at home and in their classroom, or for those without access in either place. For example, among teachers who had access in both places, the average Teacher Internet Use score for teachers who attended staff development was .41; but for those who did not attend such training, only .31.

2. INFORMAL CONTACTS AMONG TEACHERS

Each teacher was asked how frequently they had had several types of discussions with other teachers at their school—discussions about how to teach a concept; of ideas for student or group projects; discussions about computers, software, or the Internet; about personal matters; and about issues in their subject-matter field—and they were also asked about the frequency [at which] they observed another teacher's class or another teacher observed herself. Note that in contrast to our measure of formal staff development, only a small part of our measure of informal contacts dealt with conversation about the Internet per se. Instead, it is a measure of the breadth of conversation that occurs among teachers at the same school.

We divided teachers into four quartiles in terms of the overall frequency of informal contacts. We found that there were clear distinctions in Internet use between each quartile—*the higher the frequency of informal contacts, the greater the use of the Internet and the more essential its presence was regarded.* When we controlled on Internet access at home and in the classroom, to look at the relationship between Internet use and informal contacts independent of issues of access, we found that the differences between high-contact teachers and other teachers was more substantial and more widespread than the differences between in-service attenders and non-attenders. This was particularly true for the differences between teachers who were in the top quartile of informal contacts and teachers in the three other quartiles. So for example, among teachers without any Internet access, either at home or in their classroom, teachers who had frequent informal contact with other teachers were more likely to use the Internet themselves (.16) and to believe it was essential for classroom teaching (.49) than other teachers that also lacked Internet access but who didn't have that high level of informal contact with other teachers (.06 and .30, in comparison).

3. SCHOOL-PROVIDED COMPUTER RESOURCES

Having a computer on one's own desk may be another element in the support structure for facilitating a teacher's use of technology. Our data show that teachers who report that their school provided them with their own computer are more likely to believe that classroom Internet is essential to teaching, and are more likely to use the Internet as well. However, once we control on whether their classroom had Internet access, only the difference in attitudes remains. In other words, among teachers with the same level of Internet access in their classroom, those who have been provided with a computer for their own professional use are more likely to believe classroom Internet access to be essential. However, they are no more likely to use the Internet in their teaching (either themselves or by their students) than are teachers who were not given a computer for themselves.

F. Pedagogical Beliefs and Practices

Along with other applications of computers, the Internet has been seen by many people as a vehicle for teachers to carry out major changes in how they teach students. Obviously, having students use the Internet is by itself one level of change—a change in the information resources that students examine. But it may also be that the Internet enables teachers to follow a whole new approach to teaching based on a different theory of how students attain understanding or new perspectives on what it is important for students to know.

In the common view of the teaching-learning model, the teacher helps students to master a sequential set of skills, facts, and concepts primarily by (a) having the whole class read the same material in a textbook, (b) explaining the content to students using various forms of questioning and direct explanation, and (c) having students practice their understanding repetitively until they can demonstrate their competency on a test. In contrast, a "reform" or "constructivist" approach to teaching involves having students work on complex projects, often in groups, and often with different groups working on different projects. In this model, students learn skills and concepts in the context of using them to *do* something—for example, in making a product. These projects follow from a constructivist theory of learning that suggests that subject-matter becomes meaningful, and therefore understandable, only when it is *used* in context-rich activities. Teachers whose instructional plan follows from constructivist learning theory will not only use group projects more than other teachers; they will, for example, emphasize the student's own responsibility for designing their own tasks, for figuring out their own methods of solving problems, and for assessing their own work—all as a means of making learning tasks more meaningful to students.

1. MEASUREMENT OF CONSTRUCTIVIST PEDAGOGY

A number of multi-part questions in the teachers' survey asked teachers about their beliefs of what constitutes good teaching and about how they carry out instruction in one of their classes, in particular, in the class "where you are most satisfied with your teaching—where you accomplish your teaching goals most often." Factor analysis was used to select a subset of items that contributed to measures of the underlying conceptual contrast between constructivist and traditional pedagogies. Although different factor analyses yielded slightly different sets of items, the one used here incorporates 11 "belief" items (i.e., assessments of the value of different teaching practices) and 15 "practice" items (i.e., reports of the frequency [with which] they used different methods). This particular factor analysis distinguished five "factors" related to constructivist versus traditional pedagogy:

• *Disagreement with traditional pedagogy and learning theory:* opposition to statements about the value of (1) a quiet classroom; (2) basic skills being taught prior to "meaningful" instruction; (3) teacher control over the classroom agenda; (4) problems or tasks with clear correct answers; (5) teacher explanations to students based on their superior knowledge; and (6) learning being dependent on a store of background knowledge.

• *Agreement with statements about the value of . . .:* (1) the teacher being a facilitator rather than explainer; (2) multiple classroom activities rather than a common set for all students; (3) interest and effort being more important than the particular subject-matter in the prescribed curriculum; (4) student participation in setting assessment criteria; and (5) student freedom of movement within a classroom.

• *Frequent use of projects and demonstrations:* (1) demonstrating their work to an audience; (2) making a product to be used by someone else; (3) working on projects that take a week or more; (4) doing "hands-on" collaborative activities; and (5) NOT working individually to answer questions (i.e., seatwork).

• *Frequent practices requiring heavier student responsibility:* (1) deciding on their own procedures for solving a problem; (2) designing their own problems to solve; (3) working in small groups to come up with a joint solution; and (4) doing problems with no obvious solution.

• *Frequently using the following practices in their teaching:* (1) student assessment of their own work; (2) student essay-writing; (3) student journal-writing; (4) student debates; (5) assignments for which "there is no correct answer"; and (6) student participation in planning class activities.

Although all five of those "factors" are independent of each other (and thus statistically uncorrelated, a result of the factor analysis procedure), for this report we used the information provided by the factor analysis in a heuristic manner. In particular, we combined the teachers' responses on the 26 items that loaded on any one of the five factors into an overall index of constructivist pedagogy. Those constructivist pedagogy scores were then correlated with Internet use.

Overall, the "typical" teacher is almost right in the middle between the "constructivist" and the "traditional" ends of the index, scoring 2.9 on a scale whose maximum (constructivist pole) is 5 and whose minimum (traditional pole) is 1.[5]

2. CONSTRUCTIVISM AND INTERNET USE

The responding teachers were divided into four quartiles based on their "constructivist vs. traditional pedagogy" index score. *On all four measures of Internet use and valuation, the more constructivist the teacher, the greater their average use and the more positively they viewed the Internet.* For example, among the most constructivist teachers (those in the upper 19 percent on the index) nearly two-thirds (65 percent) believed Internet presence in their classroom was essential; among the most traditional teachers, only one-third (34 percent) felt it was essential. Similarly, the most constructivist teachers' average score for Teacher Internet Use was 22 times as high as the average score for the most traditional teachers (.30 vs. .12). Differences in terms of teachers' use of the Internet with their students was even greater: The average Student Research score for the most constructivist teachers was .31, compared to .11 for the most traditional teachers; and in terms of Student Projects and Publication, the respective averages were .09 versus .02. Clearly, a teacher's pedagogical beliefs and practices are strongly related to how relevant they see the Internet for their teaching and whether they use it.

Part V. Multivariate Analysis

So far we have shown that almost every variable we have examined has at least some relationship to whether teachers use the Internet and whether they regard its presence in their classroom as essential to their teaching. These variables include . . .

INTERNET ACCESS

- Classroom Internet access
- Home Internet access

---

[5] The study of teacher pedagogy is a central part of the TLC−1998 research. Later reports will discuss pedagogical differences among different groups of teachers, and will provide data on specific aspects of teachers' beliefs and practices. Those various aspects are combined here for this initial examination of the relationship between constructivist pedagogy and use of the Internet.

- Direct-LAN connectivity in their classroom
- Having many computers in the classroom with simultaneous Internet access

TEACHING RESPONSIBILITIES

- Subject-matter responsibilities and school level
- Prior achievement of students taught

TECHNOLOGY EXPERIENCE

- Whether they have used computers with students
- How long they have had a modem at home
- Self-reported computer competencies

PROFESSIONAL EXPERIENCE

- Years of teaching experience and age
- Educational background: college attended, GPA, courses and degrees since BA
- Professional leadership activities

SCHOOL SUPPORT FOR TEACHING USING TECHNOLOGY

- Formal training on Internet use
- Informal contacts among teachers on a variety of topics
- Whether the school has supplied them with a computer on their desk

PEDAGOGICAL BELIEFS AND PRACTICES

Constructivist vs. traditional pedagogical beliefs and practices

In Part V, we address two related questions:

A. To what extent do these variables in combination account for variation among teachers in their Internet use and valuation? That is, if we take into account all of the variation among teachers and in their teaching context represented by the above list of variables, how different do teachers look from one another in terms of Internet use?

B. Which variables are most strongly related to Internet use and beliefs about its value, net of all other predictor variables? We add that last phrase, "net of all other predictor variables," because some of these predictor variables are themselves correlated. For example, teachers employing constructivist pedagogies were also more involved in professional leadership activities and had more informal contacts with other teachers. Therefore, taking a somewhat conservative approach, we ask what is the contribution of each variable in predicting teacher Internet use and value, once each of the other variables is accounted for.

A. All Predictors Considered Together

To measure the combined force of Internet access, teaching responsibilities, technology expertise, professional experience, school support for teaching, and pedagogical beliefs and practices on teachers' Internet use and valuation, we established a set of criteria or conditions, one for each variable, and then calculated for each teacher how many of the conditions were present for that teacher. Specifically, we used the following twenty conditions:

INTERNET ACCESS

1. Had classroom Internet access of some kind
2. Had direct-LAN connectivity in their classroom
3. Had Internet access at home

TEACHING RESPONSIBILITIES

1. Computer class teacher
2. NOT a math teacher
3. Taught high achieving classes

TECHNOLOGY EXPERTISE

1. Had used computers with students
2. Had a modem at home for 3 years+
3. Broad computer expertise

PROFESSIONAL EXPERIENCE

1. Under 30 years of age
2. Teaching experience: 7 [years] or less
3. Educational background:
   - College GPA: 3.5+
   - Attended a selective college (SAT 1100+)

- Masters degree or higher
- Coursework since BA: 8+ courses outside education

4. Professional leadership activities: 3+ out of 6

SCHOOL SUPPORT FOR TEACHING

1. Formal training on Internet use in the last year
2. Had frequent informal contacts with other teachers at school
3. School provided teacher with computer

PEDAGOGICAL BELIEFS AND PRACTICES

Constructivist pedagogy (top 19 percent on index)

In the case of the typical (median) teacher, seven of these twenty conditions are present. However, for some teachers as many as sixteen conditions are present, and a few teachers have just one or two.

The effect of the combination of all of these predictors on teachers' use and valuation of the Internet is dramatic. *Nearly every increase in the number of conditions present is accompanied by an increase in teachers' Internet use and valuation.* Whereas the 15 percent of teachers with the fewest criteria have Perceived Value scores averaging .20 (20 percent believing the Internet is essential in their classroom), those passing at least half of the criteria have Perceived Value scores averaging .74 (74 percent). Similarly, our measure of a teacher's professional use of the Internet rises from .04 to .43, Student Research use goes from .03 to .43, and Student Projects and Publications increases from .00 to .16. Those few teachers meeting 12 or more criteria (4.4 percent of all teachers) have even higher scores, with, for example, an average Student Projects and Publication score of .25 and an average Student Research use score of .57.

There are several ways to think about these results. From one perspective, even among teachers with many things in their favor—perhaps a good educational background, good Internet access, school support for using technology, and some expertise in using computers—only about one-half of the teachers in the most favorable settings are strong Internet users or use the Internet in a substantial way with students. At most, only one-fourth of them involve classes in cross-school Internet collaborations or put up student work on the World Wide Web. On the other hand, in the absence of those conditions very few teachers are Internet users, and where fewer than one-half of these conditions apply, very few teachers use the Internet for student projects and publication. It is important to re-

Figure 6.5. Internet Use/Value by Number of Conditions Present.

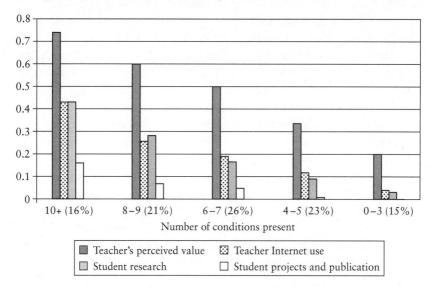

Number of conditions present

■ Teacher's perceived value ⊠ Teacher Internet use
▢ Student research □ Student projects and publication

Sources: *Teaching, Learning and Computing—1998, "Internet Use by Teachers," http://www.crito.uci.edu/TLC.*

member, though, that the Internet is a brand-new resource in most schools. Over time, one would expect all of the values in Figure 6.5 to rise. However, the *differences* in average scores for teachers experiencing different conditions may stay relatively constant.

B. Multivariate Analysis—The Factors That Most Differentiate Users and Non-Users

The previous section answered the question, "How much difference does the full set of conditions make in the likelihood of a teacher being an Internet user?" Here we address the question of which conditions make the most difference. We are essentially applying a common metric to all of the different results presented in Part IV. However, we are also taking into account the overlap that exists among multiple predictors. In other words, we are taking into account the fact that different predictors are themselves correlated. (For example, teachers who participate in formal staff development activities about the Internet are more likely to have classroom Internet access, with a measured correlation of r = .30.)

As a first step in this effort to reach an understanding of the "causal" influences on a teacher's becoming an Internet user, we applied standard multiple linear regression techniques to our data. We used the original "interval-level" measures of each predictor rather than the simpler dichotomies that were used in the previous analysis. In other words, rather than measuring Teacher's Informal Contacts by the simple contrast of whether or not a teacher was in the top quartile on that index, we used the original index scores for each teacher, which varied from 1.00 to 4.00 with many different fractional scores in-between. Our measure of the "independent effect" of a predictor variable is the standardized beta coefficient in the regression equation. Four equations were used, one for each outcome variable. All relationships discussed are statistically significant at $p > .05$ and meet an "effect size" criterion of the standardized beta coefficient being greater than .05.[6]

Out of the 18 variables examined in the multiple regression equation, eight of them have important independent relationships to teachers' Internet use and valuation outcomes:

- Level of classroom connectivity
- Teacher's computer expertise
- Constructivist pedagogy
- Participation in staff development on Internet use
- Involvement in professional leadership activities
- Having informal contacts with other teachers at their school
- The teacher's age (the younger, the more likely using and believing in its value)
- Not being a mathematics teacher

---

[6] Multiple regression analysis measures only "direct" relationships between a predictor variable and an outcome, controlling on all other inputs. Consequently, predictors that operate through other predictors in the equation are not given "credit" for their "indirect" contribution to the outcome through affecting such an intermediary (intervening) variable. For example, educational background may influence Internet use through its affect on Professional Leadership. However, in multiple regression only the effects not mediated by professional leadership or other intervening variables remain attributed to educational background. Subsequent analysis will employ path analysis to more accurately model the distinction between prior and intervening variables, and direct and indirect effects.

Figure 6.6. Most Significant Predictive Conditions of Internet Use/Value.

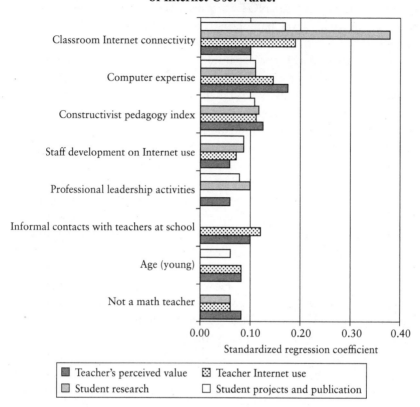

Standardized regression coefficient

■ Teacher's perceived value   ⊠ Teacher Internet use
▨ Student research   □ Student projects and publication

Source: *Teaching, Learning and Computing—1998,* "*Internet Use by Teachers,*" *http://www.crito.uci.edu/TLC.*

1. THE MAJOR THREE PREDICTORS: CONNECTIVITY, COMPUTER EXPERTISE, AND CONSTRUCTIVIST PEDAGOGY

By far the most important variable in predicting teachers' Internet use is *the teacher's level of classroom connectivity.* This variable takes on four values: no connection (0); modem connection (1); direct connection (2); direct connection with four or more computers present (3). The beta coefficients for Level of Classroom Connectivity ranged from .10, for Teacher-Perceived Value, to .36, for use in Student Research. As schools move towards connecting more classrooms to the Internet, particularly with high-speed direct connections, we can foresee parallel increases in the number of teachers who make regular use of the Internet, particularly for student research, but also for their own class preparation and for student cross-classroom projects and Web publication. For all three Internet use outcomes (but NOT for "teacher's perceived value"), classroom connectivity level had the strongest relationship of any of the predictors examined.

Other analyses performed separated out *which* aspect of connectivity is most related to Internet use—any connection at all; high-speed direct connectivity; or connectivity with many computers attached. For all four outcome variables, the biggest effect comes from having any classroom connection at all, rather than having to connect elsewhere in the school building or at home. However, both direct connectivity and direct connectivity with multiple (4+) computers contributed to explaining variation in teacher-directed Student Research use (beta coefficients of .07 and .08 respectively, in the full regression model). In addition, direct connectivity had an independent effect on teachers' professional use of the Internet (beta = .07), and direct connectivity with four or more computers had a small effect on the Student Projects and Publication variable (beta = .04). Overall, the effects of "any classroom access" were stronger than these other connectivity aspects. However, it should be recalled that the measurement of connectivity level was subject to substantial ambiguity and imputation; the result will be to underestimate the effects of direct connectivity on all of the outcome variables.

Two other predictors were also related to all four Internet use and valuation outcomes with standardized beta coefficients of +.10 or higher: the teacher's computer expertise and the teacher's pedagogical beliefs and practices.

Teacher computer expertise had the strongest association of any predictor on the "valuation" outcome—i.e., affecting how likely a teacher was to say that classroom Internet resources (e-mail and Web) were essential to good teaching. Computer expertise was measured here by excluding Internet-specific skills such as using a World Wide Web search engine, so it is simply a teacher's overall computer expertise (self-reported) that predicts beliefs about the value of the Internet for their classroom teaching. Computer expertise also predicted teachers' professional use of the Internet better than any variable besides classroom connectivity level. Thus, although the Internet is often presented as a novice-friendly area of computer use, it seems that here as well, relevant prior computer knowledge may be an important prerequisite for a teacher to make the Internet a valued resource in their classroom, and valuable in their lesson preparation activities in particular.

The third major predictor of teachers' Internet use and valuation in this analysis is the *teacher's pedagogical beliefs and practices*. Our index contrasting constructivist-compatible teaching pedagogy with traditional fact- and skills-based teaching had beta-coefficients above .10 for all four outcome variables. One conclusion of this finding is that scaling up Internet use to higher numbers of teachers may depend in part on changing the relevance that teachers perceive the Internet holds for their primary instructional goals—which in turn may require changing teachers' instructional priorities. Teachers who regard education as primarily the distribution of facts and skills to students according to a fixed curriculum sequence are much less likely to exploit the Internet than more "constructivist" teachers.

2. SCHOOL-BASED SUPPORT, LEADERSHIP EXPERIENCE, HOME ACCESS

Besides the three variables just discussed—classroom connectivity level, computer expertise, and constructivist vs. traditional pedagogy—other predictors had modestly strong beta coefficients for one or two outcome variables, but not across all outcomes. The level of a teacher's *informal contact with other teachers at their school* was associated with more positive beliefs in the Internet's value in the classroom and with a greater likelihood of using the Internet for professional tasks (beta equal to .10 and .12, respectively). However, informal contact (i.e., discussions with other teachers on a variety of topics; and mutual classroom visits) was *not* substantially related to *student* Internet use, once other predictors were taken into account. Similarly, a *teacher's home Internet access* was an important predictor of a teacher's professional use of the Internet, but not so for student use. In contrast, *involvement in professional leadership activities* was an independent predictor of *student* Internet use but not so much of teacher use or attitudes, once other predictor variables were controlled.

Participating in *staff development activities related to using the Internet* had positive beta coefficients on all four outcomes, but the coefficients were slightly weaker than those discussed so far.

It is not clear whether much should be made of the pattern in the above two paragraphs—e.g., that professional leadership is not associated with teacher professional use of the Internet, while the frequency of informal collegial relationships is not associated with more student Internet use, net of other predictors. Teachers who are active professional leaders—who mentor other teachers, do workshop presentations, and possibly even write or teach professionally—certainly do use the Internet more than other teachers do. And although a mix of informal relationships among teachers may create a climate in which teachers take the effort to become Internet users themselves, it may be that for teachers to use the Internet with students only, more specific computer-specific communication makes a difference.

3. AGE AND SUBJECT TAUGHT

Moving on to the remaining predictors in Figure 6.6, we find that the *younger the age of a teacher* the more likely the teacher was to use the Internet herself or with students, and the more she believed the Internet had an essential role in her classroom. Thus, the greater comfort with technology that younger teachers display outweighs advantages of greater teaching experience. In addition, *mathematics teachers* were clearly distinct from all other teachers in their lower likelihood of Internet use and in their lack of belief that Internet resources were "essential" to their classroom teaching. Also, there was a slightly higher likelihood for *teachers of computer classes* to be involved in having students use the Internet, after other predictors, such as level of connectivity and pedagogical beliefs, were taken into account.

4. EDUCATIONAL BACKGROUND, SCHOOL-SUPPLIED COMPUTER: RELATIONSHIPS EXPLAINED BY INTERVENING VARIABLES

If these were the variables that appeared to make a difference in discriminating among teachers in their Internet use and valuation, which variables did not. Generally speaking, once other variables were held constant, the teachers' own educational background did not have an independent effect on Internet use (but it did, still, on how much the teacher *valued* the Internet). However, the lack of an effect here is likely to mean only that the effect of educational background on Internet is *mediated* by certain intervening variables in the model, such as leadership participation or computer expertise. In other words, teachers with a more educationally advantaged background (higher degrees, higher grades, more selective schools) were more likely to undertake leadership activities within the profession and more likely to obtain computer expertise. When those intervening variables are "held constant," they "explain away" the original relationship between educational background and Internet use.

Similarly, the association between a teacher's Internet use and a school's providing that teacher with her own desktop computer evaporated in the multiple regression model. Again, however, it may be that the effect of having their own school-supplied computer is "hidden by colinearity with" (occurring to the same individuals as) high levels of classroom connectivity. However, even taking connectivity into account, teachers with a school-provided desktop computer were more likely to believe it was essential to their classroom teaching.

OTHER NEGLIGIBLE EFFECTS

In contrast to the variables discussed so far, there is relatively little effect of prior computer experience on teachers' professional use of the Internet. (This variable was excluded from the regression equations predicting student use, since, by definition, teachers who have not used computers with students have not had students use the Internet either.) Moreover, as shown earlier, how long a teacher had been having students use computers was not sufficiently predictive in the bi-variate analysis to even include that variable in these multiple regression analyses.

Finally, student ability, or prior achievement as we have called it here, was not a predictor of teacher Internet use. Teachers with both high ability classes were roughly equally likely as other teachers to use the Internet with students. The only hint of a difference was in terms of Student Projects and Publications, where teachers of high ability classes were slightly more likely to use the Internet in this way than were other teachers, net of other factors.

Part VI. Conclusions

Along with word processing, the Internet may be the most valuable of the many computer technologies available to teachers and students. In its first few years of existence, the World Wide Web has become one of the most frequently used computer technologies in schools. In addition, hundreds of thousands of teachers have become regular electronic mail users, although that same degree of taken-for-granted access has not yet been provided to many students. It is clear that, even in its most obvious manifestation as "the world's largest library," teachers find the Internet to be an incredibly useful technology. Moreover, current applications only scratch the surface of the capabilities that the world-wide digital communications infrastructure will eventually provide for teachers and their students.

In thinking about how to extend Internet use to larger numbers of teachers, it is useful to examine the conditions that our research identified as most consistently facilitative of greater levels of use—high levels of classroom connectivity; computer expertise; constructivist pedagogy;

participation in staff development; high frequency of informal contacts with other teachers; involvement in professional leadership activities; being a young teacher; and not being a mathematics teacher.

Some of these conditions tell us the kinds of teachers that are most likely (or in the case of math teachers, least likely) to be drawn to the Internet—(1) younger teachers, (2) teachers who are leaders in their profession, and (3) teachers with constructivist pedagogies.

The importance of "age" may diminish over time. What makes young teachers more likely to be Internet users is not their youth per se, but their greater comfort as a result of having grown up with ever-changing computer technologies.

Second, the relationship between Internet use and professional leadership suggests that if leaders among teachers can be encouraged to share their enthusiasm and knowledge of the Internet with other teachers, this will also have an effect of diffusing use more broadly within the profession.

The pedagogy variable may be more intractable. Other research we are conducting[7] suggests that computer technology is having an emancipating effect on teachers who believe in project-based teaching and other constructivist-compatible practices. However, changing other teachers' philosophies and beliefs to be more constructivist simply by having them use computers in their teaching may not work. It may be, then, that diffusion of Internet use to larger numbers of teachers will reach a barrier when most of the remaining non-participants hold beliefs that are not as compatible with Internet use as constructivism seems to be—in other words, teachers who believe in a skills-based curriculum, organized in a fixed, externally determined sequence, and who teach a uniform aggregation of content which all students should master.

The remaining variables related to Internet use are all, theoretically at least, within the reach of educational leaders to do something about. Certainly schools will increase the proportion of Internet-using teachers by increasing the level of classroom-located Internet connectivity—by establishing connections for classrooms that do not now have them, by having those connections be LAN-based, high-speed links, and by having at least several Internet-linked computers in each classroom. Our results about the importance of classroom-located connections suggest that

---

[7] See Becker and Ravitz, *Journal of Research on Computing in Education,* Summer 1999; and Dexter, Anderson, and Becker, *Journal of Research on Computing in Education,* Spring 1999.

schools will not increase teacher use or satisfaction with the Internet by limiting linkages to computer labs external to classrooms.

Building up the computer expertise of teachers also may produce greater use of the Internet, as would more training for teachers in how to use the Internet. However, it is the remaining "condition" in our list that is the most intriguing—frequent informal contact with other teachers at their school. As discussed earlier, teachers who use the Internet professionally report that, on average, they more frequently talk with other teachers at their school about how to teach a particular concept to a class, or about ideas for group projects, or even about personal matters, and they are more likely to have other teachers observe their own teaching. Although these differences don't extend to directly influencing student Internet use, net of other factors, frequent informal interactions among teachers may help teachers to learn enough about the Internet to apply it in their teaching in a variety of ways. The Internet thus becomes a potentially important tool in the creation of a collaborative professional culture among the teachers of a school.[8]

These findings do not represent the final word on determinants of teacher Internet use in 1998, or even the final word for this research project. Further analysis will show, for example, how the level of support for technology provided by a school (e.g., in technical troubleshooting, instructional support, and student supervision) relates to teachers' use of the Internet. The path analysis to be done will also take a second look at "distal" variables like teachers' educational background and examine how they affect eventual teacher Internet use.

WEB SITE

http://www.crito.uci.edu/TLC

---

[8] This paper has not examined the value of having teachers or students use the Internet, compared to other ways of learning or of being productive. Instead, we have taken as a starting point that use of the Internet is a worthwhile activity, and looked at the extent to which teachers are using this new technology and the conditions that make that use more likely.

7

THE LINK TO HIGHER SCORES

Jeff Archer

NEW RESEARCH ON technology's effectiveness in teaching math appears to confirm what many educators have optimistically suspected: Computers can raise student achievement and even improve a school's climate.

But they have to be placed in the right hands and used in the right ways, says Harold Wenglinsky, an associate research scientist at the Princeton, N.J.-based Educational Testing Service who carried out the analysis for *Education Week*.

In fact, used for the wrong purposes, Wenglinsky says, computers appear to do more harm than good.

"Technology, indeed, can have positive benefits," he says. "But those benefits depend on how the technology is used."

His findings are welcome news to school systems under increasing pressure to justify the nation's substantial investment in education technology—now estimated at more than $5 billion a year.

But they also present a major challenge to policymakers looking for a good return on that investment. Too often, the study finds, the total is being used for the wrong job.

UNTIL NOW, MOST RESEARCH on technology's effectiveness has taken the form of small case studies, some of which examined just a classroom or two at a time.

While several of these studies found evidence that technology can improve student achievement, researchers have been wary of presuming that

Figure 7.1. It's in the Way That You Use It . . .

The arrows below show positive relationships among school technology use, teacher technology training, a more positive school climate, and higher student math achievement. These relationships exist even when other factors that affect student achievement (teachers' qualifications, students' socioeconomic status, and class size) are taken into account.

4TH GRADE MATH

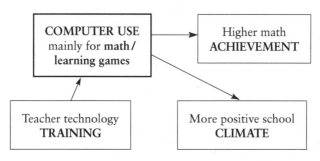

8TH GRADE MATH

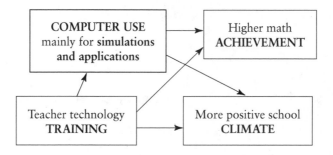

Source: *Educational Testing Service, "Does It Compute?," an analysis of 1996 National Assessment of Educational Progress.*

the same results could be replicated in other classrooms where teachers might be less motivated or knowledgeable about computers.

Wenglinsky breaks new ground by analyzing a national database of student test scores, classroom computer use, and other information, including school climate.

His study, "Does It Compute? The Relationship Between Educational Technology and Student Achievement in Mathematics," is based on the performance data of 4th and 8th graders who took the math section of

Figure 7.2. . . . Not How Often.

Educators should focus on whether teachers have training and how they use computers in the classroom, rather than how much time students spend in front of computers, an Educational Testing Service analysis suggests. The charts below show how much influence technology variables had on NAEP math scores for students in the 4th and 8th grades when other factors (teachers' qualifications, students' socioeconomic status, and class size) were taken into account. For example, 8th graders whose teachers had received technology training scored higher than students whose teachers had not received training. The difference amounted to 35 percent of a grade-level gain in scores.

4TH GRADE MATH

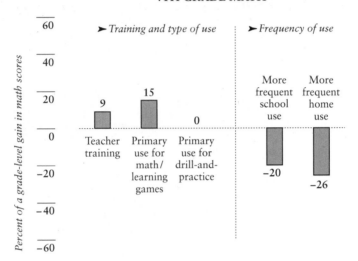

8TH GRADE MATH

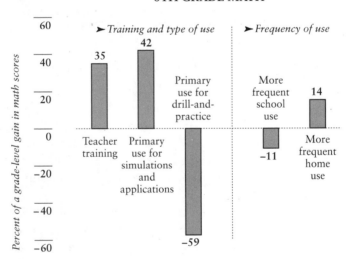

Source: *Educational Testing Service, "Does It Compute?," an analysis of 1996 National Assessment of Educational Progress.*

the 1996 National Assessment of Educational Progress. The study will also be published as an ETS policy information report, and is available at www.ets.org/research/pic.

Administered by the U.S. Department of Education, NAEP—known as "the nation's report card"—has tracked student achievement for nearly three decades. For the first time in 1996, NAEP asked students and teachers additional questions about how they used computers in math.

After factoring out the influence of several other variables that affect achievement, such as students' socioeconomic status, class size, and teacher qualifications, Wenglinsky found strong links between certain kinds of technology use, higher scores on NAEP, and an improved school climate. In every case, the gains were greater at the middle school level than in elementary school.

Among his findings:

• Eighth graders whose teachers used computers mostly for "simulations and applications"—generally associated with higher-order thinking—performed better on NAEP than students whose teachers did not. Meanwhile 8th graders whose teachers used computers primarily for "drill and practice"—generally associated with lower-order thinking—performed worse.

• Among 4th graders, students whose teachers used computers mainly for "math/learning games" scored higher than students whose teachers didn't. The research found no association, positive or negative, between 4th graders' scores and either simulations and applications or drill-and-practice.

• In both grades, students whose teachers had professional development in computers outperformed students whose teachers didn't.

• Students who spent more time on computers in school didn't score any higher than their peers; in fact, they performed slightly worse.

• The same factors that were tied to better achievement also appeared to be linked to an improved school climate. Where teachers had professional development with computers and used them for teaching higher-order skills, schools tended to enjoy higher staff morale and lower absenteeism rates.

• Low-income and black students are the least likely to have teachers who use technology to its full advantage.

Many education experts see the findings as validating their long-held beliefs about what works and what doesn't when it comes to school technology.

"We didn't know this," Douglas H. Clements, an education professor at the State University of New York at Buffalo, says of the findings. "But we had some hints from more qualitative and smaller studies. So to have a large national study with a lot of the controls that this kind of analysis allows is quite a striking confirmation."

CRITICS AND SOME SKEPTICS have long argued that computers add nothing to the education process, and may even be a distraction.

At the same time, technology's greatest proponents have portrayed computers as a potential savior of American education, with the power to increase student learning and stimulate widespread reforms in teaching practices and the way schools are structured.

Wenglinsky's research finds elements of truth in both views. What matters most, it suggests, are not the machines and the wiring themselves, but what teachers and students do with them.

"People are getting beyond the idea that this thing is magic, and that, like fire, just by sitting near it, you can get some benefit," says Christopher J. Dede, a professor of education and information technology at George Mason University in Fairfax, Va.

The benefits seem to increase as the use of the technology becomes more sophisticated.

Eighth graders whose teachers reported using computers primarily for drill-and-practice scored lower on NAEP—by more than half a grade level—than students whose teachers reported other primary uses of com-

---

Figure 7.3. 4th Grade Instructional Use: A National Look.
Other factors being equal, the largest positive effect on 4th grade math scores came from teachers using computers primarily for math/learning games. Black students, Title 1 students, and students in the Southeast are less likely to have teachers who use computers for that purpose.

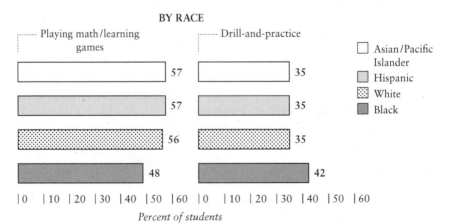

BY RACE

puters. Students whose teachers concentrated on simulations and applications, meanwhile, scored higher by two-fifths of a grade level.

A simulation can illustrate relationships for students and allow them to test the effects of changing variables; an application, such as a spreadsheet program, lets students manipulate and analyze data.

Both uses are aimed at developing higher-order thinking skills, which researcher Barbara Means of SRI International describes as being "based on multiple mental steps rather than memory and rote procedure." Means works at the Center for Technology in Learning at the Menlo Park, Calif.–based research group.

One example of this use of technology is a unit of instruction designed by researchers at the University of Massachusetts Dartmouth that allows

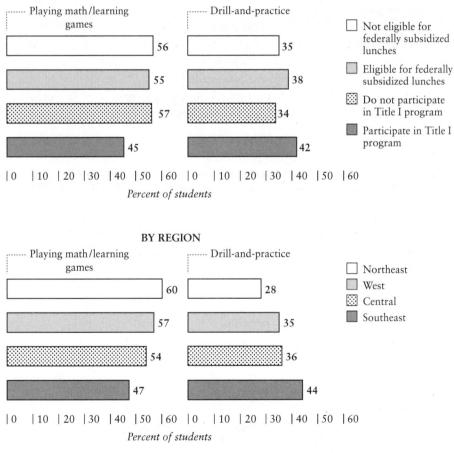

BY POVERTY

Playing math/learning games — Drill-and-practice

Not eligible for federally subsidized lunches: 56 / 35

Eligible for federally subsidized lunches: 55 / 38

Do not participate in Title I program: 57 / 34

Participate in Title I program: 45 / 42

|0 |10 |20 |30 |40 |50 |60 |0 |10 |20 |30 |40 |50 |60

Percent of students

BY REGION

Playing math/learning games — Drill-and-practice

Northeast: 60 / 28

West: 57 / 35

Central: 54 / 36

Southeast: 47 / 44

|0 |10 |20 |30 |40 |50 |60 |0 |10 |20 |30 |40 |50 |60

Percent of students

Source: *Educational Testing Service, "Does It Compute?" and unpublished tabulations from 1996 National Assessment of Educational Progress.*

students to test the concept of velocity, something most children understand intuitively but often have difficulty learning to quantify.

The program shows the up-and-down movement of an elevator alongside a graph of its changing speed in floors per second. Then, it asks where the elevator would end up based on a new graph, demonstrating that a lower velocity does not mean the elevator is going down, just that its speed is slowing. Finally, it asks students to create a new graph that makes a second elevator wind up at the same floor at the same time, but after traveling at different velocities.

"The computer's most powerful uses are for making things visual," says James Kaput, a math professor who led development of the unit. "It can make visual abstract processes that are otherwise ineffable."

Wenglinsky's research found no discernible effect of using computers primarily for simulations and applications among 4th graders, probably because there simply aren't that many teachers who regularly use technology for this purpose with young students.

But Wenglinsky did find that 4th graders whose teachers used instructional computers mostly for math/learning games posted an achievement gain equal to roughly 15 percent of a grade level.

Over the past decade, elementary school teachers have seen an explosion in the number of learning games available on the market, and many

---

Figure 7.4. 8th Grade Instructional Use: A National Look.
Other factors being equal, the largest positive effect on 8th grade math scores came from teachers using computers primarily for simulations and applications. Black students, poor students, and students in the West and Southeast are less likely to have teachers who use computers for that purpose.

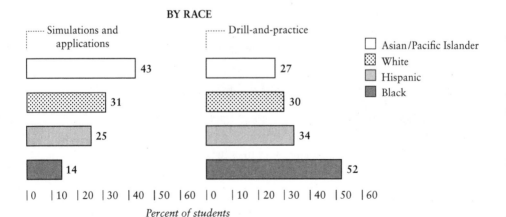

BY RACE

- Simulations and applications
- Drill-and-practice

☐ Asian/Pacific Islander
▦ White
▨ Hispanic
■ Black

Simulations and applications:
- Asian/Pacific Islander: 43
- White: 31
- Hispanic: 25
- Black: 14

Drill-and-practice:
- Asian/Pacific Islander: 27
- White: 30
- Hispanic: 34
- Black: 52

| 0 | 10 | 20 | 30 | 40 | 50 | 60 | 0 | 10 | 20 | 30 | 40 | 50 | 60

Percent of students

of these products have moved beyond computerized versions of work-sheets, says Clements of SUNY at Buffalo.

"Students are motivated by interacting with programs when they can influence the outcome of the activity," he says. "And games have the benefit of providing immediate feedback."

Clements believes the best feedback is that which is also instructive. He points to a simple program that teaches fractions by asking students to help a turtle eat a berry that sits between the reptile and a wall. When the student enters a fraction, the turtle moves that distance toward the wall, demonstrating the result of changing the numerator and the denominator.

That kind of visual response, Clements believes, is more effective than mere bells and whistles that reward a correct answer.

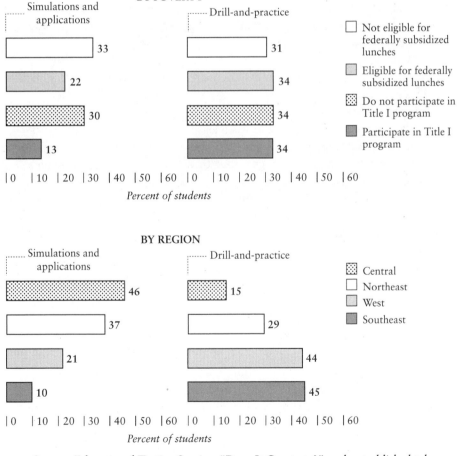

Source: Educational Testing Service, "Does It Compute?" and unpublished tabulations from 1996 National Assessment of Educational Progress.

THE SAME FACTORS that were tied to student-achievement gains were also related to a better school climate, Wenglinsky found.

In other words, where teachers used computers for more sophisticated activities than drill-and-practice, school officials were more likely to report higher teacher and student attendance, less tardiness, and better morale.

Researchers who have observed such results firsthand cite several possible reasons. One is that computers provide instantaneous, nonjudgmental feedback, a characteristic that can be especially beneficial to students with low self-esteem. Computers also can perform routine computations, giving students more time to wrestle with larger concepts.

"Technology certainly can be highly motivating," says Means of SRI International. "Teachers see it in their kids' interest. They see them come in at lunch and after school to work with it."

Technology also can liberate teachers from the traditional lecture-style of instruction by encouraging them to act instead as coaches and facilitators.

"One of the real benefits of different types of technology is the way they influence how teachers and students relate to each other," Wenglinsky says.

In fact, a growing number of education technology advocates argue that this "constructivist" approach toward learning—in which students work in rich environments of information and experience, often in groups, and build their own understandings about them—taps into the computer's greatest strengths.

"Kids learn by doing, by presenting, by displaying, by engaging," says William Fiske, the educational technology specialist at the Rhode Island department of education. "Learning happens best when the youngsters are doing the heavy lifting."

UNFORTUNATELY, MOST OF THE NATION'S SCHOOLS aren't using computers in ways that Wenglinsky's findings indicate are linked to better scores. And survey responses from the 1996 NAEP also raises serious questions about technology's role in closing the achievement gap between disadvantaged students and their peers.

Over the past decade, tremendous resources have been committed to the cause of ensuring that schools in disadvantaged communities have computer equipment and network connections on par with those serving more affluent populations. Survey results show, for example, that black students use computers in learning math somewhat more often than white students.

But the survey paints a very different picture about *how* those students use their schools' computers.

At the 8th grade level, about 31 percent of white students used computers mostly for simulations and applications, compared with just 14 percent of black students. At the same time, more than half of America's black students had teachers who used computers mostly for drill-and-practice, compared with only 30 percent of white students.

In short, black students have closed the digital divide where it matters least—the amount of time on computer. The gap persists where it matters most how the computer is used.

"It's the low-income communities that have invested the most in technology for drill-and-practice," says Margaret Honey, the deputy director of the New York City–based Center for Children and Technology. "But if this research says those investments do have the kind of impact we want them to have, then that's an important message.

"There's an expectation among many urban administrators that kids from disadvantaged backgrounds need basic skills and nothing else," she adds.

Still, even some experts who praise more sophisticated uses of education technology say it may be too soon to throw out drill-and-practice altogether, especially in the early grades.

Using computers to practice basic skills, they say, may have benefits that don't show up on NAEP scores. Several studies have suggested that computer-based exercises can raise student motivation levels, especially for children who haven't found other media engaging. Many education experts also see drill-and-practice as a useful way to build the skills needed to advance to the next level.

"A lot of people do not understand that drill-and-practice does not teach students anything," says Ted S. Hasselbring, the co-director of Vanderbilt University's Learning and Technology Center in Nashville, Tenn. "It develops fluency of an existing skill."

THE STUDY OFFERS a more encouraging result in the area of professional development.

Teachers who had received any amount of professional development with computers within the past five years were more likely to use computers in ways that Wenglinsky found to be effective than teachers who had not received such training.

In addition, 8th graders whose teachers had had technology training performed more than a third of a grade level better than those with teachers who lacked such training. The training also was linked to gains at the

4th grade level, although the effect was indirect and the difference in scores was smaller.

"The teacher has always been the key to determining the impact of innovation," says Elliot Soloway, who holds professorships in the schools of education and engineering at the University of Michigan. "It's not surprising that technology falls into this camp."

School systems appear to be waking up to the important role played by teacher training. Survey results from the 1996 NAEP show 81 percent of the nation's 4th graders had teachers who had received professional development with computers within the past five years and 76 percent of 8th graders had math teachers who had received such training within the past five years.

But the survey says little about the quality or amount of that training; it could be a one-time workshop on a piece of software or ongoing, one-on-one assistance in the classroom. And given teachers' frequent complaints about the quality of professional development in general, many education experts believe that most technology training likely leaves plenty to be desired.

Wenglinsky, in fact, says he was struck by the fact that any amount of professional development translated into student achievement gains. "Which leads one to think that more elaborate training might post even greater gains," he adds.

DESPITE HIS FINDINGS, Wenglinsky says that much about the computer's role in raising achievement remains unknown.

Because the study is based on a single year of data, it can't prove effects over time. It also can't say for certain whether certain uses of computers are causing higher student achievement, or vice versa.

Means, for instance, has observed that teachers often use games not to teach new math skills but as a reward for those students who complete their assignments early.

"The major limitation of the study is that the direction of causality is not established," Means says. "It's going to be very difficult to tease apart how much that technology adds to the quality of instruction with this study. But a more qualitative description can show classroom interactions that would just not be possible without the technology."

She also notes that the study concerns only one academic subject.

"The data might look very different with reading comprehension," Means says. "So I'd be a little bit cautious before drawing many public policy implications."

Finally, the NAEP survey didn't allow Wenglinsky to compare the effectiveness of computers with that of other educational tools, some of which might be much less expensive.

While leaving room for further research, Wenglinsky says his study does tell educators something they've been waiting a long time to hear.

"What we do know for certain," he says, "is that when teachers use the computer to teach higher-order thinking skills, students benefit."

WEB SITES

http://www.edweek.org
http://www.ets.org/research/pic/technolog.html

PART TWO

EQUITY, ACCESS, AND LITERACY

EQUITY, ACCESS, AND LITERACY are hot-button, intertwined topics in the field of education technology. Equity encompasses many contentious issues: school funding, the gap between minorities and whites in computer knowledge and usage, and how different groups of students use, or don't use, technology. In Chapter Eight, Don Tapscott, who has coined the term *Net Generation*, looks at how the information haves and have-nots will fare in the not-so-distant future. We also take a look at gender issues. Heather Kirkpatrick and Larry Cuban, in Chapter Nine, provide a meta-analysis of studies relating to how girls use technology. Chapter Ten, an excerpt from *From Barbie to Mortal Kombat*, focuses on games, but the findings of the authors' research are a fascinating comment on gender differences and are easily applied to thinking about how girls and boys approach learning via technology.

In Chapter Eleven, Chris Dede, a noted futurist, explains how, with distributed learning and reconfigured budgets, school districts can transform technological innovations into improvements in the system that are more affordable and sustainable than current technology. In Chapter Twelve, Sheldon Berman and Robert Tinker describe a project that combines high-quality instruction and technology to reach specialized groups of students at any time and place.

In Chapters Thirteen and Fourteen, scholars weigh in on how technology can assist those with special learning needs—one of the most cost-effective uses of technology in schools. With the guidance of skillful teachers and the use of innovative software and adaptive hardware, students who had been left behind due to learning disabilities or other roadblocks can move ahead and toward the mainstream. These two works are representative but barely scratch the surface of the kinds of incredible results that students—not only those with cognitive barriers to learning but also those with limited English skills or hearing or sight problems—can achieve with current technologies.

Digital literacy, or the need to be an informed consumer of digital information, is covered in Chapter Fifteen by Internet expert Paul Gilster. Gilster recognizes the need for students to be able to sift cognitively through the information they find on the Internet.

8

THE DIGITAL DIVIDE

Don Tapscott

Have-Nots, Know-Nots, and Do-Nots

THIS IS A TIME of promise and of peril. What kind of world do we want our children to inherit?

The most widely feared prediction surrounding the digital revolution is that it will splinter society into a race of information haves and have-nots, knowers and know-nots, doers and do-nots—a digital divide. This revolution holds the promise of improving the lives of citizens, but also the threat of further dividing us. As philanthropist Mario Marino says: "The technology of interactive communications will change the status quo with or without your involvement. The question is how and to what extent we will use it—to help people empower themselves and give those at every social and economic level a voice and an option, or to trigger a division among us that may never be healed."

The issue is not just access to the new media, but rather whether differences in availability of services, technology fluency, motivation, and opportunities to learn may lead to a two-tiered world of knowers and know-nots, doers and do-nots.

It is the responsibility of adults to tackle this problem for the new generation. However, there is a dialogue of the deaf on this issue, with two extreme perspectives. In one corner are the *stateists,* who argue that the Net, like the highways, is an essential service and a key infrastructure for any economy. As such it is best planned, controlled, and (in some countries) even owned by government.

In *The Digital Economy,* I argued against this view, explaining that, "because public coffers are empty and leading-edge innovation is desirable, the private sector needs to take the front-line role in financing, building, and operating the information highway." The highway analogy is a limited one. It is not feasible to plan the digital infrastructure like a highway, for many reasons, including the fact that no one knows for sure what technologies are best. Through an open, competitive market these issues will get sorted out. An open market also enables and promotes the kind of innovation that the five-year master plan cannot. The development of the digital media will be molecular. It will grow in chaotic and unpredictable ways. If its direction (technological, services, information) is left alone, it will behave like an ecosystem or organism, constantly changing, evolving, and mutating as the myriad forces within it and upon it change. An open competitive market is essential for the new media to evolve rapidly and to fulfill their potential. Countries which are bounded by old monopolistic structures are falling behind in technological innovation, penetration, and use.

The stateist view has weak support in North America. However, there are numerous suggestions for increased government control to end the "anarchy" of the Internet. The most popular theme is censorship and control of the Net through laws and other techniques. Such efforts are undesirable, unnecessary, and unfeasible.

In the other corner are the market *determinists.* The need for an open market has caused many to conclude that market forces should be the sole determinant of technology growth and use. In fact, it has become fashionable to ridicule government, corporate, or community efforts for universality. The Net, it is said, is an organic ecosystem (true), unlike a highway (true), and therefore cannot be planned (true) and should not be controlled by any force (true). From this, the market determinists conclude that there is no role for social policy and that efforts to achieve universal access are basically silly and even dangerous.

Typical of this view is an article in the Libertarian publication *Reason Magazine,* ". . . the call for universal service is a red herring. It masks a fundamental mistrust of a process that will deeply reshape society and yet is almost entirely beyond government control. A process that is chaotic and self-organizing, utterly without a central plan. In other words, a market." The author ridicules vice president Al Gore's objective of universal access. "Imagine that in 1895, some 13 years before the Model T, Al Gore's great-grandfather had correctly identified the potential importance of the new 'horseless carriage' to future employment and led the government push to ensure that we did not become a nation of 'motorized transportation haves and have-nots.'"[1]

The author continues: "A television, today's prime source of information and entertainment, can be found in upwards of 99 percent of American homes, higher even than the 93 percent of homes with a phone. Without a hint of government subsidy—let alone a domestic producer—TV reaches more homes than telephones, despite six decades of sweeping universal telephone service policy courtesy of the Communications Act of 1934."

"The best thing government can do is get out of the way," said Michael Bloomberg at the aforementioned panel discussion in Davos, Switzerland. He argued that governments are basically an obstacle to progress.

The digital media cannot be compared to the television, as the market determinists would have us believe. TV is basically a passive form of entertainment. The new media require the active, informed, literate participation of a user. The pattern of TV growth will not be replicated, because purchase and use of the new media are skewed toward those who are literate and motivated for active participation. It is precisely those children who are disadvantaged in education, family income, and personal empowerment who will be least able and least motivated to embrace the new media. While access is critical for universality, it is also inadequate. Have-nots lead to do-nots. It's not simply having access, but what you do with it that counts. As Joan Chiaramonte of Roper Starch says: "It's really important what demands people make on the technology. One group will have greater knowledge, motivation, and vision, creating [greater] possibilities." The term have-nots should not be used to mean lacking access only; rather, a growing underclass does not have fluency, motivation, and integration of digital tools with various aspects of their lives. Having, knowing, and doing go hand in hand.

By the time—if ever—the "free market" catches up to the nots, they will no longer be children. Denied the opportunity to assimilate the new media in their youth, they will, instead, have to adapt to it. They will be on the wrong end of the generation lap—lapped by those of their own generation. Moreover, their employment prospects in a knowledge economy, their potential income levels, their prospects for stable families, and their potential for a fulfilling life will all be greatly diminished. This is a downward spiral. Poverty causes digital impoverishment, which in turn contributes to continued povertization.

"Leave everything to the market," or "It'll all come out in the wash." Such statements reflect a growing belief in Social Darwinism. The economic view that competitive markets are required for economic growth and success is extended to an ideology regarding society and governance. In this ideology there is no such thing as the public interest. It is said that governments should get out of the business of social policy and helping disadvantaged people or groups and instead be defenders of individual rights. Darwin's views on the evolution of the species were extended in an earlier period—the late nineteenth century—to a social view about nations. It was argued at the time that within the human species, nations are locked in a struggle for survival in which civilized nations were supplanting barbarous nations. Advanced civilization, obviously, has inherited valuable traits from its ancestors. Underdeveloped cultures will soon die off. Therefore, natural order obligates powerful, civilized nations to appropriate the limited resources of the weak.[2]

A century later the new god is not a superior species but the market. In my debates on haves and have-nots I have heard the statement "the poor will always be with us." I have heard people say the issue is really "information haves and have-laters." I have heard people say, "don't concern yourself with these things. It'll all be fine." Many leading technology and business thinkers, who should know better, have become champions of this cause. The view is extended to the digital economy as a whole. It is argued that governments today are a legacy of the old industrial economy and need to be eliminated. It is not always clear what should replace them.

What is driving this view? Some critics have argued it is greed—the ideological rationalization for unfettered capitalism and a gold rush in cyberspace.[3] Others see it as ironic that those who favor an end to government involvement in the Net are precisely those who benefitted from initial government subsidization.[4] A kinder view is that many well-meaning thinkers are just naive—smart on technology and business issues and lacking experience on social issues.

The wealthy in America are information-rich. The poor are information-poor. Whites are generally haves. Blacks are have-nots—two-thirds less likely to have a PC in the home. The solution to this problem is not the market. The problem has been created, in part, by the market—or more precisely by the lack thereof among the dispossessed. Just as there is no market for food in areas where people are starving—because food cannot be profitably sold—so there is no market for the digital media in the inner city, the reservation, or parts of the rural south.

This situation is not improving. It is being exacerbated with every passing day as the gap grows. As Fig. 8.1 indicates, the rate of penetration for the haves is rapid, while for the have-nots it lingers. Each day that the haves get not only better access but more services, improved technology, and most important, improved fluency and motivation, the gap grows.

As Brad Fay, who led the seminal work for Roper Starch on *The Two Americas,* says, "The logical implication of this is that we are moving into two distinct societies where people have very different life experiences,

Figure 8.1. Used a Computer at Home—Grades 1–6; Grades 7–12.

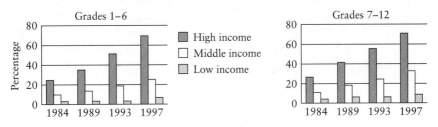

Data: *U.S. Census Bureau.*

lifestyles, and attitudes. Part of it is economically driven—what people can and cannot afford." According to their research, 24 percent of people without high school diplomas and 37 percent of low-income people are interested in using the computer to obtain product information. This compares to 64 percent of college graduates and 69 percent of those earning more than $50,000 per year. Hardly any lower-income households have a computer (7 percent), in comparison to those making between $30,000 and $50,000 (32 percent). Of those making over $50,000, usage increases to 53 percent. Households earning more than $75,000 are 10 times more likely to be surfing the Net than those making less than $30,000 per year. Most Americans know what this will lead to: 59 percent say divisions between those who understand the new technology and those who do not will be a serious problem in 25 to 50 years.[5]

Poverty begets information poverty begets poverty. Racial divides beget a racial gap in media access begets racial divides. Opposition to efforts for universality, regardless of the intentions or lofty ideologies of the perpetrators, result in actions which uphold and amplify social differences.

What Are the Facts on Universality?

The first problem with the market determinist view is one of fact. If you look at the data, there is a growing information apartheid already in the United States. Parallel to this, there is a growing polarization in the distribution of wealth. Unless a new social contract is achieved, these two gaps will continue to interact, strengthening trends toward the consolidation of a large, permanent underclass.

The problem is not limited to America, and becomes much clearer when one considers the rest of the world, particularly the developing countries.

"Picture this scenario: somewhere in South Africa a person spends two whole days manually sending out a bulletin to about two dozen subscribers by fax," writes South African journalist Gumisai Mutume. "Often the line breaks down and the process starts again. Eventually all the pages go through and then the phone calls start pouring in. 'The fax is blurred, we did not get page three of the document. Could you please resend the whole thing?' At the end of it all, a phone bill of some $150 U.S. dollars is the tab for the effort. This is the stark reality of communications between African countries."

The information gap between have and have-not countries is growing. According to Jupiter Communications, of the 23.4 million households connected to the Net in 1996, 66 percent were in North America, 16 percent in Europe, and 14 percent in the Asian Pacific.[6] The gap is not just one of developed countries versus underdeveloped countries. Amazingly, Western Europe (excluding Scandinavia) and Japan—countries which currently have some of the highest GNP per capita—are falling behind badly in terms of access and use. Sales of PCs in Europe slipped below those in Asia for the first time in 1996. "Tiger" economies in Asia are leapfrogging both Japan and Europe in their use of the new media. In Malaysia, the government has launched an "information superhighway corridor" project which will deliver high-capacity networking through core elements of the country. Asian/Pacific Rim markets will grow from 3.6 million online households from year-end 1996 to 10 million by 2000.[7]

The Myth of Universal Access at School

Additionally, market determinists argue that government and corporate programs to get technology into the schools are unnecessary. They argue that universality will be and is being achieved in the schools through market forces. They draw comfort from data that indicate that computers and Net access are flooding into the schools. For example, calculations based on a 1995 survey conducted by Grunwald Associates showed that the parents of 19 million American children believe that their kids have access to the Internet either at home or at school. According to those parents, 6 million children had Internet access at home. Of the 13 million children whose parents believe they are accessing the Internet from either the library or school, 5 million did not have computers at home. Here the phrase "believe they are accessing the Internet" becomes problematic. Access to the Internet from school, like Internet access from home, is both enabled and limited by one factor: family income.

By 1996, 65 percent of United States public schools had access to the Internet, but schools with richer student populations were still 25 percent more likely to be connected than schools with poorer student populations. According to the National Center for Education Statistics, 58 percent of schools where more than one-third of students are eligible for free or reduced-priced lunches were connected to the Internet, while 78 percent of schools where only 1 in 10 students is eligible for the same lunch discount had access.[8] President Clinton has said that the legacy of his administration will be that every K–12 public school in the United States will be hooked up to the Internet—a promise he has backed up with a pledge of $500 million dollars. There are 84,000 public schools in the United States, which means the government will pay just under 12 percent of the $50,000 cost of wiring each school. Furthermore, fewer than 5 percent of instructional classrooms have Internet connections, which means that in many schools Internet access is limited to the library or to the staff room (see Fig. 8.2). Teachers can download instructional materials but their students cannot participate in the search for those materials or learn the process of that search.

According to the Alliance for Converging Technologies, the average ratio of students to computers in United States public schools is expected to reach 9:1 by the beginning of the 1998 school year. The ratio of students to multimedia computers (with capability to access the Net), however, will only be 33:1. So charts like Fig. 8.3 below are misleading because the

Figure 8.2. Percent of Instructional Rooms* with Internet Access.

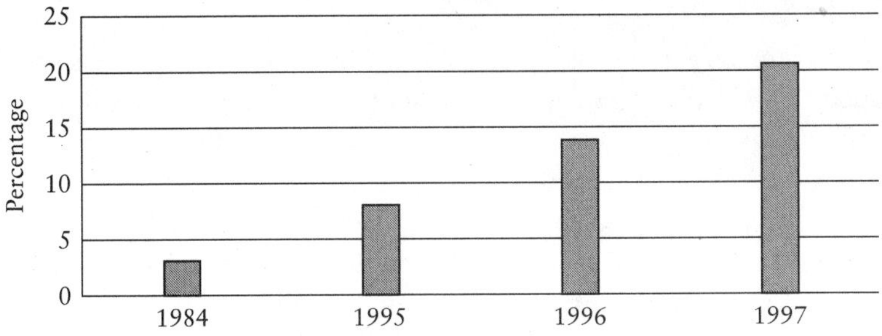

Data: *National Center for Education Statistics.*
* *The percent of instructional rooms across the country is based on the total number of instructional rooms (e.g., classrooms, computer labs, library/media centers) in all regular public and secondary schools.*

Figure 8.3. Students per Computer, U.S. Public Schools
(per School Year).

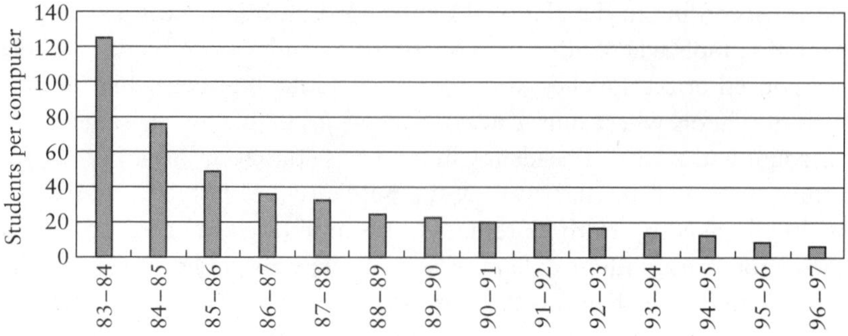

Data: *QED—Quality Education Data, Alliance for Converging Technologies.*

number of computers in the classrooms which are actually usable for the reinvention of education is tiny.

Access Is Not Enough in the Schools Either

Wiring the schools and populating them with computers is necessary but insufficient to ensure equal opportunity to share in the digital revolution. Children need access to computers and the Net, but they also need appropriate software and services. They need motivation to learn. They need a redesigned education system and teachers who have been retrained and reoriented. Innovative technologies cannot make up for educational professionals who lack innovative methods and merely replicate learning models that don't work.

In fact, programs to get technology into schools don't even ensure that students will have access, let alone relatively equal access and all the other requirements for participation. At present, more than 74 percent of schools have computers, but only 10 percent of students say they have used a computer at school in the past week. Many students who responded to our forum said that they had never seen the single computers in their classrooms used by either teacher or student. Meanwhile, many teachers do not allow their students to compose homework on computers because it would give them an unfair advantage over those students who do not have computers at home. Some teachers also mistrust words which have been typed with a computer. We discovered more than one N-Gener who purposely put spelling and formatting errors into projects so that the teacher wouldn't think their parents had done the work or that text had been cut and pasted from another source.

Two of the factors contributing to the present underutilization of the technology are the fact that only one-half of all teachers have any kind of computer training, and the widespread belief that work done on outdated computer hardware and software is useless. Is it really likely that knowledge of WordPerfect, for example, is a hindrance to learning Microsoft Word later? One certainly wouldn't say that the knowledge of French is a hindrance to learning Spanish.

"Kids here don't have the fastest processors and they don't have the most up-to-date software," says cyber arts teacher Kathy Yamashita of her school in North York, Ontario. "They have enough of the basics to allow them to fly once they get there. So I don't believe that public education should have state-of-the-art everything." Yamashita, like most teachers, is not a computer science specialist but an English literature major.

Even though not all school environments are hostile to the use of technology, there are other factors hindering schools from providing the experience with the new media their students need. Many schools are not a part of their students' neighborhoods or communities. Almost 60 percent of American students are sent to school by bus, and the vast majority of those students come from lower-income neighborhoods.[9] (The percent of instructional rooms across the country is based on the total number of instructional rooms—classrooms, computer labs, library/media centers—in all regular public and secondary schools.) It's a story Michael Bouyer, a Palo Alto, California, consultant with The Arts Resources & Talents Association (ARTA) who works with children and youth, knows well. "They take a bus across town to go to school (the bus leaves at 3:15, they get out at 3:05) and make their way back, glad to escape an environment that's not very friendly to them," Bouyer explains. "In the meantime the school has 20 computers, but those aren't really available to the students who have to take the buses."

Even when schools are wired, they are not welcoming places for many students, discouraging them from using the technology after school. In 1993, 44 percent of high school students reported that they had had something stolen from them at school and 42 percent reported that they had been threatened.[10] While the number of students who have actually been injured with weapons at school fell by almost 4 percent between 1980 and 1992, suggesting that schools are becoming physically safer, they are still not places where most kids want to be in their free time. Student participation in extracurricular activities is down. Participation in athletics, including cheerleading and drill team, has fallen from 67 percent of all seniors in 1980 to 50 percent in 1992. Remarkably, the number of students involved in academic clubs and the newspaper or yearbook dropped by only 0.5 percent and 1.1 percent during the same period.[11] One possible reason these activities have managed to retain their participants is that desktop publishing programs and computer clubs may have begun to play greater roles in school yearbook and newspaper production.

None of this means that schools do not belong online; it means that wiring schools alone is not enough to compensate for other factors that are failing to ensure that all students have free and equal access to both information technology and digitized information. That will come out of endeavors that seek to ensure that computers and connections are available after classes have been dismissed and that the model of education as a whole is changed. This requires retraining of teachers, rethinking of curricula, redesign of pedagogical models, and overall significant investment.

For those who believe in open markets and market forces, I would propose that we take precise steps to open the school market. The schools are currently a terrible "market" for the new media. They are impoverished when it comes to budgets for technology. Old cultures of teaching inhibit proliferation of the digital media. And teachers and educators have little comprehension of how to transform the schools from broadcast to interactive learning, and may lack the motivation to do so anyway. Rather than pretending that somehow schools with no technology budgets and massive cultural legacies will become magically wired, replete with glistening multimedia computers that will magically transform to interactive learning, we would do better to take radical steps to address this problem. Governments and corporations need to provide leadership to address the funding obstacle preventing the transformation of education. And the private sector needs to get beyond lip service to see that children from all walks of life have access to the Net.

Access is a critical first step. In the 1995 study on home computing conducted by Carnegie Mellon University, researchers concluded that "Once financial barriers [to access] are lowered, lower-income and less well-educated people are as likely to become [Internet] enthusiasts."[12] Race and gender, however, predicted lower usage in the study. The reasons? Culturally the Net may be seen as more foreign to women and minority races. Some blacks, for example, view the Net as a thing for white kids. And Net content is still largely oriented toward white males.

Reinforcing the myth that universal access at school is well under way are media events that suggest daily miracles in communications are happening through technology even in the worst of circumstances.

Burrville Elementary School in Washington, DC, is one of the poorest schools in Washington's inner city, but for a few brief moments it showed the world all the promise of what the digital media can do for education. In April of 1997, Canadian prime minister Jean Chrétien and his wife Aline paid a state visit to the United States president and first lady. Mrs. Clinton and Mrs. Chrétien, accompanied by dozens of reporters, visited Burrville Elementary while its students participated in an Internet exchange with students at St. Elizabeth's School in Canada's capital, Ottawa. Unbeknownst to the first lady and Mrs. Chrétien, as they, their entourage, and the journalists left Burrville, the computers the students had used during the visit were packed into boxes and taken away.

In this case only one journalist, Paul Koring of *The Globe and Mail,* covered the striking of the stage. Before and after the official visit and press event, Burrville Elementary School owned only one computer that was connected to the Internet. "That's what happens when you talk to the kids instead of just hanging around," Koring said in an interview. "The kids knew the stuff was leaving and so did the teachers, but it certainly wasn't in the press release."

Following the incident, which embarrassed both the Clinton Administration and the Canadian Embassy in Washington, Northern Telecom rescued both governments from further press scrutiny on the episode, and more importantly, saved the students from becoming part of the Not-Generation by donating 10 computers to Burrville Elementary School. Unfortunately, we don't know how many similar events held in the past have been constructed and then disassembled once the dignitaries and journalists left the classroom.

The New Responsibilities of Business

This is not some utopian call for everyone to somehow be "equal." Of course, social differences will exist for the foreseeable future based on variables like intelligence, effort, and choices in lifestyle. However, it is dangerous to polarize society further—in terms of opportunity to participate in the revolution of our times and to have a chance at a rewarding and fulfilling life.

How can we achieve universal access and take the other steps necessary to narrow the digital divide? If leaving it to the market is not a strategy, whose responsibility is it? The new media, the new economy, and the new generation are causing every institution to rethink itself and every person to reevaluate his or her values and behavior. Every institution and every person will need to get involved.

Governments can make a significant contribution. Most importantly, governments need to be one of the partners in the shift to a networked society. This means many things: for starters, taking the lead in funding the reinvention of education. Governments need to create the regulatory conditions whereby prices are fair. The best way to do this is to ensure that there is open competition—which, as a rule, drives prices down. Governments can also be model users of the digital media themselves, reinventing government to improve services and lower governmental costs. Governments can participate in projects that catalyze the kinds of partnerships which will be required to avoid the digital divide.

There is also a role for each of us as volunteers, as popularized by U.S. General (ret.) Colin Powell in the Alliance for Youth program. The program is calling on corporate America and citizens to provide their time in revitalizing the country. Another example of an important volunteer initiative is 2B1, whose goal is to break down the barriers to access, ownership, and development caused by economics, geography, gender, and culture.

The digital divide raises new imperatives for business leaders as well. Increasingly, it will be difficult and inappropriate for business people to say, "these issues are someone else's problem," or "my only responsibility is to my shareholders."

The business community needs to rethink its role in the new economy and its responsibilities to the new generation. Business should provide leadership for the broader changes to come, not only through altruism but also through self-interest. The success of businesses will depend on the rapidity and smoothness of the societal changes which are being unleashed by the N-Gen. Business in any nation state can succeed only if it has a "new-economy" workforce—one that is educated, motivated, stable, and healthy. The federal deficit is a tame problem compared to the potential social deficit lurking in the wings of a poorly managed transition to the new economy.

Is it unthinkable that business could lead in addressing the digital divide and the far-reaching issues it raises? Can the business leaders of a new generation understand their common self-interest in achieving social justice and a smooth societal transformation?

Community Computing

What concretely can be done?

One way of tackling the digital divide is by creating community computing networks—nonprofit Internet service providers (ISPs). These can use community-based computer networks or FreeNets that provide Internet access free of charge to those who cannot afford to pay for computers or connections. FreeNets, the most common of these, offer two services. They provide computers in public spaces such as libraries or Laundromats from which users can access the Internet. But they also provide dial-up access to the Internet for people who already have access to a computer, say through a friend or school, but don't have an ISP.

Homeless people online at the local library can log on to the community information bulletin board to find beds in a shelter, a hot shower, or even medical and counseling services. Children can find information about services available to them. As fashionable as the Social Darwinist stance against social services may be, arguing against the dissemination of information that prevents homeless people from freezing to death on city streets and deaths by child neglect or abuse is anything but trendy.

Those who espouse an Internet law of the jungle have another ideological predator. These predators number in the thousands of individuals who run the hundreds of community computing centers in North America. In a poll of young people living in San Francisco, "positive alternatives for youth" ranked number one as the way to reduce juvenile crime. When asked what equipment they considered most important for a youth center, the teens gave the highest priority to computers—ahead of swimming pools, pool tables, and even video games.[13]

According to Community Technology Centers' Network (CTCNet), there are over 150 nonprofit community computing centers operating in the United States. The vast majority of those that serve the needs of children are open about four hours a day, with a half-dozen computers in neighborhood community centers and Boys' and Girls' Clubs. Others are independent organizations with enough space and staff to provide access to dozens of computers for 10 to 12 hours each day. Whatever the size of the operation, the experiences of community computing centers show the potential that would be wasted if kids in low-income communities were denied access to communications technology. Such centers are also places of hope for youth where, as described by Mario Marino, "children are treated not as problems to be handled, but as resources to be encouraged."

A New Activity in the Mall

The Lakeforest Library Connection (LLC) is a computer community-access center open seven days a week in a large Rockville, Maryland, shopping mall. The access center has 127 computer terminals offering

Internet connections and educational software. It attracts more than 1000 users per week.

The project is a joint effort of the area's libraries and schools in combination with more than a dozen private-sector sponsors and supporters. Barbara Harr runs the center and says its purpose is to provide "free and equal access to electronic resources to the community at large and particularly for those in the community who do not own a computer or may have a computer but no modem.

"There is this world of information out there, and it should be freely and easily accessible to everyone in all its formats. This is the heart of the public library system. The nation is founded on this. It is at the heart of our ethics. We feel strongly about intellectual freedom and the right of access for all citizens."

The mall setting is a deliberately nontraditional library site, designed to be inviting in a way that a typical library might not be. Harr notes that many segments of the community liken libraries to fortresses, but the mall setting helps break down this perception. The LLC is open seven days a week, and is often open when regular libraries and school libraries are closed. Since opening in May 1996, the site has been tremendously popular, with the LLC relying mainly on word of mouth for promotion. There are often lines of people waiting to use a computer.

The center has received inquiries from groups around the country that would like to replicate its success. The center is appealing to all age groups, from toddlers to senior citizens. Children under 13 must be accompanied by a parent. "You will often see the parent and a four- or five-year-old working on the computer together," says Harr. "The kids are all whizzes and put us to shame. It is not unusual to see a group of kids just laughing and exploring. The older generation seems a little bit more reluctant. You can tell by the language they use.

"Middle-age users could be using the center for job hunting or looking for information to help their businesses. This is very new to them. That is where the staff come in, and they are needed to provide assistance. But the kids don't need them. In fact, the kids are thrilled with this site, and you will often see teenagers just hovering, and if they see a mature person that looks like they need help, the kids will offer their assistance." In fact, a community organization is working with Lakeforest to develop a program that will bring senior citizens to the center for courses in computer literacy that will be taught by high school students! Rather than fighting the generation lap, they will be rolling with it.

Kidzonline

Kidzonline claims it's "the coolest place for kids to hang out in a secure environment." It's also a great example of one family taking the initiative to make the cyberworld freely accessible to kids that otherwise would be shut out.

The Intranet-style site boasts 24 incoming phone lines for children who have access to a computer at home or through the Boys' and Girls' Clubs that Kidzonline works with in Washington. Kidzonline also has a 15-PC LAN available in a training center set up in donated space in the basement of a local bank.

The project began much more modestly in 1994 when Wesley Cruver, then 11 years old, thought it would be neat to set up a bulletin board system for his friends. "He is not a child genius, he is just a regular guy. But man, is he good with computers and software," says his dad, Phil.

When Sharon, Wesley's mom, saw the fun her son and his friends were having with the bulletin board, she realized that many kids would be denied this source of entertainment and learning simply because they didn't have access to computers.

Sharon asked local businesses to donate the equipment and enlisted the area's Boys' and Girls' Clubs to help make the technology available to inner city kids. The goal was to "introduce kids from all economic levels to the networking technologies that will play a major role in their futures."

Today the site is a roaring success, with teenager Wesley making sure the technology functions properly and his mom orchestrating the creation of more than 800 pages of content. The site offers file libraries, educational resources, local after-school activities, and fun things like comics, reviews, stories, e-mail buddies, and more.

Kids can post software, movie and book reviews, among other things. Commenting on the *Bailey School Kids* book series, Robyn "Tweety Bird" Andrews, age 10, says, "some of the stories are funny, some are sad, but they're cool. If you read one, you'll want to read another."

In the Girlz Only section, boys are asked what turns them off when dating. Matt, 16, writes: "The worst thing is going to a girl's house and being put through half an hour of talking to her parents because she's still getting ready." Tobin, 14, says that, "heavy makeup and smelly perfume are major turnoffs."

"A lot of the material is educational, but the curriculum isn't math or science. They are learning computer skills, how to upload, download, unzip files," says Phil Cruver. "Once those kids get that mouse in their hand, they pick it up really fast. But you've got to give them the exposure."

Plugged-In: A Model for the Future

Imagine, if you can, a miracle in which street kids give up their weapons and gang affiliations to spend time playing, learning, and doing their homework in a community computing center. Sounds like a stretch, but this is actually happening in the low-income neighborhoods of East Palo Alto, California.

Muki Izora gives kids exposure to the digital media every day, an experience that gives him the ability to speak with all the confidence of a person who really knows what he can do. "I can get kids interested enough to come in here off the street, I can teach them how to use a computer to tell a story, I can teach them how to type as quickly as they can talk, I can give them a safe place to be with their friends, and then I can give them a part-time job."

Izora, 26, is the project director for Plugged-In, a community computing center located in East Palo Alto, that is successfully working to address the issue of the technology-poor on several levels. Plugged-In has become "the community center that never was in East Palo Alto," says Izora, who has worked with the organization since 1992 when it was "six donated computers in the back room of the Boys' and Girls' Club in Menlo Park." Plugged-In now occupies three storefront offices where the organization offers classes to children, teens, and adults; gives free Internet access to members of the community; and hosts an innovative program known as "Plugged-In Enterprises" where teens apply the programming and design skills they have learned to a business in which they build and maintain Web pages.

Encircled by the cities and companies that make up Silicon Valley, East Palo Alto itself has not benefited economically from the computer industry's growth or profits. Located inside a confusing triangle created by the construction of Freeway 101, bad urban planning contributed to cutting the population off from its neighbors and many of the technological innovations that had shaped the surrounding cities. That is, until the arrival and growth of Plugged-In. According to the teens who use Plugged-In, the center has changed the city of East Palo Alto itself.

"This city is the only one that's been left out, maybe because of the violence—that's changed in the past few years though," says Dominic Bannister, 15, of East Palo Alto. "I think they should have a place like Plugged-In in every community, especially in troubled neighborhoods. Here, this has helped the community a lot and it's a great place to be at. Everybody treats you like you're family. There are no fights over here, no conflicts like that, nothing like that."

"I think it's a new way of seeing technology, especially in East Palo Alto," says Thomas Gomez, 14, of River City. "You don't see that much technology around here. It's the only place you might see a computer and access the World Wide Web, which most people around here don't know about."

Even more impressive than the changes to East Palo Alto are the changes to the kids themselves. N-Geners at Plugged-In seem almost surprised to find themselves enjoying a safe environment that encourages learning.

"When I first came here, I was sort of afraid because everybody was looking at me because I was new," says 15-year-old J. R. Organez who is relieved that Plugged-In is so different from school. "Every hour there's always fights at school, you know. . . . They judge the way you dress, the way you look." That doesn't happen at Plugged-In, says J. R. "When I came here I was like 13 years old and, like a month later, everybody knew my name and that felt good."

"I like being here because I can do my homework. Here is a bit quieter than school. They give you more access to computers and when you need help somebody comes to help you. At school, people don't do that very much," Dominic says.

"They're always on your back about your grades. I should know that," says Thomas, who has raised his GPA from 1.7 to 2.5 since he started going to Plugged-In. "I was getting a low grade in biology because I changed classes—I was taking computer science. Then they moved my whole schedule around and I didn't make up my work and stuff. Then when they found out about it, they made sure I didn't play no games. When I came in I just did my homework and stuff. That's what they made me do; they took away my privileges and stuff."

The "they" who got on Thomas's back about his homework are the dedicated staff and volunteers at Plugged-In. The people who prove that support for role models is as important as technical support for community computing centers are staff like Julian Lacey, a 25-year-old skills instructor at Plugged-In. Lacey hassles Plugged-In's students about their homework and is treated with the highest degree of respect in return. "Julian is the man," says Dominic. "He's like a psychic. He knows everything, practically. He knows when there's something wrong with me. He studies all of us. He knows when something is bothering you; he talks to you about it."

"When Julian sees me and I have homework to do," Thomas adds, "and he sees me playing a game, he's going to turn it off and make me do my homework. Or else, if I'm not doing that, he says, 'you could be learning something new,' and he makes me look up stuff on the Internet."

Lacey, who works for a courier company from 4 to 11 a.m. before he begins teaching at the center, knows he has an effect on the kids at Plugged-In and has made it his priority to help out. "There are a lot of people in Silicon Valley who have a lot of money who want to come here and help because they feel like there's something missing from their lives," Lacey explains. "I don't feel that way because I know I'm giving something back."

That sense of responsibility for the community has created a cycle of role modeling among the N-Geners at Plugged-In that challenges the belief that computers and the Net prevent kids from developing social skills. Older N-Geners help younger ones, a process that enhances their self-esteem.

Juliana Maciel, a 15-year-old East Palo Alto girl, is a student and part-time worker at Plugged-In, where she answers the phone and technical questions from the center's clientele, who range in age from 3 to 75. Juliana's favorite part of the job is helping little kids. "It's nice when little kids call you over and say, 'help me with this, show me that,' and you get to have a real friendship with them and they start liking you a lot," Juliana says. "It makes me feel important. It makes me feel wanted. It is important to have that kind of support because [without it] I probably wouldn't even be here—I would probably be somewhere else doing something bad."

At Plugged-In, Juliana says she learned more than how to program HTML to build Web pages. She says she also learned how to give speeches. "I'm a lot more talkative. I used to be shy, now I'm not." This skill, acquired through participation in the Plugged-In Enterprises program, led to Juliana's participation in Youth Community Service, where, Juliana says, "We clean out graffiti in the community, and we are filming a project about homeless people learning how to use Macintosh computers. I'm also working on another project where I talk to eighth-graders about gangs and the problems they can cause."

It is her own experience with neighborhood gangs that makes Juliana credit her parents, her friends, and the staff at Plugged-In for giving her a stronger sense of self.

"There's this gang that hangs out near where I live, and they saw me with my friends and they came up and asked me if I was claiming 'blue,'" Juliana explains, referring to the colors local gangs use to mark their allegiances and identify rivals. "Every day I used to have to confront them, most days I had to run away from them, but I put up with it. One day they were asking me to fight with them and I was like—'If you want to fight me, let's fight right here now. One by one.' They weren't used to what I said, so they stopped fighting me."

The staff at Plugged-In don't take all the credit for their students' rising levels of self-esteem. While pure skills like touch typing are taught to even very young children at Plugged-In, embedded into the center's curriculum is an emphasis on storytelling. The process begins with teenage N-Geners reading stories to the neighborhood preschoolers, who quickly become the youngest Plugged-In students, learning basic computer skills as they make slide shows about their community using storyboard software.

"Storytelling is a collaborative act that is focused around building communication and life skills," explains Muki Izora. "That's our heart and that's really what it's all about: teaching kids how to work together, tapping into their creativity and their potential to use a variety of disciplines to find solutions to problems."

While these N-Geners are learning the skills to help them navigate their generation's medium, they're also learning how to access their creativity, take on leadership roles in their communities, and survive in a business environment. In short, N-Geners at Plugged-In have access to more than just computers and the Internet. They have access to a safe environment that supports friendship and learning, and the support of staff who are both caring and knowledgeable. As a result of this access, the N-Geners of East Palo Alto have said that gang participation is down and GPAs are up. These indicators may not be related to the value of computers, but to the value of knowledge itself. Plugged-In's students use a specific compliment when someone has done something new, original, and enviable at the computer terminal: "You are Ph.D. . . . Stanford Ph.D."

What Isn't Working

East Palo Alto is a great success story, but every community computing center is not like Plugged-In. The more typical model resembles Plugged-In's origins in the back room of the Boys' and Girls' Club, but it is difficult to see how many centers will grow to replicate the good influence Plugged-In has had on its community. As with wired schools, at community computing centers access itself is crucial, but not all access is equal.

The solution to this dilemma would seem to be corporate sponsorship, but a few free computers, despite what the computer industry would have us believe, are not enough to create another Plugged-In. Microsoft's KidReach program is one body that funds community computing centers in lower-income neighborhoods. This is a positive approach, and when it comes to working to close the digital divide, Microsoft is one of the better companies. One of Microsoft's initiatives resulted in this mention in a press release: "The leading charity in the field of product philanthropy, Gifts In Kind International and Microsoft Canada, have recently opened the Technology Learning Center at the Dovercourt Boys' and Girls' Club in Toronto, giving access to technology to over 70 children in that community."

The Technology Learning Center at the club is by no means as big as its name suggests. It is five computers, donated by Compaq, running Microsoft software in an office-sized room. "When those computers came, it was like Christmas around here," says executive director Tony Puopolo. "The kids kept asking 'when are we going to get to use them?' for weeks while we got the room ready."

Three groups of 10 to 12 students use the five computers for 30 minutes each during the center's after-school program. Due to funding limitations, only one of the computers has an Internet connection, on a telephone line shared with the center's fax machine. Puopolo does not yet know where the money to pay for Internet access will come from once Microsoft's one-year funding commitment for the ISP runs out. Ensuring that there is also adequate staff is also a concern. "Supervision is really important," says Puopolo. "If I don't have a supervisor for the room, then I have to close the room. You can't just turn kids loose on equipment like that."

This limited exposure is probably adequate to teach these budding N-Geners to play an online game and do a little chatting, but not enough to build a Web page or to research and type a history report. The club members also have no access to e-mail, so they cannot build up global networks through longer-term communication.

Club members do get some other exposure to computers. The club has retained its collection of 15 Commodore 64s and 286s with equally ancient software that it acquired through donations from local businesses that upgraded their systems. They would not have had to keep these machines had the corporation involved followed its original plan to give the club 15 computers and the technical assistance of "a National network of Microsoft employee volunteers" which Microsoft told the club it had in place.

Computer industry professionals do play a significant role as volunteers in the wiring of both schools and community computing centers. NetDay serves as the best-known example of such altruism. Since 1995, NetDay has mobilized tens of thousands of computer industry and telecommunications professionals who have donated their time and expertise toward wiring U.S. schools in what has often been called "a modern-day barn raising." One organization, San Francisco-based Compumentor, provides technical assistance to schools and community computing centers that serve low-income populations. Compumentor looks at the organization's mission, resources, and technical issues and then, says Compumentor's mission statement, "we develop solutions that are appropriate in terms of affordability, sustainability, and level of technology." The organization can help beginning community computing centers, like the Dovercourt Boys' and Girls' Club, define their mandates and construct their plans for growth.

While Compumentor and other organizations like it can assist organizations, the problem of funding, not a lack of ambition, is at the root of many community computing centers' woes. Puopolo emphasizes that both he and the club are extremely grateful to have the five computers, but he doesn't have the funding for telephone lines, ISP fees, another staff member, or the equipment to take the Technology Learning Center to the next level, which Puopolo believes would be sharing its resources with the larger community. To address the shortfalls in staffing, technological support, and the communication infrastructure, corporations have to move toward a more meaningful model of funding community computing ventures.

Creating a Meaningful Model for Corporate Involvement

Often corporate donations are given to schools or community groups without the needs of the recipient being the uppermost consideration. Frequently the guiding factors are the potential tax credits stemming from the donation, or good publicity, or the thought of future sales. For example, used equipment which would otherwise be written off when discarded anyway, often doesn't have multimedia capabilities and therefore cannot use CDs or access the Net fully. Often appropriate software, which is no longer on the market, has to be found. As often happens with machines injected with shared disks, computer viruses proliferate. The machines also break down often.

Even when new equipment is donated to community computing centers, it is rarely accompanied by technical support or commitments to offer infrastructure support. One-time gifts do generate positive publicity for the corporate donor, attracting attention to the community computing center itself, which finds its service in greater demand without a greater pool of resources with which to serve the community.

"These are our future consumers," one telecommunications corporation representative said of her company's school initiatives. "So certainly we're looking to present these offers in the home, through the schools, to our future and current consumers." While this approach to corporate donations is certainly of more benefit to the community than any ad campaign, it is a disempowering one for the members of that community. It considers what products or packages the corporation wants to give, rather than what is needed by that community or the knowledge of the instructor who facilitates use of the tool by that community.

There are a number of steps corporations could take that would make a positive and meaningful contribution:

1. Wire your employees, wire a family.

The easiest way for all corporations to ensure universal access is to provide all of their employees [with] computers to take home. This proposal is not naïve. It makes good business sense to increase fluency of human capital in the knowledge economy. Computers in the home will be instantly embraced by children, who will train their parents, thereby reducing training costs and time taken away from work for training. N-Geners, the children of corporate employees, are the answer to boomer fluency. I have made this proposal to many senior management audiences over the last year and while the idea has been received well, the actions have been piecemeal and low profile. Imagine the impact of a number of leading companies jointly announcing their decision to ensure that every family of their employees would get wired! One such initiative could have a rippling effect across the economy and strike an historic blow for access, fluency, and fairness.

2. Give your employees time, give a community time.

Professionals in the computer industry are famous for the long hours they work in an extremely competitive industry. While these professionals are putting in hours of overtime, their expertise is needed elsewhere as well. Give your employees time to volunteer in their communities as well as in under-privileged communities. In community computing centers, these employees are needed to train the instructors who, while they may be expert users, are often confronted with donated software they haven't necessarily come across before. In addition, children who have no understanding of corporate culture or professionalism desperately need mentors.

3. Fund the connector to make the connection.

A community computing center needs more than just computers and Internet access. It also needs to be able to pay for staffing, telephones, and telephone lines. But even covering these expenses isn't enough to ensure that the venture is a true success. Corporations have to recognize that community computing centers provide more than just access to computers.

"Our problem is that we have to reach into the community of people who know nothing at all about—not just computers—but planning their lives," says consultant Michael Bouyer, who sits on the board of directors at Plugged-In. "Corporate sponsors need to understand that we're dealing with a huge lack of life skills. We try to put programs together for people who want to come on a regular basis. We give them the kind of jobs where they have to be finished on time and they must be consistent. We need corporations to help with the resources to get the training to the second level all the way to a job in corporate America." In other words, to get return on investments in a community, corporations must be willing to invest in teaching real skills and to stand by their own investments by hiring people from the communities they train.

"We ask corporations to deliver skills that they are going to benefit from in the end," says Bouyer. "Even if the kids don't all become computer programmers or data processors at some corporation, at least they have the dignity and self-esteem to not be out on the street, banging you on the head while you're at the ATM. If they have a job, they are doing something meaningful. They won't be so underskilled and desperate that they'll be on the street."

This means creating partnerships the right way, rather than the easy way or the way that is expedient from a short-term corporate perspective. Firms should think cooperation and partnership for closing the digital divide, rather than simply seeding fertile young minds with their products. A Kodak program is a good example of the right approach. "All of our really meaningful partnerships are cooperative," says cyber arts teacher Kathy Yamashita, whose school has made several successful partnerships with corporate sponsors. The school is not bound to purchase Kodak products because of its relationship, nor does it take what it does not need.

Yamashita notes:

> My Kodak partner's mandate does not require us to use her product. They give me stuff, for example: paper, film, the time of a chemist. If I have a project going, she will make me a CD. They also gave us a trainer who is an expert educator. She teaches the students and finds

out activities that would be profitable. For example, at the Metro Convention Centre, the kids had a booth sponsored by Kodak at the multimedia 1996–1997 event. In exchange we provide her with things she needs. We do conferences for her, but she always pays us, so the kids get something back again. Those are the kinds of partnerships that we like to form that generate really dynamic collaboration.

She runs courses for teachers and, in return, I provide her with students as TAs and so she has a ready labor force of experienced students that can go out. They have presentation leadership skills in technology and they can go out as TAs when she does her workshops. And she pays the students, so it just breeds upon itself.

Bring the Community Together: The Tech Corps and CyberEd

Some of the most successful corporate initiatives have recognized that a good program is one that brings together the energies of community-minded organizations. The corporation serves as a facilitator and can achieve far more impact with the group effort than if it just acted by itself.

When President Clinton challenged corporate America to help bring information and education technology to every classroom in the United States, communications giant MCI responded by building and equipping a state-of-the-art multimedia classroom that was completely plugged in to the Internet. What made this classroom unique is that it was built inside an 18-wheel big-rig truck. From April to September of 1996 the truck, dubbed CyberEd, traveled more than 25,000 miles, visiting 15 federal empowerment zones from New York City to Oakland, California. The tour was orchestrated by Tech Corps, a national nonprofit organization that helps K–12 schools with their technology initiatives.

The purpose of the truck was not to roll into a community, dazzle everyone with gee-whiz technology, and then depart. By itself, that would accomplish little. "We felt the truck could be most effectively used as a catalyst for schools and communities to move their educational technology agenda forward," explained Karen Smith, the executive director of Tech Corps.

At least a month before the truck would arrive in each community, Tech Corps would arrange for a meeting with the mayor's office, the superintendent's office, and the director of the empowerment zone. Tech Corps would outline the strategy it felt could make best use of the truck.

Its first recommendation was to ask the schools to send the teachers who knew the least about technology, not the most. Says Smith: "We didn't want to be preaching to the choir." Tech Corps also recommended bringing in other community stakeholders who are crucial to getting technology into the schools, such as Boards of Education, City Council, and the Chamber of Commerce. The Tech Corps view was that "to be successful, these groups will also need to know why you should have the Internet in your classrooms here."

The truck would spend a week in each community and on the last day of the visit a roundtable discussion would bring all of the stakeholders together in a setting that was open to the public. Representatives of the companies that helped sponsor CyberEd would outline what they would leave behind, such as equipment, software, or Internet accounts. Other groups who were already involved with helping implement technology in the community's schools would outline what services they were currently providing. Within this framework, recalls Smith, "someone, usually the mayor's office, would say, 'Here is our vision of what we want to do, and here is what is currently being provided. What pieces of the puzzle are we missing?' By doing this we left behind a group of people who were committed to continue working together to advocate for educational technology in the schools."

Getting Wired in the Developing World: Jimmy Efrain Morales

Even in the most difficult, poverty-plagued environments, N-Gen is rising to the challenge of the new media. This became clear to me recently when I gave the opening address to the Latin American Bankers Association conference in Bogotá, Columbia. My graphic material was organized into a fairly sophisticated multimedia presentation using a complex program called "Macromedia Director." Each time I use this presentation in such a large setting it is important to have a perfect technical setup, preferably with an on-site expert.

As I walked onto the stage for a technical rehearsal I was assured that the situation was well under control because the "chief systems engineer" was very knowledgeable and experienced. Beside the stage was a complex computer configuration with dozens of wires connecting various peripherals and, in turn, connecting to a huge video projection system. And sitting at the console was the chief systems engineer—a boy who looked about 13 years old! He was introduced to me as Jimmy Efrain Morales.

Sure enough, he was the computer expert I needed and my software ran like a top.

Jimmy's story is an amazing one. Born in Bogotá, he is the eldest of four children. His father was a watchman at the local college (University Distrital) and is now on a modest pension. By American standards, the family is poor. They had no phone in the house until Jimmy was 12 years old. His mother knits to supplement the family income. Jimmy has a growth hormone deficiency which gives him the appearance of a boy half a decade younger than his actual age. Such problems are simply treated in richer countries. Jimmy never liked school, as the teachers used rulers to beat kids who didn't perform or who misbehaved. He failed grade 9.

During high school he saw his first computer on television and became curious about the technology. When Jimmy was 16, his local library converted to a computer card index system and the boy was thrilled. He was going to get to use a computer. He entered the library, sat down in front of the terminal, and "looked up books" for the next four hours. He was exhilarated to see that it was so easy and also useful. "Kids my age don't go to libraries because it is too hard and too intimidating to find a book. Now it is easy." Every day he went back to the library to "look up books," just to be able to use the computer. He began to take friends to the library to show them this amazing new thing.

Jimmy's time in the library led to a new motivation to learn and do better in school. He managed to graduate from high school in 1993 and because his dad had worked at the college, he was able to attend college tuition-free.

To his delight, Jimmy discovered that at college there was a room where students could go to use computers. Better still, these computers did a lot more things than looking up books. There were all kinds of applications, and Jimmy learned "anything I could get my hands on." He says, "I was pretty driven to see what computers could do." There were no instruction manuals for any of these applications. As Jimmy says, "If you went into the computer room you were supposed to know what you were doing," so he had to quietly "learn for myself."

During one of his sessions Jimmy met a friend who showed him many new tools like e-mail, simulators, and computer-aided design. One day his new friend, who came from a wealthy family, announced that he was going to buy a computer and asked Jimmy to come along. The two boys stayed up all night, they were so excited to have their own machine to configure and experiment with.

Another new-found friend was asked to make a presentation about the future of education to a government committee. Jimmy decided to help him out by learning Director, a multimedia resource handler requiring strong technical skills in a number of areas. When the local production company which set up the equipment for the presentation found out that Jimmy knew Director, they were delighted to learn about this new resource. Jimmy had himself a part-time job.

Then his father took out a loan for $3500 to buy a computer for all the children. Jimmy says, "My parents felt it was the best investment they could make in their children after they saw what an impact computers had had on me."

An N-Gener in Bogotá. For Jimmy, "Computers changed my life. They are the most important tool for man ever. Computers don't replace man. Man replaces himself."

Give them access to good technology and they will find a way—not just to assimilate it but to change their life circumstances.

NOTES

1. Gibson, Steve. "Universal Disservice," *Reason Magazine,* April 1995.

2. "Social Darwinism: Reason or Rationalization?" http://www.smplanet .com/imperialism/activity.html.

3. Bennahum, David S. "Mr. Gingrich's Cyber-Revolution," *The New York Times,* 17 January 1995.

4. Borsook, Paulina. "Cyberselfish," *Mother Jones,* July/August 1996.

5. "The Two Americas: Tools for Succeeding in a Polarized Marketplace," Roper Starch, 1996.

6. Jupiter Communications, *World On-line Markets Report,* 1996.

7. Ibid.

8. National Center for Education Statistics. *Advanced Telecommunications in US Public Elementary Schools,* 1995, www.ed.gov./NCES/.

9. National Center for Education Statistics. *Digest of Education Statistics,* 1995, table 50.

10. National Center for Education Statistics. *The Condition of Education,* 1995, Indicator 47.

11. National Center for Education Statistics. *The Digest for Education Statistics,* 1996.

12. HomeNet: "A Study of Electronic Communication by Families and the Transformation of Home Computing." Human Computer Interaction Institute, Carnegie Mellon University, Pittsburgh, 1995. http://homenet .andrew.cmu.edu.

13. Survey conducted by Coleman Advocates for Children and Youth, San
    Francisco, 1996.

WEB SITES

http://www.pluggedin.org
http://www.growingupdigital.com

9

SHOULD WE BE WORRIED?

WHAT THE RESEARCH SAYS ABOUT GENDER DIFFERENCES IN ACCESS, USE, ATTITUDES, AND ACHIEVEMENT WITH COMPUTERS *

Heather Kirkpatrick, Larry Cuban

THE FACTS ARE QUITE SIMPLE. In comparison with males, females do not take as many computer courses at school; they do not spend as many hours on computers at home, at computer camps, or in after-school computer centers; and they do not select undergraduate or graduate computer majors as often. What is less simple is understanding why females are not investing as much time in computers as their male peers.

In this article, we provide a synthesis of the research findings on gender differences in the field of computers. We then examine several popular theories of why the differences exist and what to do about them. Finally, we argue that given the role that technology will play in the future and the present disparity between the genders in higher education and in the labor force, policy-makers, parents, and practitioners should be paying more attention to the issues raised here.[1]

* We thank Susan Christopher, Sondra Cuban, Elisabeth Hansot, and Susan Verducci for comments on earlier drafts, and we thank the Center for Eco-Literacy for a grant that underwrote the research for this article.

Research Findings

When females and males have had the same amounts and types of experiences on computers, studies show that females' achievement scores and attitudes are similar to those of males in computer classes and classes using computers (in primary through higher education levels).[2] Research also shows clearly that males use computers more often,[3] in more places,[4] and for more purposes[5] than do females; furthermore, these disparities increase with age.[6]

None of these latter findings alone would necessarily be cause for concern. However, in considering them collectively and in light of the dominant role that technology will play in the 21st century, there is cause for concern. The U.S. Department of Labor has predicted that between 1994 and 2005 there will be a 90 percent increase in computer engineering and computer science jobs and a 92 percent increase in systems analysis jobs, ranking these the third and fourth fastest growing industries in the United States.[7]

Presently, the computer sciences labor force is estimated to consist of between 25 percent and 33 percent females.[8] One out of every six doctoral degrees earned in the computer sciences is earned by a female and one out of every three undergraduates in the computer sciences is female.[9] It is not that women are discriminated against in hiring or acceptance at institutions of higher education. Women are admitted in approximately the same proportion in which they apply to graduate level computer science programs.[10] Moreover, they achieve at the same levels as males when they are enrolled in classes. The problem is that girls and women are not applying at the same rates or enrolling in as many computer classes throughout their education as are males.

If males and females do equally well, given similar experiences with computers, but females do not typically have the same amounts and types of experiences as males, then we can expect females as a group to be less technologically competent than their male counterparts and therefore less competitive. In public schools, where the belief in education as a tool to gain an edge in the labor market is strong, this puts females at a decided disadvantage.

This causal sequence is illustrated in research findings about today's students. Studies over the past ten years show that males and females differ in terms of their access to and use of computers—when, where, and how they use them. The disparities in *when* males and females use computers exist along three dimensions. First, males take more classes in school in which computers are used than do their female counterparts.[11] Second, males use computers more frequently in their recreational time. This includes afterschool clubs, summer camps, and at-home use. Third, males not only use computers more often but also stay on them for a longer duration.[12]

Another distinction between male and female computer use is *where* they use computers. While the majority of females (56 percent) learned how to use computers at school, a minority of males (35 percent) learned computers at school.[13] This may be due to males having had greater access to computers outside of the school than females. Home ownership of computers was significantly lower for females than males.[14]

Within the school setting, the disparities between genders is apparent in *how* males and females use computers. In comparing enrollment in high-level computer classes offered in high school and high-level computer classes offered in college, the inequalities are dramatic.[15] By the graduate level, the National Science Foundation found that 681 males compared to 116 females earned a doctorate in computer and information science in 1991. This ratio of one female to six male Ph.D.s in the field has held steady since the 1970s, when computer science emerged as a distinct field.

It is possible that the difference in enrollment in the high-level computer classes at the high school level is due not to the perceived difficulty of the class but to larger issues that are at play with females in their adolescence. Most studies have found that the gap between male and female achievement and attitude toward computers was small in the early grades but that males were at significantly higher achievement levels by grade twelve.[16] Similarly, study after study has shown that, with age, males are increasingly more confident in their ability to use computers and more positive in their attitude toward computers than are females.[17]

Not surprisingly, studies have also found differences in attitudes and achievement levels correlated to types and amounts of computer use. Differences in achievement levels most often have reflected differences in types and amount of use, not any inherent difference in preferences or ability.[18] In fact, the studies have revealed that the more time students spent learning on computers, the fewer differences there were in male and female achievement.[19] While these are not particularly startling findings, they underscore the importance of access, use, and attitudes in achieving computer competence.

Theories on Why the Differences Exist and What to Do About Them

So, why do these gender differences exist? Historically, there are three main hypotheses that have been used to answer this question: (1) gender differences are due to genetic differences; (2) gender differences are due to different learned behaviors; (3) gender differences are due to both genetic and learned differences. Biological determinism, that is, attributing differences to genetic encoding, has largely been discredited in research comparing the genders.[20] In keeping with this larger trend, and in line with studies that report females perform as well as males on computers—given equal amounts and types of experiences—researchers who study females' achievement levels and attitudes toward computers have not discussed whether the differences found between males and females were attributable to genetic differences.

Instead, researchers have generally focused on social and psychological factors to explain why girls have less access, use, and positive attitudes than boys:

• Teachers and guidance counselors encourage boys more than girls to take computer classes and to excel in this field.[21] In a historical study of coeducation, David Tyack and Elisabeth Hansot point to a long history of such institutionalized differentiation between male and female students.[22]

• Parents encourage their boys more than their girls to take computer classes and to excel in this field.[23] The work of psychologists supports this reasoning by showing the effects of parental norms on children's socialization.

• Males typically work with computers. Studies report that brothers and fathers, not sisters and mothers, use the computer at home. Further, given the disparities between the genders in access and use, more male computer-using role models exist in peer groups than female computer-using role models.[24]

• Computers and computer programs are culturally perceived as a male enterprise. Marketing, for example, is directed largely to a male audience. Research on marketing shows that magazines promoting computers and computer programs feature males significantly more often than females in both articles and advertisements.[25] Another example of the maleness of the computer culture is seen in the predominance of males in computer sites such as after-school clubs and camps. Psychologists assert that children are aware of their own gender from an early age and make conscious decisions to act according to what they understand to be the "rules" for their gender.[26] Thus, the imbalance of participation and concomitant lack of role models discourage females from expressing interest in computer clubs and camps.[27]

- Computers are often associated with math classes and math skills, since computer classes are often taught by math teachers in the higher grades (where the disparity between the genders is greatest) and computer labs are often located in math departments.[28] By pointing out the association of computers with math, these researchers lean on a body of literature that first shows that self-confidence is related to achievement, and second, that females are less confident in their math skills than are their male counterparts. If students do in fact associate computers with math, and females are less confident in their math abilities than their male classmates, then females' lack of self-confidence and the resultant smaller enrollment of females in higher-level computer classes can be partially explained. Whether girls associate computers with math or not, research indicates that adolescent girls' loss of self-confidence could explain, in part, the increase in gender differences with age.[29]

- Girls are socialized away from computers through a combination of the forces cited above.[30] Social and psychological factors combine to account for the disparities in access, use and attitudes between male and female.

The research findings and explanations for the findings indicate that females' attitudes are shaped by family, school, and the larger culture to limit their access to and use of computers. The research also shows that attitude is an outcome of previous computer experience. Hence, a self-perpetuating cycle exists—experience with computers is necessary for a more positive attitude toward computers, yet a positive attitude is necessary in order to engage students in working with computers.

How might this cycle be broken? As there are various reasons why the disparities exist, there are various recommended remedies, each according to how the problem of disparities between males and females is framed. Thus, those who argue that the inequalities are due to marketing see the solution in marketing that is geared toward females. Those who perceive the inequalities to be due to parents, teachers, and counselors see a potential remedy in the form of public-awareness campaigns and teacher-training programs. Two studies have suggested that the solutions can be found in ensuring that sufficient numbers of computers are available in schools. Where the ratio of computers to students reached 1:1 in and out of school settings, it was more likely that females were using computers as often as males.[31] The implication of such research is that low socioeconomic-economic status compounds gender inequalities.

Some studies have proposed single-sex opportunities and structured after-school activities, along the lines of intervention programs in the late 1970s that worked to improve females' achievement and attitudes in math.[32] These researchers contend that most settings are not conducive to allowing and encouraging females to use computers. They point to findings that indicate that adolescent females use computers more when single-sex computer time is available.[33] Others have found value only in a comprehensive approach, one that addresses each of the explanations.

Should We Be Worried?

Should we be worried by the research findings? *Yes.* While the gender disparities at the elementary level are small, they increase significantly by high school and are dramatic at the level of higher education. Within the working world, the inequalities are alarming. Women make up between one-fourth and one-third of the computer science labor force and only eight percent of the faculty in computer science departments.[34] There is no indication that these inequalities will necessarily decrease in the future.

The research strongly suggests that if females do not gain experience with computers, they will not be as positive about computers or be as proficient on computers as their male peers. Clearly there are exceptions —there are a number of remarkable women in the field of computer sciences. These women report overcoming stereotypes, continually proving their capability, and learning to negotiate a male-dominated culture.[35]

Attention must be paid to females' access to and use of computers at the elementary and secondary school levels if females remain underrepresented in the computer sciences. It is the early grades of schooling where the inequalities are least significant and the middle and high school grades where the discrepancy increases. The early grades could be the target of attempts to remedy the later substantial inequalities. We argue that, at their best, targeted efforts will include both a comprehensive approach, one that considers each of the contributing social and psychological factors, and ongoing research that clarifies which specific aspects of the remediation are effective.[36]

The question now is whether practitioners, parents, and policy-makers are worried enough to invest the necessary human and financial resources to address the disparities. While we focus here on the role that schools can play in bringing females into the computer sciences, there are many other factors outside of schools that contribute to the disparity between the genders—advertising and the labor market, for example. A truly comprehensive solution would focus on these factors as well. Nevertheless, schools will be an essential part in making women more competitive in the computer sciences.

In an economic system where competition is prized, in a society where individual merit is highly esteemed and schooling is viewed as a consumer good that is necessary to raise one's social status, more must be done to ensure that half of the population has the chance to wield the powerful tools that computers literally put at their fingertips. The problem is not women's alone. Knowing what is known, rounding the final bend into the 21st century, where computers are certain to dominate work lives and home lives, shouldn't we all be worried?

NOTES

1. Two caveats are important at the outset. First, while there is much debate about whether computers are effective teaching devices, in this article this question is not an issue. Here we are interested strictly in students' access and use of technologies, their attitudes, and particularly, their competency in using computers—not how well, or if, students learn math or writing better with computers than without computers. If computers are employed effectively, and do in fact work to support particular student learning, then any differences between the genders in access, use, attitude, or competency is a concern.

   Second, the majority of the studies either do not mention socioeconomic status (SES) at all or, if they do, gender and SES are reported as distinct categories. (See Hess *et al.,* 1983; Kahle & Meece, 1994; Mark, 1992; Martinez *et al.,* 1988; Sutton, 1991.) This poses a problem in interpreting the research, since studies referring to "female" or "male" imply that there are no class differences among males and among females. This leads to inaccurate understandings, given that the findings on computer use and access among students of different socioeconomic classes vary significantly.

   The general trend in the research shows, not surprisingly, that the higher the socioeconomic status (SES) of the population, the greater the access to computers. (See Becker *et al.,* 1987; Chen, 1986; Hess *et al.,* 1983; Sutton, 1991; Urban, 1986.) Studies, however, do not provide the kind of details that research looking at gender across socioeconomic strata could. For example, on computer literacy achievement tests, girls of upper SES may score lower than boys of upper SES while girls of lower SES may score higher than boys of lower SES, or vice versa. By and large, the research omits such variations in the data that could illuminate these important distinctions.

Given the available research, we cannot distinguish between the role that gender plays and the role that SES plays in females' access, use, achievement, and attitudes toward computers.

2. Anderson, 1987; Arch *et al.*, 1989; Chen, 1986; Clarke, 1990; Clarke *et al.*, 1989; Colley *et al.*, 1994; Hattie, 1987; and Woodrow, 1994.

3. Becker *et al.*, 1987; Chen, 1986; Cole, 1997; Colley *et al.*, 1994; Cooper *et al.*, 1996; Hess *et al.*, 1983; Joiner *et al.*, 1996; Shashaani, 1994; Sutton, 1991; Urban, 1986; and Winkle-Williams *et al.*, 1993.

4. Cheek *et al.*, 1995; Chen, 1986; Colley *et al.*, 1994; Culley, 1988; Levine *et al.*, 1995; Martinez *et al.*, 1988; Sanders, 1985; Shashaani, 1994; and Winkle-Williams *et al.*, 1993.

5. Cheek *et al.*, 1995; Chen, 1986; Levine *et al.*, 1995; Martinez *et al.*, 1988; and Riggs, 1994.

6. Chappell, 1996; Chen, 1986; Durndell *et al.*, 1995; Fetler, 1985; Hattie, 1987; Hess *et al.*, 1983; Martinez *et al.*, 1988; Shashaani, 1995; Urban, 1986; and Woodrow, 1994.

7. United States Department of Labor, *Occupational Outlook Quarterly*, 1995.

8. Computer Professionals for Social Responsibility, 1997; Fryer, 1994; Kahle & Meece, 1994; National Science Foundation, 1994; and United States Department of Labor, *Monthly Labor Review*, 1995.

9. Fryer, 1994; National Science Foundation, 1994; and United States Department of Education, 1992.

10. Humphreys, 1982.

11. Chen, 1986; Cole, 1997; Colley *et al.*, 1994; Hess *et al.*, 1983; Shashaani, 1994; Sutton, 1991; Urban, 1986; and Winkle-Williams *et al.*, 1993.

12. Becker *et al.*, 1987; Cooper *et al.*, 1996; Hess *et al.*, 1983; Joiner *et al.*, 1996; and Shashaani, 1994.

13. Shashaani, 1994.

14. Cheek *et al.*, 1995; Chen, 1986; Colley *et al.*, 1994; Culley, 1988; Levine *et al.*, 1995; Martinez *et al.*, 1988; Sanders, 1985; Shashaani, 1994; and Winkle-Williams *et al.*, 1993.

15. Cheek *et al.*, 1995; Chen, 1986; National Science Foundation, 1991; and Sackrowitz, 1995.

16. Chappell, 1996; Chen, 1986; Durndell *et al.*, 1995; Fetler, 1985; Hattie, 1987; Hess *et al.*, 1983; Martinez *et al.*, 1988; Shashaani, 1995; Urban, 1986; and Woodrow, 1994.

17. Arch *et al.*, 1989; Ayersman, 1996; Bunderson, 1995; Chen, 1986; Clarke *et al.*, 1989; Colley *et al.*, 1994; Fetler, 1985; Hattie, 1987; Sackrowitz, 1995; Shashaani, 1994, 1995; Wilder *et al.*, 1985; and Winkle-Williams *et al.*, 1993.

18. Anderson, 1987; Arch *et al.*, 1989; Chen, 1986; Clarke, 1990; Clarke *et al.*, 1989; Hattie, 1987; and Woodrow, 1994.

19. Note that achievement was measured by: self reporting in Arch *et al.*, 1989; Clarke *et al.*, 1989; Woodrow, 1994; computer literacy tests in Anderson, 1987; and class grades in Chen, 1986.

20. Bleier, 1984; Fausto-Sterling, 1992; and Hubbard, 1990.

21. American Association of University Women, 1992; Chen, 1986; Humphreys, 1982; Riggs, 1994; and Tyack & Hansot, 1990.

22. Tyack & Hansot, 1990.

23. Chen, 1986; Kahle & Meece, 1994.

24. Clarke, 1990; Clarke *et al.*, 1989; Colley *et al.*, 1994; Fetler, 1985; and Shashaani, 1994.

25. Chappell, 1996; Clarke, 1990; Hattie, 1987; Huff *et al.*, 1987; Lockheed, 1985; Sanders, 1985; and Wilder *et al.*, 1985.

26. American Association of University Women, 1992; Kohlberg, in Maccoby, 1966; and Maccoby in Maccoby, 1966.

27. Clarke, 1990; Colley *et al.*, 1994; Culley, 1988; Hattie, 1987; Hess *et al.*, 1983; Kahle & Meece, 1994; Lockheed, 1984, 1985; Sackrowitz, 1995; Sutton, 1991; Urban, 1986; and Wilder *et al.*, 1985.

28. Chen, 1986; Culley, 1988; Fetler, 1985; Hattie, 1987; Lockheed, 1984, 1985; and Shashaani, 1995.

29. American Association of University Women, 1992; Chodorow, 1978; and Rogers & Gilligan, 1988.

30. Campbell, 1991; Kahle & Meece, 1994; and Tyack & Hansot, 1990.

31. Anderson, 1987; Ayersman, 1996.

32. Kahle & Meece, 1994.

33. Cheek *et al.*, 1995; Clarke, 1990; Cooper *et al.*, 1996; Culley, 1988; Jones *et al.*, 1995; Lockheed, 1984; and Sanders, 1985.

34. Computer Professionals for Social Responsibility, 1997; Fryer, 1994; Kahle & Meece, 1994; National Science Foundation, 1994; United States Department of Education, 1992; United States Department of Labor *Monthly Labor Review*, 1995.

35. Fryer, 1994; Gornick, 1984; and Steinkemp & Maehr, 1984.

36. Kahle & Meece (1994) determine that two decades of intervention programs in math were successful in improving girls' participation and achievement in math. It is possible that intervention programs in the technological sciences could work similarly.

REFERENCES

American Association of University Women. (1992). *How schools shortchange girls*. New York: Marlowe and Company.

Anderson, R. (1987). Females surpass males in computer problem solving: Findings from the Minnesota Computer Literacy Assessment. *Journal of Educational Computing, 3*(1), 39–51.

Arch, E. *et al.* (1989). Structured and unstructured exposure to computers: Sex difference in attitude and use among college students. *Sex Roles, 20*(5), 245–254.

Ayersman, D. (1996). Effects of computer instruction, learning style, gender, and experience. *Computers in the Schools, 12*(4), 15–30.

Becker, H. *et al.* (1987). Equity in school computer use: National data and neglected considerations. *Journal of Educational Computing Research, 3*(3), 289–311.

Bleier, R. (1984). *Science and gender*. New York: Pergamon Press.

Bunderson, E. (1995). An analysis of retention problems for female students in university computer science programs. *Journal of Research on Computing in Education, 28*(1), 1–18.

Campbell, J. (1991). The roots of gender inequality in technical areas. *Journal of Research in Science Teaching, 28*, 251–264.

Chappell, K. (1996). Mathematics computer software characteristics with possible gender-specific impact. *Journal of Educational Computing Research, 15*(1), 25–35.

Cheek, D. *et al.* (1995). Gender and equity issues in computer-based science assessment. *Journal of Science Education and Technology, 4*(1), 75–79.

Chen, M. (1986). Gender and computers: The beneficial effects of experience on attitudes. *Journal of Educational Computing Research, 2*(3), 265–282.

Chodorow, N. (1978). *The reproduction of mothering*. Berkeley: University of California.

Clarke, V. (1990). Sex differences in computing participation: Concerns, extent, reasons, and strategies. *Australian Journal of Education, 34*(1), 52–66.

Clarke, V. *et al.* (1989). Gender-based factors in computing enrollment and achievement: Evidence from a study of tertiary students. *Journal of Educational Computing Research, 5*(4), 409–429.

Cole, N. (1997). *ETS gender study: How females and males perform in educational settings*. Princeton: ETS.

Colley, A. *et al.* (1994). Effects of gender role identity and experience on computer attitude components. *Journal of Computing Research, 10*(2), 129–137.

Colley, A. *et al.* (1995). Gender effects in the stereotyping of those with different kinds of computing experience. *Journal of Educational Computing Research, 12*(1), 19–27.

Computer Professionals for Social Responsibility. (1997). Web site (www.cpsr .org/program/gender/index.html).

Cooper, J. *et al.* (1996). Gender, computer assisted learning, and anxiety: With a little help from a friend. *Journal of Educational Computing Research, 15*(1), 67–91.

Culley, L. (1988). Girls, boys, and computers. *Educational Studies, 14*(1), 3–8.

Durndell, A. *et al.* (1995). Gender and computing: Persisting differences. *Educational Research, 37*(3), 219–227.

Fausto-Sterling, A. (1992). *Myths of gender*. New York: Basic Books.

Fetler, M. (1985). Sex differences on the California statewide assessment of computer literacy. *Sex Roles, 13*(3/4), 181–191.

Fryer, B. (1994, April). Sex and the superhighway. *Working Woman*.

Gornick, V. (1983). *Women in science*. New York: Simon and Schuster.

Hattie, J. (1987). Sex differences in attitudes, achievement, and use of computers. *Australian Journal of Education, 31*(1), 3–26.

Hess, R. *et al.* (1983). *Gender and socioeconomic differences in enrollment in computer camps and classes*. ED 237 610.

Hubbard, R. (1990). *Politics of women's biology*. New Brunswick, NJ: Rutgers University Press.

Huff, C. *et al.* (1987). Sex bias in educational software. *Journal of Applied Social Psychology, 17*(6), 519–532.

Humphreys, S. (1982). *Women and minorities in science*. Boulder: Westview Press.

Joiner, R. *et al.* (1996). Gender, computer experience, and computer-based problem solving. *Computer Education, 26*(1–3), 179–187.

Jones, T. *et al.* (1995). Explanation of the apparent advantages of single sex settings. *Journal of Educational Computing Research, 12*(1), 51–64.

Kahle, J., & Meece, J. (1994). Research on gender issues in the classroom. In D. Gabel (Ed.), *Handbook of research in science teaching and learning*. New York: Macmillan.

Kohlberg, L. (1966). A cognitive development analysis of children's sex-role concepts and attitudes. In E. Maccoby (Ed.), *The development of sex differences*. Stanford: Stanford University Press.

Levine, T. *et al.* (1995). Computer experience, gender, and classroom environment in computer-supported writing classes. *Journal of Educational Computer Research, 13*(4).

Lockheed, M. (1984). Sex equity: Increasing girls' use of computers. *Computing Teacher, 11*(8), 16–18.

Lockheed, M. (1985). Women, girls, and computers: A first look at the evidence. *Sex Roles, 13*(4), 337–357.

Maccoby, E. (1966). Sex differences in intellectual functioning. In E. Maccoby (Ed.), *The development of sex differences.* Stanford: Stanford University Press.

Mark, J. (1992). *Beyond equal access: Gender equity in learning with computers.* Newton, MA: Education Development Center.

Martinez, M. *et al.* (1988). *Computer competence: First national assessment.* Princeton, NJ: Educational Testing Service.

National Science Foundation. (1991). *Surveys of science resources series.* Washington, DC.

National Science Foundation. (1994). *Women, minorities, and persons with disabilities in science and engineering.* Washington, DC.

Riggs, A. (1994). Gender and technology education. In F. Banks (Ed.), *Teaching technology.* London: Routledge Press.

Rogers, A., & Gilligan, C. (1988). *Translating girls' voices.* Harvard Project on the Psychology of Women and the Development of Girls. Harvard University Graduate School of Education.

Sackrowitz, M. (1995). *An unlevel playing field: Women in the introductory computer sciences courses.* ED 384 389.

Sanders, J. (1985). Making the computer neuter. *Computing Teacher, 12*(7), 23–27.

Shashaani, L. (1994). Gender differences in computer experience and its influence on computer attitudes. *Journal of Educational Computing Research, 11*(4), 347–367.

Shashaani, L. (1995). Gender differences in mathematics experience and attitude and their relation to computer attitude. *Educational Technology, 35*(3), 32–38.

Steinkemp, M., & Maehr, M. (1984). *Women in science.* (Vol. 2). Greenwich, CT: JAI Press.

Sutton, R. (1991). Equity and computers in the schools: A decade of research. *Review of Educational Research, 61*(4), 475–503.

Tyack, D., & Hansot, E. (1990). *Learning together: A history of co-education in American schools.* New Haven: Yale University Press.

United States Department of Education. (1992). *Characteristics of doctorate recipients,* National Center for Educational Statistics, Office of Educational Research and Improvement, Washington, DC.

United States Department of Labor. (1995). *Occupational outlook quarterly*, Bureau of Labor Statistics, Washington, DC.

United States Department of Labor. (1995). *Monthly Labor Review, 118*(12), Bureau of Labor Statistics, Washington, DC.

Urban, C. (1986). *Inequalities in computer education due to gender, race, and SES*. ED 279 594.

Wilder, G. *et al.* (1985). Gender and computers: Two surveys of computer related attitudes. *Sex Roles, 13*(3/4), 215–228.

Winkle-Williams, S. *et al.* (1993). Gender roles, computer attitudes, and dyadic computer interaction performance in college students. *Sex Roles, 29*(8), 515–525.

Woodrow, J. (1994). Development of computer related attitudes of secondary students. *Journal of Educational Computing Research, 11*(4), 307–338.

10

GIRL GAMES AND
TECHNOLOGICAL DESIRE

Cornelia Brunner, Dorothy T. Bennett, Margaret Honey

Gender and Technological Desire

DURING THE PAST TEN YEARS, a research and design group at the Center for Children and Technology has spent time investigating issues of gender and diversity as they relate to the ways in which students, particularly girls, use and engage with technologies. Our approach to these issues has been both psychological and sociological: we have investigated the ways in which children and adults construct meanings in relation to different technological environments, and we have examined the social and cultural barriers that tend to affect the ways we engage with technologies. We have also experimented with designing technological environments that can engage diverse populations of learners—not just the white boys.

It has become clear to us over time that the problem of designing for gender and diversity is quite complicated, particularly with respect to technology. A variety of forces affect our understanding of gender and make it very hard for us to think our way out of more or less conventional understandings of "masculinity" and "femininity." They include such sociological issues as the fact that girls and students of color still opt out of advanced-level science and math courses at a greater rate than do Caucasian males. As a result, scientific, engineering, and technological fields that are responsible for technological design are still largely dominated by white men. They also include economic factors, such as the fact that successful interactive "edutainment" products, often linked to other commercially successful products such as television series, are the ones to find shelf space in CompUSA and other large retail outfits. And they include psychological factors, such as the ways in which we as consumers have been strongly encouraged to collude in the kinds of narratives that the vast majority of interactive products offer, particularly in the gaming industry. In this paper we focus on the latter point: the *psychological paradox,* the question of how we address issues of concern to young women that are glaringly absent in technological design without colluding in stereotypical understandings of femininity.

One of our strategies in exploring the psychological complexities that surround technological design has been to start with ourselves. We noticed that the women in our office seemed to respond quite differently to the sight of boxes of high-tech equipment arriving in the office than most of our male colleagues. The men seemed magnetically drawn to the boxes, tearing them open, practically salivating at the sight of the shiny, new machines emerging from their styrofoam nests. Then there would be the sound of happily boastful speculation about the speed, the power, the number of bips per bump the machine could produce or consume, and how it compared to a range of other machines with whose model numbers everybody seemed intimately familiar. We women tended to stay back and watch this frenzy with some amusement and a strong dose of skepticism, best summarized in the polite request that they let us know when they had put the thing together and had figured out what it was good for. We knew that there was no difference in technical expertise to explain this difference in attitude. Several of the women were more technically sophisticated than some of the men who were spitting stats at the new machine, and these women would probably end up setting up the machine, figuring out how to make good use of it—and then explaining it to the men.

As researchers and designers we decided to explore some of these casually observed differences in more depth. The Spencer Foundation funded a series of studies involving interviews with users of technology, from architects to NASA scientists, from filmmakers to programmers (Bennett, 1993; Brunner, Hawkins, and Honey, 1988; Brunner, 1991; Hawkins, Brunner, Clements, Honey, and Moeller, 1990; Honey, Moeller, Brunner et al., 1991; Honey, 1994). All of these individuals were deeply engaged in computer-related activities, including programming, multimedia design and authoring, computer-assisted design, and engineering. We asked them about a wide range of topics, from their career paths and their mentoring experiences to their personal feelings about their work. We also selected a subsample of twenty-four respondents, balanced by gender and profession, and asked them to participate in a study of their technology fantasies.

In the fantasy study, we were interested in exploring women's and men's feelings about technology—the nonrational aspect of how we interpret technological objects. Assuming that people might be less self-conscious about sharing such fantasies with a computer than with a human interviewer, we made a software program that invited our respondents to spin fantasies directly into the computer. We made the program look fanciful rather than serious, hoping to invite respondents to censor themselves as little as possible. We posed the following question: "If you were writing a science fiction story in which the perfect instrument (a future version of your own) is described, what would it be like?" Our analysis of the adult fantasies focused on five major topics: (1) the role of technology in integrating people's home and work lives; and the technology's relationship to (2) nature, (3) the human body, (4) the process of creation, and (5) the process of communication.

What emerged from this study were two distinct and highly gendered perspectives on technology. Across our sample, women fantasized about small, flexible objects that facilitate sharing ideas and staying in touch, that can be used anywhere and fulfill a number of quite different functions—something that can be a camera one minute, for instance, and a flute the next. For the women in our sample, technology is a fellow creature on the earth, a child of humanity, promising but problematic (because, like all good things, there can be too much of it), needing care and guidance to grow to its best potential within the balance of things surrounding it, within the social and natural network in which it lives. The women wrote stories about tools that allow us to integrate our personal and professional lives and to facilitate creativity and communication. The following is typical of the fantasies written by women:

> The "keyboard" would be the size of a medallion, formed into a beautiful piece of platinum sculptured jewelry, worn around one's neck. The medallion could be purchased in many shapes and sizes. The keyed input would operate all day-to-day necessities to communicate and transport people (including replacements for today's automobile). The fiber-optic network that linked operations would have no dangerous side effect or byproduct that harmed people or the environment.

In contrast, men's fantasies were about mind-melds and bionic implants that allow their owners to create whole cities with the blink of an eye, or to have instant access to the greatest minds in history, to check in and see, as they get dressed in the morning, what Gandhi might have thought about a problem they are facing in the office that day. In their stories technology frees us from the earth, from social problems, possibly from humanity itself. The men praised technology because it increases our command and control over nature and each other. It allows us to extend our instrumental power into god-like dimensions, to transcend the limitations of time, space, and our physical bodies. For the men technology is a magic wand (pun intended), and scenarios like the following were typical:

> A direct brain-to-machine link. Plug it into a socket in the back of your head and you can begin communications with it. All information from other users is available and all of the history of mankind is also available. By selecting any time period the computer can impress directly on the user's brain images and background information for that time. In essence a time-machine. The user would not be able to discern differences between dreams and reality and information placed there by the machines.

Table 10.1 illustrates how we chose to summarize some of the most striking differences in how men and women fantasized about technology (Bennett, Brunner, and Honey, 1996).

During the past decade, we have also conducted similar studies investigating children's technology fantasies and have collected fantasy machines, mostly from elementary and middle school students. In an analysis of the fantasy tasks of forty-seven preadolescent boys and girls, we asked children to create a blueprint for a machine of their own creation. Boys tend to make vehicles that take them wherever they want to go instantaneously. Typically, these vehicles have elaborate model numbers. Figure 10.1 represents what boys tend to imagine. The New 1994 Mazing Hover Carr is further illustrated in Figure 10.2. This one has a "twin valve seven rotor 4 class booster rocket," hidden turbo jets—and a snack bar.

Girls' fantasies about technology differed in nature from those of boys. The machines that girls typically invented tended to be human-like household helpers or improvements to existing technologies that aimed to solve real-life problems. They often highlighted functions rather than the features of their machines, and they were situated in context. Figure 10.3 shows an example of what girls typically imagine: instead of features, there are functions.

The Season Chore Doer (Figure 10.4) is a sophisticated, multifunctional device. It senses what is needed and provides just the right tool: a

Table 10.1. Technology.

Women	Men
fantasize about it as a	fantasize about it as a
MEDIUM	PRODUCT
Women	Men
see it as a	see it as a
TOOL	WEAPON
Women	Men
want to use it for	want to use it for
COMMUNICATION	CONTROL
Women	Men
are impressed with its potential for	are impressed with its potential for
CREATION	POWER
Women	Men
see it as	see it as
EXPRESSIVE	INSTRUMENTAL
Women	Men
ask it for	ask it for
FLEXIBILITY	SPEED
Women	Men
are concerned with its	are concerned with its
EFFECTIVENESS	EFFICIENCY
Women	Men
like its ability to facilitate	like its ability to grant them
SHARING	AUTONOMY
Women	Men
are concerned with	are intent on
INTEGRATING	CONSUMING
Women	Men
talk about wanting to	talk about using it to
EXPLORE	EXPLOIT
worlds	resources and potentialities
Women	Men
are	want
EMPOWERED	TRANSCENDENCE
by it	

Source: *Brunner, 1994.*

Figure 10.1.

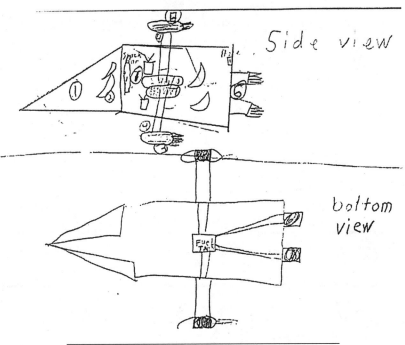

seeder in spring, an umbrella in summer, a rake in the fall, and a shovel in winter. It does not, however, eliminate the need for the chore itself. If this gadget had been designed by a boy, chances are it would not provide a rake to collect the leaves—it would probably pulverize them.

Implications for the Design of Girl Games

One way of summarizing the implications of our research for the development of new technologies is to say that women and girls are much more likely to be concerned with how new technologies can fit into the social and environmental surroundings, whereas men are much more likely to be preoccupied with doing things faster, more powerfully, and more efficiently regardless of social and environmental consequences. Women are also far less likely to push the technological envelope and tend to be willing to make do with available tools. Men, in contrast, tend to draw upon their technological imaginations to extend the capabilities of technologies and to attempt to "go where no man has ever gone before."

Figure 10.2.

① The New 1994 Mazing Hover Carr

triangle wind shield

② moon seats

③-⑤ Twin valve seven rotor 9 class boster rocket

⑥ Hidden turbo jets!

⑦ .snack ,bar and tv's.

Figure 10.3.

SEASON CHORC DOER

What are the implications of these differences for girl-friendly electronic games?

When thinking about the design of technological environments—particularly in relation to entertainment and educational projects—it has been exceedingly difficult for us to imagine our way out of antithetical positions. The common approach in interactive design, or perhaps the path of least resistance, is to develop story lines that reinforce extreme notions of gender. The result is that "Mortal Kombat" becomes the archetypal video game for boys. In the girls' arena, programs like "McKenzie & Company" are beginning to emerge. This product presents scenarios that revolve around how to handle problems with boyfriends or would-be

Figure 10.4.

boyfriends, and how to dress and what kind of makeup to wear. These kinds of stories are not bad in and of themselves, but if they are the only available options, they run the danger of reinforcing stereotypic thinking about gender. Just as the fantasy life of boys who enjoy playing games like "Mortal Kombat" should not be curtailed by scenes of mindless violence, the social decision-making options in a game like "McKenzie & Company" are too simplistic to represent the kind of human problem-solving situations girls think about all the time. Products such as these enlarge an already gaping gender divide, making it harder for us to imagine approaches that do not privilege an either/or paradigm: Conquest or A Day at the Mall. We have to engage both boys and girls with electronic games that can incorporate multiple perspectives and varying themes.

To consider what our research means for designing a new genre of game that is not rigidly overdetermined, we first have to consider the function of games and play. One of the functions of playing games, as Henry Jenkins notes, is to rehearse and explore what it means to have a gender. Games provide a safe place to explore issues of femininity and masculinity. Game playing can deliberately expand our sense of who we are. The appeal of role-playing games among both children and adults is testimony to this fact. The kinds of worlds represented in electronic games tend to be one dimensional. Typically these games appeal to boys. They are about conquest, winning, scoring points, assertion, and domination. The player becomes the active protagonist, whether the game is played from a first- or third-person perspective. The player is central, makes things happen, and determines the outcome. There usually are no other roles. There are few partner roles, few helper roles, few participant-observer roles. Making ourselves so big and so powerful that nobody can touch us is hardly preparation for the multiplicity of roles that people, particularly women, play in life. We need to make games that stretch the potential of different play paradigms.

Games have traditionally privileged:

- Victory over justice.
- Competition over collaboration.
- Speed over flexibility.
- Transcendence over empathy.
- Control over communication.
- Force over facilitation.

We need game environments that offer players options—where you can pick and choose from a range of personas, decide on varying strategies, and discover that different actions result in variable outcomes. We need a more complex relationship between actions taken and results obtained, and we need contexts that offer rich and varied opportunities for exploration.

Based on our research, and on a variety of experiments with designs that are deliberately open-ended (such as leaving choice in the hands of the user), we have conditional faith in the following generalizations about designing games for both boys and girls. It must be stressed, however, that these observations are speculative. We have never actually investigated the design features that make games more attractive to girls. We are merely applying the characteristics we have found to make for good electronic learning environments for girls to the domain of electronic games. What follows, then, is a nonprescriptive attempt to transform traditionally privileged design elements, and imagine alternative scenarios for play.

- *Technological sophistication.* The kinds of games that encourage flexibility in decision making require a more sophisticated technology than current games. Mitchel Resnick (Resnick, 1991) learned years ago that girls wanted to build Lego Logo devices that could interact with each other. Instead of thinking about a single object that did one thing very well, designers had to pay attention to multiple objects that would interact with each other.
- *Winning and losing.* It probably matters more to girls what you win and what you lose than whether you win or lose. Girls are not that interested in conquering the world. Girls really prefer triumphs of a more personal sort. Many girls are seriously preoccupied with perfecting themselves, which is quite different from a more masculine desire to become stronger and more powerful, or with having total control over some part of the universe. This preoccupation with self-improvement and perfection is a tricky business, no simpler nor more beneficial than the masculine focus on power over others, except, perhaps, that the damage is more likely to be internal than external. It is, however, a rich ground for interesting stories and meaningful problems to solve.
- *Success and sacrifice.* Girls are interested in thinking about the issues that adult women must face these days, including how to juggle career and family, how to be successful at work while helping others, and how to stay part of the group. Girls want to figure out what the issues are and what sacrifices one may have to make. They want to anticipate and rehearse the complex dance that adult women, particularly those in nontraditional professions, must perform in order to make their lives work. This is good material for all kinds of adventure games.

• *The contradictions of femininity.* What constitutes femininity is open to question these days. For the young women we interviewed, femininity is linked to notions of social justice. Defining femininity is a live issue and a complicated one. Theories that absolve girls from the need to be feminine are of no help in the real world of their everyday lives. Things have not changed that much in junior high school, and popularity and traditional femininity still go together. Not much help is given to young women on how to rethink these issues. We believe that one function of role-playing games could be to help provide an imaginary space allowing girls to fool around with the notions of femininity that make sense to them, and offer rich, complex stories that raise questions about the consequences of the social prescriptions for femininity.

• *Persuasion versus conquest.* Women and girls tend to value persuasion, not conquest. Persuading is a more complex act than conquering. It is easy to simulate shooting somebody dead. It is harder to simulate persuading somebody—the interaction is more nuanced. Persuasion cuts both ways, of course. We have always wanted to make a game in which rumors create both havoc and opportunity. Instead of pulling out a sword when confronted with a complex situation, we want to let fly a rumor and have interesting things happen as a result of it—as in real life.

• *Humor.* Girls are very interested in humor. We think girls have less tolerance for humorlessness when it comes to games than boys do, because boys have something else they can fool around with even in the absence of humor—weapons and victory. They still get to rack up points and shoot off weapons. The humor girls appreciate is based on character and situation rather than putdown. A certain level of sarcasm can be a lot of fun, but when the humor is based on pointing out people's shortcomings, it no longer appeals to girls as much.

• *Adventure.* What is adventure for girls? Rescue and romance are adventures. There is plenty of rescue and romance in current games, but the females in the story rarely get to experience that adventure directly. Girls do not just want to get rescued, they want to do the rescuing—without having to abandon femininity to do it. And they want to do more than come up with the right approach to get a guy to ask them out! Adventure means risk. In many games, the payoff is getting more strength, accumulating wealth or power, and figuring out what risks to take to achieve those gains. The kinds of risks that interest girls may have to do with defying conventions rather than gaining authority. Let us have some games about that—more romantic heroines striking out to make a place for themselves and their kind in a world that misunderstands or undervalues them.

- *Puzzles and obstacles.* Let us also have more games in which you play at outwitting your opponent rather than vanquishing the enemy. Many games have puzzles that occasionally are very clever and require real thought. They are, however, rarely integral to the story. There are exceptions, of course, including "Myst." The puzzle solving is fun, even when it is just an artificial obstacle to pursuing the story, but it might be a lot more entertaining to girls if the puzzles contributed to the story. Since girls are less motivated by winning than by following the flow of the story, such unintegrated puzzles can be frustrating and discouraging. Boys, on the other hand, often appreciate the opportunity to rack up more points.

- *Writing.* Girls are very interested in letter-writing and in other forms of communication across a variety of media. They like to think about what to say and how to say it. Girls enjoy analyzing responses, mulling over phrasings, and testing alternatives. They like to illustrate their messages, comment on them, and compare and contrast them with other statements. Girls might be interested in games that focus on how things are communicated, not just on what is being said.

- *Design.* Girls like designing living spaces—not blueprints, but actual spaces. With VRML and VR technologies, it should be possible to see people move through a space you have designed, to report on how it feels, to look at it from their perspective, and to watch which kinds of interactions the design privileges and which are prohibited.

- *Being chosen.* The girls we interviewed often mentioned that they might like games about being chosen. But girls are not nearly as interested in thinking about how to seduce someone into choosing them as they are in the complexity that results once you have been chosen. Being chosen, as we all know, is a complicated thing. You lose some friends, you gain some things, stuff happens. Games that focus on dealing with that stuff might be extremely interesting to young women.

- *Mysteries.* Girls like mysteries because they have complex plots and intelligent action. There is something to think about and to talk over with friends. The kinds of action required to solve a mystery—keeping track of information, sifting through it, thinking it over, trying it again, looking at it from a different perspective—are the kinds of adult skills girls want to rehearse. It is what we like to do.

Some existing software, though not necessarily intended for girls, is designed in ways that seem compatible with the kind of feminine perspective on technology we have described here. Interactive comics, for instance, are an interesting new use of the electronic medium. The interactive features are a good fit with the way kids actually read comics, bringing each panel to life with sound and movies or animation. The comics provide a strong, linear narrative structure but utilize the nonlinear nature of the medium to offer a choice between multiple perspectives. The plot remains the same, the speech bubbles and the images inside the panels don't change, but the context and commentary in the descriptive labels changes, as does the accompanying information. This makes for a complex narrative of multiple voices, which lends itself beautifully to interactive storytelling. Unfortunately, this feature is not used in most of the interactive comics for children. These comics may include multimedia but they don't offer any conceptual interactivity. They are more like Living Books. Moreover, the comics we have seen, such as "Reflux" by Inverse Ink, are interesting to look at and beautifully designed, but their content is strongly masculine. Nonetheless the genre makes a lot of sense for girls. Looking at a situation from multiple perspectives is a very attractive activity for girls.

Rather than leaving their mark on the world by conquering territory or even by amassing resources, girls might like to make a difference in a social situation, right an injustice, save a whale or two, or discover a cure for cancer. Some educational games allow for this kind of thinking, including the SimGames by Maxis and the Trail games by MECC. In the entertainment realm, there are some adult games, such as "Voyeur II" by Philips, that allow you to solve a mystery and thus prevent a murder rather than to avenge one. In "Voyeur II" you are a private eye, observing the shenanigans of a wealthy family in a fancy mansion through your fabulous binoculars. Sex, romance, and family tensions are the main elements of the plot, rather than war, violence, or world domination.

The themes matter, and so do the activities themselves. In "The 1st Degree" by Broderbund, a game for adults in which you are the district attorney (male, with a young, white, smart-alecky woman assistant who develops much of the context information), you have to make a case for first-degree murder. You interview witnesses in their surroundings to get an idea of the context in which they live. The point of the game is not to solve the mystery but to make the case, which requires figuring out people's motivations and relationships, rather than establishing facts. Witnesses from whom you have learned the truth will lie on the stand if you have not persuaded them to join you. The story is more about the underlying emotional realities than about the grisly deed. This makes sense to girls.

Games with an electronic doll-house "feel" seem to be attractive to girls. An example is "SimTown" by Maxis, an environmental problem-solving game that lets you customize your own character, find out how the population feels, and lift the roof off the houses to see what's going on inside.

"Hollywood" by Viacom is another kind of electronic doll house. Here, you can make animated movies with a set of characters and settings. You can write dialogue, select actions for character animation, customize the characters by giving them personality traits, and then record and play the movie. "Imagination Express" by Edmark is another doll house with good backgrounds, plenty of characters and objects, and the ability to add a little animation as well as captions. This program makes constructing settings fun because the objects, people and things, have a good deal of intelligence built into them. They twist and turn and place themselves appropriately behind, in front of, over or under things, and change size to maintain the illusion of depth.

Some of the new software coming out for girls, such as "Let's Talk About Me" by Simon & Schuster Interactive, are not exactly games. "Let's Talk About Me" is marketed as a handbook, and provides some activities girls might like. As for the other new electronic girls' games, some are good, some are not so good. The main differences are in the content rather than in the kind of activity they privilege. Most puzzles are still too unintegrated, and the choices are too few. The interactivity is still not conceptual enough. And we worry that the folks likely to have the money to develop complex activities may confuse content with marketing and end up reaffirming stereotypes. They may fail to realize that the desired forms of activity can be applied to a wide range of content girls are interested in, not just to catching a boyfriend. But at least somebody's finally working on the problem.

Our final thought is this. Boys can use games to escape into a fantasy world which allows them to prepare themselves for the requirements of adult masculinity. They can gird their digital loins with magical potencies and vanquish enemies with their limitless strength. They can also get killed, over and over, along the way, until they have achieved the degree of mastery that makes them champions. Then they can reach into the full storehouse of boy games and accept another challenge. The cultural prescriptions for masculinity are harsh and exacting. Few boys can feel secure about achieving a sufficient degree of masculinity. The pressure is relentless—and these games provide a fun, painless opportunity to boost their sense of masculinity and let off some steam.

The cultural prescriptions for femininity are equally stringent—and they are also internally contradictory. Girls are expected to be both frail and enduring, helpless and competent, fun loving and sensitive, emotional and available, needy and nurturing, vain and moral. Girls need games in which they can rehearse and express the ambiguities and contradictions of femininity. Navigating the shoals of femininity is the stuff girls think about. It is an endless conundrum: how to do the right thing when all the available options force you to choose against yourself; how to maintain a sense of pleasure and confidence in yourself when all the paths before you lead to danger; how to satisfy everybody without calling undue attention to yourself. Girls need games in which they can take their own side, act out, throw caution to the winds and watch what happens. They need games in which they survive, again and again, until they have achieved a state of grace that makes them happy. Then they need to reach into a growing storehouse of girl games and play another story. The pressure on girls is relentless, too. Becoming a woman is a tricky business. Girls could use some games that provide a fun, painless opportunity to bolster their sense of femininity and to stretch their wings.

REFERENCES

Bennett, D. 1993. "Voices of Young Women in Engineering." Paper presented at the 10th International Conference on Technology in Education. Cambridge, MA: Massachusetts Institute of Technology.

Bennett, D., Brunner, C., and Honey, M. 1996. "Gender and Technology: Designing for Diversity." Paper written for the Regional Equity Forum on Math, Science and Technology Education. Cosponsored by EDC's WEEA Equity Resource Center, Northeastern University Comprehensive Resource Center for Minorities, TERC, and Mass Pep.

Brunner, C. 1991. "Gender and Distance Learning." In L. Roberts and V. Horner, eds., The Annals of Political and Social Science. Beverly Hills: Sage Press, 133–145.

Brunner, C., Hawkins, J., and Honey, M. 1988. "Making Meaning: Technological Expertise and the Use of Metaphor." Paper presented at the American Educational Research Association, New Orleans.

Hawkins, J., Brunner, C., Clements, P., Honey, M., and Moeller, B. 1990. "Women and Technology: A New Basis for Understanding." Final report to the Spencer Foundation. New York: Center for Children and Technology, Bank Street College of Education.

Honey, M. 1994. "Maternal Voice in the Technological Universe." In D. Bassin, M. Honey, and M. Kaplan, eds., Representations of Motherhood. New Haven: Yale University Press.

Honey, M., Moeller, B., Brunner, C., Bennett, D. T., Clements, P., and Hawkins, J. 1991. "Girls and Design: Exploring the Question of Technological Imagination." Tech Rep. No. 17. New York: Bank Street College of Education, Center for Technology in Education.

Resnick, M. 1991. "Xylophones, Hamsters, and Fireworks: The Role of Diversity in Constructionist Activities." In I. Harel and S. Papert, eds., Constructionism. Norwood, MA: Ablex Publishing, 151–158.

II

RETHINKING HOW TO INVEST IN TECHNOLOGY

Chris Dede

NEW TECHNOLOGY-BASED MODELS of teaching and learning have the power to dramatically improve educational outcomes. An important question is, How can districts scale up scattered, successful "islands of innovation" into universal improvements in schooling?

Such improvements can take place only within the larger context of systemic reform—sustained, large-scale, simultaneous innovations in curriculum, pedagogy, assessment, professional development, administration, incentives, and partnerships for learning among schools, businesses, homes, and community settings. Systemic reform requires policies and practices different from fostering pilot projects for small-scale educational improvement. As it relates to technology-based improvements in education, systemic reform involves at least two major shifts: (1) rethinking the organization of learning to include the possibility of "distributed learning"—the use of information technologies outside the school setting to enhance classroom activities; and (2) moving from using special, external resources to reconfiguring existing budgets to free up money for innovation. Before undertaking these shifts, however, schools should consider some underlying concerns.

Moving Beyond Naive Conceptions

Giving all students continuous access to computers with Internet connections and multimedia capabilities is currently quite fashionable. For politicians, the Internet in every classroom has become the modern equivalent of the promised "chicken in every pot." Communities are urging volunteers to participate in "Net Days" to wire the schools. Information technology vendors are offering special programs to encourage massive educational purchases. States are setting aside substantial amounts of money for building information infrastructures dedicated to instructional usage.

As an educational technologist, I am more dismayed than delighted by how this enthusiasm about the Internet is being expressed. Some of my nervousness comes from the "first-generation" thinking about information technology that underlies these visions. Many people see multimedia-capable, Internet-connected computers as magical devices, silver bullets to solve the problems of schools. They assume that teachers and administrators who use new media are automatically more effective than those who do not. They envision classroom computers as a technology comparable to fire: Students benefit just by sitting near these devices, as knowledge and skills radiate from the monitors into their minds.

Yet decades of experience with technological innovations based on first-generation thinking have demonstrated that this viewpoint is misguided. Unless other simultaneous innovations occur in pedagogy, curriculum, assessment, and school organization, the time and effort expended on instructional technology produce few improvements in education outcomes —a result that reinforces many educators' cynicism about fads based on magical machines.

Additional concerns about attempts to supply every student with continuous access to high-performance computing and communications technology relate to the likely cost of this massive investment. Depending on the assumptions made about the technological capabilities involved, estimates of the financial resources needed for such an information infrastructure vary (Coley et al., 1997). Extrapolating the most detailed cost model (McKinsey and Company, 1995) to one multimedia-capable, Internet-connected computer for every two to three students yields a price tag of about $94 billion of initial investment and $28 billion per year in ongoing costs—a financial commitment that would drain schools of all discretionary funding for at least a decade.

For several reasons, this is an impractical approach for improving education. First, putting this money into computers and cables is too large an investment in just one part of the infrastructure improvements that many schools desperately need. Buildings are falling apart, furnishings are dilapidated, playgrounds are in disrepair. If these needs are ignored, the machines will cease to function, as their surroundings deteriorate.

Also, educational researchers and developers need substantial funding for other types of innovations required to make instructional hardware effective, such as standards-based curricular materials for the World Wide Web and alternative kinds of pedagogy that link teachers and tools. (The McKinsey cost estimates do include some funding for content development and staff training, but in my judgment it is too little to enable effective technology integration and systemic reform.)

Second, without substantial and extended professional development in the innovative models of teaching and learning that instructional technology makes possible, many educators will not use these devices to their full potential. "Second-generation" thinking in educational technology does not see computers as magical, but it does make the mistake of focusing on automation as their fundamental purpose. It envisions computers as empowering "teaching by telling" and "learning by listening." In this view, the computer serves only as a fire hose that sprays information from the Internet into learners' minds. Even without educational technology, classrooms are already drowning in data. Adding additional information, even with multimedia bells and whistles, is likely to worsen rather than improve educational settings. Professional development needs are more complex than increasing educators' technical literacy (training in how to use Web browsers, for example). They involve building teachers' knowledge and skills in alternative types of pedagogy and content. Such an increase in human capabilities requires substantial funding that will be unavailable if almost all resources are put into hardware.

Third, the continuing costs of maintaining and upgrading a massive infusion of school-based technology are prohibitive. High-performance computing and communications systems require high-tech skills to remain operational, and, moreover, they will become obsolete in five to seven years as information technology continues its rapid advance. Taxpayers now see computers as similar to chalkboards: Buy them once, and they are inexpensively in place for the lifetime of the school. School boards quickly become restive at sizable yearly expenditures for technology maintenance and usage—especially if, several months after installation, standardized test scores have (unsurprisingly) not yet dramatically risen—and they will become apoplectic if the replacement of obsolete equipment consumes additional substantial sums only a few years after a huge initial expenditure. For all these reasons, investing an exorbitant amount in information infrastructures for schools is impractical and invites a later backlash against educational technology as yet another failed fad.

I would go further, however, and argue that we should not make such an investment even if a technology fairy were to leave billions under our virtual pillows, no strings attached. Kids continuously working on machines with teachers wandering around coaching the confused is the wrong model for the classroom of the future. In that situation—just as in classrooms with no technology—too much instructional activity tends to center on presentation and motivation, building a foundation of ideas and skills as well as some context that helps students understand why they should care about learning the material. Yet this temporary interest and readiness to master curricular material rapidly fade when no time is left for reflection and application, as teachers and students move on to the next required topic in the overcrowded curriculum, desperately trying to meet all the standards and prepare for the tests.

Helping students make sense out of something they have assimilated but do not yet understand is crucial for inducing learning that is retained and generalized, much research documents (Schank and Jona, 1991). Learners must engage in reflective discussion of shared experiences from multiple perspectives if they are to convert information into knowledge and master the collaborative creation of meaning and purpose (Edelson et al., 1996).

But what if much of the presentation and motivation that is foundational for learning occurred outside of classroom settings, via information technologies that are part of home and workplace and community contexts? What if students arrived at school already imbued with some background and motivation, ripe for guided inquiry, ready for interpretation and collaborative construction of knowledge? By diverting from classroom settings some of the burden of presenting material and inducing motivation, learning activities that use the technology infrastructure outside of schools would reduce the amount of money needed for adequate levels of classroom-based technology. Such a strategy also would enable teachers to focus on students' interpretation and expressive articulation without feeling obligated to use technology in every step of the process.

Putting Distributed Learning to Work

Distributed learning involves orchestrating educational activities among classrooms, workplaces, homes, and community settings (Dede, 1996). This pedagogical strategy models for students that learning is a part of all aspects of life—not just schooling—and that people adept at learning use many types of information tools scattered throughout our everyday context. Such an educational approach can also build partnerships for learning between teachers and families, activating a powerful lever for increasing student performance.

A district that exemplifies this model of distributed learning is Union City, New Jersey. This district emphasizes integrating Internet resources into the curriculum, as well as giving students skills in authoring techniques and design principles for building World Wide Web resources. As part of the learning process, students create Web sites that provide information about various local government agencies and social service organizations, including the public housing authority, the mayor's office, and a day-care provider. The school district also sponsors a Parent University to facilitate parental involvement. Parent University's evening learning experiences in schools help families and taxpayers understand investments in educational technology as one vital part of the district's extensive educational reform process. The Parent University partnerships are reinforced by electronic newsletters, by computers in public libraries used to teach basic skills to adults, and by School Improvement Teams that give participants a voice in shaping schools' policies and innovations.

A partnership between Bell Atlantic–New Jersey and the school district has aided the district's efforts by expanding the community's telecommunications connections. Among other things, the partnership has provided students and teachers with computers at both home and school to link the two learning environments and allow communication via e-mail. In addition, technology-based instructional materials funded by the National Science Foundation that emphasize student inquiry projects in community settings also are helping educational reform in Union City. Locally developed Web-based curriculums also address the specific needs of this urban, ethnically diverse, low-income locality.

The district has dramatically improved its student learning outcomes through this model of distributed learning. Specific outcomes include significantly higher standardized test scores, improved writing and research skills, and decreased absenteeism.[1]

Even without a sophisticated infrastructure, readily accessible new media can facilitate large-scale educational innovation. People are spending lots of money on devices purchased for entertainment and information services: televisions, videotape players, computers, Web TV, videogames. Many of the underlying technologies are astonishingly powerful and inexpensive: The Nintendo 64 machine available now for a couple hundred dollars is the equivalent of a graphics supercomputer that cost several hundred thousand dollars a decade ago. What if these devices—many of them common in rich and poor homes, urban and rural areas—were also used for educational purposes? For example, videogame players are widely available in poor households and provide a sophisticated but inexpensive computational platform for learning—if we develop better content than the mindless material that constitutes most videogames. My research in virtual reality illustrates how multisensory, immersive virtual environments could be used to help students learn complex scientific concepts on computational platforms as commonplace as the videogames of the next decade.[2]

Districts can leverage their scarce resources for innovation, as well as implement more effective educational models, by using information devices outside of classrooms to create learning environments that complement school-based technology. The question remains, however: How can schools afford enough computer and telecommunications technology to sustain new models of teaching and learning and curriculum essential for systemic reform?

Finding the Dollars

In the past, money for technology improvements has come largely from special external sources: grants, community donations, bond initiatives. To be sustainable over the long run, however, resources for technology must come from reallocating existing budgets by reducing other types of expenditures. Of course, those groups whose resources are cut resist such shifts in financing, and district administrators and school boards have been reluctant to take on the political challenges of changing how money is spent. An easy way to kill educational innovations is to declare that of course they will be implemented—as long as no existing activities must be curtailed to fund new approaches.

Educational organizations are unique, however, in demanding that technology implementation be accomplished via add-on funding. Other institutions—factories, hospitals, retail outlets, and banks, for example—recognize that the power of information devices stems in part from their ability to reconfigure employee roles and organizational functioning. These establishments use the power of technology to alter their standard practices, so that the cost of computers and communications is funded by improvements in effectiveness within the organization, by doing more with less. If educators were to adopt this model—reallocating existing resources to fund technology implementation—what types of expenditures would drop so that existing funds could cover the costs of computers and communications?

Visions presented in the forthcoming 1998 ASCD yearbook (Dede and Palumbo, in press) depict how altered configurations of human resources, instructional modalities, and organizational structures could result in greater effectiveness for comparable costs—even with the acquisition of substantial school-based technology. This case is also made at greater length in Riel (1995) and in Hunter and Goldberg (1995). One specific example would involve a reordering of roles. Currently teachers all have comparable roles with similar pay structures—unlike other societal organizations, which have complementary staff roles with a mix of skill levels and salaries.

In the commercial sector, these types of institutional shifts too often result in layoffs. Because of the coming wave of retirements among educators, however, districts have a window of opportunity to accomplish structural changes without major adverse impacts on employees. As large numbers of baby boom educators leave the profession, a concurrent process of organizational restructuring could occur. Coordinating technology expenditures as an integral part of that larger framework for institutional evolution is vital as districts plan for the future. Using technology to implement new types of content and pedagogy attracts a new generation of teachers with a broad range of skills and knowledge that instructional media can complement.

Thinking Differently

Technology-based systemic reform is hard in part because our ways of thinking about implementation are often flawed. Large-scale educational innovation will never be easy, but it can be less difficult if we go beyond our implicit assumptions about teaching, learning, technology, schooling, and society. The conceptual framework of distributed learning, coupled with reconfigured budgets, is not a blueprint for universal educational improvement based on information technology—no one yet has such a recipe—but it is a vision that is affordable, generalizable, and sustainable. By balancing investments in advanced technology with investments in sophisticated curriculum, assessments, and educators—in and out of school—we can successfully prepare children for the tremendous challenges of the 21st century.

NOTES

1. Readers can view the city's Web site (www.union-city.k12.nj.us) for further information.

2. For more information, see the Web site for Project ScienceSpace (http://www.virtual.gmu.edu).

REFERENCES

Coley, R. J., J. Cradler, and P. K. Engel. (1997). *Computers and Classrooms: The Status of Technology in U.S. Schools.* Princeton, N.J.: Educational Testing Service.

Dede, C. (1996). "Emerging Technologies and Distributed Learning." *American Journal of Distance Education* 10, 2: 4–36.

Dede, C., and D. Palumbo, eds. (in press). *Learning with Technology.* The 1998 ASCD Yearbook. Alexandria, Va.: ASCD.

Edelson, D. C., R. D. Pea, and L. M. Gomez. (1996). "Constructivism in the Collaboratory." In *Constructivist Learning Environments: Case Studies in Instructional Design,* edited by B. Wilson. Englewood Cliffs, N.J.: Educational Technology Publications.

Hunter, B., and B. Goldberg. (1995). "Learning and Teaching in 2004: The BIG DIG." In *Education and Technology: Future Visions* (OTA-BP-EHR–169), edited by the Office of Technology Assessment. Washington, D.C.: U.S. Government Printing Office.

McKinsey and Company. (1995). *Connecting K–12 Schools to the Information Superhighway.* Palo Alto, Calif.: McKinsey and Company.

Riel, M. (1995). "The Future of Teaching." In *Education and Technology: Future Visions* (OTA-BP-EHR–169), edited by the Office of Technology Assessment. Washington, D.C.: U.S. Government Printing Office.

Schank, R. C., and M. Y. Jona. (1991). "Empowering the Student: New Perspectives on the Design of Teaching Systems." *The Journal of Learning Sciences* 1, 1: 7–35.

12

THE WORLD'S THE LIMIT IN THE VIRTUAL HIGH SCHOOL

Sheldon Berman, Robert Tinker

Combining high-quality instruction and current technology, net-courses in virtual high schools are uniquely able to reach specialized groups of learners—any time and any place.

○

THE INSTRUCTIONAL POTENTIAL of the Internet is extraordinary. Yet schools have hardly scratched its surface. With the assistance of a five-year U.S. Department of Education Technology Innovation Challenge Grant, the Hudson (Massachusetts) Public Schools, the Concord Consortium Educational Technology Lab, and 30 collaborating high schools across the nation have begun a bold and far-reaching experiment to realize this potential through the development of a virtual high school over the Internet. Through Internet-based courses, Virtual High School significantly enhances the curricular offerings of each school and integrates the best that technology can offer into the academic curriculum.

Virtual High School is built on a simple concept. Each school in the collaborative selects one or two innovative and technologically adept faculty members to teach over the Internet. These teachers receive training in how to teach netcourses, engage students, maximize the use of Internet-based resources, and utilize the best in multimedia technology. In exchange for releasing each teacher to teach one netcourse, the school is able to register 20 students to take netcourses offered by any of the participating schools. Because the teachers for these 20 students may be in 20 different schools, each school provides release time for a site coordinator who acts as a guidance counselor and technical advisor for students in that school who are taking netcourses.

In the future, our university and corporate partners will also offer courses, at times even for university credit. In this way, we bring the world into schools by tapping the knowledge and experience of corporations, universities, and individuals anywhere. This instructional medium is particularly effective for four types of courses.

1. Advanced courses, including advanced placement courses; advanced electives such as "Modeling and Calculus"; or advanced literature courses in any language.

2. Innovative core academic courses that maximize the use of technology, such as "Writing Through Hypertext," a simulations course on "Economics and the Budget Debate," or the "Global Lab" environmental studies course that uses online collaboration among students worldwide.

3. Courses for language minorities, so that small groups of students from a particular language background for whom individual schools are not able to offer a bilingual program can take courses in their native language.

4. Technical courses built around the very technology we are using, such as "Network Operations" and "Robotics."

In September 1997, Virtual High School teachers began offering 29 courses to more than 550 students from 27 high schools. The initial set of courses includes such titles as "Microbiology," "Model United Nations," "Informal Geometry," "Writing through Hypertext," "Business in the 21st Century," "Stellar Astronomy," "Bioethics," "Advanced Placement Statistics," "Economics and the Budget Debate," "Poetics and Poetry for Publications," "Programming in C++," and "Music Composition."

Virtual Classes, Real Benefits

Virtual High School provides four unique benefits for schools and students. First, it significantly expands curricular offerings. For example, many high schools cannot offer advanced or specialized courses because enrollment is too low to economically justify the course. Through netcourses, however, small groups of students at a number of high schools can fill these courses.

Second, it provides technology-rich instruction. Netcourses give students experience in telecollaboration and the use of software tools in the context of serious academic instruction. Netcourses provide learners with experience with e-mail, online working groups, and online conferencing. They challenge students to learn how to use the medium to communicate well, present data authoritatively, and demonstrate effective research skills.

Third, Virtual High School brings unprecedented resources to schools. Students learn how to access the wealth of data on the Internet. From exploring primary source material at the Library of Congress to accessing scientific databases to conversing with experts, students can take their learning far beyond textbooks into the real world of open-ended problems and unanswered questions.

Finally, Virtual High School significantly enhances teachers' skills in technology that can extend to their regular classroom instruction. There is probably no better way for teachers to become adept at telecollaboration and using a wide range of software tools than to make daily use of them in their instruction.

New Approaches to Instruction

Although netcourses provide unique benefits for education, they are a challenge to organize and teach. Netcourse instruction is different from regular classroom instruction and requires a particular approach to be successful. One cannot simply transfer a traditional course into the Internet environment. A number of netcourse design characteristics that match technology and quality education have emerged:

Asynchronous communication. Netcourses need to make effective use of asynchronous communication that does not require the sender and receiver to be present at the same time. These asynchronous technologies include electronic mail, conferencing, and news groups. Synchronous technologies, such as two-way voice and video, real-time chats, and shared applications, require two or more users to be present at the same time. Asynchronous communication is more adaptable to a person's schedule, works far better across time zones, and usually requires less technology.

Seminar model. Many teachers who experiment with online courses report being overwhelmed with enrollments of only 10 or 12 students because they set up e-mail conversations with each student. The better model is more like a seminar, in which the teacher determines the topic and activities, encourages substantive interactions among students, monitors and shapes the conversation, and promotes an atmosphere in which students respond to one another's work. This model results in more conversation, is far more likely to be constructivist, and builds on the rich learning that takes place in groups.

Technology-rich instruction. Access to the Internet and multimedia computing is a requirement for netcourses. Participants need to utilize all the resources of the Internet—data, images, references, current events, and expertise. Because of the general isolation that a student taking a netcourse may experience, a text-based course will not hold interest. Teachers need to use all available technology resources—including digitized images, short audio and video clips, graphics, conferencing, and multimedia presentations—to bring students in contact with one another and the reference world within the network.

Project-based learning. In addition to maximizing the use of technology to engage students, netcourses need to create forms of instruction that actively involve students. Projects that are posted for the whole class, simulations and gaming that involve the class in role-playing, and collaborative investigations are strategies that provide the kind of hands-on engagement that breaks away from the static medium of text-based communication.

Netcourses have some obvious disadvantages as well, the most significant being the lack of face-to-face communication. Interpersonal communication is far richer than electronic communication. Responses are immediate, nonverbal cues enhance communication, and group dynamics become an important part of the message.

The lack of this kind of communication, however, may serve some students well. Often in classrooms, the social dynamics of the group dictates who responds and who is acknowledged.

In the rapid-fire exchanges of the classroom, those who think the most quickly are often the most vocal. A netcourse brings freedom from these restraints. Virtual High School students enter a new social environment that does not carry their personal history into each course. It gives students the time to think through an answer and shifts attention from articulate speech to articulate writing and presentation. Netcourses offer opportunities for students to demonstrate unique abilities that they may not have been able to exhibit in the regular classroom.

Freedom from Time and Place

Netcourses have a number of built-in advantages compared to traditional courses. The asynchronous communication can be more inclusive than classroom discussions, the seminar model provides for stronger collaborations, and the full use of information technologies gives teachers and students facility in their application.

But one of the greatest advantages is that netcourses can be offered any time and any place. Thus they can reach new audiences, utilize new teachers, and tailor instruction. Homeschooled students, students who are too ill to attend school, and students who live in rural communities can have the same rich curriculum as anyone else. A netcourse faculty can easily be a worldwide team of experts, as netcourses make it feasible for far more people to share their time and knowledge with interested learners. Because netcourses have a global reach, teachers can tailor them to serve learners, from special needs students to language-minority students to students interested in a highly specialized topic. The ability to use new kinds of teachers to reach new, widely scattered and specialized audiences means that netcourses can have an impact both within the traditional structure of the high school and far beyond that structure as well.

Virtual High School can never replace the experience of being in a positive social learning environment within a school. Yet this project opens a new medium for education that can merge the best on instructional practice with the best in current technology.

WEB SITE

http://www.concord.org

13

COMPUTER TECHNOLOGY, SCIENCE EDUCATION, AND STUDENTS WITH LEARNING DISABILITIES

David Kumar, Cynthia L. Wilson[1]

Introduction

THIS PAPER WILL EXPLORE ways of improving the quality of science education for students with learning disabilities (LD) using computer technology. According to national science organizations such as the American Association for the Advancement of Science (1989), K–12 science education should benefit all students. Holahan, McFarland, and Piccillo (1994), in a summary of studies [by Gregory, Shanahan, and Walberg (1985); Ysseldyke, Thurlow, Christenson, and Weiss (1987); Harnish and Wilkinson (1989); Patton, Polloway, and Cronin (1990)] reported the following picture of science education for students with disabilities. Among high schoolers, students with disabilities scored significantly lower grades on science tests than students without disabilities. The instructional time devoted to students with mild disabilities in science was less than that in reading. About 42 percent of special education teachers had no science training and 38 percent of children in self-contained classes received no

[1] Florida Atlantic University, College of Education, 2912 College Avenue, Davie, Florida 33314.

science instruction. Less than 60 minutes per week was devoted to teaching science by half the special educators who teach science. As Holahan, et al. (1994) stated, despite calls for making science beneficial for "all," very little effort has been made to make science available to students with disabilities.

One potential tool for making science available to all students is computer technology. For example, the electronic "information super highway" is capable of bringing scientific information to the fingertips of all learners and teachers in the U.S. While these efforts are purported to be improving the quality of science education for all, they are often biased and serve only the average pupils, referred to as the "normal students." Unfortunately, very little has been done with respect to improving the quality of science education to meet the needs of students with disabilities.

Students with Learning Disabilities

In defiance of normal intellectual functioning, students with LD exhibit academic deficits that impede their progress in the general education classroom. While they have the same needs as other students, their access to creative and challenging learning opportunities often is impaired. Their deficient skills in the basic areas affect their abilities to understand and enjoy learning in the sciences. For example, these students may find it difficult to read content-area textbooks, listen and take notes in class, produce coherent written work, or take tests. Furthermore, they may lack the experiences, vocabulary, and study strategies necessary for school success. Yet most teachers rely on lectures, textbooks, and written tests as the primary means of delivering and evaluating instruction in content-area classes such as science. Even when students with LD are able to get passing grades in their general education content-area classes, such as science, they still receive lower grades than do their low-achieving peers. For example, Donahoe and Zigmond (1990) found that ninth-grade youngsters with LD received lower grades than did their low-achieving peers in the same general education social studies and health classes and 69 percent of ninth-grade students with LD earned a D or below in science.

Additionally, research has shown that LD students are generally slower in executing basic mathematics problems; this poses a deficit that could impede their progress in science (Goldman, Pellegrino, and Mertz, 1988). According to one study (Goldman *et al.*, 1988), such deficiencies, at least in mathematics, are largely due to delayed learning as opposed to developmentally different reasoning from normal students. Therefore, the skills and reasoning strategies of students with LD have been found to be largely the same as normal students', but they occur at later ages.

A large portion of the energy of students with LD is focused on the solution of simple tasks; thus, less cognitive energy is available for the development of the complex reasoning skills required in science. These same students often have low self-esteem and low motivation associated with prior frustrating learning experiences. Technological tools such as those described in this paper contain several unique features that address the aforementioned concerns.

Why Science Education for Students with Learning Disabilities?

There are two major reasons for providing science education for students with LD. The first reason is constitutional and the second pedagogical. The Americans with Disabilities Act (ADA), often referred to as the "most comprehensive civil rights legislation since the 1960s" (Stinson, 1993, p. 71), along with the Individuals with Disabilities Education Act (IDEA), give the constitutional justification for providing access to science education for all students. Therefore, it is not out of charity that students with LD be provided as solid an education as those without LD, but it is the legal right of students with LD that they must be given access to all available educational opportunities in the United States.

From a pedagogical perspective, science is a subject which is cognitive and affective in nature (Lawson, 1994; Simpson, Koballa, Oliver, and Crawley, 1994). Science is a subject quite suitable for developing thinking and problem solving skills and enhancing the affective attributes, such as better attitudes toward the world among students with disabilities. In effect, science is both hands-on and minds-on in practice. As Aldridge (1992) said, "science is needed by everyone and everyone [including those with LD] is capable of learning and enjoying science" (p. 14). However, with the existing traditional instructional practices such as lecture, teacher demonstration and rote learning, it is difficult to make science interesting and appealing to students with LD. This present condition of a lack of opportunities for involvement of students with LD in science education was obvious when Reith and Polsgrove (1994) opined that there is very little emphasis on science education in special education. On the other hand, considering the advantages of science education mentioned earlier, it is critical to search for alternative instructional tools for teaching science to students with LD. In this context, how computer technology could be used to deliver science education and make science more appealing to students with LD is worth exploring.

An examination of the literature in science education, technology education and special education revealed that scant attention was given to how computer technology could be used to deliver science education to students with LD. A search of the Educational Resource and Information Center (ERIC) database showed that there was a paucity of published studies discussing and/or presenting computer-assisted instruction as one of the effective intervention techniques for making science education a meaningful experience for students with disabilities. Therefore, other more direct sources of information were consulted for this paper.

The Role of Computer Technology

Computer technology is gaining wide acceptance in science teaching and learning. Interactive videos, hypermedia/multimedia environments, and virtual reality are replacing earlier educational computing applications like low level drill and practice software. These newer technologies have not only improved the quality of computer applications in education, but have also provided a basis for understanding human cognition and learning. Using computer environments for teaching science to students with disabilities has both cognitive and affective implications. Computer technology could provide cognitively challenging environments for the development of analytical, critical thinking, reasoning and problem solving skills in students. Also technology could provide students with interesting and motivating learning experiences that would help them to stay on task. Using computer technology, science educators and researchers can facilitate the teaching of science to students with learning disabilities through: individualizing the mode of delivery; developing expert tutors; anchoring instruction; integrating science with other subjects; reducing cognitive load on working memory; and motivating students to stay on task. Further discussion will highlight these instructional attributes of computer technology with reference to students with LD.

Individualizing the Mode of Delivery

Textual information may often not be appreciated by students with LD. In this respect, computers are ideal tools for individualizing the mode of delivery of presentation and the style of interaction (Hythecker, Rocklin, Dansereau, Lambiotte, and O'Donnel, 1985; Bristor and Drake, 1994; Lovitt and Horton, 1994). For example, in biology lessons, students may be presented with the option of choosing information in the form of text, still pictures or videos depending upon their individual level of attention and comprehension. Hypermedia software such as HyperCard (TM) and Linkway (TM) provide enormous opportunities for improving presentation modes to suit the individual needs of learners.

These computer tools have the potential for providing additional support for students when learning through the use of multimedia involving audio (e.g., pronunciation and explanation of words) and animation and video to demonstrate complex concepts. Multimedia presentations are highly visual in nature, providing step-by-step highly pictorial instruction rather than prose. Because of students' impaired learning abilities, a teacher cannot always assume students have read and understood traditional laboratory science instructions. Therefore, students with impaired reading or math skills are less disadvantaged than they might be in a traditional science curriculum. For example, in a study involving students with LD, Higgins and Boone (1990) found that those students who received hypertext-based instruction scored the highest on a daily quiz compared to those who received lecture and lecture plus hypertext-based instructions. Through the use of flexible hypertext instructional tools that emphasize simple, sequential, and pictorial instructions, teachers can be more assured that students are understanding the instructions given. In addition, students have the power to re-run, retest, or practice ideas as often as they wish, and at a time of their choosing. Individuals can work at their own pace through a lesson doing whatever level of work their learning allows.

Developing Expert Tutors

In traditional classroom settings it may be practically impossible for a teacher to give individual help or attention to students with LD. With computer technology, it is possible to develop expert tutors to provide higher cognitive level learning experiences on an individual basis. Expert tutors are known to improve student thinking and problem-solving skills to the level of the experts modeled by the tutor (Lajoie and Lesgold, 1989; Dori, Dori, and Yochim, 1992). For example, Lajoie and Lesgold (1989) described "SHERLOCK," a computer-based tutor to train Airforce trainees in troubleshooting. Novice trainees who used SHERLOCK were able to perform at a level equal to that of their colleagues with four more years of on-the-job experience.

Advantages of expert tutors for students with LD include the ability of expert tutors to present instruction in small sequential steps for problem solving, to provide variable levels of difficulty and review of concepts, and to allow students to work independently (Bos and Vaughn, 1994). However, critical to the success of expert tutors used by students with LD is the analysis of student performance and use of effective instruction (Bos and Vaughn, 1994). The program should provide the student and teacher with specific corrective feedback. For applications of expert systems for the diagnosis and treatment of learning problems please refer to Hofmeister and Lubke (1988) and van Geldern, Ferrara, Parry, and Rude (1991).

Anchoring Instruction

"Anchored instruction" is an instructional technique whereby videodiscs of real-world problem situations are used as "anchors" to provide a macro context for students to gain a meaningful understanding of the topic they learn (Cognition and Technology Group at Vanderbilt, CTGV, 1990). According to Bransford, Sherwood, Hasselbring, Kinzer, and Williams (1990), "the major goal of anchored instruction is to enable students to notice critical features of problem situations and to experience the changes in their perception and understanding of the anchor as they view the situation from new points of view" (p. 135). In this respect, the use of videodiscs helps students revisit problem situations and overcome "inert knowledge," that is the knowledge people possess but often fail to recall spontaneously for problem solving due to a lack of meaningful context (Whitehead, 1929).

The potential to provide students with an array of concrete visual representations of concepts and relationships through the use of videodiscs is particularly promising for teaching students with learning problems (Hofmeister, Engelmann, and Carnine, 1989). The images can be presented in slow motion, fast motion, or frame by frame, allowing students with LD to critically view (and review as necessary) the features of problem situations at their own learning pace. The ability to store and randomly access large amounts of information is an added advantage.

Integrating Science with Other Subjects

Computer technology is an ideal tool for removing the barriers that separate science and other disciplines such as language arts and reading. Integrating science with other disciplines has cognitive and affective implications, because integrated approaches to instruction demand the use of both the right and left brain hemispheres (Fortner, 1990). Thus, for example, students with LD are encouraged to use their linear and nonlinear metaphoric ways of thinking, leading to meaningful understanding of the concepts and principles discussed in science courses. The multiple modes of presentation of information using multimedia can help students to see any information beyond the boundaries of subject matters. Bristor and Drake (1994) reported a five-year study of integrating science and language arts in which they have employed several modes of information presentation with the aid of technology.

Science telecommunications networks provide excellent opportunities for integrating science with other disciplines. Student enthusiasm for Kids Network (a science telecommunications network) resulted in student-initiated activities of writing to other students at different lab stations, bringing in newspaper clippings, verifying data through comparison with supplemental professional data, and improved collaborative writing of reports via word-processing packages (Tinker, 1987). For students with LD, science telecommunications networks can give "expanded access to the physical and social world, bringing it closer to them—even if indirectly—to be examined as it has not been before" (Cuffaro, 1984, p. 565).

Reducing Cognitive Load on Working Memory

Students with LD experience difficulties doing mental operations involving several variables at a time. Thinking and problem solving involving more than one variable at a time is a skill necessary for survival in science at higher grade levels, and might pose a problem for students with LD due to their limited working memory. Computers have been credited with functioning like an external human memory, and are thus believed to be reducing the load on working memory in situations involving computer interactive learning and problem solving in science (Champagne and Klopfer, 1984; Kumar, White, and Helgeson, 1994a). For example, in a study of novice and expert high school chemistry students solving stoichiometric problems, Kumar, et al. (1994a) found that novice students using computers performed at a level similar to expert students using the paper-and-pencil method. In a physics problem-solving experiment Staver (1986) found that the performance level of students increased as the number of independent variables was decreased, leading one to believe that the amount of memory space required to think while solving a problem has direct consequences on the outcome. Considering this viewpoint in light of the poor working memory students with LD possess, it could be constructively argued that computers have a lot to offer in aiding their working memory via interactive computer tasks. In this context, the role of innovative input devices such as induction pen (used in pen-point computers) in reducing the human-computer interaction at the cognitive-psychology-computer-technology interface (Kumar, Helgeson, and White, 1994) should not be overlooked. Input devices like the induction pen might improve the performance of students with LD in computer interactive problem-solving tasks in science by enabling them to convey their cognitive processes better than traditional paper-and-pen methods.

Motivating Students to Stay On Task

Computers are excellent motivational tools to keep students on task. According to Jackson (1988), computer features such as immediate formative feedback to students about their performance play a significant role in motivating students to stay on task and complete their assignment. In a study, Kumar, et al. (1994a) noticed that the time-on-task for the novice chemistry problem solvers using computers was significantly higher than their counterparts using traditional paper-and-pencil methods.

Maintaining attention on learning tasks is often a problem for students with LD. Lack of attention frequently leads to impaired and frustrated learning. Teaching strategies that can encourage students with LD to remain interested and working are therefore especially beneficial. For example, students with LD often remain more cognitively engaged when using technological tools than without them, particularly when corrective feedback is immediately provided (Goldenberg, Russell, and Carter, 1984).

Summary

A few ways computer technology could be used to facilitate the teaching of science to students with LD from that of rote practice to higher level thinking have been presented in this paper. They include individualizing the mode of delivery, developing expert tutors, anchoring instruction, integrating science with other subjects, reducing cognitive load on working memory, and motivating students to stay on task. The salient features of each of these were discussed.

The instructional attributes of computer technology discussed in this paper have tremendous potential to improve the cognitive and affective aspects of science education for students with LD. Authoring systems and multimedia permit teachers and students to prepare individualized lessons and examinations. The capabilities for individualizing instruction using technology can lead not only to engaged learning but also to more meaningful knowledge acquisition (Songer, 1989; Tinker, 1987). Expert systems and anchored instruction provide opportunities for simulations that emphasize problem-solving abilities and the development of knowledge. Application systems such as word processing and database management are ideal for the integration of science with other disciplines and allow students to be active planners and communicators. Learning environments containing multiple sources of information and multiple viewpoints can be provided for student exploration and integration into a personal construction of meaning. In effect, active participation of students with LD in science using technology exposes them to meaningful learning and enables them to appreciate science, and could result in more students with LD making science a possible career choice.

Additionally, computer-enhanced classrooms could lead to greater teacher innovation and more positive interactions between students with LD and science teachers. Teachers may find themselves spending more time encouraging individual students rather than lecturing or providing all the information themselves. The role of the teacher may change from provider of all information to that of an "idea coach" (Songer, 1989, p. 38). Teacher education programs must provide teacher candidates with experiences in teaching science to students with LD by using technology (Egelston-Dodd, 1995).

If science education is for all students, then it is necessary to devise strategies for involving students with LD in science. As discussed in this paper, computer technology provides a powerful tool for getting students with LD actively engaged in learning science. Technology can be used to engage students with learning disabilities in meaningful learning instead of rote practice with discreet scientific concepts. Technologies provide students with mechanisms for accessing data and understanding complex problems, or with opportunities for dialogue and discussion. Once they are adept at using technology, students have quick access to multiple resources and tools for combining those resources. They can spend less time looking for answers and information, and more time analyzing, reflecting and developing an understanding.

There is a lack of attention in the research, development and implementation of technology to teaching science to students with LD (Egelston-Dodd, 1995). Science educators, special educators and technology educators should make collaborative efforts to develop innovative computer technology tools for making science both cognitively and affectively appealing to students with LD. More research and development efforts are needed to accomplish this task with a genuine concern for making science instruction available to students with LD.

REFERENCES

Aldridge, B. G. (1992). Project on Scope, Sequence, and Coordination: A synthesis for improving science education. *Journal of Science Education and Technology,* 1(1), 13–21.

American Association for the Advancement of Science. (1989). *Science for all Americans: A project 2061 report on literacy goals in science, mathematics, and technology.* Washington, DC.

Bos, C. S., and Vaughn, S. (1994). *Strategies for teaching students with learning and behavioral problems (3rd ed.).* Allyn and Bacon. Boston, Massachusetts.

Bransford, J. D., Sherwood, R. D., Hasselbring, T. S., Kinzer, C. K., and Williams, S. M. (1990). Anchored instruction: Why we need it and how technology can help. In Nix, D., and Spiro, R. (eds.), *Cognition, education, and multimedia.* Lawrence Erlbaum. Hillsdale, New Jersey.

Bristor, V. J., and Drake, S. V. (1994). Linking the language arts and content areas through visual technology. *Technological Horizons in Education Journal,* 22(2), 74–77.

Champagne, A. B., and Klopfer, L. E. (1984). Research in science education: Cognitive psychology perspective. In D. Holdzkom and P. B. Lutz (Eds.), *Research within reach: Science education.* National Science Teachers Association. Washington, DC.

Cognition and Technology Group at Vanderbilt. (1990). Anchored instruction and its relationship to situated cognition. *Educational Researcher,* 19(6), 2–10.

Cuffaro, H. K. (1984). Microcomputers in education: Why is earlier better? *Teachers College Record,* 85(65), 559–568.

Donahoe, K., and Zigmond, N. (1990). Academic grades of ninth-grade urban learning disabled students and low-achieving peers. *Exceptionality,* 1, 17–27.

Dori, Y. J., Dori, D., and Yochim, J. E. (1992). Characteristics of an intelligent computer-assisted instruction shell with an example in human physiology. *Journal of Computers in Mathematics and Science Teaching,* 11(3/4), 289–302.

Egelston-Dodd, J. (1995). *Proceedings. Working Conference on science for persons with disabilities.* University of Northern Iowa. Cedar Falls, Iowa.

Fortner, R. W. (1990). How to combine language arts and science in the classroom. *Science Activities,* 27(4), 34–37.

Goldenberg, E., Russell, S., and Carter, C. (1984). *Computers, education and special needs.* Addison-Wesley. Reading, Massachusetts.

Goldman, S., Pellegrino, J., and Mertz, D. (1988). Extended practice of basic addition facts: Strategy changes in learning-disabled students. *Cognition and Instruction,* 5(3), 223–265.

Gregory, J., Shanahan, T., and Walberg, H. (1985). Learning disabled 10th graders in mainstreaming settings: A descriptive analysis. *Remedial and Special Education,* 6(4), 25–33.

Harnisch, D., and Wilkinson, I. (1989). *Cognitive return of schooling for the handicapped: Preliminary findings from high school and beyond.* Paper presented at the Annual Meeting of the American Educational Research Association, San Francisco.

Higgins, K., and Boone, R. (1990). Hypertext computer study guides and the social studies achievement of students with learning disabilities, remedial students, and general education students. *Journal of Learning Disabilities,* 23, 529–540.

Hofmeister, A. M., Engelmann, S., and Carnine, D. (1989). Developing and validating science education videodiscs. *Journal of Research in Science Teaching,* 26, 665–677.

Hofmeister, A. M., and Lubke, M. M. (1988). Expert systems: Implications for the diagnosis and treatment of learning disabilities. *Learning Disabilities Quarterly,* 11, 287–291.

Holahan, G., McFarland, J., and Piccillo, B. A. (1994). Elementary school science for students with disabilities. *Remedial and Special Education,* 15(2), 86–93.

Hythecker, V., Rocklin, T., Danseraeu, D., Lambiotte, J., and O'Donnel, A. (1985). A computer-based learning strategy training module: Development and evaluation. *Journal of Educational Computing Research,* 1, 275–283.

Jackson, B. (1988). A comparison between computer-based and traditional assessment tests, and their effects on pupil learning and scoring. *School Science Review,* 96(249), 809–815.

Kumar, D. D., White, A. L., and Helgeson, S. L. (1994a). A study of the effect of HyperCard and pen-paper performance assessment methods on expert-novice chemistry problem solving. *Journal of Science Education and Technology,* 3(3), 187–200.

Kumar, D. D., Helgeson, S. L., and White, A. L. (1994). Computer technology-cognitive psychology interface and science performance assessment. *Educational Technology Research and Development,* 42(4), 6–16.

LaJoie, S. P., and Lesgold, A. (1989). Apprenticeship training in the workplace: Computer-coached practice environment as a new form of apprenticeship. *Machine-Mediated Learning,* 3, 7–28.

Lawson, A. E. (1994). Research on the acquisition of science knowledge: Epistemological foundations of cognition. In Gabel, D. (ed.), *Handbook of research on science teaching and learning*. Macmillan Publishing Company, 131–176. New York.

Lovitt, T. C., and Horton, S. V. (1994). Strategies for adapting science textbooks for youth with learning disabilities. *Remedial and Special Education, 15*(2), 105–116.

Patton, J., Polloway, E., and Cronin, M. (1990). *A survey of special education teachers relative to science for the handicapped.* Unpublished manuscript, University of Hawaii, Honolulu.

Reith, H. J., and Polsgrove, L. (1994). Curriculum and instructional issues in teaching secondary students with learning disabilities. *Learning Disabilities Research and Practice, 9*(2), 118–126.

Simpson, R. D., Koballa, Jr., T. R., Oliver, J. S., and Crawley, III, F. E. (1994). Research on the affective dimension of science learning. In Gabel, D. (ed.), *Handbook of research on science teaching and learning*. Macmillan Publishing Company, 211–234. New York.

Songer, N. B. (1989). Technological tools for scientific thinking and discovery. *Reading, Writing, and Learning Disabilities, 5*, 23–41.

Staver, J. R. (1986). The effects of problem format, number of independent variables, and their interaction on student performance on a control of variables reasoning problem. *Journal of Research in Science Teaching, 23*(6), 533–542.

Stinson, B. (1993). Getting started with adaptive technology: Meeting the needs of disabled students. *Florida Technology in Education Quarterly, 6*(1), 71–76.

Tinker, R. (1987). In our view: Real science education. *Hands On!* 10(1), 2. (Technical Education Research Centers, Cambridge, Massachusetts).

van Geldern, L., Ferrara, J. M., Parry, J. D., and Rude, H. (1991). Local validation of mandate consultant: An expert system for assuring compliance in the IEP process. *Journal of Special Education Technology, 11*, 113–120.

Whitehead, A. N. (1929). *The aims of education.* Macmillan Publishing Company. New York.

Ysseldyke, J., Thurlow, M., Christenson, S., and Weiss, J. (1987). Time allocated to instruction of mentally retarded, learning disabled, emotionally disturbed and nonhandicapped elementary students. *The Journal of Special Education, 21*, 23–42.

14

THE COMPUTER DOESN'T
EMBARRASS ME

Ted S. Hasselbring, Laura Goin, Rose Taylor,
Brian Bottge, Patrick Daley

FOR ADOLESCENTS WHO STRUGGLE to read and write, being chosen to read aloud in class can be a wrenching experience.

> If I thought the teacher was going to call on me to read, my heart would start pounding real hard. I kept saying to myself, "Don't call on me, don't call on me." It could be cold in the classroom, but I'd be sweating all over. Then if she called on me, I always came up with some good excuse to get out of reading, like, "I've got a headache," or "My eyes are bothering me and I can't see the words."

Thanks to a joint effort between the Orange County, Florida, schools and Peabody College of Vanderbilt University, middle school students like this young man are improving their reading and writing skills in more than 120 classrooms. Recognizing that many students entering middle school could not read and write at even basic levels, administrators and teachers launched the Orange County Literacy Project. The project combines the benefits of computer technology, sound principles of literacy instruction, an accommodating schedule, and small class sizes to help students develop the skills and confidence they need to be successful in content area classes.

A New Approach to Literacy Instruction

For many Orange County students, the inability to read and write resulted in embarrassment, defiance, truancy—and failure. For these learners, common classroom activities simply compounded feelings of shame. One student recalls how he tried to be the last person to read because he hoped class would end before his turn came. Unfortunately, as he put it, "my last name began with an 'A' and so I was often picked first." Other adolescents who could not understand what they read reported skipping school because they did not consider it to be of much use to them.

Teachers and administrators realized they needed a new approach to literacy instruction to help growing numbers of young people with serious reading and writing difficulties. These learners, both native and non-native speakers of English, did not qualify for special education services. Many of the students had low self-esteem, poor school attendance, and serious discipline problems. In an ambitious response to these needs, three middle school classrooms piloted the Orange County Literacy Project during the 1994–95 school year. The program grew to 13 classes the following year, and it was implemented districtwide last year.

Although each school used slightly different approaches in the experimental program, all schools built their efforts on several key elements. First, for students identified as having serious reading and writing difficulties, schools allocated two-hour time blocks for daily literacy instruction. No more than 20 students were scheduled into a classroom during this block of time. Second, the teachers selected for these classes knew how to teach literacy and were committed to teaching students in the program. Third, teachers based their instruction on two complementary approaches to developing literacy: (1) The Peabody Learning Lab, a computer-based program in which a virtual tutor guides students through a series of skill-development activities in reading, spelling, and writing (CTGV, 1994), and (2) the Literacy Workshop (Allen, 1995), a method of teaching that encourages students in reading, writing, speaking, and listening. Finally, each participating classroom was supplied with five computers capable of running the Learning Lab software, and all teachers participated in more than a week of professional development for the literacy project.

Peabody Learning Lab

In a central feature of the program, students participate in daily literacy instruction with the multimedia Peabody Learning Lab software. The Learning Lab uses video to provide a meaningful context for learning content and applying important literacy skills. The software is designed to improve the word recognition, reading comprehension, and spelling skills of middle-level students. Melvin, an animated tutor, leads learners through instructional activities in a virtual laboratory, and he supports them throughout the program.

As the middle schoolers work on the computer each day for 20–30 minutes, Melvin guides them through the reading lab, the word lab, and the spelling lab. Each time students enter the reading lab, they watch a segment of a video and then read a passage about it. The video gives students some background for their upcoming reading and provides a mental model of the text passage. After students view the video, Melvin instructs them to read a related text passage. Melvin provides individualized help on an as-needed basis. If they need help, students can ask Melvin to read the passage slowly (word by word) or fluently (sentence by sentence) to them. Or if students attempt to read the passage themselves, they can get help from Melvin by clicking on individual words for the pronunciation or definition.

After reading the text passage several times, students move on to the word lab. The words presented in this lab are taken from the reading passage. Melvin asks students which words they can read without help. Melvin puts a short list of words on the board, and as quickly as possible students click on the word that Melvin pronounces. The computer records accuracy and speed. In all three labs, the computer keeps track of individual assessment and performance data. When the assessment is complete, Melvin lists the words that the student needs to practice and begins a series of interactive exercises to help the student become fluent in decoding and recognizing these words.

Finally, students proceed to the spelling lab, where they spell words that were presented in the reading and word labs. Following a pretest, Melvin pronounces each word, uses it in a sentence, breaks it into parts, and then pronounces it again. Melvin then asks students to type the word. During each attempt at spelling the word, Melvin analyzes a student's spelling and, if incorrect, provides specific corrective feedback to the student. Students must correct their errors to continue. Following the initial instruction, learners do additional guided practice to develop spelling fluency. Students see a graph of their results after each session.

Once students have mastered the words from the original reading passage in the word and spelling labs, they engage in comprehension activities back in the reading lab. The first activity presents three passages similar to the one that had accompanied the video. Only one of the passages accurately describes the video segment. Students must read the passages and select the appropriate one. The last activity is a cloze exercise in which students must fill in missing words that have been deleted from the comprehension passage.

In addition to their work on the computer, students participate in other literacy activities. Janet Allen describes some of these instructional approaches, designed to motivate reluctant secondary students to become active readers and writers, in her book *It's Never Too Late* (1995). Allen contends that by the time students with reading and writing difficulties reach middle school, they are so used to meaningless exercises that they no longer have any interest in print.

Much of Allen's approach to reading instruction for middle school learners centers on literacy exploration, motivation, and self-esteem. She asserts that students must learn to love reading to become readers. The Orange County Literacy Project introduces students to many forms of literature, uses techniques including books-on-tape and guided reading, and encourages students to select their own reading.

Measures of Success

The data collected during the first two years of the pilot study included measures of reading achievement, overall school achievement, and student attitudes and behaviors. The average scores of the 376 students on the vocabulary and reading comprehension subtests of the Stanford Diagnostic Reading Test improved significantly over the course of the program. Students also made significant gains on the Culture-Free Self-Esteem Inventory and the Test of Written Spelling. And their school attendance and grade point averages improved. The number of disciplinary referrals continued to grow, but close inspection of the records revealed that this trend was due to a few students with chronic misbehavior problems.

As pleased as we were by the statistical data, it was the comments of students and their families that led us to believe that the program should continue. We interviewed 24 participating students about their reading problems and their attitudes toward school. More than half of the students made comments like, "My reading and study habits have improved" and "I no longer fear or dislike reading." Many of the students addressed their feelings of avoidance and shame about their reading problems. For example, one boy said, "I don't have to avoid being called on anymore. I can work all the time without being criticized." Other students gave high marks to their teachers: "My teacher makes sure that each student learns words. She has high expectations for me."

The middle schoolers also discussed how the Peabody Learning Lab had helped them read and spell better. One young man wrote an entire page about his experience. Other students commented on how the software had affected their self-esteem: "The computer corrects me without making me feel ashamed." "Students don't pick on me anymore." "I will succeed."

In our telephone interviews with the families of 19 participating students, many parents described improvements in the behavior and attitudes of their children. They indicated that their children read more, were happier about school, earned better grades, and did not get into as much trouble. Several families also reported that students had begun to read to their younger brothers and sisters.

Critical Factors

One of the most serious problems in teaching reading to students from disadvantaged backgrounds is their lack of compatible prior knowledge and experience. Students without this rich base find it exceedingly difficult, if not impossible, to attach meaning to what they read. The Learning Lab supplied some of this experience through the videos displayed in the software. Because reading passages, word recognition practice, and spelling exercises were all based on a common frame of reference provided by the videos, students quickly found meaning in their reading.

Reduced class size was another important factor of our success. We are quick to point out, however, that smaller classes do not automatically lead to higher achievement. Our teachers knew how to take advantage of smaller class sizes by structuring learning activities that offered students the greatest amount of individual attention.

Vital to the success of the program was the belief that all students could make significant gains in reading and writing. This belief guided practice. First, classroom teachers—and Melvin—gave students individual attention and high-quality instruction. This instruction communicated to the middle schoolers that they were important and capable of improving their reading and writing skills. Teachers made frequent home contacts and encouraged families to initiate communication. Second, the administration supported the program by providing time for staff development, necessary software and computers, and reduced class sizes. Finally, staff from the school district and Vanderbilt University collaborated to design and carry out a program based on the effective use of technology and a solid foundation of literacy research.

Shame to Pride

We tend to underestimate the shame and embarrassment that older students feel about their reading and writing difficulties. Often, these feelings are masked by any number of discipline problems. The Orange County Literacy Project gave students the opportunity to improve their skills in a risk-free environment. Students knew that Melvin would not criticize or make fun of their responses. The combination of talented teaching and well-designed software helped students improve their skills and strengthen their fragile self-concepts. As one student put it, "I don't mind reading now because the computer doesn't embarrass me."

REFERENCES

Allen, J. (1995). *It's Never Too Late: Leading Adolescents to Lifelong Literacy.* Portsmouth, N.H.: Heinemann.

Cognition and Technology Group at Vanderbilt University (1994). Multimedia environments for developing literacy in at-risk students. In B. Means (Ed.), *Technology and Education Reform* (pp. 23–56). San Francisco, Calif.: Jossey-Bass.

WEB SITE

http://www.peabody.vanderbilt.edu/ctrs/ltc

15

DIGITAL LITERACY

Paul Gilster

Literacy for the Internet Age

THE GREAT PHYSICIST Ernest Rutherford, frustrated by the self-important airs of his peers, once told a colleague that a scientist who couldn't explain his theories to a barmaid didn't really understand them. An idea, in other words, should correspond to a recognizable reality, explainable to an audience larger than a handful of specialists. Digital literacy—the ability to access networked computer resources and use them—is such a concept. It is necessary knowledge because the Internet has grown from a scientist's tool to a worldwide publishing and research medium open to anyone with a computer and modem.

Digital literacy is the ability to understand and use information in multiple formats from a wide range of sources when it is presented via computers. The concept of literacy goes beyond simply being able to read; it has always meant the ability to read with meaning, and to understand. It is the fundamental act of cognition. Digital literacy likewise extends the boundaries of definition. It is cognition of what you see on the computer screen when you use the networked medium. It places demands upon you that were always present, though less visible, in the analog media of newspaper and TV. At the same time, it conjures up a new set of challenges that require you to approach networked computers without preconceptions. Not only must you acquire the skill of finding things, you must also acquire the ability to use these things in your life.

The skills of the digitally literate are becoming as necessary as a driver's license. The Internet is the fastest growing medium in history—like it or not, it will affect you and those around you at home and on the job, from the merging of your television set's images with network data to the emergence of communities of users whose activities will change the shape of commerce and education. The Net's growing universality will create priceless resources for learning and self-advancement. If these won't overwhelm your life overnight, they will change it, subtly, continually, and with irresistible force.

Acquiring digital literacy for Internet use involves mastering a set of core competencies. The most essential of these is the ability to make informed judgments about what you find on-line, for unlike conventional media, much of the Net is unfiltered by editors and open to the contributions of all. This art of critical thinking governs how you use what you find on-line, for with the tools of electronic publishing dispersed globally, the Net is a study in the myriad uses of rhetoric. Forming a balanced assessment by distinguishing between content and its presentation is the key.

Other competencies branch inevitably from your ability to think critically. You will have to target your reading using the model of the electronic word—hypertext and its cousin hypermedia, the linking of the individual noun or phrase to supporting text or other forms of media. Sequential reading is supported by nonlinear jumps to alternative idea caches, with inevitable repercussions for comprehension. The journey through text becomes enriched with choices. Consequently, you need to learn how to assemble this knowledge, that is, build a reliable information horde from diverse sources. You must choose an environment within which to work and customize it with Internet tools.

And because the journey through text is flush with choices, developing search skills is the final core competency; it engages you in strategies for using the rapidly proliferating search engines that can hunt through millions of pages of information as you watch, returning a list of targets for your consideration. With the help of these researchers, you can learn how to learn anew; widen an education, support a career change, join a community of like-minded individuals in pursuit of a hobby or an idea. How to pursue is the ultimate issue. Ungoverned and perhaps ungovernable, the Internet's vast holdings catalyze your thinking only if you master the primary skills of the digitally literate searcher.

Today these skills are an adjunct to our normal lives, for the novelty of networking is a long way from wearing off. But the powerful changes in media now occurring throughout the planet argue for a future in which digital literacy is essential. Internet access has been broadened from the original research laboratories that built it to universities worldwide and now to the modem-using public, a public that is signing up for accounts in the millions. On-line services like CompuServe and America Online are acknowledging the Internet's power through their own gateways to the Net. Cable television companies are developing modems that will let them deliver digital data through the cables that already run into your house, while telephone companies and content providers are merging in an effort to pump everything from movies to video games to educational programming through an Internet-enhanced telephone wire.

Content Evaluation

When is a globe-spanning information network dangerous? When people make too many assumptions about what they find on it. For while the Internet offers myriad opportunities for learning, an unconsidered view of its contents can be misleading and deceptive. This is why critical thinking about content is the Internet competency upon which all others are founded. You cannot work comfortably within this medium until you have established methods for judging the reliability of Web pages, newsgroup postings, and mailing lists, a task complicated by the nature of the international data flow.

Consider this story, discussed recently at an awards dinner for the American Association for Forensic Science. A man reportedly jumped from the tenth floor of a building, but before hitting the ground he was killed by a shotgun blast fired out a ninth floor window. The shooter on the ninth floor was a man threatening his wife with the shotgun—which he believed to be unloaded. But in fact the gun had been loaded six months earlier by the man's son, angry at his disinheritance by his mother and intending to trick his father into killing his mother with it. When his plan failed, he decided to commit suicide by jumping from the tenth floor, but was thus killed by the very gun he had loaded.

Sound unbelievable? Nevertheless, this story was widely propagated on the Internet newsgroups.[1] From an initial posting on the Internet, at a time and place now lost, the tale gained a life of its own. Credibility grew as it echoed around the world by e-mail and newsgroup. Newspapers picked up on the plot; in fact, I first ran across it in my local paper, *The News & Observer,* here in Raleigh. Thousands of people accepted this myth as reality. The truth is that the past president of the American Academy of Forensic Sciences made up the story as part of a speech he gave in 1987.

I relate this story to illustrate the power of electronic networking. If even a small percentage of the people who read this account assumed it was true, they could use the Net to circulate it. One convincing poster could cause a ripple effect as other people read and accepted his or her conclusions uncritically. People are remarkably malleable; they tend to believe what they are told by whatever medium they're accessing, presumably out of their implicit trust in the editorial function of editors and news organizations. Unfortunately, because the Internet lacks such editorial functions, its decentralization makes the idea of news "organization" in the on-line sense a dubious proposition, as Pierre Salinger ought to have known.

This is not to say that there are no reputable news sites on the Internet; in fact, the number of trustworthy sources for everything from world affairs to financial analysis and political commentary is growing daily. But we must come to terms with the fact that for every *Wall Street Journal* and *New York Times* on the Net, there are thousands of individuals who have the opportunity to publish with impunity and certainly without editorial scrutiny. The Net is a straight shot for anyone to use sophisticated (and often free) software as a conduit of content. This puts the onus upon the reader to develop the critical skills necessary to evaluate such materials.

Separating Form from Content

Much of the Internet's spin on information is deceptively enticing. For while the World Wide Web has opened numerous doors for the providers of content, multimedia has also put the digitally illiterate user at a disadvantage. When image becomes substance, and the picture all too often substitutes for the thousand words that would more accurately describe an event or an idea, the audience is in danger of being misled. Dress up a bogus story with professional-looking fonts and photographs, blend in a snippet of audio or video, and you lend your tale a verisimilitude that it may not in fact possess.

Let's say you read an article in *Fortune* or *Investor's Business Daily* about a hot stock prospect. Chances are you'd give it some credence. But what if you saw the same tip reported in a cheaply printed flyer delivered through the mail or posted on a bulletin board at your grocery store? The same information is available in each, but we view the content differently based on presentation. Assumptions thus become an inseparable part of how we read. We must track this tendency as we explore the Internet, for — on the World Wide Web in particular — implied content can be deceptive. One of the challenges of Internet publishing is that it turns our conventional expectations, built upon years of experience with newspapers and magazines, on their head. We can no longer assume that the appearance of a publication is necessarily relevant to the quality of its information.

For instance, I can create a handsome Web page with a little study of the nondemanding HTML language and a variety of freeware editors that allow me to create content on the fly. I have seen Web pages that rival those of the most experienced developers implemented by one-person offices with a determination to use the Internet for commerce. Extremists defend everything from the Oklahoma City bombing to the Holocaust on finely tuned Web pages. Simply put, the Internet demands that our judgments about content be affected less by appearance than by our ability to evaluate and verify what we see. The diversity of Web content and its ability to be linked to other information sources provides us with unique challenges in this regard, but fortunately it also furnishes us with the set of digital tools we need to solve the problem.

Ironically, the same issue is raised *in reverse* with text-based network resources. For most of its life, the Net has been a carrier of textual information; until recently, what you saw on the screen was simple ASCII code, unadorned with pictures and incapable of carrying the professional-looking format of Web pages. Straight text is a transparent carrier; alike for all concepts, it fades behind the idea, yielding to the force of the thing expressed. For these reasons, text seems to be both more honest and thus safer than multimedia.

But the problem of perception remains. While text flattens the reading space so that content can be evaluated for what it is, the written word is nonetheless composed of a limited number of symbols. When imposed on a screen's glowing phosphors, text loses the subtle cues that give us indications about how much work went into the job of publishing, and hence how seriously the publisher took his or her mission. These are judgments we make as a matter of course with printed materials; without them, we must acquire the critical skills that allow us to question attribution, authority, and references.

The modern Internet, design-rich, performs the same feat. Make multimedia ubiquitous and you flatten the perspective by enabling anyone to create a richly developed context for his or her work. Thus a willingness to challenge ideas must prevail, a deliberate and thoughtful effort to separate form from content to consider the clockwork of meaning within.

Any teacher who has used the Internet in a classroom setting can tell you how troubling it is to see children taking World Wide Web pages at face value, without the evaluative skills to place them in context. In that sense, the Internet can, in the wrong hands, become a tool of propaganda. You could consider the Internet as a wire service, at least on a superficial level. The amount of content it offers is remarkable, so that hunting through it in search of particular information requires the same kind of filtering on the part of the individual that news organizations provide on a professional level. But—and this is a big but—unlike a wire service, its content has not been chosen by professionals who can distance themselves from the motives of the creators of the news. The Internet is like a raw data stream, an open microphone for every interest group, corporation, fan club, professional organization, or fanatic that wants to use it. And if you've ever been near a karaoke club, you know how painful an open microphone can be.

Hyperlinks: Guidance or Manipulation?

Hyperlinks are shown through underlining and color changes; most browsers highlight the links to related content in blue. The reader sees text with certain elements clearly labeled as significant; these are the ones to which the eye is drawn, while other words and phrases lose emphasis because they are not selected for linkage. In a similar fashion, a newspaper can, by its choice of subheads and placement of stories on a page, determine your perception of the importance of a particular news item. It's important to keep this framework in mind as you read. Appropriate questions to ask of all Web content are: What should I be seeing here that I am not? Is there another side to this issue that's not being presented?

I could, for example, present the news about China in entirely different ways than Asia Inc. Imagine a portion of my earlier paragraph, now set up as a hyperlinked Web page: "Other media sources—CNN, The Economist, The New York Times—tell me that among the Asian mergers and acquisitions, tensions have yet to be resolved about China's relationship with the United States, particularly as it relates to the infringement of intellectual rights covering CDs and computer software. That subtext bubbles fitfully beneath the surface chatter about economic growth, affecting other stocks I own, like Boeing, whose sales in China are hurt by political uncertainty. Taiwan continues to be an issue: Would China dare invade the island? Nor is T'ienanmen Square a distant memory, leaving me to wonder in whose hands I'm putting so much of my capital. And what about the sweatshops, where women and even young children are exploited for the sake of cheap exports?"

This paragraph acts as a set of pointers, but the choice of hyperlinks (shown by underlining) says everything about my viewpoint. If you wanted to learn more about the broad term *sweatshops,* for example, you could put your cursor over it in this hypothetical hypertext document, clicking to be whisked to, perhaps, a news account of abuses in a textile factory. A click on T'ienanmen Square might take you to a video about the brutal crackdown that ended (temporarily, at least) the democracy movement in China, while my link to CNN might provide a less than flattering story about censorship in that country. Clearly, a page constructed with these kind of links is making a different rhetorical statement about China's economy than one like Asia Inc.'s, which is filled with hyperlinks to stock market tables and corporate profiles. Both appear to forge necessary connections to the background information supporting their particular positions; both leave out links to information that calls that position into doubt.

The point is, your view of hypertext should be considerably different from your experience of the printed page. When you read text in a book or newspaper, the only visual emphasis is the occasional use of bold or italics, or the clear marking of a chapter head. Good writing rarely requires additional emphasis; it should present its ideas in such a way that the reader understands where the weight of the paragraph falls, and knows how to interpret the focus of a sentence. Accenting these things with too promiscuous a use of italics and bolding is thus a kind of copout, an easy way to make points without building the requisite rhetorical skills.

Hypertext puts emphasis back into the text by turning certain words and phrases blue and underlining them. These emphases are determined by a programmer with a hypertext editor who creates hyperlinks in specific places. Thus we see hypertext emerging as a new kind of rhetorical tool. Rhetoric considers the question of how to use media to influence the judgment or the emotions of the intended audience. Style is part of this, as is design. Whenever we decide where we want to place a particular image on a World Wide Web page, we're engaging in a rhetorical exercise, speculating about the image's impact on the reader who is viewing that page. Whenever we choose the links that we deem significant enough to bear linkages, we make a similar judgment. Hence, rhetoric, being about persuasion, can succeed through means fair and foul; we can consider how to move an audience by appealing directly to their worst instincts, or we can shape an argument around principles of truth seeking.

Read through a typical home page and you will be taken along a route that has been determined for you by that page's creator. The question about hypertext that people fail to ask is, who creates the hyperlinks? Their very presence signals which ideas are important and which, by being unlinked, are not. The critical reader must note which is which, and ask whether these choices are authoritative or arbitrary. A range of possible actions exists for making such determinations, but the point is that hypertext as a reading medium is unusually sensitive to manipulation. It's far too easy for a page designer to neglect a key objection to a particular point simply by not hyperlinking anything to it; the alternative viewpoint is therefore never seen. For the unwary reader, the experience of reading hypertext is all too often a search for the next hyperlink and a quick exit.

A key component of digital literacy, then, is wariness. Sequential reading allows an author to build an argument, buttressing the case with examples and taking advantage of the arts of persuasion. Hypertextual reading puts the rhetorical arts into an odd tension; the reader, rather than the author, is the one who charts a course through the document. This being the case, the author of hypertext has to consider which routes the reader will be allowed to take. In doing so, he or she can lay out an argument through the omission or addition of particular items that support the point being made. If I create a hypertextual document about the Holocaust in which every link points to a site that supports people who think it never happened, I am creating a phony information path, but one that, by the number of its links to outside sources, looks authoritative. Blithely ignoring the testimony of survivors, of the soldiers who entered the concentration camps after their liberation, of the jurists at Nuremberg, I can show you only the dubious "scholarship" of those who deny that these events ever happened.

Knowledge Assembly

In the dark days of the Iran hostage crisis in 1979–1980, I often turned to shortwave radio for information. As the presidential election neared, U.S. networks were reporting that a deal was in the works to free the hostages in time to save the flagging Carter campaign. I tuned my receiver to Radio Tehran to see if the Iranian position was softening, only to find that the deal, if indeed it was pending, was well concealed. The stream of propaganda continued unabated, mixed with martial calls to continue the revolution. And sure enough, the hostages weren't released until the day Carter left office.

Good information gathering is often a balancing act. In this case, Radio Tehran, a less than reliable source, provided an antidote to the usually more accurate Western media. But Tehran's declarations of victory over the United States, in turn, needed balancing by the Voice of America, which itself needed balancing by the BBC, an excellent news source, but one that, during the Falklands War in 1982, needed balancing from Radio Argentina Exterior, and so on. Even in those days, history had already become a multimedia exercise. All these radio stations could be checked against print sources like *The Washington Post* or *The New York Times*— the former balanced politically by *The Washington Times,* the latter by other dissident voices on the right, like the *National Review*. Television could bring photographs and live video of the drama, which could be explicated at length in feature articles and editorials. It's fascinating to speculate on how the Internet would have covered the hostage story.

We can view the Internet as yet another source in the ever rising torrent of journalistic chatter, or we can see it as a necessary filter that helps us get to the underlying issues. Used properly, networked information possesses unique advantages. It is searchable, so that a given issue can be dissected with a scalpel's precision, laid open to reveal its inner workings. It can be customized to reflect our particular needs. Moreover, its hypertextual nature connects with other information sources, allowing us to listen to opposing points of view and make informed decisions about their validity.

And its data sources are remarkably broad. The increasingly convergent nature of the Net provides access to archives from the world of broadcast media, such as databases of radio shows and, soon, television news reports, which we will be able to search for using keywords and replay as needed. Newspaper accounts can be read on-line and weighed against previous articles on the subject stored in the site's archives. Discussions by people directly affected by events can be monitored on the newsgroups and mailing lists. Meanwhile, customizable datafeeds allow us to target a particular story and receive daily updates about its progress. Using these tools and evaluating the results is a process I call *knowledge assembly*.

Agents and Intelligence

While the ability to search will remain a key Internet competency, how you run the search will change. Imagine you are tracking the ongoing hunt for peace in the Middle East. As you compose words on-screen, a software "agent" is active on the Internet examining Web sites. Having made multiple sweeps through the various search engines, the agent knows to look only for sites that have gone on-line since your last foray on the Net. Targeting these, it looks for select keywords, basing its search pattern not only on the terms you give it—say, "israel," "arafat," "palestine"—but also on words that have appeared frequently on sites to which you keep returning. The document you're composing in your word processor may suggest keywords as you compose your argument, for the agent can scan relevant materials looking for patterns in your writing. Perhaps you'll leave the agent out on the Net when you stop work for the day. Unlike you, the agent can keep searching all night long to monitor developments; you can review its results over your morning coffee.

An agent like this automates the search process; it's a digital tool that can locate information, bring it back, sort and catalog it, and even assist in your analysis. But more significantly, software agents of the sort now being contemplated will "learn" from their experience. Detecting patterns in your work, themes that interest you, or concepts to which you return, the agent will adapt by strengthening its searching on those parameters, while abandoning less productive channels of inquiry. Theoretically, a good agent should be able to track down things you may not have realized you needed. In doing so, the agent has analyzed what you do (as opposed to what you think you do), and has sculpted its search strategy accordingly.

Already we've examined the earliest examples of agents, tools that in their various ways attempt to customize our search operations. Many of the search engines now available allow customized searching or generate personal news pages, while services like PointCast or NewsPage allow us to set up filters against which their database is run. The true agent, however, is more personal still; in the future, it will reside on our machines, becoming one of the essential software tools that link us to the Net. Ultimately, it becomes the hinge that connects our various applications, binding the information in word processor files to database records and Net-based research sites. Agents reflect a changing relationship between individual and machine. The computer has been successful insofar as it has allowed us to commit intensive tasks, particularly in terms of number crunching, to its processors. Tomorrow's desktop machine will be powerful enough to reproduce human behaviors, using heuristic algorithms to mimic our intellectual habits and research patterns. While content verification will remain the domain of the researcher, content exploration will increasingly be managed by digital means. This expansion of computer power grows by necessity out of the stunning surge in available data. If it is true, as George Gilder says, that the amount of raw data will increase by a factor of 19 between the years 1990 and 2000, then researchers will have no choice but to automate their explorations.[2]

Agents are challenging because they seem to point to a change in the way we find information. But in fact, agent software simply takes existing technology and extends it. The issues of content verification that so dominate Web researchers today remain emphatically in force, whether the content we've downloaded comes from our own hunt through a Web site or from a list retrieved by an agent. The agent, much like today's search engines with their relevancy rankings, can only make informed guesses as to what we need. Even the most sophisticated agent may misinterpret our preferences, retrieving information that's wide of the mark. With agents, as with other kinds of searching, it will take experience and experiment to see how satisfactorily a particular product works, and how far it should be trusted to deliver useful content.

NOTES

1. As reported by Tracy Thompson in *The Washington Post* and reprinted in *The News & Observer* (Raleigh, N.C.), February 26, 1996.

2. Gilder, George, *Life After Television* (New York: WW Norton & Co., 1994), p. 79.

PART THREE

TECHNOLOGY AND SCHOOL CHANGE

PART THREE INTRODUCES the reader to the theories, programs, and critiques that have shaped the introduction and increasingly complex use of technology in the schools, and the change that has resulted from that introduction. We begin in Chapter Sixteen with a piece from Seymour Papert. *Mindstorms* was originally published in 1980 to much acclaim and adoption. Although some of the references and ideas mentioned in this piece may seem like ancient history in the fast-paced world of technology, the reader must understand that Papert's programming language, LOGO, traces the beginning of the partnership between technology and constructivist learning—the conventional wisdom in today's most advanced classrooms. *Mindstorms* was written at a turning point in the development of educational computing. At that time, only a handful of classrooms were using personal computers, mainly in research settings. A decade later, thousands of individual classrooms were integrating technology into the curriculum. Although Papert has written much since the publication of *Mindstorms,* it is a seminal work and one that begins to form a basis for judgment of how technology can be used to improve learning.

We also look at what critics have to say about technology's use in education. Neil Postman (Chapter Twenty) and Larry

Cuban and David Tyack (Chapter Seventeen) are well-tempered voices in the critique of technology in schools. Costs versus benefits, lack of training and overburdening of teachers, and the all too common belief that technology is the silver bullet that will transform education overnight are most frequently cited as the perils of embracing technology in learning.

Balancing these arguments are such pieces as Andrea Gooden's chapter on the Ralph Bunche school in Harlem (Chapter Twenty-One). This chapter gives ample evidence of technology making an unprecedented difference in the lives of teachers and students. Chapter Twenty-Three is an applied view of technology in learning, showing how technology can improve assessment and provide innovative ways to give students feedback on their work.

We also provide an introduction to several projects that have integrated technology into school populations and the preliminary results of these efforts. Among these projects is the Apple Classroom of Tomorrow (ACOT) (Chapters Eighteen and Nineteen). A ten-year experiment, ACOT began in 1985 with a question: What happens to students and teachers when they have access to technology whenever they need it? ACOT was quite fruitful in researching technology's effects on student outcomes, the vocabulary and modes of practice that technology introduced into the mainstream, and the relationship between learning and technology. In Chapter Twenty-Two, Marlene Scardamalia and Carl Bereiter tell about their work with a "knowledge society," another noteworthy project that involves students in creating and maintaining a learning network.

16

COMPUTERS AND
COMPUTER CULTURES

Seymour Papert

IN MOST CONTEMPORARY educational situations where children come into contact with computers the computer is used to put children through their paces, to provide exercises of an appropriate level of difficulty, to provide feedback, and to dispense information. The computer programs the child. In the LOGO environment the relationship is reversed: The child, even at preschool ages, is in control. The child programs the computer. And in teaching the computer how to think, children embark on an exploration about how they themselves think. The experience can be heady: Thinking about thinking turns the child into an epistemologist, an experience not even shared by most adults.

This powerful image of child as epistemologist caught my imagination while I was working with Piaget. In 1964, after five years at Piaget's Center for Genetic Epistemology in Geneva, I came away impressed by his way of looking at children as the active builders of their own intellectual structures. But to say that intellectual structures are built by the learner rather than taught by a teacher does not mean that they are built from nothing. On the contrary: Like other builders, children appropriate to their own use materials they find about them, most saliently the models and metaphors suggested by the surrounding culture.

Piaget writes about the order in which the child develops different intellectual abilities. I give more weight than he does to the influence of the materials a particular culture provides in determining that order. For example, our culture is very rich in materials useful for the child's construction of certain components of numerical and logical thinking. Children learn to count; they learn that the result of counting is independent of order and special arrangement; they extend this "conservation" to thinking about the properties of liquids as they are poured and of solids which change their shape. Children develop these components of thinking preconsciously and "spontaneously," that is to say, without deliberate teaching. Other components of knowledge, such as the skills involved in doing permutations and combinations, develop more slowly, or do not develop at all without formal schooling. Taken as a whole this book is an argument that in many important cases this developmental difference can be attributed to our culture's relative poverty in materials from which the apparently "more advanced" intellectual structures can be built. This argument will be very different from cultural interpretations of Piaget that look for differences between city children in Europe or the United States and tribal children in African jungles. When I speak here of "our" culture I mean something less parochial. I am not trying to contrast New York with Chad. I am interested in the difference between precomputer cultures (whether in American cities or African tribes) and the "computer cultures" that may develop everywhere in the next decades.

I have already indicated one reason for my belief that the computer presence might have more fundamental effects on intellectual development than did other new technologies, including television and even printing. The metaphor of computer as mathematics-speaking entity puts the learner in a qualitatively new kind of relationship to an important domain of knowledge. Even the best of educational television is limited to offering quantitative improvements in the kinds of learning that existed without it. "Sesame Street" might offer better and more engaging explanations than a child can get from some parents or nursery school teachers, but the child is still in the position of listening to explanations. By contrast, when a child learns to program, the process of learning is transformed. It becomes more active and self-directed. In particular, the knowledge is acquired for a recognizable personal purpose. The child does something with it. The new knowledge is a source of power and is experienced as such from the moment it begins to form in the child's mind.

I have spoken of mathematics being learned in a new way. But much more is affected than mathematics. One can get an idea of the extent of what is changed by examining another of Piaget's ideas. Piaget distinguishes between "concrete" thinking and "formal" thinking. Concrete thinking is already well on its way by the time the child enters the first grade at age 6 and is consolidated in the following several years. Formal thinking does not develop until the child is almost twice as old, that is to say, at age 12, give or take a year or two, and some researchers have even suggested that many people never achieve fully formal thinking. I do not fully accept Piaget's distinction, but I am sure that it is close enough to reality to help us make sense of the idea that the consequences for intellectual development of one innovation could be qualitatively greater than the cumulative quantitative effects of a thousand others. Stated most simply, my conjecture is that the computer can concretize (and personalize) the formal. Seen in this light, it is not just another powerful educational tool. It is unique in providing us with the means for addressing what Piaget and many others see as the obstacle which is overcome in the passage from child to adult thinking. I believe that it can allow us to shift the boundary separating concrete and formal. Knowledge that was accessible only through formal processes can now be approached concretely. And the real magic comes from the fact that this knowledge includes those elements one needs to become a formal thinker.

This description of the role of the computer is rather abstract. I shall concretize it by looking at the effect of working with computers on two kinds of thinking Piaget associates with the formal stage of intellectual development: combinatorial thinking, where one has to reason in terms of the set of all possible states of a system, and self-referential thinking about thinking itself.

In a typical experiment in combinatorial thinking, children are asked to form all the possible combinations (or "families") of beads of assorted colors. It really is quite remarkable that most children are unable to do this systematically and accurately until they are in the fifth or sixth grades. Why should this be? Why does this task seem to be so much more difficult than the intellectual feats accomplished by seven and eight year old children? Is its logical structure essentially more complex? Can it possibly require a neurological mechanism that does not mature until the approach of puberty? I think that a more likely explanation is provided by looking at the nature of the culture. The task of making the families of beads can be looked at as constructing and executing a program, a very common sort of program, in which two loops are nested: Fix a first color and run through all the possible second colors, then repeat until all possible first colors have been run through. For someone who is thoroughly used to computers and programming there is nothing "formal" or abstract about this task. For a child in a computer culture it would be as concrete as matching up knives and forks at the dinner table. Even the common "bug" of including some families twice (for example, red-blue and blue-red) would be well-known. Our culture is rich in pairs, couples, and one-to-one correspondences of all sorts, and it is rich in language for talking about such things. This richness provides both the incentive and a supply of models and tools for children to build ways to think about such issues as whether three large pieces of candy are more or less than four much smaller pieces. For such problems our children acquire an excellent intuitive sense of quantity. But our culture is relatively poor in models of systematic procedures. Until recently there was not even a name in popular language for programming, let alone for the ideas needed to do so successfully. There is no word for "nested loops" and no word for the double-counting bug. Indeed, there are no words for the powerful ideas computerists refer to as "bug" and "debugging."

Without the incentive or the materials to build powerful, concrete ways to think about problems involving systematicity, children are forced to approach such problems in a groping, abstract fashion. Thus cultural factors that are common to both the American city and the African village can explain the difference in age at which children build their intuitive knowledge of quantity and of systematicity.

While still working in Geneva I had become sensitive to the way in which materials from the then very young computer cultures were allowing psychologists to develop new ways to think about thinking.[1] In fact, my entry into the world of computers was motivated largely by the idea that children could also benefit, perhaps even more than the psychologists, from the way in which computer models seemed able to give concrete form to areas of knowledge that had previously appeared so intangible and abstract.

I began to see how children who had learned to program computers could use very concrete computer models to think about thinking and to learn about learning, and in doing so enhance their powers as psychologists and as epistemologists. For example, many children are held back in their learning because they have a model of learning in which you have either "got it" or "got it wrong." But when you learn to program a computer you almost never get it right the first time. Learning to be a master programmer is learning to become highly skilled at isolating and correcting "bugs," the parts that keep the program from working. The question to ask about the program is not whether it is right or wrong, but if it is fixable. If this way of looking at intellectual products were generalized to how the larger culture thinks about knowledge and its acquisition, we all might be less intimidated by our fears of "being wrong." This potential influence of the computer on changing our notion of a black and white version of our successes and failures is an example of using the computer as an "object-to-think-with." It is obviously not necessary to work with computers in order to acquire good strategies for learning. Surely "debugging" strategies were developed by successful learners long before computers existed. But thinking about learning by analogy with developing a program is a powerful and accessible way to get started on becoming more articulate about one's debugging strategies and more deliberate about improving them.

My discussion of a computer culture and its impact on thinking presupposes a massive penetration of powerful computers into people's lives. That this will happen there can be no doubt. The calculator, the electronic game, and the digital watch were brought to us by a technical revolution that rapidly lowered prices for electronics in a period when all others were rising with inflation. That same technological revolution, brought about by the integrated circuit, is now bringing us the personal computer. Large computers used to cost millions of dollars because they were assembled out of millions of physically distinct parts. In the new technology a complex circuit is not assembled but made as a whole, solid entity—hence the term "integrated circuit." The effect of integrated circuit technology on cost can be understood by comparing it to printing. The main expenditure in making a book occurs long before the press begins to roll. It goes into writing, editing, and typesetting. Other costs occur after the printing: binding, distributing, and marketing. The actual cost per copy for printing itself is negligible. And the same is true for a powerful as for a trivial book. So, too, most of the cost of an integrated circuit goes into a preparatory process; the actual cost of making an individual circuit becomes negligible, provided enough are sold to spread the costs of development. The consequences of this technology for the cost of computation are dramatic. Computers that would have cost hundreds of thousands in the 1960s and tens of thousands in the early 1970s can now be made for less than a dollar. The only limiting factor is whether the particular circuit can fit onto what corresponds to a "page"—that is to say, the "silicon chips" on which the circuits are etched.

But each year in a regular and predictable fashion the art of etching circuits on silicon chips is becoming more refined. More and more complex circuitry can be squeezed onto a chip, and the computer power that can be produced for less than a dollar increases. I predict that long before the end of the century, people will buy children toys with as much computer power as the great IBM computers currently selling for millions of dollars. And as for computers to be used as such, the main cost of these machines will be the peripheral devices, such as the keyboard. Even if these do not fall in price, it is likely that a supercomputer will be equivalent in price to a typewriter and a television set.

There really is no disagreement among experts that the cost of computers will fall to a level where they will enter everyday life in vast numbers. Some will be there as computers proper, that is to say, programmable machines. Others might appear as games of ever-increasing complexity and in automated supermarkets where the shelves, maybe even the cans, will talk. One really can afford to let one's imagination run wild. There is no doubt that the material surface of life will become very different for everyone, perhaps most of all for children. But there has been significant difference of opinion about the effects this computer presence will produce. I would distinguish my thinking from two trends of thinking which I refer to here as the "skeptical" and the "critical."

Skeptics do not expect the computer presence to make much difference in how people learn and think. I have formulated a number of possible explanations for why they think as they do. In some cases I think the skeptics might conceive of education and the effect of computers on it too narrowly. Instead of considering general cultural effects, they focus attention on the use of the computer as a device for programmed instruction. Skeptics then conclude that while the computer might produce some improvements in school learning, it is not likely to lead to fundamental change. In a sense, too, I think the skeptical view derives from a failure to appreciate just how much Piagetian learning takes place as a child grows up. If a person conceives of children's intellectual development (or, for that matter, moral or social development) as deriving chiefly from deliberate teaching, then such a person would be likely to underestimate the potential effect that a massive presence of computers and other interactive objects might have on children.

The critics,[2] on the other hand, do think that the computer presence will make a difference and are apprehensive. For example, they fear that more communication via computers might lead to less human association and result in social fragmentation. As knowing how to use a computer becomes increasingly necessary to effective social and economic participation, the position of the underprivileged could worsen, and the computer could exacerbate existing class distinctions. As to the political effect computers will have, the critics' concerns resonate with Orwellian images of a 1984 where home computers will form part of a complex system of surveillance and thought control. Critics also draw attention to potential mental health hazards of computer penetration. Some of these hazards are magnified forms of problems already worrying many observers of contemporary life; others are problems of an essentially new kind. A typical example of the former kind is that our grave ignorance of the psychological impact of television becomes even more serious when we contemplate an epoch of super TV. The holding power and the psychological impact of the television show could be increased by the computer in at least two ways. The content might be varied to suit the tastes of each individual viewer, and the show might become interactive, drawing the "viewer" into the action. Such things belong to the future, but people who are worried about the impact of the computer on people already cite cases of students spending sleepless nights riveted to the computer terminal, coming to neglect both studies and social contact. Some parents have been reminded of these stories when they observe a special quality of fascination in their own children's reaction to playing with the still rudimentary electronic games.

In the category of problems that are new rather than aggravated versions of old ones, critics have pointed to the influence of the allegedly mechanized thought processes of computers on how people think. Marshall McCluhan's dictum that "the medium is the message" might apply here: If the medium is an interactive system that takes in words and speaks back like a person, it is easy to get the message that machines are like people and that people are like machines. What this might do to the development of values and self-image in growing children is hard to assess. But it is not hard to see reasons for worry.

Despite these concerns I am essentially optimistic—some might say utopian—about the effect of computers on society. I do not dismiss the arguments of the critics. On the contrary, I too see the computer presence as a potent influence on the human mind. I am very much aware of the holding power of an interactive computer and of how taking the computer as a model can influence the way we think about ourselves. In fact, the work on LOGO to which I have devoted much of the past ten years consists precisely of developing such forces in positive directions. For example, the critic is horrified at the thought of a child hypnotically held by a futuristic, computerized super-pinball machine. In the LOGO work, we have invented versions of such machines in which powerful ideas from physics or mathematics or linguistics are embedded in a way that permits the player to learn them in a natural fashion, analogous to how a child learns to speak. The computer's "holding power," so feared by critics, becomes a useful educational tool. Or take another, more profound example. The critic is afraid that children will adopt the computer as model and eventually come to "think mechanically" themselves. Following the opposite tack, I have invented ways to take educational advantage of the opportunities to master the art of *deliberately* thinking like a computer, according, for example, to the stereotype of a computer program that proceeds in a step-by-step, literal, mechanical fashion. There are situations where this style of thinking is appropriate and useful. Some children's difficulties in learning formal subjects such as grammar or mathematics derive from their inability to see the point of such a style.

A second educational advantage is indirect but ultimately more important. By deliberately learning to imitate mechanical thinking, the learner becomes able to articulate what mechanical thinking is and what it is not. The exercise can lead to greater confidence about the ability to choose a cognitive style that suits the problem. Analysis of "mechanical thinking" and how it is different from other kinds of thinking, and practice with problem analysis, can result in a new degree of intellectual sophistication. By providing a very concrete, down-to-earth model of a particular style of thinking, work with the computer can make it easier to understand that there is such a thing as a "style of thinking." And giving children the opportunity to choose one style or another provides an opportunity to develop the skill necessary to choose between styles. Thus, instead of inducing mechanical thinking, contact with computers could turn out to be the most conceivable antidote to it. And for me what is most important in this is that through these experiences these children would be serving their apprenticeships as epistemologists, that is to say, learning to think articulately about thinking.

The intellectual environments offered to children by today's cultures are poor in opportunities to bring their thinking about thinking into the open, to learn to talk about it and to test their ideas by externalizing them. Access to computers can dramatically change this situation. Even the simplest Turtle work can open new opportunities for sharpening one's thinking about thinking: Programming the Turtle starts by making one reflect on how one does oneself what one would like the Turtle to do. Thus, teaching the Turtle to act or to "think" can lead one to reflect on one's own actions and thinking. And as children move on, they program the computer to make more complex aspects of their own thinking.

In short, while the critic and I share the belief that working with computers can have a powerful influence on how people think, I have turned my attention to exploring how this influence could be turned in positive directions.

I see two kinds of counterarguments to my arguments against the critics. The first kind challenges my belief that it is a good thing for children to be epistemologists. Many people will argue that overly analytic, verbalized thinking is counterproductive even if it is deliberately chosen. The second kind of objection challenges my suggestion that computers are likely to lead to more reflective self-conscious thinking. Many people will argue that work with computers usually has the opposite effect. These two kinds of objections call for different kinds of analysis and cannot be discussed simultaneously. The first kind raises technical questions about the psychology of learning. The second kind of objection is most directly answered by saying that there is absolutely no inevitability that computers will have the effects I hope to see. Not all computer systems do. Most in use today do not. In LOGO environments I have seen children engaged in animated conversations about their own personal knowledge as they try to capture it in a program to make a Turtle carry out an action that they themselves know very well how to do. But of course the physical presence of a computer is not enough to ensure that such conversations will come about. Far from it. In thousands of schools and in tens of thousands of private homes children are right now living through very different computer experiences. In most cases the computer is being used either as a versatile video game or as a "teaching machine" programmed to put children through their paces in arithmetic or spelling. And even when children are taught by a parent, a peer, or a professional teacher to write simple programs in a language like BASIC, this activity is not accompanied at all by the kind of epistemological reflection that we see in the LOGO environments. So I share a skepticism with the critics about what is being done with computation now. But I am interested in stimulating a major change in how things can be. The bottom line for such changes is political. What is happening now is an empirical question. What can happen is a technical question. But what will happen is a political question, depending on social choices.

The central open questions about the effect of computers on children in the 1980s are these: Which people will be attracted to the world of computers, what talents will they bring, and what tastes and ideologies will they impose on the growing computer culture? I have described children in LOGO environments engaged in self-referential discussions about their own thinking. This could happen because the LOGO language and the Turtle were designed by people who enjoy such discussion and worked hard to design a medium that would encourage it. Other designers of computer systems have different tastes and different ideas about what kinds of activities are suitable for children. Which design will prevail, and in what sub-culture, will not be decided by a simple bureaucratic decision made, for example, in a government department of education or by a committee of experts. Trends in computer style will emerge from a complex web of decisions by foundations with resources to support one or another design, by corporations who may see a market, by schools, by individuals who will decide to make their career in the new field of activity, and by children who will have their own say in what they pick up and what they make of it. People often ask whether in the future children will program computers or become absorbed in pre-programmed activities. The answer must be that some children will do the one, some the other, some both and some neither. But which children, and most importantly, which social classes of children, will fall into each category will be influenced by the kind of computer activities and the kind of environments created around them.

As an example, we consider an activity which may not occur to most people when they think of computers and children: the use of a computer as a writing instrument. For me, writing means making a rough draft and refining it over a considerable period of time. My image of myself as a writer includes the expectation of an "unacceptable" first draft that will develop with successive editing into presentable form. But I would not be able to afford this image if I were a third grader. The physical act of writing would be slow and laborious. I would have no secretary. For most children, rewriting a text is so laborious that the first draft is the final copy, and the skill of rereading with a critical eye is never acquired. This changes dramatically when children have access to computers capable of manipulating text. The first draft is composed at the keyboard. Corrections are made easily. The current copy is always neat and tidy. I have seen a child move from total rejection of writing to an intense involvement (accompanied by rapid improvement of quality) within a few weeks of beginning to write with a computer. Even more dramatic changes are seen when the child has physical handicaps that make writing by hand more difficult than usual or even impossible.

This use of computers is rapidly becoming adopted wherever adults write for a living. Most newspapers now provide their staff with "word processing" computer systems. Many writers who work at home are acquiring their own computers, and the computer terminal is steadily displacing the typewriter as the secretary's basic tool. The image of children using the computer as a writing instrument is a particularly good example of my general thesis that what is good for professionals is good for children. But this image of how the computer might contribute to children's mastery of language is dramatically opposed to the one that is taking root in most elementary schools. There the computer is seen as a teaching instrument. It gives children practice in distinguishing between verbs and nouns, in spelling, and in answering multiple-choice questions about the meaning of pieces of text. As I see it, this difference is not a matter of a small and technical choice between two teaching strategies. It reflects a fundamental difference in educational philosophies. More to the point, it reflects a difference in views on the nature of childhood. I believe that the computer as writing instrument offers children an opportunity to become more like adults, indeed like advanced professionals, in their relationship to their intellectual products and to themselves. In doing so, it comes into head-on collision with the many aspects of schools whose effect, if not whose intention, is to "infantilize" the child.

Word processors *can* make a child's experience of writing more like that of a real writer. But this can be undermined if the adults surrounding that child fail to appreciate what it is like to be a writer. For example, it is only too easy to imagine adults, including teachers, expressing the view that editing and re-editing a text is a waste of time ("Why don't you get on to something new?" or "You aren't making it any better, why don't you fix your spelling?").

As with writing, so with music-making, games of skill, complex graphics, whatever: The computer is not a culture unto itself but it can serve to advance very different cultural and philosophical outlooks. For example, one could think of the Turtle as a device to teach elements of the traditional curriculum, such as notions of angle, shape, and coordinate systems. And in fact, most teachers who consult me about its use are, quite understandably, trying to use it in this way. Their questions are about classroom organization, scheduling problems, pedagogical issues raised by the Turtle's introduction, and especially about how it relates conceptually to the rest of the curriculum. Of course the Turtle can help in the teaching of traditional curriculum, but I have thought of it as a vehicle for Piagetian learning, which to me is learning without curriculum.

There are those who think about creating a "Piagetian curriculum" or "Piagetian teaching methods." But to my mind these phrases and the activities they represent are contradictions in terms. I see Piaget as the theorist of learning without curriculum and the theorist of the kind of learning that happens without deliberate teaching. To turn him into the theorist of a new curriculum is to stand him on his head.

But "teaching without curriculum" does not mean spontaneous, freeform classrooms or simply "leaving the child alone." It means supporting children as they build their own intellectual structures with materials drawn from the surrounding culture. In this model, educational intervention means changing the culture, planting new constructive elements in it and eliminating noxious ones. This is a more ambitious undertaking than introducing a curriculum change, but one which is feasible under conditions now emerging.

Suppose that thirty years ago an educator had decided that the way to solve the problem of mathematics education was to arrange for a significant fraction of the population to become fluent in (and enthusiastic about) a new mathematical language. The idea might have been good in principle, but in practice it would have been absurd. No one had the power to implement it. Now things are different. Many millions of people are learning programming languages for reasons that have nothing to do with the education of children. Therefore, it becomes a practical proposition to influence the form of the languages they learn and the likelihood that their children will pick up these languages.

The educator must be an anthropologist. The educator as anthropologist must work to understand which cultural materials are relevant to intellectual development. Then he or she needs to understand which trends are taking place in the culture. Meaningful intervention must take the form of working with these trends. In my role of educator as anthropologist I see new needs being generated by the penetration of the computer into personal lives. People who have computers at home or who use them at work will want to be able to talk about them to their children. They will want to be able to teach their children to use the machines. Thus there could be a cultural demand for something like Turtle graphics in a way there never was, and perhaps never could be, a cultural demand for the New Math.

Throughout the course of this chapter I have been talking about the ways in which choices made by educators, foundations, governments, and private individuals can affect the potentially revolutionary changes in how children learn. But making good choices is not always easy, in part because past choices can often haunt us. There is a tendency for the first usable, but still primitive, product of a new technology to dig itself in. I have called this phenomenon the QWERTY phenomenon.

The top row of alphabetic keys of the standard typewriter reads QWERTY. For me this symbolizes the way in which technology can all too often serve as a force not for progress but for keeping things stuck. The QWERTY arrangement has no rational explanation, only a historical one. It was introduced in response to a problem in the early days of the typewriter: The keys used to jam. The idea was to minimize the collision problem by separating those keys that followed one another frequently. Just a few years later, general improvements in the technology removed the jamming problem, but QWERTY stuck. Once adopted, it resulted in many millions of typewriters and a method (indeed a full-blown curriculum) for learning typing. The social cost of change (for example, putting the most used keys *together* on the keyboard) mounted with the vested interest created by the fact that so many fingers now knew how to follow the QWERTY keyboard. QWERTY has stayed on despite the existence of other, more "rational" systems. On the other hand, if you talk to people about the QWERTY arrangement they will justify it by "objective" criteria. They will tell you that it "optimizes this" or it "minimizes that." Although these justifications have no rational foundation, they illustrate a process, a social process, of myth construction that allows us to build a justification for primitivity into any system. And I think that we are well on the road to doing exactly the same thing with the computer. We are in the process of digging ourselves into an anachronism by preserving practices that have no rational basis beyond their historical roots in an earlier period of technological and theoretical development.

The use of computers for drill and practice is only one example of the QWERTY phenomenon in the computer domain. Another example occurs even when attempts are made to allow students to learn to program the computer. Learning to program a computer involves learning a "programming language." There are many such languages—for example, FORTRAN, PASCAL, BASIC, SMALLTALK, and LISP, and the lesser known language LOGO, which our group has used in most of our experiments with computers and children. A powerful QWERTY phenomenon is to be expected when we choose the language in which children are to learn to program computers. I shall argue in detail that the issue is consequential. A programming language is like a natural, human language in that it favors certain metaphors, images, and ways of thinking. The language used strongly colors the computer culture. It would seem to follow that educators interested in using computers and sensitive to cultural influences would pay particular attention to the choice of language. But nothing of the sort has happened. On the contrary, educators, too timid in technological matters or too ignorant to attempt to influence the languages offered by computer manufacturers, have accepted certain programming languages in much the same way as they accepted the QWERTY keyboard. An informative example is the way in which the programming language BASIC[3] has established itself as the obvious language to use in teaching American children how to program computers. The relevant technical information is this: A very small computer can be made to understand BASIC, while other languages demand more from the computer. Thus, in the early days when computer power was extremely expensive, there was a genuine technical reason for the use of BASIC, particularly in schools where budgets were always tight. Today, and in fact for several years now, the cost of computer memory has fallen to the point where any remaining economic advantages of using BASIC are insignificant. Yet in most high schools, the language remains almost synonymous with programming, despite the existence of other computer languages that are demonstrably easier to learn and richer in the intellectual benefits that can come from learning them. The situation is paradoxical. The computer revolution has scarcely begun, but it is already breeding its own conservatism. Looking more closely at BASIC provides a window on how a conservative social system appropriates and tries to neutralize a potentially revolutionary instrument.

BASIC is to computation what QWERTY is to typing. Many teachers have learned BASIC, many books have been written about it, many computers have been built in such a way that BASIC is "hardwired" into them. In the case of the typewriter, we noted how people invent "rationalizations" to justify the status quo. In the case of BASIC, the phenomenon has gone much further, to the point where it resembles ideology formation. Complex arguments are invented to justify features of BASIC that were originally included because the primitive technology demanded them or because alternatives were not well enough known at the time the language was designed.

An example of BASIC ideology is the argument that BASIC is easy to learn because it has a very small vocabulary. The surface validity of the argument is immediately called into question if we apply it to the context of how children learn natural languages. Imagine a suggestion that we invent a special language to help children learn to speak. This language would have a small vocabulary of just fifty words, but fifty words so well chosen that all ideas could be expressed using them. Would this language be easier to learn? Perhaps the vocabulary might be easy to learn, but the use of the vocabulary to express what one wanted to say would be so contorted that only the most motivated and brilliant children would learn to say more than "hi." This is close to the situation with BASIC. Its small vocabulary can be learned quickly enough. But using it is a different matter. Programs in BASIC acquire so labyrinthine a structure that in fact only the most motivated and brilliant ("mathematical") children do learn to use it for more than trivial ends.

One might ask why the teachers do not notice the difficulty children have in learning BASIC. The answer is simple: Most teachers do not expect high performance from most students, especially in a domain of work that appears to be as "mathematical" and "formal" as programming. Thus the culture's general perception of mathematics as inaccessible bolsters the maintenance of BASIC, which in turn confirms these perceptions. Moreover, the teachers are not the only people whose assumptions and prejudices feed into the circuit that perpetuates BASIC. There are also the computerists, the people in the computer world who make decisions about what languages their computers will speak. These people, generally engineers, find BASIC quite easy to learn, partly because they are accustomed to learning such very technical systems and partly because BASIC's sort of simplicity appeals to their system of values. Thus, a particular subculture, one dominated by computer engineers, is influencing the world of education to favor those students who are most like that subculture. The process is tacit, unintentional: It has never been publicly articulated, let alone evaluated. In all of these ways, the social embedding of BASIC has far more serious consequences than the "digging in" of QWERTY.

There are many other ways in which the attributes of the subcultures involved with computers are being projected onto the world of education. For example, the idea of the computer as an instrument for drill and practice that appeals to teachers because it resembles traditional teaching methods also appeals to the engineers who design computer systems: Drill and practice applications are predictable, simple to describe, efficient in use of the machine's resources. So the best engineering talent goes into the development of computer systems that are biased to favor this kind of application. The bias operates subtly. The machine designers do not actually decide what will be done in the classrooms. That is done by teachers and occasionally even by carefully controlled comparative research experiments. But there is an irony in these controlled experiments. They are very good at telling whether the small effects seen in best scores are real or due to chance. But they have no way to measure the undoubtedly real (and probably more massive) effects of the biases built into the machines.

We have already noted that the conservative bias being built into the use of computers in education has also been built into other new technologies. The first use of the new technology is quite naturally to do in a slightly different way what had been done before without it. It took years before designers of automobiles accepted the idea that they were cars, not "horseless carriages," and the precursors of modern motion pictures were plays acted as if before a live audience but actually in front of a camera. A whole generation was needed for the new art of motion pictures to emerge as something quite different from a linear mix of theater plus photography. Most of what has been done up to now under the name of "educational technology" or "computers in education" is still at the stage of the linear mix of old instructional methods with new technologies. The topics I shall be discussing are some of the first probings toward a more organic interaction of fundamental educational principles and new methods for translating them into reality.

We are at a point in the history of education when radical change is possible, and the possibility for that change is directly tied to the impact of the computer. Today what is offered in the education "market" is largely determined by what is acceptable to a sluggish and conservative system. But this is where the computer presence is in the process of creating an environment for change. Consider the conditions under which a new educational idea can be put into practice today and in the near future. Let us suppose that today I have an idea about how children could learn mathematics more effectively and more humanely. And let us suppose that I have been able to persuade a million people that the idea is a good one. For many products such a potential market would guarantee success. Yet in the world of education today this would have little clout: A million people across the nation would still mean a minority in every town's school system, so there might be no effective channel for the million voices to be expressed. Thus, not only do good educational ideas sit on the shelves, but the process of invention is itself stymied. This inhibition of invention in turn influences the selection of people who get involved in education. Very few with the imagination, creativity, and drive to make great new inventions enter the field. Most of those who do are soon driven out in frustration. Conservatism in the world of education has become a self-perpetuating *social* phenomenon.

Fortunately, there is a weak link in the vicious circle. Increasingly, the computers of the very near future will be the private property of individuals, and this will gradually return to the individual the power to determine patterns of education. Education will become more of a private act, and people with good ideas, different ideas, exciting ideas will no longer be faced with a dilemma where they either have to "sell" their ideas to a conservative bureaucracy or shelve them. They will be able to offer them in an open marketplace directly to consumers. There will be new opportunities for imagination and originality. There might be a renaissance of thinking about education.

NOTES

1. The program FOLLOW is a very simple example of how a powerful cybernetic idea (control by negative feedback) can be used to elucidate a biological or psychological phenomenon. Simple as it is, the example helps bridge the gap between physical models of "causal mechanism" and psychological phenomena such as "purpose."

Theoretical psychologists have used more complex programs in the same spirit to construct models of practically every known psychological phenomenon. A bold formulation of the spirit of such inquiry is found in Herbert A. Simon, *Sciences of the Artificial* (Cambridge: MIT Press, 1969).

2. The critics and skeptics referred to here are distillations from years of public and private debates. These attitudes are widely held but, unfortunately, seldom published and therefore seldom discussed with any semblance of rigor. One critic who has set a good example by publishing his views is Joseph Weizenbaum in *Computer Power and Human Reason: From Judgment to Calculations* (San Francisco: W.H. Freeman, 1976).

Unfortunately Weizenbaum's book discusses two separate (though related) questions: whether computers harm the way people think and whether computers themselves can think. Most critical reviews of Weizenbaum have focused on the latter question, on which he joins company with Hubert L. Dreyfus, *What Computers Can't Do: A Critique of Artificial Reason* (New York: Harper & Row, 1972).

A lively description of some of the principal participants in the debate about whether computers can or cannot think is found in Pamela McCorduck, *Machines Who Think* (San Francisco: W.H. Freeman, 1979).

There is little published data on whether computers actually affect how people think. This question is being studied presently by S. Turkle.

3. Many versions of BASIC would allow a program to produce a shape like that made by the LOGO program HOUSE. The simplest example would look something like this:

```
10 PLOT (0,0)
20 PLOT (100,0)
30 PLOT (100,100)
40 PLOT (75,150)
50 PLOT (0,100)
60 PLOT (0,0)
70 END
```

Writing such a program falls short of the LOGO program as a beginning programming experience in many ways. It demands more of the beginner; in particular, it demands knowledge of cartesian coordinates. This demand would be less serious if the program, once written, could become a powerful tool for other projects. The LOGO programs SQ, TRI, and HOUSE can be used to draw squares, triangles, and houses in any position and orientation on the screen. The BASIC program allows one particular house to be drawn in one position. In order to make a BASIC program that will draw houses in many positions, it is necessary to use algebraic variables as in PLOT (x,y), PLOT $(x + 100, y)$, and so on. As for defining new commands, such as SQ, TRI, and HOUSE, the commonly used versions of BASIC either do not allow this at all or, at best, allow something akin to it to be achieved through the use of advanced technical programming methods. Advocates of BASIC might reply that: (1) these objections refer only to a beginner's experience and (2) these deficiencies of BASIC could be fixed. The first argument is simply not true: The intellectual and practical primitivity of BASIC extends all along the line up to the most advanced programming. The second misses the point of my complaint. Of course one could turn BASIC into LOGO or SMALLTALK or anything else and still call it "BASIC." My complaint is that what is being foisted on the education world has not been so "fixed." Moreover, doing so would be a little like "remodeling" a wooden house to become a skyscraper.

WEB SITE

http://www.mamamedia.com

17

TEACHING BY MACHINE

David Tyack, Larry Cuban

MANY AMERICANS RELISH technological solutions to the problems of learning. It has long been so. Hear the rhetoric of another era: "The inventor or introducer of the system deserves to be ranked among the best contributors to learning and science, if not among the greatest benefactors of mankind." The time was 1841. The "system" was the blackboard, which another salesman forty years later described as "the MIRROR reflecting the workings, character and quality of the individual mind." And so it went, as advocates of educational radio, film, television, and programmed learning predicted pedagogical Nirvanas that never materialized.[1]

Worry as well as hope has fueled waves of enthusiasm for educational technology. Reformers have turned to machines when they were concerned about the competence of teachers, or the high cost of schooling, or some external threat to American security or prosperity that gave special urgency to education.

The people who promised educational moonshots through technology were an assorted lot. Not surprisingly, many were business people who wanted to market their wares up to the schools. Some were scholars and academic entrepreneurs—psychologists, for example, who thought that programmed instruction would streamline pedagogy. Foundation officials seeking a quick impact on schooling sometimes saw the new media as a way around the briar patch impeding educational change. Some educational administrators who wanted their schools to be up to date embraced new technologies. A new specialist who had a vested interest as well as a faith in technology appeared in colleges, state departments of education, and school districts: the audiovisual expert.[2]

In the top-down process of advocating and implementing technology, teachers were rarely consulted, though it was mainly their job to make it work in the classroom. A small minority of teachers welcomed media such as radio and films, believing that they would motivate their reluctant students and make their own instruction easier and more effective. Most, however, used the new devices minimally or not at all. As new forms of pedagogy by machine appeared, a familiar cycle of reform recurred: hyperbolic claims about how a new invention would transform education; then research showing that the technology was generally no more effective than traditional instruction and sometimes less; and finally, disappointment as reports came back from classrooms about the imperfections of the reform and as surveys showed that few teachers were using the tool.[3]

Whom to blame? The obvious scapegoat was the teacher unwilling to climb onto the new bandwagon. Whatever the audiovisual reformers might have hoped, behind the classroom door teachers remained the key influence on instruction. By and large, they used the technologies that fit familiar routines and classroom procedures—in other words, that helped them solve their problems of instruction. The rest they mostly ignored.[4]

Many technical inventions have in fact made their way into classrooms and are now so familiar that few people even notice them. Consider these: the blackboard, of course; cheap paper, which replaced slates; books for each child made possible by sharp drops in production costs; paperbacks, which supplemented hardcover textbooks; globes and maps; ballpoint pens, which replaced the steel-nib pens that had replaced quill pens; and though they were controversial, cheap hand-held calculators. More complex technologies have had much less impact on everyday teaching than the simple, durable, reliable improvements like the chalkboard that enhanced what teachers were already doing. Teachers have regularly used technologies to enhance their regular instruction but rarely to transform their teaching.[5]

Advocates of film as a mode of instruction saw it as the very emblem of progressive pedagogy, for it promised to breathe visual reality into the spoken and printed word. But again the companies that wanted to sell technical solutions and the educators enjoined to use them tended to live in different worlds. One advocate of films reported that teachers "failed to make their problems articulate to the commercial producers," while business people "failed to grasp or to study the nature of instruction and the complexity of educational institutions." Many of the early "free" films were thinly disguised commercials for products and resented as such by teachers. Especially to blame for the cool reception teachers gave film was "the stupidity which has characterized the advertising, propaganda, and sales methods of companies" that claimed that moving pictures might supplant textbooks and even teachers.[6]

The early projectors were expensive and required constant maintenance, and films themselves were costly and needed to be shared by many teachers. For these reasons, film was first used in large cities and wealthy suburbs. Most districts had no projectors; rural schools often lacked electricity. In 1936, after a decade of florid claims about educational motion pictures, a survey of 21,000 districts (9,000 replied) found that across the nation there were only about 6,074 silent-film projectors and 458 sound-film projectors (it did not say how many of these were in good repair and actually in use). By 1954, when equipment was cheaper and more reliable, the National Education Association estimated that schools had one projector for every 415 students.[7]

But even when districts had the necessary equipment and films, teachers used educational films sparingly, except for a small cadre of enthusiasts: A study of 175 elementary teachers in New Haven, Connecticut, discovered that teachers ordered about fifteen hundred films in one year, but two-thirds of the orders came from twenty-five mediaphiles. When researchers investigated obstacles to the use of moving pictures, they pinpointed the teachers' lack of skills, the cost of purchase and upkeep of the equipment, and the inability to find the right fit between films and class lessons.[8]

On its face, radio was a simpler medium to use than film. But again, lack of equipment originally limited diffusion of the reform. In the mid-1930s superintendents reported only about one radio per district. An expert on educational radio estimated in 1945 that only 5 percent of children heard radio regularly in their classrooms. When principals in Ohio were asked what were the blocks to greater use of radio, they listed lack of radios (50 percent), poor equipment or reception (30 percent), and lack of coordination of radio programs with the curriculum. But advocates of radio education instead blamed teachers' "indifference and lethargy, even antagonism, toward this revolutionary means of communication."[9]

Television was going to be different, said reformers. In the 1950s, when the Ford Foundation entered the arena of electronic teaching with its subsidies and publicity, the campaign for instructional television gained momentum. Soon an airplane was circling over the Midwest beaming down programs to six states. Hagerstown, Maryland, developed a model system of closed-circuit television that promised a richer curriculum at less cost. By 1961 the Ford Foundation had spent $20 million for classroom television, and the next year Congress appropriated another $32 million for that purpose.[10]

Despite unprecedented public attention and enthusiastic promotion, instructional television made slow headway. A survey of public schools in 1961 found only 1.65 TV sets per district. In the mid-1960s, as federal dollars flowed into the schools, districts that had been too poor to buy adequate audiovisual equipment were able for the first time to acquire television sets along with many other kinds of machines and software. But the machines often sat idle in closets. In the 1970s teachers reported that they showed TV programs only 2 to 4 percent of classroom time. A decade after classroom television was introduced with a flourish, a fervent advocate lamented: "If something happened tomorrow to wipe out all instructional television, America's schools and colleges would hardly know it was gone."[11]

The history of film, radio, and television in the public schools shows a common pattern. Initially, nonteachers who pushed teaching by machine made extravagant claims. When a minority of teachers responded enthusiastically, technophiles were pleased. But this rarely happened, for electronic learning was marginal to most instruction in classrooms. How might this historically dominant pattern be interpreted?

Explanations abound. Disappointed reformers complained that teachers were laggard and fearful if not incompetent. Teachers gave other reasons. They pointed to problems with hardware: there was not enough, or it was broken or complicated, or it took too much time to arrange for its use. They criticized the content of the films or television and radio programs as inappropriate to the curriculum, as not fitting the class schedule, or as of poor quality. Top-down implementation provoked many teachers to dig in their heels or simply to put technology in the closet.[12]

But perhaps the most fundamental block to transforming schooling through machines has been the nature of the classroom as a work setting and the ways in which teachers define their tasks. We have suggested that the regularities of institutional structure and of teacher-centered pedagogy and discipline are the result of generations of teachers' experience in responding to the imperatives of their occupation: maintaining order and seeing that students learn the standard curriculum. Teachers have been willing, even eager, to adopt innovations such as chalkboards or overhead projectors that help them do their regular work more efficiently and that are simple, durable, flexible, and responsive to the way they define their tasks. But they have often regarded teaching by machines as extraneous to their central mission.[13]

Will teaching and learning by personal computers suffer the same fate of hyperbolic claims by advocates and then marginalization in schools? Certainly there has been plenty of hyperbole about the educational uses of computers, but computers are different in important ways from the other machines and media we have examined.

Computers are tools that are sweeping across workplaces as diverse as offices, stores, airlines, steel plants, hospitals, and the military. Increasingly, families use computers at home for a variety of tasks. Citizens have put pressure on schools to familiarize the young with the uses of this powerful new tool, believing that if they do not, the next generation will be handicapped in getting jobs in an age of information. No public urgency compelled such attention to the media previously used in schools.

As a result of this public concern, computers have spread far more rapidly in schools than did any earlier forms of electronic hardware. From 1984 to 1992 over a billion dollars was spent on equipping schools with computers. A few statistics suggest the broad outlines of a rapidly changing picture:

> In 1981, only 18 percent of schools had computers, but by 1993, 99 percent had them.
>
> In 1981, only 16 percent of schools used computers for instructional purposes. By 1993, 98 percent reported that they did so.
>
> The number of students per computer decreased from 125 in 1981 to 14 in 1993.[14]

Although substantial progress has been made in installing computers in schools and in convincing the public that facility in using them is vital to students' success in school and jobs, there are serious social inequalities in the use of computers in schools. Students from high-income families have far more access to computers and to sophisticated uses of them than do students from low-income families. Black students use them less than whites, females less than males, and pupils whose native language is not English less than those who are proficient in English. Charles Pillar, who investigated use of computers in schools for the magazine *Macworld,* lamented "the creation of the technological underclass in America's public schools." He observed that "computer-based education in poor schools is in deep trouble. Inner-city and rural school districts rarely have the skills or funds to maintain their machines. These districts lack the training and social support to use computers effectively. In most cases, computers simply perpetuate a two-tier system of education for rich and poor." [15]

Simply having access to computers and learning to use them as tools is only part of the story of the educational use of computers. To what degree are they actually employed as sophisticated teachers' aides and integrated into instruction? A study reveals that when students do use computers (and not all do), they spend only a little more than an hour per week on the machines. What students do on computers varies greatly. Eleventh-grade students, for example, mostly go to computer laboratories to learn about computers and seldom use them in their academic subjects. Low-income students are more likely to do drill and practice on computers than to use them for problem solving and complex thinking. Excellent software for classroom learning is scarce; typically it lags far behind the capacity of the hardware. Computers can communicate efficiently and enhance learning, but often what humans place in them is pedestrian.[16]

A significant minority of teachers have welcomed computers as an aid to learning and incorporated them in imaginative ways in their classrooms. These serious users, like colleagues in earlier generations who welcomed film, radio, and television, are outnumbered by those who are content to have students leave their classes to go to the computer lab down the hall. The overall picture that emerges after over a decade of advocates' claims and public urgency is that computers play a marginal role in regular instruction in public schools. A one-line summary of the situation to date might be: computers meet classroom; classroom wins.[17]

The educational potential of the computer is already apparent, but the jury is out on how soon and how extensively the computer will be incorporated in everyday instruction. Computers are by far the most powerful teaching and learning machines to enter the classroom. Students and teachers can interact with computers in ways impossible with film, radio, and television. Depending on the software, preschoolers through graduate students can write and edit, learn languages, have a machine "tutor" in algebra, retrieve a great variety of information from electronic disks or distant libraries, receive E-mail from students a continent away, prepare multimedia reports, and use state-of-the-art technology in drafting, auto mechanics, and office work. In special education, computers help blind, deaf, and multiply-disabled students read, write, and communicate in ways that heretofore were unavailable. These various uses of the computer, valuable in themselves, will still require the integration and sense-making that a good teacher can provide. And whether teachers will embrace this new technology depends in good part on the ability of technologically minded reformers to understand the realities of the classroom and to enlist teachers as collaborators rather than regarding them as obstacles to progress.[18]

NOTES

1. Josiah F. Bumstead, *The Blackboard in the Primary Schools* (Boston: Perkins and Marvin, 1841), p. viii, and Andrews & Co., *Illustrated Catalogue of School Merchandise* (Chicago, 1881), p. 73, as quoted in Charnel Anderson, *Technology in American Education, 1650–1900* (Washington, D.C.: GPO, 1962), pp. 18, 32; David Tyack, "Educational Moonshot?" *Phi Delta Kappan* 58 (February 1977): 457; Philip W. Jackson, *The Teacher and the Machine* (Pittsburgh: University of Pittsburgh Press, 1967).

2. By 1931 twenty-five states and many large cities had departments devoted to audiovisual instruction—Larry Cuban, *Teachers and Machines: The Classroom Use of Technology Since 1920* (New York: Teachers College Press, 1986), p. 12; Paul Saettler, *A History of Instructional Technology* (New York: McGraw-Hill, 1968), ch. 7; David Tyack and Elisabeth Hansot, "Futures That Never Happened: Technology and the Classroom," *Education Week,* September 4, 1985, pp. 40, 35.

3. Cuban, *Teachers and Machines;* Anthony Oettinger and Selma Marks, "Educational Technology: New Myths and Old Realities," *Harvard Educational Review* 38 (Fall 1968): 697–717; the *Education Index,* described earlier, charts the rise and decline of hyperbolic claims about instruction by various technologies.

4. Larry Cuban, "Determinants of Curriculum Change and Stability," in Jon Schaffarzick and Gary Sykes, eds., *Value Conflicts and Curriculum Issues* (Berkeley: McCutchan, 1979), pp. 139–196.

5. Anderson, *Technology.*

6. Saettler, *History,* pp. 110–111, 127.

7. Cuban, *Teachers and Machines,* ch. 1; Saettler, *History,* pp. 302–303.

8. Mark May and Arthur Lumsdaine, *Learning from Films* (New Haven: Yale University Press, 1958), p. 206.

9. William Levenson, *Teaching Through Radio* (New York: Farrar and Rinehart, 1945), p. 181; Norman Woelfel and Keith Tyler, *Radio and the School* (Yonkers-on-Hudson: World Book Co., 1945), pp. 3, 4–5.

10. *Decade of Experiment: The Fund for the Advancement of Education, 1951–1961* (New York: The Ford Foundation, 1962); Cuban, *Teachers and Machines,* ch. 2.

11. Cuban, *Teachers and Machines,* pp. 38–39 (advocate quoted on p. 50).

12. Ibid., ch. 3.

13. Ibid.

14. U.S. Department of Commerce, *Statistical Abstract of the United States, 1991* (Washington, D.C.: GPO, 1991), p. 150; Peter West, "Survey Finds Gaps in U.S. Schools' Computer Use," *Education Week,* December 15, 1993, p. 8; Gina Boubion, "Technology Gap Frustrates Schools," *San Jose Mercury,* March 14, 1993, pp. 1, 8A; Charles Pillar, "Separate Realities: The Creation of the Technological Underclass in America's Public Schools," *Macworld,* September 1992, pp. 218, 218–231.

15. Pillar, "Separate Realities," pp. 218–219.

16. U.S. Congress, Office of Technology Assessment, *Power On: New Tools for Teaching and Learning* (Washington, D.C.: GPO, 1988), p. 6, passim.

17. Larry Cuban, "Computers Meet Classroom; Classroom Wins," *Teachers College Record* 95, no. 2 (Winter 1993): 185–210.

18. Susan Russell, *Beyond Drill and Practice: Expanding the Computer Mainstream* (Reston, Va.: The Council for Exceptional Children, 1989); Office of Technology Assessment, *Power On.*

18

THE EVOLUTION
OF INSTRUCTION IN
TECHNOLOGY-RICH
CLASSROOMS

Judith Haymore Sandholtz, Cathy Ringstaff, David C. Dwyer

*"One thing I have a hard time with as a traditional classroom
teacher is to let them go, let the students try a new way."*

The Promise of Technology for Education

IN THE EARLY DAYS of the introduction of computers to classrooms,
there was unbridled hope that technology would bring about the same
kind of successful transformation that had been seen in science, industry,
and business. In these arenas, technology's role seemed obvious from the
start. In science, automated computation allowed measurement and
comparisons never before possible. Simulations made whole classes of
natural phenomena accessible and opened them to experimentation. In
industry, repetitive and well-specified processes suggested computerized
and roboticized solutions, eliminating the errors and hazards that come
with human boredom. In business, the flexibility of the word processor
over the typewriter was immediately obvious. In each of these fields,
clear procedures combined with technology led to quantum leaps in
efficiency.

Technology's role in schooling is not so obvious, in part because the process and product of formal education remain largely unspecified. Learning and teaching may be the fundamental processes of schooling, but perspectives on learning are constantly changing and images of teaching vary widely (Greene, 1979). Some argue that teaching is a clinical pursuit, where practitioners control instructional variables (Smith, 1963). Others view it as an enterprise, where teachers create learning communities and focus on social processes (Dewey, 1963). Or to some, the practice of teaching might be more like therapy, where a teacher recognizes unique moments that present students with opportunities for growth and capitalizes on them (Buber, 1957). None of these images of teaching has proven superior to any other. To some extent, they all coexist in schools today.

Learning outcomes are equally subject to debate. Witness the raucous clash over educational standards. What are they, and who should define them? Should standards be set by local, state, or national groups? Should parents, professional educators, policymakers, or business and industry leaders drive the process? How do you factor in conservative and liberal perspectives or religious and secular interests? How do you account for regional differences?

Adding more complexity to this picture, children arrive at classroom doors in countless shades of physical, emotional, social, and cognitive readiness. Still, teachers greet their students year after year and attempt to help them develop their intellectual and emotional potential and provide some sense of greater purpose and social responsibility. No wonder that school reformers responded optimistically to the introduction of educational technology. At some level, perhaps, dealing with hardware and software seemed so much simpler than contending with issues as complex as human cognition, politics, and values.

When computers were first introduced to classrooms, reformers focused on the innovation—computers and software. They gave little thought to how technology would integrate into instruction and influence assessment. In many ways, ACOT (Apple Classroom of Tomorrow) repeated the same error. The addition of large numbers of computers, peripherals, and software to ACOT classrooms did catalyze change, but their contribution was clearly mediated by familiar human, organizational, and educational issues. Technology by itself was not the silver bullet. In fact, it added yet another layer of complexity, a whole new set of things for already overworked and stressed teachers to learn and manage. Yet, as the project continued, teachers found strategic ways to use the technology. Its use in instruction and learning changed as teachers themselves changed. The speed and direction of this evolution were closely tied to changes in teachers' beliefs about learning, about teacher-student roles, and about instructional practice.

The Importance of Personal Beliefs
to Instructional Evolution

Beliefs play an important part in human endeavors, particularly in situations where there is a great deal of uncertainty, as in schools (Nespor, 1987). Beliefs are personal and are individually derived; they form the basis for individuals' perspectives about right and wrong, and they predispose individuals to certain modes of conduct (Rokeach, 1975). From a cultural perspective, the potency and permanence of beliefs are greatly heightened when groups share common beliefs (Schein, 1985). Teachers enter the profession with deeply held notions about how to conduct school—they teach as they were taught. If these beliefs are commonly held and help teachers negotiate the uncertainty of work in schools, no wonder teachers are reticent to adopt practices that have not stood the test of time. If beliefs govern behavior, the process of replacing old beliefs with new becomes critically important in changing educational practice in schools. Schein describes how beliefs are replaced in groups:

> When a group faces a new task, issue, or problem . . . someone in the group, usually the founder, has convictions about the nature of reality and how to deal with it, and will propose a solution based on those convictions . . . If the solution works, and the group has a shared perception of success . . . group members will tend to forget that originally they were not sure and that the values were therefore debated and confronted. As the values begin to be taken for granted, they gradually become beliefs and assumptions and drop out of consciousness, just as habits become unconscious and automatic [pp. 15–16].

This perspective explains the approach-avoidance behavior of some teachers as they struggle to integrate technology into their daily activities with students. Replacing old teaching habits took time and repeated success. It also required recognition from their peers and administrators that they were being successful with new practices and technology. New beliefs were reluctantly forged.

Schein's perspective about how beliefs are replaced in groups helped us understand the significance of the changes we watched unfold across the entire project. In the next section, we look at patterns of teaching and learning that emerged over time and describe our conceptual framework through the stories of ACOT teachers' classroom experiences.

Stages of Instructional Evolution

Our model includes five stages: entry, adoption, adaptation, appropriation, and invention. In this model, text-based curriculum delivered in a lecture-recitation-seat work mode is first strengthened through the use of technology and then gradually replaced by far more dynamic learning experiences for students.

Entry

At the time the project began, an instructional technology already existed in each of the ACOT classrooms. This technology was text based, and the common tools were blackboards, textbooks, workbooks, ditto sheets, and overhead projectors. These tools were used in combination to support lecture, recitation, and seat work. "Real school" was firmly in place. Teachers who were beginning with the project had little or no experience with computer technology and were in various stages of trepidation and excitement. At each site, teachers spent the first weeks of the project unpacking boxes, running extension cords, untangling cables, inserting cards, formatting disks, checking out home computers, and generally trying to establish order in radically transformed physical environments.

During this unavoidable initiation, experienced teachers found themselves facing problems typical of first-year teachers: discipline, resource management, and the personal frustration that comes from making time-consuming mistakes in already crowded days. Their audiotape journals were full of comments that expressed serious reservations about students' access to computers and about whether the new technology would ever "fit in." One of the project's elementary teachers commented, "There's too much fooling around with the computer—mousing around—when students are supposed to be listening." Another noted:

> Time is always going to be a problem. Teachers need help just to get equipment up and running sometimes. I do not seem to have enough time to meet the needs of everyone. I keep up by going in on weekends to complete the technical work.

Occasionally, ACOT teachers had second thoughts about the wisdom of their mission. After a number of months, however, equipment was finally in place, and teachers and students had mastered the technology basics. With more certainty about simple technical matters, there was less concern about time, and teachers began to focus again on instruction, the signal that they had entered a new phase, which we call adoption.

Adoption

While technology issues for ACOT teachers were far from over during the adoption stage, teachers—in their conversations, weekly reports, and audiotape journals—showed more concern about how technology could be integrated into daily instructional plans. Interspersed among traditional whole-group lectures, recitations, and seat work, teachers incorporated computer-based activities aimed primarily at teaching children how to use technology. Keyboarding instruction, for example, got under way at all of the sites. It typically occurred in 15-minute increments for a six-week period; at the end of this time, even eight-year-olds were typing 18–20 words per minute. Training on how to use word processors was a common next step, progressing in all instances far faster than teachers imagined. For example, high school teachers developed a multiweek unit on word processing. Instead of students taking weeks, teachers found students rushing ahead through feature after feature on their own and mastering the use of the software in a few hours over a number of days. Another common instructional agenda was learning how to save, store, and organize work.

At the elementary level, teachers spent inordinate amounts of time evaluating any of the hundreds of software programs that were available at that time for the Apple IIe computer, searching for just the right content and approach for a specific lesson. High school teachers, because they had chosen to work with Macintosh computers, skipped the time-consuming step of software evaluation; there simply were no educational software programs available at that early point in the Macintosh development. Consequently, sooner than their elementary colleagues, the ACOT high school teachers investigated other tool-based software such as databases, graphics programs, and spreadsheets for use in their classrooms. But in both instances, the teachers searched for software they could adapt to their established curricular and pedagogical preferences. Although much had changed physically in the classrooms, more remained the same.

With hindsight, there is little surprise that change was not faster and more dramatic. Given their lack of experience with the technology, teachers attempted to blend its use into the most familiar form of classroom practice, direct instruction. There were, in the beginning of the program, no successful experiences powerful enough to displace more comfortable patterns of operating. In addition to teachers' internal reticence, external forces influenced their instruction as well. At the high school site, an observer hired by the district noted the heavy emphasis on the official course of study and just how little leeway teachers perceived they had in varying from that guide (Damarin & Bohren, 1987). The same was true at the elementary sites, where teachers felt pressure to make sure their students would perform well on standardized tests of basic skills. At two elementary sites, annual teacher evaluations created concern. Would district observers allow for messier, noisier classrooms where children were not necessarily all doing the same things at the same time? Parents, too, voiced their concerns: "Will my child's handwriting develop naturally?" and "Will they do anything with this technology other than play games?" Teachers were very aware of the contextual constraints in which they worked.

Given frequent disruptions to normal classroom operation that came with beginning attempts to use the computers, we anticipated short-term declines in student performance in the adoption stage. Traditional measures of achievement, however, showed no significant decline or improvement in student performance aggregated at the classroom level (Baker, Herman, & Gearhart, 1989). Teachers reported that individual students performed better and were more motivated. What we witnessed during this period was the adoption of the new electronic technology to support text-based drill-and-practice instruction. ACOT staff hoped for more and began to see it in the next stage of teachers' progress with technology— adaptation.

Adaptation

In this phase, the new technology became thoroughly integrated into traditional classroom practice. Lecture, recitation, and seat work remained the dominant form of student tasks; but students used word processors, databases, some graphic programs, and many computer-assisted-instructional (CAI) packages for approximately 30–40 percent of the school day. More frequent and purposeful use of technology began to return dividends.

Productivity emerged as a major theme. Teachers reported that their students produced more and at a faster rate. In a self-paced, computational math program, for example, sixth-grade students completed the year's curriculum by the beginning of April, creating a quandary of what to do in math for the remainder of the year. The mere suggestion that these children start the seventh-grade math curriculum early created an uproar among seventh-grade teachers: "What will we do when we get the children next fall?" The solution was to use the balance of the year to focus the sixth-graders on application and problem solving. A revelation to the teachers was that students who were not usually enamored of math and rarely performed well became engaged in the hands-on, problem-solving approach. These students then became recognized as creative math-problem solvers. In future years, teachers at this site assigned most of the more traditional computational math activities as homework to be completed on the home computers and used class time for application and problem-solving activities.

At an elementary site, teachers focused on basic math and language-arts skills and used their computers purposefully to raise student test scores. For two years in a row the district reported that ACOT students scored significantly higher on the California Achievement Test than non-ACOT students in vocabulary, reading comprehension, language mechanics, math computation, and math concepts and application (Memphis Public Schools, 1987). At other sites, which were less focused on basic skill development, teachers still expressed fears that time spent on developing technology skills (rather than on covering the standard curriculum) might erode student test scores. Less time spent on basics, however, did not have a negative impact on student performance on tests at these sites (Baker, Herman, & Gearhart, 1989).

The productivity theme emerged at the high school level as well. In chemistry, students learned to use a simple graphics program to illustrate molecules and the exchange of atoms in chemical reactions. As a result, the teacher reported that students learned how to write and balance chemical formulas faster and more accurately than in his previous experience. As he explained, "It is great to be able to compress lesson time because of the software tools we now have." The chemistry teacher's supervisor also noted a change in the efficiency of the instructional process:

> The students have access to the total assignment on the network and are working through it much more quickly and with more understanding. Many of them never use paper and pencil on the assignment at all. They download the teacher's handouts to their computers, work on the tasks assigned, and send the final copy of their work to the printer to be picked up by the teacher. No more pages and pages of handouts that are lost, replaced, and lost again.

Writing was another area that drew frequent comment from the sites in the adaptation phase. A weekly report from a fourth-grade classroom read:

> I was amazed at the speed at which some of the students could use the word processor. I have noticed that increasingly this word-processing

program has become the preferred manner of preparing assignments. Many of the students can now type faster than they can write.

A special education teacher reported:

> Students are writing with a great deal more fluency now, thanks to keyboarding skills. Following a prewriting exercise, they now type their stories directly into the computer, rather than writing out the whole story and then copying it.

Researchers who examined writing in one third-grade ACOT classroom determined that children maintained a high level of enthusiasm for and interest in writing during the six-month study; that computers made compositions more presentable to others, thus encouraging writing; and that students wrote more and better as a function of the accessibility of computers (Hiebert, Quellmalz, & Vogel, 1987). Increased productivity in writing led to a bounty of text that allowed teachers to work with even young students on narrative skills. Willingly, students reworked their papers, a rare occurrence in paper-and-pencil classrooms. The same outpouring of text overwhelmed the project teachers and led to the need for new strategies for instruction, feedback, and evaluation.

During the adaptation phase, teachers also noted changes in the quality of student engagement in classroom tasks. The following reports from elementary sites are representative of those observations. As one teacher described:

> On Monday, when I announced that it was time for recess, the students wanted to continue to work in the classroom. One said, "You know, I can't believe it's really recess. When you're having a good time, time goes by so fast." They are really involved . . . They work really quietly without a lot of running around. They seem to be setting up standards for themselves to judge their own work.

Another teacher noted:

> This class is made up of children who had difficulty with the third grade and were not quite ready for the fourth. They are easily distracted. . . . They are less inclined to get off task when working on the computer and less intimidated with math problems than when working from a book.

In addition, teachers reported that students were increasingly more curious and assertive learners in the technology-rich classrooms, taking on new challenges far beyond the normal assignments (Fisher, 1991).

Appropriation

Appropriation is less a phase in instructional evolution and more a milestone.[1] It is evidenced less by change in classroom practice and more by change of personal attitude toward technology. It comes with teachers' personal mastery of the technologies they are attempting to employ in their classes. Appropriation is the point at which an individual comes to understand technology and use it effortlessly as a tool to accomplish real work. Perhaps it is best described in the words of two ACOT teachers. The first teacher is on the doorstep of appropriation:

> I'm still getting more confident in my use of computers. Seems that my day unconsciously revolves around the use of computers. I do lesson plans, notes and correspondence, report card information, history information, current events—all on the computer. I appreciate how it lets me function better as a teacher, when it's working. I don't think it's more important than any other teaching tool. However, it has a wide variety of uses.

The second teacher has crossed the threshold:

> Last spring, when I was taking a course at the university, I borrowed a computer and I did my whole term paper on it. I could not believe how labor saving it was, and now I believe, like many other teachers who have discovered the same thing, that it would be hard to live without a computer. If you had to take the computer I have at home, I would have to go out and buy one. I would have to have a computer. It has become a way of life.

The teachers' comments underscore the process of replacing old habits with new. When individuals have a shared perception of success, they forget their original doubts and their new values gradually become beliefs that are taken for granted (Schein, 1985). Teachers' new habits reveal a change in beliefs about the usefulness of technology. This milestone is a necessary and critical step before one can move onto more imaginative uses of technology for teaching and learning.

---

[1] In earlier descriptions of appropriation (e.g., Dwyer, Ringstaff, & Sandholtz, 1991), we discussed appropriation as a stage in the evolutionary process and included much of the description of interdisciplinary and project-based activities in the classrooms in it. In retrospect, we want to emphasize the personal nature of appropriation and assign the classroom shifts to the invention stage.

In the pioneering days of the ACOT project, few teachers in the world, much less their students, had enough access to technology to truly appropriate it (Becker, 1987; Office of Technology Assessment, 1988). In our view, lack of access to technology and little opportunity for appropriation underlie much of the criticism about technology use in schools. Teachers are simply unable to move on to more innovative uses and demonstrate new kinds of outcomes for students. Computers remain tools for efficiency, an underwhelming justification for their broader deployment (Cuban, 1986). Appropriation is the turning point for teachers—the end of efforts simply to computerize their traditional practice. It leads to the next stage, invention, where new teaching approaches promote the basics yet open the possibility of a new set of student competencies.

Invention

> I was so excited after the first day, I thought it was too good to be true. The students were using page layout software to make a publication in a 40–minute class period using the network. . . . All students saved and quit within three minutes before the bell. It runs like a charm. . . . Now we can simulate a newspaper company. Eventually, students will work in groups, each with their own task, some for art, business graphs, articles, and the editing group. Students can place finished work on a public share disk for the editing group to retrieve and complete the publication.

One of ACOT's high school teachers had developed so much confidence with networking technology and a professional page layout program that he ignored company warnings that his plan would never work. Guided by a vision of an ambitious writing project that would engage his students in a highly collaborative and creative activity, he doggedly continued until he succeeded. That success opened the way to an annual publication of students' writing that became as important to them as their yearbook at graduation. This is one example of what happens beyond appropriation.

In the invention stage, teachers experimented with new instructional patterns and ways of relating to students and to other teachers. As more teachers reached this stage, the whole tenor of the sites began to change. Interdisciplinary project-based instruction, team teaching, and individually paced instruction became common. Students were busier, more active; the classrooms buzzed.

At the high school site, students and teachers joined in a study of the renovation effort under way in their own city's business and government center. They began to design a large-scale model of the downtown, animated with robotics and controlled by a dozen or more computers. The final construction sat on a 10-by-20-foot base and incorporated 4-foot-tall models of buildings complete in every detail. A weekly electronic memo shared among all the ACOT sites described the project in progress in its late stages:

> The district art teacher will be with the ACOT students the entire six periods Monday as they put their model of the city together. The applications teacher has conned the rest of the team into giving up their classes so the students can have a full day of Computer Applications. . . . This has been a wonderful, integrated activity for students. They are using the robotics they have to build parts of our city. . . . The students researched the actual height of the buildings downtown and followed that by doing the mathematical proportions that must be done to determine the heights and widths of the model building accurately.

The success of this first big event led to subsequent projects the next school year, including an embellished return of the city project that included field trips to specific buildings and research about the individuals and businesses that occupied them.

At both the elementary and secondary levels, this type of teamed, project-based learning activity created opportunities for teachers to step back and observe their students. They saw their students' highly evolved skill with technology, their ability to learn on their own, and their movement away from competitive work patterns toward collaborative ones. For example, one teacher said:

> It's amazing to me how much these kids are learning. . . . Kids are doing things that are not assigned. The excitement is that they are motivated, seeing the power of the things which they are learning how to use, creating for themselves solutions to problems for other things. That is the goal of the educator. That the student be motivated to solve problems important to him, not to go after points. You never see this in regular classes.

Another teacher, describing a project in which students designed a calculator using a hypermedia application, reported:

> It was just so gratifying to see that as soon as one student finished, they would go look at another student's, saying, "How did you get it to do that?" They shared strategies. "Didn't you do the extra credit?" "You know how to do square root? Let me show you." It was just that sort

of give and take, that sort of excitement, contagious enthusiasm, high level of engagement that makes me feel that this really is a good model for the classroom of the future.

In yet another classroom, a teacher reflected on changes in the students' interactions:

> I tried to stand back today and take an overall view of what our classroom looks like. Some students were working on the board with each other in small groups. Sue was working with Joe; they've never worked together before. Joe's mother has talked to me because she's upset that he's not succeeding in the math part of our program. One of his problems is that he is so shy; he just won't ask questions. So, Sue was helping Joe and he seemed to be understanding. . . . I went and asked if she needed help. As soon as I left, I noticed Joe sought her out again for help. I thought, wow, this is something that would not happen in a traditional high school math classroom.

Students helped other students over hurdles with the technology, and they helped their teachers. Some teachers were a bit defensive at first about their students' growing expertise, but they later adapted to the more empowered status of students.

Others noted changes as well. An independent observer studying one of the elementary sites commented on changes in communication patterns and on the extent of collaborative work among even the youngest students. She reported that the children interacted differently at the computers. They talked to each other more, frequently asked for assistance from their neighbors, quickly interrupted their own work to help someone else, and displayed tremendous curiosity about what others were doing (Phelan, 1989). A district technology supervisor at the high school site, observing the extent of peer interaction in the ACOT classroom, noted that by allowing students to teach each other, teachers' roles were changing as well.

> The students really enjoy these group activities and, as we all know, learn more since they are actively rather than passively participating in the learning experience. Our teachers are learning to be facilitators rather than the total dispensers of knowledge. Everyone benefits.

The most important change in this phase was an increasing tendency of the ACOT teachers to reflect on teaching, to question old patterns, and to speculate about the causes behind changes they were seeing in their students. At the beginning of her third year with the project, one of ACOT's high school English teachers recorded in her audiotape journal: "It is all individualized and there is such a businesslike hum going on; there is such a good feel to it. It seems like what schools ought to be."

These types of changes in the learning environment benefited students. For instance, a longitudinal study of ACOT students at a high school site showed considerable differences when compared with their non-ACOT peers. ACOT students' absentee rate was 50 percent less, and they had no dropouts, compared with the school's 30 percent rate. Although half of the students who joined ACOT as freshmen had not planned to go to college, 90 percent of them graduated and went on to college compared with 15 percent for the non-ACOT graduates. Moreover, this ACOT graduating class amassed 27 academic awards in addition to recognitions for outstanding accomplishments in history, calculus, foreign language, and writing.[2] The greatest difference in these students, however, was the manner in which they organized for and accomplished their work. They routinely employed inquiry, collaborative, technological, and problem-solving skills uncommon to graduates of traditional high school programs (Tierney, Kieffer, Whalin, Desai, & Gale, 1992). These skills are remarkably similar to competencies argued for by the U.S. Department of Labor (Secretary's Commission on Achieving Necessary Skills [SCANS], 1991). This report maintains that in addition to basic language and computational literacy, high school graduates must master the abilities to organize resources; work with others; locate, evaluate, and use information; understand complex work systems; and work with a variety of technologies.

The invention stage is the climax in the evolution of teachers' instructional strategies and beliefs. In ACOT's research, most but not all teachers reached this new plateau as classroom leaders. They demonstrated their comfort with a new set of beliefs about teaching and learning that was not common among teachers at the project's outset. Though there was variation, the ACOT teachers became more disposed to view learning as an active, creative, and socially interactive process than when they entered the program. Knowledge came to be viewed more as something that children must construct for themselves and less as something that can be transferred intact.

---

[2] This graduating class was not a technical random sample of the high school students. We believe, however, that it was representative of the school as a whole. The magnitude of difference between the ACOT students' performance and that of their peers is provocative. Moreover, we have seen similar outcomes in subsequent graduating classes.

Reaching the invention stage, however, was a slow and arduous process for most teachers. In the following section, we describe the types of supports that can help teachers as they progress through the evolutionary stages.

Building Support for Instructional Change

Technology is a catalyst for change in classroom processes because it provides a distinct departure, a change in context that suggests alternative ways of operating. It can drive a shift from a traditional instructional approach toward a more eclectic set of learning activities that include knowledge-building situations for students. In this chapter, we discussed five common stages in that transition, highlighting changes in teachers' actions, in the way they employed technology at each stage, and in the resulting transformations in their students' work. Underlying this model is our view that such changes will occur only if there is a concomitant change in teachers' beliefs about their practice. However, instructional evolution is not simply a matter of abandoning beliefs but one of gradually replacing them with more relevant ones shaped by experiences in an altered context. Beliefs are a source of guidance in times of uncertainty; they are important in defining teaching tasks and organizing relevant information. They are an irreplaceable element in the process of imagining alternative futures—"envisioning and trying to establish instructional formats or systems of classroom relations of which there is no direct personal experience" (Nespor, 1987, p. 319).

The idea that deeply held beliefs are pivotal to change in practice frequently emerges in educational research (Baldridge & Deal, 1975; Chin & Benne, 1961; Cuban, 1986; Fullan, 1982; Giacquinta, 1973; Paul, 1977). However, the challenge lies in finding ways to help teachers confront their instructional beliefs.

Contextual Forms of Support

What can be done to foster the generation of values and attitudes that support innovations? Two conditions seem essential. First, before teachers can reflect on their beliefs, they must somehow bring them to a conscious level, and they must see and understand the connection between their beliefs and their actions. They must also be aware of alternative belief systems and experience positive consequences of those alternatives. Second, administrators must be willing to implement structural or programmatic shifts in the context or working environments of teachers who are instructionally evolving.

The process of change in ACOT classrooms involved more than introducing the technology and waiting for change to occur. Certain aspects of the project, such as data collection requirements and close working relationships among teachers and project researchers, gave teachers opportunities for reflection, which promoted changes in their personal beliefs about instruction. In addition, institutional and project supports altered the teachers' working environments.

At the same time that teachers transformed the structure of their classrooms, ACOT staff worked closely with school and district administrators to change the larger context in which the teachers worked. Institutional supports, including technical training on the use of hardware and software, and release time for collaboration and team planning, became routine for project teachers. Teachers also had opportunities to attend or present at professional conferences and to participate in workshops on instructional issues in which they expressed interest.

At each site, coordinators provided ongoing technical and instructional support. Whenever possible, administrators permitted daily schedules to be flexible, allowing for peer observation and team teaching. Teachers and coordinators also had access to a telecommunications network—linking participants, ACOT staff, researchers, and other educators. Teachers frequently used the network to discuss instructional issues, provide emotional support, and share experiences with participants at other sites. These forms of contextual support promoted change by decreasing teacher isolation. As teachers grappled with difficult instructional issues, they found it helpful to discuss their concerns with others in similar situations:

> James commented at our meeting that he is not comfortable at all with having the students work together. I felt uncomfortable with that last year, but ACOT has broken me away from that feeling, realizing that they can be very productive being instructional aides to each other. We pointed out to James that in our program if a student is having another student do their work for them, it's going to show on the test. Unlike the normal classroom, they can't just take their F and go on.

Opportunities for teacher reflection complemented these contextual changes and further promoted teacher change. The process of reflection helped teachers to see for themselves the benefits and drawbacks of different instructional approaches. Unlike many programs aimed at educational reform, this project provided built-in mechanisms that cultivated teacher reflection over the long term. For example, the data collection strategy requiring teachers to complete audiotapes provoked their analysis of classroom experiences. Although some teachers grumbled about the time necessary to comply with this requirement, many recognized the value of the exercise:

> These tape requirements that you have given us were the pits at first. Now I am really into them as a means of mental release. . . . Anyhow, I'll stop beating around the bush. My tape recorder is broken. I now have nothing to talk into every day and I am feeling very panicky. Is there any way you could bring a new tape recorder to the conference? I would really appreciate it.

The process of completing weekly reports about major events and developments, which were telecommunicated to other sites, gave teachers further opportunities to reflect upon their teaching.

Another research component of the project involved having individual teachers work closely with university-based investigators on issues such as student empowerment, multimedia instruction, and mathematics software. Once again, teachers sometimes complained about the time they had to commit to these activities, but they also acknowledged that working closely with researchers had important benefits:

> This experiment with Cornell University is really forcing me to think through my thought processes about what I am doing and questions I am asking. It is really good and healthy for me to experience these challenges. I feel I am growing and learning more about myself, and becoming more aware of what is happening in the classroom.

Not only did working closely with researchers increase the opportunities for teachers to confront their own beliefs about teaching and learning, but it also validated their efforts to change:

> Working with researchers lets me know that I am not doing such a bad job, that I do come up with some good questions, and that I am becoming more secure about myself as I become more experienced at using a new teaching approach.

Similarly, periodic visitors to the classrooms provided an important audience for ACOT teachers. The visitors served as a source of valuable feedback, increasing teachers' reflections on their practices and reinforcing their experimentation with new methods. Being constantly observed by colleagues, particularly those from other schools, reemphasized the importance and value of their innovative strategies. Moreover, the changes teachers made in their instructional techniques were pervasive enough to be noted over time, rather than being temporary alterations meant to impress occasional visitors.

Incremental Steps to Altering Contexts

Recognizing that change is evolutionary, we suggest an incremental approach to altering contexts and providing needed supports. Table 18.1 delineates the kinds of training, activities, and support that parallel our five stages and can help expedite teachers' passage through them.

In the early stages of implementing technology in classrooms, teachers' needs center around their concerns over the technology itself: central processing units, disk drives, software, and other peripherals. Technical training, therefore, is a key ingredient that can reduce stress and boost confidence. But it will remain an isolated exercise, soon forgotten, unless it is situated in a context with purpose. As teachers learn technological basics, they need to be immersed in an environment that builds the links between technology and instruction and learning. They must have enough access to technology for themselves and for their students to make the exercise relevant. We also hold that teachers will more likely be successful if they engage in this process as volunteers and as members of teams. The first serious organizational shift comes with the need to schedule time for teams to meet routinely. Besides providing technology, allowing teachers time to acquire skills and assist one another is a clear indicator of any administrator's seriousness about this form of change.

We recommend forms of support for teacher change that are increasingly interactive as teachers progress through the evolutionary stages and that expand to include more and more teachers, mentors, and even researchers. Teachers need increased and varied opportunities to see other teachers, to confront their actions and examine their motives, and to reflect critically on the consequences of their choices, decisions, and actions. They need opportunities for ongoing dialogue about their experiences and for continuous development of their abilities to imagine and discover more powerful learning experiences for their students. Finally, both for teachers' own personal affirmation as well as for the creation of bodies of craft knowledge to support novice teachers, we recommend that teachers write about and publish their experiences as innovators. The advent of the World Wide Web and numerous teacher bulletin boards and chat areas provides a perfect opportunity.

There are important caveats to the strategy of focusing on changing teachers' beliefs as a condition for instructional change. First, there are

Table 18.1. Support for Instructional Evolution in Technology-Rich Classrooms.

Phase	Expectation	Support
Entry	Volunteer team	Provide routine planning time to develop shared vision and practice
	Critical mass of technology present for teachers and students	Excuse staff from as many district requirements as possible
		Create opportunities for staff to share experiences with nonparticipant colleagues
Adoption	Keyboarding	Provide nuts-and-bolts technical support to develop teacher's confidence and ability to maintain hardware and facilitate children's use
	Use of word processors for writing	
	Use of CAI (computer-assisted instruction) software for drill and practice of basic skills	Provide CAI, keyboarding, and word-processing software and training
Adaptation	Many basic instructional activities individualized and self-paced	Develop flexible schedule to permit peer observation and team teaching
	Students composing on computers	Introduce and discuss alternative pedagogies
	Course of study evolving as result of student productivity and changing expectations of teachers	Train staff in use of tool software: spreadsheets, databases, graphics, hypermedia, communications
		Introduce video disc and scanner technology

Table 18.1. (*continued*).

Phase	Expectation	Support
Appropriation	Increased focus on higher-order skills	Routinize peer observations and group discussions of events and consequences
	Experimentation with interdisciplinary, project-based instruction	Reexamine project mission and goals
	Experimentation with team teaching	Build awareness of alternative student assessment strategies, i.e., performance-based assessment and portfolio assessment strategies
	Experimentation with student grouping	
	Conflict with traditional schedules and assessment techniques	Encourage and support conference attendance and teacher presentations
	Experimentation with scheduling and assessment strategies	
Invention	Establishment of higher learning standards	Encourage collaboration between teachers and researchers
	Implementation of integrated curriculum	Encourage teachers to write about and publish their experiences
	Balanced and strategic use of direct teaching and project-based teaching	Explore telecommunications as way to keep teachers in contact with innovators outside of district
	Integration of alternative modes of student assessment	Create opportunities for teachers to mentor other teachers

risks associated with making successful change efforts a matter of achieving a series of personal triumphs rather than recognizing the process as an organizational, systemic, or cultural phenomenon. Any teacher in the process of change is an actor surrounded by other actors and institutionalized principles. If there is no change in the larger system, the struggling teacher is doomed to frustration and the innovation to abandonment (Bowers, 1973; Schiffer, 1979). Second, beliefs are an inherently complex concept. Although plans for reform may appear rational, reformers must accept that beliefs, tied as they are to personal insights, to significant personal moments, and to significant others, affect behavior in outwardly irrational ways. "There are no clear, logical rules for determining the relevance of beliefs to real world events and situations" (Nespor, 1987, p. 321). Third, groups bound by commitment to change, sharing reflections and shaping new beliefs, can lose their objectivity and create new problems (Dwyer, 1981; Hoffer, 1951; Janis, 1972; Smith & Dwyer, 1979).

In sum, instructional change can proceed only with a corresponding change in beliefs about instruction and learning. Teachers' beliefs can only be modified while teachers are in the thick of change—taking risks and facing uncertainty. Bringing significant change to the way we do schooling is a complex proposition fraught with setbacks. The experience of the ACOT project demonstrates the value of taking a long-term perspective on change and making the necessary personal and organizational commitments to bring about that change. To the observer, hoping for quick evidence of the efficacy of innovations, computers or otherwise, the process can only be frustrating and inconclusive. To those dedicated enough to make the commitment, the process can be very rewarding.

REFERENCES

Baker, E. L., Herman, J. L., & Gearhart, M. (1989). *The ACOT report card: Effects on complex performance and attitude.* Paper presented at the meeting of the American Educational Research Association, San Francisco.

Baldridge, B. J., & Deal, T. E. (1975). *Managing change in educational organizations.* Berkeley, CA: McCutchan Publishing Corporation.

Becker, H. J. (1987, July). *The impact of computer use on children's learning: What research has shown and what it has not.* Baltimore, MD: Center for Research on Elementary and Middle Schools.

Bowers, D. G. (1973). OD techniques and their results in 23 organizations: The Michigan ICL study. *Journal of Applied Behavioral Science, 9,* 21B41.

Buber, M. (1957). *Between man and man.* Boston: Beacon Press.

Chin, R., & Benne, K. D. (1961). General strategies for effecting changes in human systems. In W. G. Bennis, K. D. Benne, & R. Chin (Eds.), *The planning of change*. New York: Holt, Rinehart & Winston.

Cuban, L. (1986). *Teachers and machines: The classroom use of technology since 1920*. New York: Teachers College Press.

Damarin, S., & Bohren, J. (1987). The evolution of the ACOT-Columbus classroom. In S. Damarin, & J. Bohren (Eds.), *Reaching for tomorrow: A study of a computer-saturated classroom*. Unpublished manuscript.

Dewey, J. (1963). *Experience and education*. New York: Collier Books.

Dwyer, D. (1981). *Ideology and organizational evolution: A comparative study of two innovative educational projects*. Unpublished doctoral dissertation, Washington University, St. Louis, MO.

Dwyer, D. (1994). Apple Classrooms of Tomorrow: What we've learned. *Educational Leadership, 51*(7), 4–10.

Dwyer, D., Ringstaff, C., & Sandholtz, J. H. (1991). Changes in teachers' beliefs and practices in technology-rich classrooms. *Educational Leadership, 48*(8).

Fisher, C. W. (1991). Some influences of classroom computers on academic tasks. *Journal of Computing in Childhood Education, 2*(2), 3–16.

Fullan, M. G. (1982). *The meaning of educational change*. New York: Teachers College Press.

Giacquinta, J. B. (1973). The process of organizational change in schools. In F. N. Kerlinger (Ed.), *Review of Research in Education, 3* (pp. 178–208). Itasca, IL: Peacock.

Greene, M. (1979). Teaching: The question of personal reality. In A. Lieberman & L. Miller (Eds.), *Staff development: New demands, new realities, new perspectives* (pp. 23–35). New York: Teachers College, Columbia University.

Hiebert, E. H., Quellmalz, E. S., & Vogel, P. (1989). *A research based writing program for students with high access to computers* (ACOT Report No. 2). Cupertino, CA: Apple Computer.

Hoffer, E. (1951). *The true believer: Thoughts on the nature of mass movements*. New York: Perennial Library Harper & Row.

Janis, I. (1972). *The victims of group think: A psychological study of foreign-policy decisions and fiascoes*. Boston: Houghton-Mifflin.

Memphis Public Schools. (1987). ACOT: Right here in Memphis. *Memphis District Newsletter*, Memphis, TN.

Nespor, J. (1987). The role of beliefs in the practice of teaching. *Journal of Curriculum Studies, 19*(4), 317–328.

Office of Technology Assessment. (1988). *Power on! New tools for teaching and learning*. Washington, DC: U.S. Government Printing Office.

Paul, D. A. (1977). Change processes at the elementary, secondary and post secondary levels of education. In N. Nash & J. Culbertson (Eds.), *Linking processes in educational improvement: Concepts and applications* (pp. 7–73). Columbus, OH: University Council for Educational Administration.

Phelan, P. (1989). *The addition of computers to a first-grade classroom: A case study of two children.* Unpublished report.

Rokeach, M. (1975). *Beliefs, attitudes and values.* San Francisco: Jossey-Bass.

Schein, E. H. (1985). *Organizational culture and leadership: A dynamic view* (1st ed.). San Francisco: Jossey-Bass.

Schiffer, J. (1979). A framework for staff development. In A. Lieberman & L. Miller (Eds.), *Staff development: New demands, new realities, new perspectives* (pp. 4–23). New York: Teachers College Press.

Secretary's Commission on Achieving Necessary Skills (SCANS). (July, 1991). *What work requires of schools: A SCANS Report for America 2000.* Washington, DC: U.S. Department of Labor.

Smith, B. O. (1963). Toward a theory of teaching. In A. A. Bellack (Ed.), *Theory and research in teaching.* New York: Bureau of Publications, Teachers College.

Smith, L. M., & Dwyer, D. C. (1979). *Federal policy in action: A case study of an urban education project.* Washington, DC: Occasional Paper of the National Institute of Education.

Tierney, R. J., Kieffer, R. D., Whalin, K., Desai, L., & Gale, A. (1992). *A longitudinal study of the influence of high computer access on students' thinking, learning, and interactions* (ACOT Report No. 16). Cupertino, CA: Apple Computer.

WEB SITE

http://www.apple.com/education/k12/leadership/acot

19

REDEFINING COMPUTER APPROPRIATION

A FIVE-YEAR STUDY OF ACOT STUDENTS

Robert J. Tierney

MUCH HAS BEEN WRITTEN about ACOT teachers and the technology used in their classrooms. While this is valuable information, I contend that the real strength of ACOT lies in the vision of technology that the students themselves have discovered and appropriated. The teachers, staff, and researchers at ACOT support and influence student development, but the most significant changes have actually occurred on the margins of classrooms, in conjunction with what students have realized for themselves. What happens to the students in ACOT has not been limited to gaining proficiency in the mechanics of computer use; the entire learning process has been enhanced as students' access to multimedia tools and other technologies has increased. As the students have recognized the potentials of multimedia, their individual perceptions and innovations have moved to center stage. This shift has involved more than the showiness of the projects. Students' conceptions of and acquisition of knowledge as well as their understandings of how media might be employed have become more flexible and dynamic. Furthermore, technology has become woven into the fabric of who they were and what they do both individually and within their classrooms, schools, and wider communities. Technology has played an important role in how these students view themselves, the roles they assume in their various communities, and the cultural practices they have come to value.

Over a six-year period, I was involved in a longitudinal study of computer literacy acquisition.[1] In my research, I was specifically interested in literacy acquisition that emerges from the experiences of students with high computer access. My goal was to explore student development in a manner that was observational, open-ended, and not constrained by predetermined views of outcomes, and so I have focused on development rather than on a single set of measures or comparisons with equivalent groups. The study involved two sets of students who attended ACOT classrooms for the entire four years of their high school experience. The extended duration of this investigation allowed my colleagues and me to achieve a developmental perspective, and it enabled us to assess shifts in student learning across time.

From a rather unique exploration of students' appropriation of computer literacy, we gleaned strong evidence that the circumstances of ACOT had a major, significant, positive, and sustained impact upon student learning and ways of knowing. Indeed, I feel that the data warrants some rather bold claims about the impact of computer appropriation upon students involved in ACOT. These students discovered *genres of power* in new texts, new ways of negotiating meaning, and new ways of knowing that allowed them to develop and test a variety of approaches and hypotheses. This phenomenon is at the core of ACOT and is what makes attempts at systemic reform and efforts to replicate the success of ACOT worthwhile. If we ignore the magnitude of the shifts in perspective that occurred, or if we fail to consider the nature of computer appropriation, then we will trivialize the significance of ACOT.

Computer Appropriation in an ACOT Studio Setting

In their review of research on media and learning, Clark and Salomon[2] suggest that one of the drawbacks to studies of the impact of media is that very few situations provide for the sustained daily engagement that would allow for a reasonable assessment of the impact of technology. ACOT affords students as much access to computers as students in regular classrooms have to books and pen and paper. Students are able to interact with a community of learners in various subject areas within a context that enables them to explore and learn with a range of multimedia software, databases, and word processing software. At the ACOT site in Columbus, we were involved with students who have had access to state-of-the-art software and hardware, as well as technical support. We were therefore able to look at the impact of computers on a cohort of students over the course of four years, during which time students had more than four hours per day of access to a computer at school and free access at home. The ACOT site permitted the level of investment that Clark and Salomon called for, and therefore provided a unique opportunity to study the impact of computer media upon learning.

Participants in ACOT's Columbus site are selected by lottery each year from over a hundred applicants. Class sizes are kept to thirty and students represent a cross-section in terms of ability and background. The students came from primarily working class homes of a variety of racial and cultural heritages. Students selected for the case studies were drawn from the first two cohorts of students to complete the ACOT high school program. From these two classes, students of varying abilities were identified for inclusion in this study and agreed to participate.

The physical arrangement of the high school classrooms was largely self-contained. Most of the class periods were taught in one of three or four rooms involving team-teaching situations (for example, science and math, English and history). Within each classroom, every student had a variety of workspaces that afforded opportunities for individual or group use of computers, printers, and other media equipment, and access to a range of software.

Observations and interviews served as the cornerstone for our investigation into computer literacy acquisition. General interviews were used in hopes of providing details of the students' attitudes, expectations, perceptions of learning experiences, engagement of thinking, and learning outcomes. Within twenty-four hours of each lesson, classroom observers debriefed individual students. Records of classroom and student activities were transcribed from both videotapes and running records.

In conjunction with our open-ended orientation, we struggled with ways to discern and account for patterns in the data. The difficulty of so doing was compounded by the masses of data we had collected from each year. For some students, we accumulated over seventy-five thousand words across the four years. To cope with the enormity of data and as a way of identifying themes, we developed a coding system using FileMaker to help organize the data. First, each student's comment was coded in terms of learning activities, such as process (planning, drafting, revising, sharing, and so on), type of activity (seventeen types were included), nature of support (peer, teacher, and so on), mode (computer or noncomputer), and overall effect.

Our second pass—colloquially referred to as "the wall"—consisted of displays of all the data on the walls of our offices. It was at this point that we began to discern the types of shifts. Themes were identified by examination of these data across different years and by various procedures that we used to achieve alternative perspectives on the data. The multiyear nature of the data allowed us to examine developmental issues for each individual. As data were reorganized by years, we were able to see differences from one year to the next.

The use of TEX, a HyperCard application, afforded frequency counts for each word by year. For example, the frequency of each and every word for each student provided a comparative distribution of the number of times students used different words, such as graphics, friends, interface, and so on. These collagelike distributions provided a take on the data that served as a cross-check on some of the trends that were originally identified by other means. While these counts were seen as complementary to our other analyses, it should be obvious that such counts have limitations: they represent what was said, not what was felt, thought, or done; and decontextualized words sometimes render interpretation problematic. However, what was apparent in both the interviews and the word counts was that students were appropriating technology on its own terms. It was not until we listened closely to what students were saying and began rethinking the data in terms of the symbol systems actually used that we realized that our adopted lens was restricting our view of what was occurring.

Initially, we had unwittingly adopted the view of technology as merely an adjunct to learning. With the introduction of desktop publishing, scanning capabilities, and hypermedia, some major shifts occurred in how students represented and approached the integration of ideas from various sources. To capture these dimensions, we found it useful to characterize the shifts that occurred according to: the students' ways of representing ideas and thinking about issues symbolically; students' approaches to developing projects and problem solving; certain social dimensions of students' learning, including their collaborations and nature of support; and students' ongoing goals and attitudes. To this end, we labeled each shift as pertaining to one or more of the following: view of text, process, self-evaluation, learning goals, task demands, and social concerns. In addition, these comments were examined across time and in terms of whether they pertained to a student's expectation, perception, or outcome.

Some Findings

During the first year of the project, most students approached texts in a rather limited fashion. They would proceed with little regard to integrating graphics or other media, layout would be largely predetermined and conventionalized, text would be rather linear and nonlayered, and audience was considered somewhat as an afterthought. In accordance with this tendency, computers were perceived as tools for expediting revision to ensure accuracy. Audience served the function of offering general reactions and correcting errors. The computer-generated copy was for presentation rather than involvement.

These tendencies can be seen in students' comments during year one and in word counts conducted across the four years for the two cohorts of students. Students often made remarks in which the role of the computer was diminished. For example, one student stated: "It helps you to just write down or type out what you're thinking about, and then lets you get the rough idea out, and then you can just go back and change or add to it." Another referred to "accuracy and neatness" as the major advantages of using the computer. Very few students mentioned graphics and the use of other media; nor did students discuss alternate formats or layouts for presenting ideas in a multilayered fashion.

At the end of year two, all students reported an improvement in their ability to write as a result of using the computer. They felt that their final products looked better and were easier to revise. The computer was now thought of as a tool for efficiency. But by years three and four, student involvement with multimedia became more prevalent, especially via HyperCard. And in turn, major shifts occurred. Accompanying the shift to multimedia was the unearthing of a new, more powerful set of genres and text forms. With these texts, students seemed less verbocentric. They were more likely to include graphics and appeared to display a greater willingness to experiment. There was also a shift in their approach to developing ideas.

These new genres and possibilities brought to the surface a desire to develop electronic texts with multifaceted appeals and different relationships to both the ideas themselves and the possible readers' responses. Their developing understandings of technology altered how students used symbol systems (that is, graphics and print) to explore, represent, and share ideas. The students moved beyond the incorporation of text and graphics to consciously stretch the capabilities of the software to create a form that mirrored the dynamics of their ideas and the messages they wished to convey. Students realized the possibility of developing texts that, to use their words, were "dynamic rather than static." Their approaches to ideas became less verbocentric, less linear and unidimensional. In conjunction with being able to explore the integrated use of various graphics (animation, video segments, scanned images or various ways to graphically depict data), they began to utilize diverse media as a way of achieving different perspectives on issues as they explored physics, history, and other subjects.

Some students were not engaged in using multimedia technology extensively, yet their shift to graphics was still notable in terms of the possibilities they saw and the thinking they did. Whereas, in years one and two, texts were largely devoid of graphics except to enhance the look of a page, in years three and four graphics had become an integral symbol system for exploring and sharing ideas. The students were exploring ways to integrate images with written text to achieve different takes and twists. They found themselves free to develop texts that were nonlinear and multilayered. They embedded buttons in their texts and graphics that, if clicked upon, accessed other layers of information. By year four, students would experiment with graphics, sound, animation, and text so that their projects were integrated, aesthetically pleasing, and engaged the attention of fellow students and others. As the students stated:

> "A lot of times I'll work with graphics and experimenting. I'll create new graphics or new drawings like I did like that and then figure out new ways to put it in there so it catches the person's eye and they want to read more or try to get away with—a picture is worth a thousand words. Try to—I work experimentally a lot with that. Trying to make it so my report only has to be a picture."

> "I thought it would be kind of hard to get the graphics and text together at first. And especially when we were doing HyperCard. To get the graphics so they would look good. So they didn't just look like a stack. I wanted it to look like a computer program and not a HyperCard stack. It wasn't as hard as I thought it was either. Just putting your ideas down and just doing it a little differently than you first expected to."

> "The things that we created weren't really something that could be done on a page. They could be printed out but they still wouldn't be the same, clicking on a button. It wasn't something you could look at; it was something you had to become involved with. . . . I think it makes it more nonlinear sometimes. . . . Like they'll be showing a process on a computer screen."

> "I tried to find some graphics that would appeal. I tried to figure out how to do animation so it wouldn't be too boring. I tried to make it as fresh as I could."

Their strategies had shifted toward using the computer to crisscross their explorations of a topic or issue as they enlisted various media in search of different but complementary perspectives. For example, one student described how his process of developing projects had evolved throughout the years. He labeled each year: ninth grade as the year to work on writing; tenth grade as the scripting year; eleventh grade as working with graphics; and the twelfth grade as "combining it all together in one big media project."

Technology appears to have increased the likelihood of students' being able to pursue multiple lines of thought and entertain different perspectives. Ideas were no longer treated as unidimensional and sequential; the technology allowed students to embed ideas within other ideas, as well as pursue other forms of multilayering and interconnecting ideas. Students began spending a great deal of time considering layout, that is, how the issues that they were wrestling with might be explored across an array of still pictures, video segments, text segments, and sound clips. It was apparent that students in the high-access classroom had begun exploring texts in very complex ways. These tendencies are also apparent in the terms used by students in assessing their own learning. In year one, words such as *type, read,* and *write* were among the most frequent terms used when they assessed their learning. By year four, words such as *graphic, layout, multimedia, project, show,* and *see* had become much more prevalent.

Literacy is a social act. Oftentimes, what is read, written, dramatized, or symbolized is intended for others; usually it has involved others in the selection and formation of ideas, and at the very least it involves a negotiation with oneself amidst a community of co-learners. These social dimensions are not an offshoot of what is involved in literacy experience, they are integral. Students' engagement with computers is no different. Whereas computers may be viewed as isolating students and minimizing interaction with others, data from our case studies suggest this is not the case. All of the current case-study students both were engaged in and viewed their experiences with computers as involving complex social dimensions. Students interacted and collaborated with others in a variety of ways, including joint construction of projects, cooperative ventures involving differential expertise, coauthoring, parallel development of similar work, and side-by-side consultation and group sharings. In these processes, students assumed a range of roles such as demonstrator, partner, helper, sounding board, advisor, mediator, supervisor, and decision maker. In other words, the social facts of computer literacy in ACOT were pervasive, dynamic, and complex. Students were engaged in literacy that was socially transforming for themselves, their friends, and sometimes their families. In high school, students' views of themselves as learners often decline together with their appreciation of the relevance of their experience. ACOT seems to have afforded students an experience that is different in direction and kind—especially in relation to community building.

Students were well aware of the extent to which ACOT encouraged students to work together. They often noted the social dimension of the program in regard to both the bonuses of cooperation and the effect interaction had on their relationships. As one said, "Well, one thing, especially when the class is new, it helps build confidence and friendship among the people, because no one knows what they're doing. But there'll be a few people who catch on quicker and people will be asking them 'how do you do this' or they'll be offering help—the ones who have learned it faster. So it's one way to meet people."

Students often found themselves cast in the role of experts advising others on software use, and this interaction with others enhanced their own pursuits. Their expertise was also accessed in the wider community. For example, one student asserted: "My friends in ACOT, they're in it so they understand what it's all about. I have a lot of friends who aren't in it. And they think it's neat too. That I can do some stuff. Sometimes I work with them on projects using the computer, like I just got done working on a newspaper where I worked with a lot of people I knew. Sometimes I'll offer suggestions like—'I could show you how to do that on the computer a lot easier'—things like that. It's kind of just the sharing of ideas." Similar sentiments were expressed by other students who valued the exchange of ideas and the support, as well as the efficiency in completing tasks.

Students in ACOT constantly worked together in groups. Sometimes they worked with friends, other times with assigned partners. The groups generally worked by meeting and discussing an idea or topic and then dividing up the work. They would go their separate ways and then come back together to compile their findings into an integrated whole. During the compilation process they often sat together as a stack was created and took turns controlling the mouse. Finally, they presented their work together as a group.

Working together in groups gave students opportunities to interact, provide assistance, and share ideas. The sharing of ideas was emphasized by many students as being important to the success of a project. This was, one student asserted: "Because they all chip in and work together and you are basically doing the same amount of work but you've got so much more put into it."

Having spent four years together, the students knew each other very well and were comfortable using each other for support, as well as for academic help. "Most of the time we divide the work together because outside of school we don't really get to do things together so each person has different tasks and then when we go back to school when we have time to work in class we'll get together and then kind of tell each other what we have. Or ask for ideas or help." The fact that everyone had different ideas sometimes caused difficulties, but students felt that in the long run projects were improved by cooperative efforts.

The classrooms assumed the feel of studios and think-tanks where artists and scientists work together on various projects. The shift toward a dynamic multimedia studio for learning was supported by the collaborations among students and teachers in the classrooms. As one student stated: "I think it increases your ability to communicate and to take criticism, because you just get used to it after a while. People are always saying, 'Hey, try it this way. That might work out better.' And you just kind of look at it, 'OK, I'll try it like that.'"

The social dynamics became pervasive as students were engaged in their own projects and projects for others. They worked with and for others and technology was seen as an important part of the process.

On another level, ACOT is a project involving working relationships with various groups—researchers, computer hackers, and businesses. This involves the students in diverse discourses, as one student noted: "I think ACOT definitely helps just because they come into contact with so many more people, so many more different types of people. You've got the students for most of the day but you're communicating with business executives and you meet people in educational fields. Just so many types of people. That's one thing that will be helpful."

The longitudinal data suggested that over the course of their involvement in ACOT students shifted from cautious optimism about themselves to what might be viewed as a connoisseurship of their computer-based learning experiences and respect for their own capabilities. Their involvement with computers was not seen as superfluous, but rather as integral to and having the potential to socially transform their lives. The comments of the students support an appreciation of the meaningfulness of their learning experiences, including an attitude toward computers as a tool that afforded them ways of achieving their ends. That is not to say that they might not be able to achieve these ends by other means, but that computers had become a vehicle for achieving a range of goals, both immediate and long term. Students improved their ability to solve problems and communicate ideas effectively, use alternative symbol systems, establish goals for themselves, and perceive strengths and weaknesses of their work. They also recognized the long-term advantages of newly acquired skills for their career aspirations and achievement of personal goals. At the same time, their experiences were also individualized. All of these students have different goals and dispositions that define to some extent what they gained, as well as where they saw themselves headed.

While these observations and interviews of the students are not comprehensive, they suggest that students engaged in a range of different forms of collaborations for a variety of purposes. Moreover, these collaborations are an integral dimension of their learning. It would seem that if we are to come to grips with understanding computer literacy, then we need to understand its dynamics, especially the social dimensions.

Discussion

The ACOT site was a platform where the envelope was pushed in lots of ways: how student learning was defined, what was entailed in teaching and learning with technology, how technology might be enlisted in classrooms governed by constructivist learning tenets, how students might work together in such environments, how technology might be appropriated by teachers and students, and how systemic change occurs. The longitudinal study at the Columbus site explored some of these issues.

Students in both cohorts became independent and collaborative problem solvers, theorists, communicators, record keepers, and learners with the computers. They developed a repertoire of abilities with which they could explore possibilities that would be too cumbersome or difficult to attain without the technology. Furthermore, their ways of thinking shifted to align with options afforded by multilayered texts. While they had the capability of achieving independent agendas, their approach to learning was collaborative. The studio environment at ACOT contributed to their visions of the future and to their sense of authority.

Certainly, the complex nature of computer appropriation and the differences that exist across individuals and groups over time should not be dismissed. For example, different literacies are apt to be appropriated in different ways and variations are apt to exist in the social dimensions associated with different literacies. While our general findings apply across students, individuals vary in expertise, experience using particular software applications, and the ways in which expertise developed over time. Various factors appear to contribute to these differences, including motivation, goals, exposure, and interests.

As should be apparent from our observation and debriefing procedures, we approached our data without a rigidly fixed agenda. One of the advantages of so doing was that we did not establish boundaries of our study *a priori*. If we had done so, we would not have uncovered what we uncovered. However, rather than clone ACOT, we would encourage sites to emerge in accordance with local situations and stress the need for the investment of energy, resources, and time befitting the vision. The kind of computer appropriation that we witnessed is not something that one can prepackage.

It is essential that the vision of technology that emerged not be slighted. Sometimes new media predispose students to superficially engage in activities that have doubtful value. This was not what occurred with multimedia at ACOT. The software and teaching goals afforded generative —rather than tightly constrained and predictable—pursuits. Indeed, the media prompted the pursuit of ways of knowing aligned with complex knowledge acquisition. This involved multilayered explorations, including extensive use of resources as well as more in-depth pursuit of topics. It promoted an appreciation of the perspectives that different media provide. In some ways, students became critics of text as vehicles for communication and management as they began to view knowledge in terms of the media used in accessing and presenting ideas.

In closing, the results from our research shed some light on the integration of technology in education and might guide others in this arena. In many ways, the ACOT research provides possibilities for a major shift in education toward constructivist views of knowledge, use of multiple symbol systems, and use of integrated technologies in the context of generative learning tasks. Furthermore, it represents a study of community development in which technology became woven into the fabric of everyday teaching and learning and extended students' sense of community beyond school boundaries.

NOTES

1. This chapter is based on a multiyear research project carried out at the Columbus ACOT site. Additional information on the study can be found in Tierney, R. J. (1989). *The influence of immediate computer access on students' thinking*. ACOT Report Number 3. Cupertino, CA: Apple Computer; and Tierney, R. J., Kieffer, R. D., Stowell, L., Desai, L. E., Whalin, K., & Moss, A. G. (1992). *Computer acquisition: A longitudinal study of the influence of high computer access on students' thinking, learning, and interactions*. ACOT Report Number 16. Cupertino, CA: Apple Computer. Related studies: Galindo, R., Tierney, R. J., & Stowell, L. (1989). Multimedia and multilayers in multiple texts. In S. McCormick & J. Zutell (Eds.), *Cognitive and social perspectives for literacy research and instruction* (pp. 311–322). Chicago: National Reading Conference; Sidorenko, E. B., Tierney, R. J., & Kaune, C. (1990). *Emergent video: The integration of student-mediated video technology into a high computer access classroom*. Paper presented at the International Reading Association, Orlando, Florida.

2. Clark, R. E., & Salomon, G. (1986). Media in teaching. In M. C. Wittrock (Ed.), *Handbook of research on teaching* (3rd ed.). New York: Macmillan, pp. 464–478.

WEB SITE

http://www.apple.com/education/k12/leadership/acot

20

SOME NEW GODS THAT FAIL

Neil Postman

IF ONE HAS A TRUSTING RELATIONSHIP with one's students (let us say graduate students) and the subject under discussion is the same as the subject of this text, it is not altogether gauche to ask them if they believe in God (with a capital G). I have done this three or four times, and most students say they do. Their answer is preliminary to the next question: If someone you love were desperately ill and you had to choose between praying to God for his or her recovery or administering an antibiotic (as prescribed by a competent physician), which would you choose?

Most say the question is silly, since the alternatives are not mutually exclusive. Of course. But suppose they were; which would you choose? God helps those who help themselves, some say in choosing the antibiotic, and thereby getting the best of two possible belief systems. But if pushed to the wall (for example, God does not always help those who help themselves; God helps those who pray and who believe), most say the antibiotic, after noting that the question is asinine and proves nothing. Of course, the question was not asked, in the first place, to prove anything, but to begin a discussion of the nature of belief. And I do not fail to inform the students, by the way, that there has recently emerged at least some (though not conclusive) evidence of a scientific nature that when sick people are prayed for, they do better than those who aren't.[1]

As the discussion proceeds, important distinctions are made among the different meanings of "belief," but at some point it becomes far from asinine to speak of the god of Technology—in the sense that people believe technology works, that they rely on it, that it makes promises, that they

289

are bereft when denied access to it, that they are delighted when they are in its presence, that for most people it works in mysterious ways, that they condemn people who speak against it, that they stand in awe of it, and that, in the born-again mode, they will alter their lifestyles, their schedules, their habits, and their relationships to accommodate it. If this be not a form of religious belief, what is?

In all strands of American cultural life, one can find so many examples of technological adoration that it is possible to write a book about it. And I would if it had not already been done so well. But nowhere do you find more enthusiasm for the god of Technology than among educators. In fact, there are those, like Lewis Perelman, who argue (for example, in his book *School's Out*) that modern information technologies have rendered schools entirely irrelevant, since there is now much more information available outside the classroom than inside. This is by no means considered an outlandish idea. Dr. Diane Ravitch, former Assistant U.S. Secretary of Education, envisions, with considerable relish, the challenge that technology presents to the tradition that "children (and adults) should be educated in a specific place, for a certain number of hours, and a certain number of days during the week and year." In other words, that children should be educated in school. Imagining the possibilities of an information superhighway offering perhaps a thousand channels, Dr. Ravitch assures us that:

> In this new world of pedagogical plenty, children and adults will be able to dial up a program on their home television to learn whatever they want to know, at their own convenience. If Little Eva cannot sleep, she can learn algebra instead. At her home-learning station, she will tune in to a series of interesting problems that are presented in an interactive medium, much like video games. . . . Young John may decide that he wants to learn the history of modern Japan, which he can do by dialing up the greatest authorities and teachers on the subject, who will not only use dazzling graphs and illustrations, but will narrate a historical video that excites his curiosity and imagination.[2]

In this vision, there is, it seems to me, a confident and typical sense of unreality. Little Eva can't sleep, so she decides to learn a little algebra? Where did Little Eva come from, Mars? If not, it is more likely she will tune into a good movie. Young John decides that he wants to learn the history of modern Japan? How did young John come to this point? How is it that he never visited a library up to now? Or is it that he, too, couldn't sleep and decided a little modern Japanese history was just what he needed?

What Ravitch is talking about here is not a new technology but a new species of child, one that, in any case, hasn't been seen very much up to now. Of course, new technologies do make new kinds of people, which leads to a second objection to Ravitch's conception of the future. There is a kind of forthright determinism about the imagined world described in it. The technology is here or will be; we must use it because it is there; we will become the kind of people the technology requires us to be; and whether we like it or not, we will remake our institutions to accommodate the technology. All of this must happen because it is good for us, but in any case, we have no choice.

This point of view is present in very nearly every statement about the future relation of learning to technology. And as in Ravitch's scenario, there is always a cheery, gee-whiz tone to the prophecies. Here is one produced by the National Academy of Sciences, written by Hugh McIntosh.

> School for children of the Information Age will be vastly different than it was for Mom and Dad.
>
> Interested in biology? Design your own life forms with computer simulation.
>
> Having trouble with a science project? Teleconference about it with a research scientist.
>
> Bored with the real world? Go into a virtual physics lab and rewrite the laws of gravity.
>
> These are the kinds of hands-on learning experiences schools could be providing right now. The technologies that make them possible are already here, and today's youngsters, regardless of economic status, know how to use them. They spend hours with them every week—not in the classroom, but in their own homes and in video game centers at every shopping mall.[3]

It is always interesting to attend to the examples of learning, and the motivations that ignite them, in the songs of love that technophiles perform for us. It is, for example, not easy to imagine research scientists all over the world teleconferencing with thousands of students who are having difficulty with their science projects. I can't help thinking that most research scientists would put a stop to this rather quickly. But I find it especially revealing that in the preceding scenario, we have an example of a technological solution to a psychological problem that would seem to be exceedingly serious. We are presented with a student who is "bored with the real world." What does it mean to say someone is bored with the real world, especially one so young? Can a journey into virtual reality cure such a problem? And if it can, will our troubled youngster want to return to the real world? Confronted with a student who is bored with the real world, I don't think we can get away so easily by making available a virtual-reality physics lab.

The role that new technology should play in schools or anywhere else is something that needs to be discussed without the hyperactive fantasies of cheerleaders. In particular, the computer and its associated technologies are awesome additions to a culture, and they are quite capable of altering the psychic, let alone the sleeping, habits of our young. But like all important technologies of the past, they are Faustian bargains, giving and taking away, sometimes in equal measure, sometimes more in one way than the other. It is strange—indeed, shocking—that with the twenty-first century so close on our heels, we can still talk of new technologies as if they were unmixed blessings, gifts, as it were, from the gods. Don't we all know what the combustion engine has done for us and against us? What television is doing for us and against us? At the very least, what we need to discuss about Little Eva, Young John, and McIntosh's trio is what they will lose, and what we will lose, if they enter a world in which computer technology is their chief source of motivation, authority, and, apparently, psychological sustenance. Will they become, as Joseph Weizenbaum warns, more impressed by calculation than human judgment? Will speed of response become, more than ever, a defining quality of intelligence? If, indeed, the idea of a school will be dramatically altered, what kinds of learning will be neglected, perhaps made impossible? Is virtual reality a new form of therapy? If it is, what are its dangers?

These are serious matters, and they need to be discussed by those who actually know something about children from the planet Earth, and whose vision of children's needs, and the needs of a society, go beyond thinking of school mainly as a place for the convenient distribution of information. Schools are not now and have never been chiefly about getting information to children. That has been on the schools' agenda, of course, but it has always been way down on the list. In a moment, I will mention a few school functions that are higher, but here it needs saying that for technological utopians, the computer vaults information access to the top. This reshuffling of priorities comes, one might say, at a most inopportune time. The problem of giving people greater access to more information, faster, more conveniently, and in more diverse forms was the main technological thrust of the nineteenth century. Some folks haven't noticed it, but that problem was largely solved, so that for almost one hundred years there has been more information available to the young outside the school than inside. That fact did not make the schools obsolete, and it does not make them obsolete now. Yes, it is true that Little Eva, the insomniac from Mars, could turn on an algebra lesson, thanks to the computer, in the wee hours of the morning. She could also, if she wished, read a book or magazine, watch television, pop a video into the VCR, turn on the radio, or listen to music. All of this she could have done before the computer. The computer does not solve any problem she has but exacerbates one. For Little Eva's problem is not how to get access to a well-structured algebra lesson, but what to do with all the information available to her during the day, as well as during sleepless nights. Perhaps this is why she couldn't sleep in the first place. Little Eva, like the rest of us, is overwhelmed by information. She lives in a culture which has 260,000 billboards, 17,000 newspapers, 12,000 periodicals, 27,000 video outlets for renting tapes, 400 million television sets, and well over 500 million radios, not including those in automobiles. There are 40,000 new book titles published every year, and each day 41 million photographs are taken. And thanks to the computer, over 60 billion pieces of advertising junk mail arrive in our mailboxes every year. Everything from telegraphy and photography in the nineteenth century to the silicon chip in the twentieth has amplified the din of information intruding on Little Eva's consciousness. From millions of sources all over the globe, through every possible channel and medium—light waves, airwaves, ticker tapes, computer banks, telephone wires, television cable, satellites, and printing presses—information pours in. Behind it in every imaginable form of storage—on paper, on video, on audiotape, on discs, film, and silicon chips—is an even greater volume of information waiting to be retrieved. In the face of this, we might ask, What can schools do for Little Eva besides making still more information available? If there is nothing, then new technologies will indeed make schools obsolete. But in fact, there is plenty.

One thing that comes to mind is to provide her with a serious form of technology education, something quite different from instruction in using computers to process information, which, it strikes me, is a trivial thing to do, for two reasons. In the first place, approximately 35 million people have already learned how to use computers without the benefit of school instruction. If the schools do nothing, most of the population will know how to use computers in the next ten years, just as most of the population learned how to drive cars without school instruction. In the second place, what we needed to know about cars—as we need to know about computers, television, and other important technologies—is not how to use them but how *they* use us. In the case of cars, what we needed to think about in the early twentieth century was not how to drive them but what they would do to our air, our landscape, our social relations, our family life, and our cities. Suppose that in 1946 we had started to address similar questions about television: What would be its effects on our political institutions, our psychic habits, our children, our religious conceptions, our economy? Wouldn't we be better positioned today to control television's massive assault on American culture?

I am talking here about making technology itself an object of inquiry, so that Little Eva and Young John in using technologies will not be used or abused by them, so that Little Eva and Young John become more interested in asking questions about the computer than in getting answers from it.

I am not arguing against using computers in school. I am arguing against our sleepwalking attitudes toward it, against allowing it to distract us from more important things, against making a god of it. This is what Theodore Roszak warned against in *The Cult of Information:* "Like all cults," he wrote, "this one has the intention of enlisting mindless allegiance and acquiescence. People who have no clear idea of what they mean by information, or why they should want so much of it, are nonetheless prepared to believe that we live in an Information Age, which makes every computer around us what the relics of the True Cross were in the Age of Faith: emblems of salvation."[4] To this, I would add the sage observation of Alan Kay of Apple Computer. Kay is widely associated with the invention of the personal computer, and certainly has an interest in the use of computers in schools. Nonetheless, he has repeatedly said that any problems the schools cannot solve without computers, they cannot solve with them. What are some of those problems? There is, for example, the traditional task of teaching children how to behave in groups. You cannot have a democratic—indeed, civilized—community life unless people have learned how to participate in a disciplined way as part of a group. One might even say that schools have never been essentially about individualized learning. It is true, of course, that groups do not learn; individuals do. But the idea of a school is that individuals must learn in a setting in which individual needs are subordinated to group interests. Unlike other media of mass communication, which celebrate individual response and are experienced in private, the classroom is intended to tame the ego, to connect the individual with others, to demonstrate the value and necessity of group cohesion. At present, most scenarios describing the uses of computers have children solving problems alone. Little Eva, Young John, and the others are doing just that, and in fact they do not need the presence of other children. The presence of others may, indeed, be an annoyance. (Not all computer visionaries, I must say, take lightly the importance of a child's learning to subordinate the self. Seymour

Papert's *The Children's Machine* is an imaginative example of how computers have been used to promote social cohesion, although, as I have had occasion to say to him, the same effects can be achieved without computers. Naturally, he disagrees.)

Nonetheless, like the printing press before it, the computer has a powerful bias toward amplifying personal autonomy and individual problem-solving. That is why, Papert to the contrary, most of the examples we are given picture children working alone. That is also why educators must guard against computer technology's undermining some of the important reasons for having the young assemble in school, where social cohesion and responsibility are of preeminent importance.

Although Ravitch is not exactly against what she calls "state run schools," she imagines them as something of a relic of a pre-technological age. She believes that the new technologies will offer all children equal access to information. Conjuring up a hypothetical Little Mary who is presumably from a poorer home than Little Eva, Ravitch imagines that Mary will have the same opportunities as Eva "to learn any subject, and to learn it from the same master teachers as children in the richest neighborhood."[5] For all its liberalizing spirit, this scenario contains some omissions that need to be kept in mind. One is that though new technologies may be a solution to the learning of "subjects," they work against the learning of what are called "social values," including an understanding of democratic processes. If one reads the first chapter of Robert Fulghum's *All I Ever Really Needed to Know I Learned in Kindergarten,* one will find an elegant summary of a few things Ravitch's scenario has left out. They include learning the following lessons: share everything, play fair, don't hit people, put things back where you found them, clean up your own mess, wash your hands before you eat, and of course, flush.[6] The only thing wrong with Fulghum's idea is that no one actually has learned all these things at kindergarten's end. We have ample evidence that it takes many years of teaching these values in school before they are accepted and internalized. That is why it won't do for children to learn in isolation. The point is to place them in a setting that emphasizes collaboration, as well as sensitivity to and responsibility for others. That is also why schools require children to be in a certain place at a certain time and to follow certain rules, such as raising their hands when they wish to speak, not talking when others are talking, not chewing gum, not leaving until the bell rings, and exhibiting patience toward slower learners. This process is called making civilized people. The god of Technology does not appear interested in this function of schools. At least, it does not come up much when technology's virtues are enumerated.

The god of Technology may also have a trick or two up its sleeve about something else. It is often asserted that new technologies will equalize learning opportunities for the rich and poor. It is devoutly to be wished, but I doubt it. In the first place, it is generally understood by those who have studied the history of technology that technological change always produces winners and losers—which is to say, the benefits of new technologies are not distributed equally among the population. There are many reasons for this, among them economic differences. Even in the case of the automobile, which is a commodity most people can buy (though not all), there are wide differences between rich and poor in the quality of what is available to them. It would be quite astonishing if computer technology equalized all learning opportunities, irrespective of economic differences. One may be delighted that Little Eva's parents could afford the technology and software to make it possible for her to learn algebra at midnight. But Little Mary's parents may not be able to, may not even know such things are available. And if we say that the school could make the technology available to Little Mary (at least during the day), there may be something else Little Mary is lacking—two parents, for instance. I have before me an account of a 1994 Carnegie Corporation Report, produced by the National Center for Children in Poverty. It states that in 1960, only 5 percent of our children were born to unmarried mothers. In 1990, the figure was 28 percent. In 1960, 7 percent of our children under three lived with one parent. In 1990, 27 percent. In 1960, less than 1 percent of our children under eighteen experienced the divorce of their parents. In 1990, the figure was almost 50 percent.[7]

It turns out that Little Mary may be having sleepless nights as often as Little Eva, but not because she wants to get a leg up on algebra lessons. Maybe it is because she doesn't know who her father is, or if she does, where he is. Maybe we now can understand why McIntosh's lad is bored with the real world. Or is he confused about it? Or terrified? Are there educators who seriously believe that these problems can be addressed by new technologies?

I do not say, of course, that schools can solve the problems of poverty, alienation, and family disintegration. But schools can *respond* to them. And they can do this because there are people in them, because these people are concerned with more than algebra lessons or modern Japanese history, and because these people can identify not only one's level of competence in algebra but one's level of rage and confusion and depression. I am talking here about children as they really come to us, not children who are invented to show us how computers may enrich their lives. Of course, I suppose it is possible that there are children who, waking at night, want to study algebra or who are so interested in their world that they yearn to know about Japan. If there be such children, and one hopes there are, they do not require expensive computers to satisfy their hunger for learning. They are on their way, with or without computers—unless, of course, they do not care about others, or have no friends, or have little respect for democracy, or are filled with suspicion about those who are not like them. When we have machines that know how to do something about these problems, that is the time to rid ourselves of the expensive burden of schools or to reduce the function of teachers to "coaches" in the uses of machines (as Ravitch envisions). Until then, we must be more modest about this god of Technology and certainly not pin our hopes on it.

We must also, I suppose, be empathetic toward those who search with good intentions for technological panaceas. I am a teacher myself and know how hard it is to contribute toward the making of a civilized person. Can we blame those who want to find an easy way, through the agency of technology? Perhaps not. After all, it is an old quest. As early as 1918, H. L. Mencken (although completely devoid of empathy) wrote, "there is no sure-cure so idiotic that some superintendent of schools will not swallow it. The aim seems to be to reduce the whole teaching process to a sort of automatic reaction, to discover some master formula that will not only take the place of competence and resourcefulness in the teacher but that will also create an artificial receptivity in the child."[8]

Mencken was not necessarily speaking of technological panaceas, but he may well have been. In the early 1920s, a teacher wrote the following poem:

> Mr. Edison says
> That the radio will supplant the teacher.
> Already one may learn languages by means
> of Victrola records.
> The moving picture will visualize
> What the radio fails to get across.
> Teachers will be relegated to the backwoods.
> With fire-horses,
> And long-haired women;
> Or, perhaps shown in museums.
> Education will become a matter
> Of pressing the button.
> Perhaps I can get a position at the switchboard.[9]

I do not go as far back as the introduction of the radio and the Victrola, but I am old enough to remember when 16-millimeter film was to be the sure cure, then closed-circuit television, then 8-millimeter film, then teacherproof textbooks. Now computers.

I know a false god when I see one.

NOTES

1. Although I find myself reluctant to accept such studies, there are three or four that claim that when hospitalized patients are prayed for (without their knowledge or the knowledge of their physicians), they tend to improve at a greater rate than those who are not prayed for. See *Healing Words* by Larry Dossey, M.D. (HarperCollins, 1993).

2. Diane Ravitch, "When School Comes to You," *The Economist,* September 11, 1993, 45–46.

3. Hugh McIntosh, *National Research Council News Report,* Summer 1993, 2.

4. Theodore Roszak, *The Cult of Information: The Folklore of Computers and the True Art of Thinking* (New York: Pantheon), x.

5. Ravitch, *The Economist,* 46.

6. See Robert Fulghum, *All I Ever Really Needed to Know I Learned in Kindergarten* (New York: Villard).

7. *New York Times,* April 12, 1994, A13.

8. H. L. Mencken, *A Mencken Chrestomathy* (Philadelphia: The Franklin Library), 334.

9. Quoted in Larry Cuban, *Teachers and Machines: The Classroom Use of Technology Since 1920* (New York: Teachers College Press), 5.

COMPUTER MINI-SCHOOL

TECHNOLOGY BUILDS COMMUNITY

Andrea R. Gooden

JUST BEFORE 8:00 A.M., nearly an hour before classes begin, they start filtering in: children wearing dark blue uniforms with an insignia bearing the name Ralph Bunche School. It is a public elementary school, with a sea of matching pleated skirts, slacks, and sweaters. But the room seems suddenly filled with an elite (if diminutive) corps.

The students rush to computer workstations and log on. It is a blustery, early winter morning in New York City, with freezing rain coming down in diagonal sheets. The windows of the fourth-floor corner room register the force of the storm, but all attention is focused inward. The kids from Harlem are calculating how close to Oregon they'll get in a covered wagon with a particular allotment of hay, flour, and sugar.

Paul Reese sits in front of his Macintosh at the head of several rows of Apple II and Macintosh computers. He sifts through volumes of electronic mail, trying to get a jump on the day as more kids fill the room.

There are messages from schools in Canada and Norway, notes from former students and colleagues, and inquiries from academics, researchers, and software companies. Reese's determination to dispense with these electronic missives is eventually thwarted by reality: he is even more in demand in person than he is on-line.

"You don't know what to do now? Go ahead, take the 'caps lock' off, I don't want it all in capital letters," he advises a third-grader working on an essay for the school newspaper. A nearby laser printer begins popping out multiple copies of someone's drawing. Reese checks the network on-screen, finds no clue as to the source of the abstract image, and the printer continues to churn it out.

"In addition to being a teacher, and sort of the lead teacher in the computer school, I am the technical assistant, and the technical assistant to the assistant," explains Reese, the guiding force behind the Computer Mini-School at P.S. 125, also known as Ralph Bunche, in Central Harlem.

This school-within-a-school evolved out of a three-year experiment with Bank Street College researchers who were looking at ways to improve elementary science education through the use of local area networks. Now Reese and eight other teachers in grades three through six have incorporated the technology across the entire curriculum, taking over a floor of the post–World War I brick building.

Reese had been a teacher here for more than a decade when the school purchased its first computer in 1980. A fourth-grade teacher with a specialty in math and science, he taught himself how to use the technology, started a computer club at the school, and eventually gave up his regular class to become the computer teacher. Now he also serves as technical adviser for sixteen other schools in Community School District 5.

His career as an educator began directly out of college in the 1960s, in Rhodesia (now known as Zimbabwe), teaching secondary math and science for three years. On his return to the United States, and after a stint as a summer youth worker in East Harlem, Reese joined the Urban Teacher Corps and became a faculty member at P.S. 125, where he has remained for more than two decades.

In that time, the school has been honored with numerous corporate grants and awards and has gained a reputation for innovation among technologists and academics. In 1990, Reese was named *Electronic Learning* magazine's "Educator of the Year."

"There are few things in this world more rewarding than watching kids in the process of discovering and learning," he said. "That 'aha!' when a student makes a connection is a wonderful sight, and our computer program has offered more than the average share of these moments."

In 1987, when researchers from Bank Street College were looking for a location to conduct their studies on students and technology, they found a natural partner in Paul Reese and Ralph Bunche School. With support from the National Science Foundation and twenty computers from Apple Education Grants, they installed an innovative computer network called Earth Lab. The objective was to see what would happen when grade-school students were given the same kind of communications tools that scientists use for collaborative study.

○

Harlem History

In 1919, at the end of World War I, a new school was established in Central Harlem with great expectation. The Lincoln School on West 123rd Street in Central Harlem was a private, progressive, Dewey-inspired high school dedicated to educating young Rockefellers and other children of the elite.

In his memoir *Death Be Not Proud,* author John Gunther noted that his son, whose life and early death the book chronicles, had attended Lincoln School, "which he loved with all his heart."

In 1948 the building was sold to the City of New York, and the former Lincoln School became Public School 125. The name of statesman Ralph Bunche was added to the school's title in 1969, the result of a citywide initiative to give public schools an identity beyond their traditional numeric designation.

Bunche, the first African American to receive a Ph.D. in political science, received the 1950 Nobel Peace Prize for his work in negotiating an end to the Arab-Israeli war of 1948. At the time, Bunche was principal secretary of the United Nations Palestine Commission. He had previously served as a division head in the U.S. Department of State. Bunche died in 1971.

Ralph Bunche School is bounded by disparate landmarks several blocks in each direction. To the west and south is Columbia University, whose closest satellite building is just two blocks from the school. Also nearby are Barnard College and the Union Theological Seminary.

West, toward the Hudson River, are Grant's Tomb and Riverside Church. To the north, and visible from some classrooms, is one of Harlem's most celebrated structures, the Apollo Theatre.

Half the classrooms of the Computer Mini-School face a massive skyline to the north: the nine brick buildings of the General Grant Houses, a public housing project that is home to many of the students of P.S. 125.

Across the street, on the south side of the school, is Morningside Park. In the 1960s, Columbia University proposed building a gymnasium on the park's hilly acreage, and the plan became the focus of a turbulent student protest. After a great deal of public outcry, the proposal was abandoned, and today the park forms the backdrop for Ralph Bunche's sister school for students in kindergarten through second grade.

○

They chose weather patterns as the primary subject focus for the science curriculum and installed a weather station on the roof of the five-story building. A network was set up to enable students and teachers to call up common files and applications on any computer in the school and to communicate using electronic mail.

Students collected daily weather data, compiled it on a network database, and exchanged information and observations electronically amongst themselves and with other schools. Herbert Williams, now a student at Bronx High School of Science and Technology, remembers the routine.

"Every morning we'd go up to the roof and take weather data. Then we'd go onto the computer and put that data into the database and keep a record of it, and use that information to compare and analyze. After a while we started to see patterns, and then," he recalled matter-of-factly, "we would be able to predict the weather."

When Hurricane Hugo began winding through the southern states in 1989, Earth Lab students used on-line weather data to predict its path—ahead of National Weather Service reports.

"The news was saying it was going to turn and go up the coast, and we were concerned it was coming to New York," Reese recalled. Students tapped into the raw weather data, which is updated hourly on CompuServe, and carefully plotted the path of the storm. It appeared to them that the hurricane would be moving back toward sea.

"We were almost uncomfortable with the data we had, because it contradicted what the news was saying," said Reese. As it turned out, the student forecasters were correct, and the hurricane bypassed New York.

Many Earth Lab students, including Williams, got an extra boost in mastering the technology through a computer home-loan program, which encouraged families to work together to learn computer skills. In one student's family, the program inspired a father to learn to read and subsequently return to school to pursue an education.

For Reese's students, the technology was also used to explore personal and emotional issues as well as science, math, and language. Reese related a story of two students, engaged in a dispute, who were asked to send "incident reports" to the teacher over the network. Ten minutes later the teacher found the two working at adjacent computers, carefully checking each other's versions, and essentially resolving the conflict. As a result of this episode, students who would otherwise be sent to the main office for discipline are now routinely asked to resolve their problems in electronic reports to their teachers.

Teachers involved in the Earth Lab project also began collaborating more and sharing information on the network. "I like the symbolic nature of computers and the ability to go with ideas no matter where they may be," said Reese, displaying a characteristic enthusiasm for technology's potential to transform learning.

At the conclusion of the three-year Earth Lab project in 1990, Reese and several colleagues developed a plan for a "computer mini-school." In part a response to persistent classroom problems, the plan proposed a reduction in class sizes, elimination of disruptive pull-out programs, and integration of technology across the entire curriculum.

After rather lengthy negotiations, the proposal for the mini-school was approved. Six teachers agreed to give up their contractual preparation periods in exchange for smaller class size; they then worked out ways to integrate remedial work and other mandated programs into their classroom routine. "When you talk about school restructuring, it's not just about the technology," said Reese. "Basically we created a community that's supportive—a common approach."

"When you have thirty-five kids in your room, you so much want to do your best, but you are juggling," said computer school teacher Kathy De la Garza, recalling her frustrations with the regular program before joining the mini-school. "You try to set up a routine, and it gets broken all the time. You have kids being pulled out for reading, pulled out for math, then the whole class is pulled out for science. It's just like a merry-go-round: it never stops."

Fifth-grade teacher Donna Stewart also found the realities of teaching in a traditional classroom different from what she had hoped. "Basically, I was a glorified baby-sitter," she said. "When you're in college, they don't tell you these things. They tell you that you're going to go in and essentially save the world. You're lucky if you can reach a few in the interim, because of the environment and what's happening. You try, and you do the best you can."

Stewart saw the mini-school, with its focus on technology and smaller class size, as an opportunity to "reach the children, teach them something that is going to help them in the future as far as modern technology, keep discipline problems at a minimum, and put into practice some of the things I had gone to college for."

With eight full-time teachers and two hundred students, the Computer Mini-School dominates one floor of classrooms. Each class spends two periods a week in the computer room on a variety of tasks: writing, working on spreadsheets, creating animations, or logging and editing videotape. Many students also gravitate back to the computer room before and after school and during lunch.

Several of the teachers also have computers in their classrooms, where students can work and transmit data over the network. Mona Monroe's sixth-graders use the classroom computer as a management tool. "The class itself has a class notebook," she said, describing her electronic ledger system. "Class officers have access to that notebook, which they jealously guard the password of—despite the fact that almost everybody at some time during the year gets to be a class officer and knows the password."

Her students use the electronic class notebook to manage their classroom in much the same way the school's office, or any business office, would. "If we collect money to go on a trip or to buy books for the book club, the treasurer keeps a record on the computer rather than a paper record," explained Monroe. "If we go on trips and the children bring permission slips, the class secretary makes a list that says who has brought their permission slip, and prints that out for the office the day we go on the trip."

Monroe, who has taught at Ralph Bunche since 1960, was the first teacher at the school to have a networked computer installed in her classroom. The class notebook was an idea she implemented during the first year of Earth Lab: "It's not teaching computers, not doing lessons on computers, and not doing school work, but it's a 'real world' use of computers."

The mini-school's alternative approach to learning quickly proved its value in test scores, according to Assistant Principal John Diopoulos. "In the first year," he said, "the mini-school classes outperformed the regular school by almost 20 percent. The test results were remarkable, to say the least."

Diopoulos would like to see the program expanded if the school's physical structure could handle it; "I have more teachers who want to come in, but the problem becomes space." For every two classrooms that convert from the regular school, he explained, three classrooms are required to accommodate reduced class sizes.

"Right now we're at a critical stage where I can't add another classroom," he said. "I had to vacate a room because of water damage, and it takes forever to get things fixed. When they open up one problem, there's another problem behind it." As an example, it had been three years since the Earth Lab weather station was used because of damage to the school's roof.

Undeterred, students and teachers have pursued other forms of collaborative data collection, including a global "shadows" project. Students calculate the time of "solar noon" by taking sunrise and sunset data from the daily newspaper. At the appointed hour (assuming there is sunlight), they go to the schoolyard armed with a tripod and meterstick to measure their own shadows. Then they enter the collected data into a spreadsheet and forward it to other schools involved in the project, including sites in Boston, Australia, and Sweden.

"We're asking them to develop their own theories for the explanation of seasonal changes," said Reese. Weekly weather logs received from schools around the world also broaden the students' knowledge of geography and global weather patterns:

> 10/19–25/92
> On Saturday evening, October 24, we had a time change. This shows up significantly in the time the sun rises and sets. The weather was extremely nice for this week. Now the weather has changed! We have snow!
>
> Maple Leaf School, Winnipeg, Manitoba, Canada
>
> 10/19–25/92
> After warm weather in the beginning of October, very quick cooling snow almost reached Vienna. The mountains are sometimes not passable because of snowstorms.
>
> Bundesgymnasium, Vienna, Austria

In addition to students and researchers from Columbia Teachers College and Bank Street College, Ralph Bunche School attracts a steady stream of visitors. Corporate executives, local dignitaries, congressional staffers, and even superstar athletes have all made the trip to the school on West 123rd Street.

Any encounter inside or outside the school becomes potential material for the student-produced newspaper and video news reports, including a visit by photographer Julie Chase for this book. Student Valerie Idehen wrote:

> The kids in class 401 were showing Julie Chase and her assistant Ron [Schreier] their science projects. Many of the projects needed the use of a flashlight. Julie took a picture of Isiah Meek's science project, "How much rock can moving water carry?" and of Matrice Brown's project, "The earth is like an egg."
> But I have one question for Matrice. Since the Earth is like an egg in many ways, will the earth crack? And does it have yolk inside?

Student reports have featured such notables as former Democratic Party national chair and commerce secretary Ron Brown, former Canadian prime minister Brian Mulroney, baseball star Darryl Strawberry, Olympic medalists Matt Biondi and Diane Dixon, and singer Julio Iglesias.

Production of the monthly newsletter, also under the direction of teacher Mona Monroe, is not unlike that in a professional newsroom.

Fifth-grader Veronica Rivera described the process: "You write words, you save it. Later on, you go back and correct the mistakes. You do whatever you want." To submit your work for publication, she explained, you send it electronically to the newspaper's network address. Student editors then download the articles and decide which ones to publish.

Rivera and classmate Greg Streeter collaborated on a story about a class visit to Fraunces Tavern, a historic landmark on the city's downtown waterfront:

> On our trip, we had a tour guide that helped us around and told us about the different monuments inside the tavern. We did something special. Each of us were different people from the past. For example, Greg was a slave and Veronica was an insurance agent. Although we had fun, it was difficult to do.

Their story appeared not only in the Ralph Bunche *Computer School News* but also in *This Week in AGE,* an international newsletter published by schools involved in the Apple Global Education project. Next to their story, on the front page, was a story about a ninth-grade Norwegian boy with AIDS. It described an informational meeting held at the boy's school in Norway:

> Finally Odd Kåre's mother stepped forward and told us about Odd Kåre, how he got the infection and about the bleeder illness. Then one person, Solveig from grade 9, stood up and said those words that she became famous for: "Go home and say good night to Odd Kåre from us. Tomorrow we will all meet him like a friend."

Ralph Bunche students also address issues of concern to their own neighborhood. Bulletin boards in the school hallways are decorated with colorful student artwork expressing messages such as "We Need Peace in Harlem East!" and "Stop the Violence: Love Each Other." Sixth-grader Renso Vasquez spoke at a school assembly, following an antiviolence march, and later published his speech in the school paper. It concluded with this passage:

> A lot of bad people go around your neighborhood and they just come there just to be selling drugs or to rob a store. We can solve that problem by sending in more policemen and women. And the shootings? These can be stopped when the police arrest people selling guns because those guns are just like throwing your life away. These are my wishes and if they happen, this city would be safer for the children of the future.

Newsroom activity also involves the creation of video news reports for "KidWitness News," an educational initiative sponsored by Panasonic. Reports have ranged from interviews with local politicians and sanitation workers to coverage of the funeral mass for a popular school superintendent.

Students in the mini-school are selected from the student body by lottery, which, according to Assistant Principal Diopoulos, makes the mini-school "a true representation of the school as a whole."

"We really have a diversity of ability in our classrooms," confirmed teacher De la Garza. "I see children who come into my classroom who are at a lower level, and by the time they leave at the end of the year they know they're not. They have really pulled up because they see what's happening around them. They see what other people are capable of doing; they push themselves more and they expect more of themselves."

Through Earth Lab and the mini-school, Ralph Bunche School has set a standard for the integration of technology in the classroom. But Reese believes the school "can't just live on its laurels." In that spirit, he has installed new networking technology to expand their telecommunications potential. Over one hundred students now have their own Internet addresses. "Earth Lab was designed to be a model for how kids would use electronic computers," said Reese. "I'm interested in making sure that that model is not a dead model." Only a few weeks after the students were up on the Internet, one of Reese's students had already exchanged several electronic messages with a correspondent at Penn State.

Two of his former students are assisting Reese in his quest to make the technology more relevant. Working after school and on weekends, Herbert Williams and Hamidou Diori maintain the network for Reese, doing everything from installing new equipment to compiling school attendance records.

"On Wednesdays, I help Mr. Reese with special network problems, because the networks have been going down and up," explained Diori, a 1992 Ralph Bunche graduate. "Something's wrong with our cabling on the Ethernet."

Diori also consults with the sixth-graders as a senior editor on the mini-school newspaper. After helping Reese install the Internet server four years ago, he wrote about the experience for his eighth-grade English class:

> I left my house knowing that I had enough skill to be able to assist my former teacher in helping him and a person from BBN [Bolt Beranek and Newman Inc., a high-tech company] support staff, Susan Mills, in

helping put up a network. This was no ordinary network, it was going to become a node on the Internet. . . . Mr. Reese gave me the okay to check the router. The leased line was not in yet but we still could connect via ordinary phone lines. . . . My job was to set up all the Macs that had hard drives with MacTCP, then configure their IP (Internet protocol) address, then configure the gateway address (the router). Finished that, no problem. Now to check it. Can I say it any better? It worked nicely.

"I like using telecommunications a lot, and especially on the Internet," said Diori. "When I get to one of these UNIX computers, I like messing around at the prompt, trying to find stuff." He subscribes to several "lists" on the Internet, where he engages in electronic discussions on a variety of subjects, including rap music, bicycles, and of course networking.

"I always wanted to learn to use computers," he said. His fascination with technology began in early childhood in Africa. He recalled that representatives from a computer company once came to his older sister's classroom in Nigeria to teach students how to use their system. "I always wanted to sneak in to see what they were doing, but they wouldn't let me in."

Once, while awaiting a flight in the West African country of Ivory Coast, his mother got permission for him to tour the airport's computer system. When he typed his name on a keyboard and saw it come up on the monitor, he was mesmerized. "It was such a little thing, but I was so excited about it," he said.

In 1989, he and his family emigrated from Nigeria, landing in the Central Harlem neighborhood of predominantly African American, Hispanic, and Caribbean residents. The young computer fan got a lucky break when he enrolled at his neighborhood school: "The first day I came into the computer room I was so surprised. I saw all these kids on computers and I said, 'Wow, kids actually get to use computers over here.'"

Now he regularly scans computer bulletin boards and online services to find such items as the "top ten" music list for his sister and a new disk drive for his mother. He added: "I keep in contact with Mr. Reese on the Internet."

He described finding articles on the subject of recycling for a Hyper-Card stack he was creating for his seventh-grade Earth Sciences class. Using the Wide Area Information Service, he first typed in *recycling*. "It gave me a directory of servers on the Internet that have articles on recycling or have *recycling* in the database. I typed in *recycling* a second time, and I got the actual article—and it was all real-time."

The HyperCard stack will also incorporate a QuickTime video clip from an interview Diori did on the subject of recycling while still a student at P.S. 125. "I'm going to upload it to various BBSs [bulletin board systems] when I'm done, so that people can look at it," he said.

Since leaving Ralph Bunche School, Herbert Williams repeatedly found himself in a quandary that may be common to other graduates of Reese's computer program: he was overqualified for most computer classes offered at the junior high school and high school level.

In his first year at the Bronx High School for Science and Technology, Williams was allowed to waive the required freshman computer literacy course after taking a skills test. The computer coordinator asked if he would like to take a course in the BASIC programming language instead, but he already knew BASIC. The only course left was telecommunications —a class reserved for seniors. As the only freshman in the class he felt slightly out of place, but he "got used to it." By the end of that first year, he had completed the school's computer science curriculum.

Now, most of his time on the computer is spent at the Ralph Bunche mini-school, or at his job with a children's rights organization called Kids Meeting Kids. For this group, among other tasks, he helps administer an electronic conference about children's rights on the PeaceNet, "sharing information about what's happening to children around the world, and what young people and adults can do to help."

With two years of high school left to go, his goals for college are remarkably clear: a double major in journalism and psychology. He already contributes to special electronic forums for writers.

If those plans change, he said, he'll always have computing to fall back on. "In the future, every career is going to involve a computer," he said, adding that students who don't have the opportunity to develop good computer and keyboard skills will be missing out. "It's a really useful tool, and soon it's just going to be within all our lives."

When Williams returns to Ralph Bunche School and sees what the younger students are doing, he is impressed. "It's a lot of fun to see what the people after me are doing. They do a lot of work, even the third graders—a lot of work." Williams believes many of them know more about technology than most computer professionals, and he gives Paul Reese a lot of credit: "He had a lot of projects that helped us."

JoAnne Kleifgen, a faculty member at Columbia Teachers College and director of a bilingual teaching project at Ralph Bunche for Spanish-speaking and Haitian students, reaffirmed the value of the Computer Mini-School approach. "My students and I have volunteered a lot because we are learning. It's not just out of the goodness of our hearts. We're learning from Paul, and from the kids, and the teachers."

○

Ellen Clare

"That woman who was in here yelling at me, which she does all the time, keeps me in line and honest," said Paul Reese about Ellen Clare, a thirty-five-year veteran of P.S. 125, who seems to have the same effect on her students.

When you encounter her class of twenty-two fourth-graders in the hall, you can hear a pin drop. Although she is lagging behind and out of view, they wait for her obediently, all lined up in their neat blue uniforms according to height.

As she comes down the corridor on this wintry Friday, her tall, black, reed-thin frame is decked out in cowboy boots, long narrow blue jeans, and a blue velour top. Her hair is cropped close to the head, and a single sterling silver pendant hangs from her neck. Her bearing is regal and stylish. She peers at her charges through oversized spectacles, and only when she gives the word do they march.

In the classroom, she emotes an uncanny blend of fire, brimstone, and humor. The children are, to use one of Clare's fourth-grade vocabulary words, "mesmerized"—although some might argue that "terrorized" is more like it.

Her traditional teaching style was even the subject of an editorial in the school newspaper under the title "Is Mrs. Clare a Great Teacher?" Student Edward Velasquez wrote, "The children think that Mrs. Clare is mean. So I interviewed Mrs. Clare. Mrs. Clare likes being a teacher because she wants to make sure that the children will get a good education so they can meet their needs when they are adults."

Ellen Clare surprised some colleagues when she became a member of the Computer Mini-School in 1992. Assistant Principal John Diopoulos did not expect one of the school's staunchest traditionalists to embrace the mini-school concept, but he admitted, "even the senior teachers see the benefits, because they get so much done." While noting that Clare is still relatively computer-phobic, Reese has high praise for her contribution to the mini-school, saying simply, "She's marvelous."

In her classroom, that delicate balance of discipline and whimsy is reflected in the attentiveness and enthusiasm of her students. In a discussion of the book *The Witches,* students are eager to be called on to read and explain parts of the story. They speak loudly and slowly, sounding out the syllables.

"This is much more than a job," Clare said, citing the many long afternoons and Saturdays spent there. "Many of my students have a lot of anger. They don't really know they can do this."

It's Clare's job to tell them they can.

○

"To me, and a whole lot of kids here, school is like a home," said Jour-nelle Clark, a student in Doris Parker's sixth-grade class. "The teachers are very good at trying their best to provide the best for the kids."

Reese adds: "We have a lot of kids who do not have any order in their life, and some of them very much need a clear sense of order. I don't mean a repressive order, but I mean a predictable, reliable source of routine and limits."

Computer Mini-School newcomer but longtime Ralph Bunche teacher Ellen Clare considers herself "one of the luckiest people in the world" to be part of the program. She described a difficult, chronically defiant student who, toward the end of the term, scored at the top of the class. "That face," she said, remembering his reaction, "is worth ten salaries."

For Reese, the rewards are also intangible. "Clearly, I get a lot out of it. I enjoy working with the kids, I like the world of ideas," and the mini-school, he said, gives him the opportunity to explore that world.

Reese quickly shifted away from a discussion about teaching to eagerly return to the work at hand. "This week there's pressure to get the news-paper out," he said, listing several other projects including an upcoming video competition and a classroom greenhouse that are currently de-manding his attention. "Some day I have to take care of the paperwork in here," he sighed, gesturing toward a cluttered corner of the room, "and . . . uh . . . clean my desk." But for Reese and his colleagues, the students obviously come first.

"It takes a special type of teacher," Diopoulos said, reflecting on the success of the Computer Mini-School. "I've been to a number of different schools at different times in my career; this works because of the staff."

Herbert Williams testified to the power of such care and dedication with a simple declaration: "I'll never forget what happened there."

22

ENGAGING STUDENTS IN A KNOWLEDGE SOCIETY

Marlene Scardamalia, Carl Bereiter

IMAGINE A NETWORK OF NETWORKS—*people from schools, universities, cultural institutions, service organizations, businesses—simultaneously building knowledge within their primary groups while advancing the knowledge of others. We might call such a community network a knowledge-building society.*

Electronically networked environments expand the possibilities for what such productive, mutually supportive communities can produce. These environments also alter the working dynamics of these communities. We are creating a miniature version of a knowledge-building society, using Computer Supported Intentional Learning Environment (CSILE™) software.

○

CSILE Software: Passport to the Knowledge Society

CSILE™ (Computer Supported Intentional Learning Environment) has been under development since 1986 by a team of cognitive research and computer scientists in Toronto, and teachers across North America. It is the first network system to provide general support for collaborative learning and inquiry in school environments. As such, it is the beacon technology for the K–12 sector of Canada's TeleLearning Research Network. CSILE has been used successfully at all educational levels from the 1st grade to university, in all areas of the curriculum, and with many different kinds of student populations.

At the system's core is a community database, constructed by the users. Items in CSILE's shared work space are called *notes*. Notes may include text, graphics, and links to other media. All notes can be read by all users, but edited only according to set rules. Users create notes or comment on another note, in which case the original author is notified and can immediately view the comments and respond to them. Participants can link notes to any organizational framework created with the CSILE graphics program, thus producing high-level visualizations of work on a particular problem or issue. They can also create special-purpose discussions or conference notes.

Users access CSILE on locally networked or remotely connected computers. (WebCSILE uses a Web browser in lieu of client software.) The typical school installation consists of eight computers in each classroom, attached via a local area network to a CSILE server, which maintains the shared workspace.

As links among notes emerge, participants begin to recognize higher-order concepts and view the accumulating knowledge and ways of synthesizing it. In the business world, Lotus Notes is the prime example of such an approach, and is being widely adopted by businesses setting out to become "learning organizations." In the education world, CSILE is the prime example, antedating Lotus Notes by several years.[1]

The CSILE network system is based on a decade of basic and applied cognitive research. Controlled studies show that students who use CSILE excel in a number of areas. They do better on standardized language and reading tests and are better able to comprehend difficult informative texts. They demonstrate advantages in the quality of the questions they ask, their portfolio commentaries and general depth of explanation, and their facility with graphics. They even demonstrate more mature beliefs about learning. The studies show, too, that students at the high and low ends of ability spectrums are equally engaged, and typical gender biases have not appeared.[1]

For further information, visit the CSILE Web site at http://www.csile.oise.on.ca.

1. M. Scardamalia, C. Bereiter, R. S. McLean, J. Swallow, and E. Woodruff (1989), "Computer-Supported Intentional Learning Environments," *Journal of Educational Computing Research* 5: 51–68.

We are carrying out this work as part of the Canada-wide TeleLearning Network of Centres of Excellence.[1] Our project is distinctive from the many devoted to educational uses of network technology, however. Our own aim is to enhance knowledge building and understanding in all sectors simultaneously, with particular emphasis on K–12 education.

Linking "Society" Members

The network we are creating in Toronto brings together a diverse group of participants. It includes elementary and high school students and their parents, and postsecondary teacher education and medical school students, all of whom can be doing coursework; museum staff, who are planning exhibits; engineering firm staff, who are tackling design problems; and staff from a science center and an art gallery. Also participating will be project researchers and software developers, who will be interpreting what is happening throughout the network and improving the technological infrastructure to support increasingly effective interactions.

Each of these groups carries out its own work. The work takes the form of entries stored in CSILE databases. Parts of this multimedia database can be closed off as private; but as much as possible, each database is open to people in other parts of the Knowledge Society network. The different open databases are listed, and can be visited, much as one visits Web sites on the Internet.

Students and other network members can do more than merely visit various databases, however. They can become actively involved, entering text and graphic notes or comments in all content areas. They also may use information they see to create links between notes on different databases, pointing out discrepant information or contributing new information or ideas. (Notification systems inform participants of activity related to the ideas they have contributed.)

A group of 5th and 6th graders, for instance, might be working on the problem "How does electricity work?" At the same time, curators in a science museum might be planning an exhibit on electricity. By visiting the student's databases, the curators will gain an understanding of students' conceptions (and misconceptions) of electricity, and the students will have input to the design of the exhibit.

CSILE also supports other forms of interaction. Participants can perform keyword searches and extend them across databases. Thus, if a student searches by the keyword *electron*, the search would bring together the work of all participants who had assigned this keyword to any note they created. The student could then study, cull, or link the new collection of electron notes, or use it as a basis for forming a new study group. The student could also search by "views," and see that electrons are viewed quite differently by different groups.

It is also possible to organize cross-sector interaction, so that, for example, a medical school class might work with elementary school classes on health-related topics. Other kinds of engagement will be fortuitous, but everyone joining the network is expected to take an interest in and, where appropriate, make contributions to the work of people in other sectors.

Through a variety of linking, searching, commenting, and visiting activities, the network encourages the formation of new groups and the consideration of ideas from different perspectives. The aim is to enable participants to gain knowledge and understanding and also form important new working relationships, but without being overwhelmed by long lists of notes requiring responses.

Contrasting Models

To put our Knowledge Society model in perspective, consider two other models for an educational network. In all such models there is a concern for *scalability* (Can small-scale trials go systemwide?) and *sustainability* (Can the model survive without heroic efforts?). Two further issues are whether the model supports a *constructivist approach* to knowledge, and whether it brings about *involvement* of students in the work of the larger society.

Model 1. Ask the Expert

> *Volunteer scientists at a petrochemical company agree to answer students' questions about chemical pollutants and additives. Students (or indirectly the teacher) submit questions by e-mail. They then share the information they've obtained in class discussions or reports.*

This person-to-person approach sometimes works very well. As a model for network use, however, it has three important drawbacks. First, it isn't *scalable*. That is, it may work for a few classrooms, but there aren't enough expert resources to make it work systemwide. Second, it often is not *sustainable*. Typically the relationship is increasingly burdensome for the volunteers. And their initial enthusiasm wanes as they find themselves responding repeatedly to the same questions, or to questions so basic that the students should be able to find answers themselves. (In one case, students became impatient waiting for an e-mail response and so telephoned an expert at work to find out whether a milliliter was a hundredth of a liter or a thousandth!)

Third, this approach goes against *constructivist* principles. It tells students that knowledge is out there in the heads of specialists, not that it is something to be constructed through their own efforts. Finally, although scientists are *involved* in the work of the schools, students are not involved in the work of the scientists. Thus schools continue to be isolated from the workings of a Knowledge Society.

Model 2. Cross-School Research Projects

> Schools in a wide area collaborate on a research project. Designed by the participating teachers or a central organization, the project calls for students to collect data locally, then put what they've found together and draw inferences.

Successful projects of this kind have involved climate, dialect differences, and even the design of a space colony. Unlike Model 1, this model has the virtue of supporting *constructivist* principles. When well organized, such projects have proved to be *sustainable*—typically lasting for three to nine weeks. They are, however, significantly limited in their *scalability*. Only certain topics lend themselves readily to this approach, and they often require considerable advance organization in order to succeed.

Thus, Model 2 is likely to remain a model for special purposes, not for achieving the core objectives of a subject-matter curriculum. Finally, although cross-school research projects do much to break down the barriers among schools, they maintain the isolation of schools from other sectors of a Knowledge Society, and thus fail the *involvement* criterion.

Engaging the Larger Society

Our new Knowledge Society model allows for the person-to-person relationships of Model 1 and the distributed projects of Model 2, but it is not limited to them. It is *constructivist* in a deeper sense: it involves people in the actual work of a society engaged in constructing, using, and improving knowledge. Indeed, this *involvement* is our network's outstanding virtue: Students can do more than merely contact people outside the school; they gain entry into their working worlds.

We cannot be sure how *sustainable* the model will be or how much energy will go into sustaining it. But we believe that, because responsibilities are so widely distributed and participants have so many opportunities to organize their knowledge, our model will not be as vulnerable as others that depend on key players.

As for technical requirements, the Knowledge Society model is best served by network databases that students and other participants build and contribute to, instead of communicating through point-to-point messages. As centers of activity and ideas emerge, participants gain new perspectives on the information. This contrasts with Model 1, which requires only e-mail. Model 2 has worked with e-mail, but Web-based technology offers many advantages for coordinating research inputs.

New Teachers' Give-and-Take

At best, technology can facilitate the Knowledge Society model. As in all communication, however, human efforts are the crucial elements. In our networks, preservice teachers play a pivotal role. They are involved in both a learning and teaching capacity. Through contacts with experts in many areas—science, mathematics, history—they stretch their understanding of subject matter while serving as mediators between their students and the experts. They also gain a better understanding of learning in TeleLearning environments. And they engage in virtual practice worldwide.

Preservice teachers use their growing pedagogical expertise to come up with approaches that will be particularly productive for their students. For example, a science teacher might realize that students could learn about endangered species in a more integrated way by organizing their collective notes by phylum. Accordingly, the teacher would enter a diagram of a phylogenetic tree and ask students to link their notes to this tree, as appropriate. The tree now provides a new view of their notes. Two other ways of organizing the same notes are a map organizer and a "Reasons for Endangerment" organizer that students generate.[2] By linking their notes to several integrative frameworks, students come to see their ideas in several contexts, each view revealing a new way to discuss their work.

The scientist whose work is linked may or may not have time to join this new discussion group, but will already have played an important role by demonstrating to students that their work relates to that of a practicing scientist.

A Role for Academia

Graduate students in education seminars also have a role to play. They study conceptual change and curriculum development by visiting databases throughout the world in which students are learning about everything from photosynthesis to medieval history. The graduate student not only studies the literature of conceptual change, but also views it in the context of society's expectations, as represented in curriculum guidelines.

For example, one graduate student in physics reviewed a unit on "How Heat Affects Matter," produced by 5th and 6th graders. He noticed a great deal of animistic thinking—that is, students said that molecules were "wanting to escape" from heat, "running to get free," and so forth. the physics student created a view of the database that highlighted the different animistic accounts of molecules, a view that could then be studied by students, teachers, science education students, or any other participants in the network who had obtained permission from the student and teacher to work with their database.

The physics student also wrote a scholarly paper on issues of curriculum development and conceptual change, an article that was available, not just to a select group of readers but to a network of participants worldwide. As a result of this give-and-take, the graduate student said that he himself learned more about matter and molecules.

Undergraduate students provide another resource by using worldwide networks as a new form of field study. Like the graduate student, they could, for example, provide faculty and professional development students with valuable information by constructing views of the database that help to identify misconceptions, highlight promising new directions for research, bring participants from different sites into new working groups, or offer explanations that may be extremely helpful to others.

Strength in Diversity

A Knowledge Society should favor these kinds of mutually supportive efforts. There is strength in diversity as schools, businesses, and cultural institutions share a common medium. This is true, too, of other kinds of connections. Secondary schools have a stake in the outcomes of elementary education. So why not have the contributions of younger children flow to secondary or postsecondary students, and from there to teachers and teachers in training, and from any of these contributors to those who formulate curriculum guidelines and standards?

Some might consider this Knowledge Society model impractical. But we must overcome the obstacles for three main reasons. First, the model is inevitable. Ideas and inventions, not labor and manufacturing, are already beginning to rule world economies.

Second, the skills and technology for a Knowledge Society are here, and school networks that run counter to it are likely to be short-lived. These wide-ranging networks cost no more than more limited networks, so there is little reason for schools to confine themselves within more limited technologies or networks of participants.

Finally, this is a model of mutually reinforced high achievement, in which students encounter directly the excitement of working with ideas and advancing knowledge over a lifetime, and feel a part of it.

NOTES

1. For further information, visit http://www.telelearn.ca/telelearn.

2. Examples are from D. R. Ward and E. L. Tiessen (1994), "(Re)modeling Uses of Multimedia and Hypermedia in Education, Paper presented at the World Conference on Educational Multimedia and Hypermedia (ED-MEDIA94) (Vancouver, British Columbia: Association for the Advancement of Computers in Education).

WEB SITE

http://csile.oise.utoronto.ca

23

USING TECHNOLOGY
TO SUPPORT INNOVATIVE
ASSESSMENT

Karen Sheingold, John Frederiksen

AT THE CORE OF CURRENT EFFORTS to reform education is a commitment to changing what students learn in school and how they learn it, in order to improve student achievement. It is now widely recognized by leaders, policymakers, and practitioners in education that schools must help students learn to think strategically, to understand concepts and ideas in curricular domains, to apply what they learn, and to pose questions and devise and solve problems. Such goals are viewed as mandatory for all of the nation's children (see, for example, National Governors' Association, 1990). At the same time, there is broad recognition that to change our expectations about what students should know and be able to do will involve also changing both the standards by which student achievements are judged and the methods by which students' accomplishments are assessed. For this reason, the redefinition of assessment is playing a pivotal role in the reform of education in the United States (National Council on Education Standards and Testing, 1992; Resnick & Resnick, 1992; U.S. Congress, Office of Technology Assessment, 1992). In the context of education reform, assessment matters more than it has in the past. It is more than simply one element that must change in order to transform teaching and learning. Instead, education reformers now find that assessment standards and methods have considerable power as the *agents* (or *inhibitors*) of such change.

We, moreover, believe it unlikely that any strong link can be forged between assessment and reform without considerable help from technologies such as computers, telecommunications, and multimedia databases. In what follows, we argue that there are several ways in which assessment can foster reform: through the forms of the assessments, through the criteria and standards for judging student work, and most importantly, through the processes by which large numbers of people learn to apply criteria in judging, reflecting on, and valuing good work. Technologies are critically important to school reform because they increase the range of student work that can be used in instruction and assessment and because they provide the media through which students and teachers can have conversations that lead to shared understandings of the values and standards for student performance.

Forms of Performance Assessment

The power of assessment to assist in bringing about reform derives in part from the nature of new performance-based assessments that model challenging learning activities for students. Performance assessments (sometimes also referred to as *authentic* or *alternative* assessments) differ from traditional short-answer paper-and-pencil assessments in that they take as the object of assessment the actual work that students (or teachers) do. Moreover, standards and curricular guidelines now being developed increasingly emphasize such activities as carrying out research, constructing arguments, and debating conclusions, rather than recalling facts and applying algorithms in solving well-structured problems. Like tasks or activities that individuals carry out in the real world, the performance tasks to be assessed are expected to encompass extended activities that allow for multiple approaches and a range of acceptable products and results. In contrast, traditional forms of assessment examine single problems that call for particular, circumscribed elements of knowledge and problem-solving skill (Resnick & Resnick, 1992).

Performance tasks often require collaborative effort rather than only individual work. Performance assessment tasks may also require students to write investigative reports and debate conclusions (as history/social science assessments in the California Learning Assessment System do) or to carry out inquiry projects in a chosen subject and create exhibitions that culminate in assessments in which students describe their projects to an audience and answer questions about them (Collins, Hawkins, & Frederiksen, 1990; Hawkins, Collins, & Frederiksen, 1990; McDonald, 1993). In other performance assessments, students solve open-ended problems in mathematics that include the application of knowledge and the building of mathematical models (Lesh & Lamon, 1992) or, as in the Arts Propel project in the Pittsburgh public schools, write critiques of their own ensemble musical performances (J. Waanders, personal communication, Nov. 1992). (For an excellent review of performance assessment activities being developed nationwide, see Mitchell, 1992.)

The new approaches to assessment also employ portfolios of student work, which include a collection of performances and products produced by a student over a school year or, in some cases, over several years. Portfolios contain work that students and/or teachers select according to a set of criteria. Because portfolios can include the full range of activities and projects the student has worked on, they provide useful evidence of the student's growth and development, as well as of the final levels of performance attained. Educators view portfolios as particularly valuable for the opportunities they give to students and teachers to reflect on a student's progress in a domain over a period of time. In assessment programs that rely on portfolios, students are often encouraged to consider what should go into their portfolios, why they have made their particular choices, and how their work has evolved over the period their portfolios cover (see, for example, Camp, 1992; Wolf, 1989).

A specific example of an extended, technology-enhanced performance assessment comes from a research project that Educational Testing Service (ETS) is carrying out in collaboration with the national Center for Technology in Education (Hawkins, Collins, & Frederiksen, 1990). At an alternative high school in New York City, students in a combined math/ science course are given a phenomenon in physics to explain, such as the motion of a projectile. They are provided with a computer simulation environment in which they can manipulate variables so as to carry out experiments leading to an explanation of the phenomenon. Students keep records of their reasons for doing experiments, their library search for information pertinent to the problem, their hypotheses and experimental designs for testing the hypotheses, and their final results. They generate data using the computer simulation and graph their data in multiple ways using computer facilities. They also write a report that integrates their results using an explanatory model. And finally, from the materials they have developed in their project, they prepare and give an exhibition of the project to their teachers and fellow students (as they would at a science fair). The exhibition includes a question-and-answer session and is videotaped. Overall, the project may take from one to several weeks to complete. All the performance records (students' process documents, written reports, recorded data and graphs, and videotaped exhibitions) are sources of evidence for the assessment.

Performance Standards

The power of assessment as a reform agent derives as much from the standards for performance used in evaluating work as from the value of performance tasks themselves as learning activities. Performance assessments must provide evidence about students' learning and performance in relation to established standards. It is this evaluative perspective on student performance that makes assessments particularly powerful vehicles for learning as well as sources of information for students, teachers, and other audiences. In the context of the larger goals for education reform, it is through standards that the educational community defines what is valued.

Standards for Knowing and Doing

What, then, are the performance standards students are to meet? Educators are currently developing new standards in many disciplines. Importantly, these standards include both the content and the processes that students are expected to master. Within such domains as history, mathematics, and science, educators are attempting to define the "big ideas" and central themes that are worth knowing, along with the key methods for working, thinking, and applying knowledge within those disciplines (see, for example, American Association for the Advancement of Science, 1989; National Council of Teachers of Mathematics, 1989).

California is one state that is currently developing standards for its performance-based assessment system. State assessment guidelines for students' mathematical problem solving include such factors as producing clear and coherent diagrams and explanations, communicating effectively, understanding important mathematical ideas and processes, and presenting strong arguments that include effective examples and counterexamples (California State Department of Education, 1989). The standards that are being developed, therefore, extend well beyond considering a student's knowledge of the mathematics needed to solve a particular problem.

Defining and Applying Standards

The importance of standards, however, lies not only in what the standards are but also in the processes of defining and interpreting them. Across the nation, teachers, parents, curriculum specialists, policymakers, and businesspeople are all reconsidering what students should know and be able to do. This process of grappling with, arguing about, and coming to agreement on what matters is itself central to advancing the goals of reform. Indeed, it has been argued that this very process may be an essential component of what teachers do when they implement a performance assessment in their school (Darling-Hammond, 1992) or participate in assessment design.

To be more specific, in the math/science assessment project referred to earlier, the researchers are learning about how performance standards are interpreted by a group of high school teachers. When these science teachers met with project researchers to consider how to score students' physics projects, they first surrounded themselves with actual student performance records. As a group, they then began generating a list of valued features for science projects, including such desired characteristics as "makes connections," "makes use of knowledge," "gives detailed graphs and explanations," "tests preconceptions and assumptions," "takes a reflective stance," "uses hypothetical thinking," and so forth. The list grew quite long, reaching twenty-six separate features they were looking for in projects. In suggesting features, they used the students' projects to identify examples of the kind of performance taken as evidence of the presence of each feature.

At the end of the day-long meeting, the science teachers took this long list home with them and, several weeks later, produced a scoring rubric in which they had organized the twenty-six features under the following three broad categories:

1. "Organization of Work—the work as a whole. Does it hang together? Does it make its point? Is it easily understood?"

2. "Understanding of Math/Science Ideas—using 'habits of mind' to explore and develop Math/Science ideas and concepts."

3. "Process Skills—used to develop evidence, transferable to other academic investigations."

There was a strong feeling among the science teachers that this activity of considering how to value performance was at the heart of what their school was about. It is a testimony to the quality of the rubric they developed that state education departments have requested copies of this scoring guide.

Another example is the research and development the ETS is doing for the California Learning Assessment System. Teachers from throughout the state are being brought together to design performance assessments that are to be embedded in the ongoing curriculum and to become part of a statewide assessment system. Using the state's curricular frameworks as guides, the teachers are designing learning activities that will reveal what students know and can do, as called for within those frameworks. As part of the design process, teachers are asking themselves how these activities can generate valued performances, and by what criteria teachers will judge the evidence these activities provide. Having to work back and forth between the design of the activities and the criteria by which performances and products will be judged requires teachers to consider from the beginning what they are trying to help their students accomplish. They consult state frameworks, model curriculum guides, and state scoring rubrics to ensure that what they design will contribute to the definition of statewide standards for student performance.

Transparency: What Good Work Looks Like

We have argued thus far that performance-based assessments provide a lever for reform because of their link to standards for student performance and because the evidence that is assessed is drawn from exemplary learning tasks and activities. More specifically, because they are designed to instantiate standards for student learning and performance, the new forms of assessment allow students to be evaluated with respect to valued goals and criteria. At the same time, assessments that invite students to demonstrate well-chosen "habits of mind" allow assessment itself to model and encourage valued activities and reflections on performance by students and teachers.

But achieving the goals of reform will require much more than creating new types of assessment activities and standards consistent with reform goals. Unless students and teachers genuinely come to understand what good work looks like and how they can foster it, the move to performance-based assessment will not succeed as a lever for change. The positive systemic effects of the performance assessments depend critically on the *openness* or *transparency* of the values and criteria used in those assessments.

What do we mean by transparency? To be transparent, an assessment must make students and teachers keenly aware of those characteristics of outstanding performance that exemplify shared values within the community and of the reasons these characteristics are valued. Criteria for outstanding performances do not become transparent simply by definition. Rather, they take on meaning the way most concepts do—by their use in describing instances and noninstances of the concept. Take, for example, one criterion for good writing: a sense of audience. Teachers and students learn what this "sense of audience" is by looking at writing and its effects (both intended and unintended) on its readers, and by discussing how particular examples meet or do not meet the criterion for "sense of audience."

Learning to describe performances is a social process in which meanings for concepts are negotiated between individuals and groups as they consider various performances in which the concepts may be found. Thus, the assessment system must provide examples of the ways values and criteria for good writing, painting, or scientific investigation are realized in actual performances at different levels of accomplishment. The system must also foster ongoing evaluation by teachers and students of their work in the light of these values, as well as continual refinement of the values themselves. An assessment system in which values and criteria are open and transparent is, by definition, a system in which these values and criteria are openly and widely disseminated and discussed.

Openness and transparency, then, are central requirements for an assessment system that can fuel education reform. What is evaluated in the assessment must reflect what is valued in student learning and, thus, what is emphasized in classrooms. Criteria and values become transparent to teachers and students, and to others who participate in the assessment system, both through materials (that is, examples, along with evaluations) and through multiple and varied opportunities to participate in the process of evaluation and reflection.

The goal of transparency is important precisely because it requires reflective practice. In order for the assessment to be transparent, students and teachers must participate in the process of understanding and valuing qualities of student performance. In addition, students and teachers must consider what kinds of tasks and projects allow students to develop and display the required qualities. For students, understanding and participating in the performance assessment process should encourage reflection on their own work—the personal style, strengths, and weaknesses it may reveal and the ways it can be improved. For teachers, understanding the performance assessment process should encourage reflection on their own and others' classroom practices and on ways to support students' development in a manner consistent with what is valued in the assessment system.

Conversations About Student Work

At the heart of assessment linked to reform are conversations about student work as evidence for learning and accomplishment. These conversations go on within and between school communities, and include all participants in the assessment system. They take place at the most informal level within classrooms, as teachers and students talk with each other about a piece of work in progress, and at completion, as students consult with each other about why and how to revise a joint project or as they reflect on their own progress over time in, say, history or physics. The conversations also take place when teachers share among themselves ideas for new assessment activities and their experiences with those activities already under way, and when teachers use student work as the basis for examining their own teaching and how it might change. The conversations occur when teachers work together in the construction and/or application of criteria to student work as they evaluate and score such work for assessments in their districts, regions, or states. The conversations occur as well when teams of people, including members of the larger community, make judgments about the quality of student work presented in public exhibitions of student accomplishment, or when teams of auditors review a school district's assessment process (Rothman, 1992). It is through inspecting, scoring, talking about, constructing, and internalizing standards for student work that communities come to agree on what constitutes good work.

It is only when educators, students, and the community develop a shared language about student work and a shared set of values and criteria that assessment can affect the larger educational system with the power and in the direction that reformers advocate. Thus, the design of a performance assessment system must involve many people. Teachers, in particular, must be enlisted as designers of tasks and rubrics, as scorers and judges of student work, and as central participants in the process of standards development. The task of designing and implementing an assessment system can become a catalyst for teachers, parents, and students to reconsider how valued habits of mind are acquired and how the achievement of standards can be demonstrated (Alverno College Faculty, 1979/1985).

Moreover, this activity of social construction should be an ongoing one, allowing for the constant renewal of the assessment system through the invention of new activities, the improvement of scoring frameworks, and the incorporation of new ideas about the goals of teaching and learning. Ideally, the resulting socially distributed assessment system will be a self-improving process for enriching the view of competence incorporated within the educational system.

To summarize, if assessment is to be linked with reform, all those involved in assessment's development must view it as a social process grounded in the following actions:

- Conversations about student work as evidence of learning and accomplishment

- Development of a common language for discussing learning, accomplishments, and standards
- Development of shared values and transparent criteria for evaluating student work

Given the foregoing analysis of the key characteristics of an assessment system that can be an instrument for educational change, how can technology be developed and used to promote the linking of assessment to reform? And if the development of a community of shared values is essential to this linkage, how can technology be enlisted to support its development?

Functions of Technology

As we see it, there are five central functions that technology can perform to help link assessment with education reform:

1. Support students' work in extended, authentic learning activities.
2. Create portable, accessible copies of performances and replay performances in multiple media.
3. Provide libraries of examples and interpretive tools.
4. Expand the community of assessment participants.
5. Publish selected student work and thus recognize accomplishments.

Supporting Extended, Authentic Learning Activities

Computer, communication, and video technologies support the kind of learning activities that link assessment and reform. The current dependence on text-based activities and products for student work limits both what students can do and the kind of evidence available for assessment. Technology can significantly broaden students' involvement in challenging, extended activities that require students' active participation and application of knowledge (Sheingold, 1991).

The technological possibilities include computer-based simulation tools; microcomputer-based laboratories; computer tools for representing knowledge and findings (such as graphing or drawing software); data analysis tools (such as video analysis software, spreadsheets, and statistics programs); writing and presentation tools; recording tools; tools that support collaborative inquiry and collaborative writing; databases that contain data and phenomena not otherwise available in the classroom (videodisc databases for example); and tools that facilitate remote collaboration (Sheingold, Roberts, & Malcom, 1992).

Creating Portable, Accessible Copies and Replayable Performances

In the past, and to a large extent in the present, performance assessment has been constrained in two ways. Either the work to be judged must be in written form, or the audiences/judges must be physically present to witness the performance or observe the products. Technology can help teachers and students overcome both of these hurdles.

MAKING WORK PORTABLE AND ACCESSIBLE. Technology allows the original versions of student work to take many different forms that include but go well beyond print media, including, for example, handwritten drawings and papers, group planning sessions, musical performances, demonstrations of mechanisms students have designed and/or built, question-and-answer sessions, student-developed computer programs or simulations, and students' reflective oral or written commentaries on their own or each other's work. Through photographs, videotape, film, audiotape, computer disks, and scanners, all these and many other forms of student work can be captured and preserved. Interactive multimedia formats can integrate many forms of information on one disk, and will become increasingly valuable for creating portfolios of student work in multiple media. Thus, technology permits assessments of products and processes that are not limited to text and writing.

Technology makes student work transportable to audiences and judges distant in time and place from the original performance or demonstration. And technology can ease problems of routing and transferring records of student work. The very physical problem of storing and moving around paper-based student portfolios from one year to the next is challenging to even the most inventive administrators. Technology can produce much less bulky versions of these portfolios, and ultimately network technologies will largely eliminate the need for physically transporting student work to be assessed. However, the portability of recorded performances will be a boon to students and educators only if the performances are easily accessible to all parties. Of equal importance to schools' possessing appropriate recording technologies, therefore, will be their careful construction of databases for holding and accessing recordings of performances. They will find it particularly important to create a user interface that will be accessible and understandable to the widest community of users.

Technological support will also be needed so that groups of system users can view recordings of performances together, for it is the social activity of interpreting performances in groups that leads to a common understanding of education's goals and standards. Group presentation technologies that will be needed include video image projection devices linked to a multimedia database. Groups using such a system should be able to access and replay a recorded performance, as well as to classify and annotate that performance.

MAKING PERFORMANCES REPLAYABLE. Analyzing and evaluating complex human performances such as students' presentations or teachers' lessons requires that the evaluators have multiple opportunities to observe the performances of interest, to develop and apply categories to these performances (we discuss this requirement more fully later in the chapter), and to reflect on the performances in relation to the categories. For these purposes, and also because analyses and judgments will often be made by several individuals in each case, it is very important for performances to be replayable. Conversations about student performance can be problematic if the performance is witnessed only once. Individual judges or audience members may have different recollections of what they saw or heard. And students or teachers who actually participated in the performance may have only a poor sense of how it affected others, because they were focused on moment-to-moment presentation issues. When performances are replayable, discussions about their merits can be significantly relieved of the burden of memory. If judges can see and/or hear again questionable parts of the performance, their discussions can focus appropriately on interpretation rather than on what actually occurred. For example, they may want to revisit a performance in order to view it with an alternative perspective. Videotape and audiotape technologies are most useful for these purposes.

OWNERSHIP AND ACCESS. In individual schools and school districts where performance-based assessment is taken seriously, one of its effects is to engage students in complex tasks and projects that become very important to them. Indeed, anecdotal reports from many districts around the United States reveal that, particularly where students are involved in creating, selecting, and reflecting on work in portfolios, the students value their work highly. They care about what they have accomplished, as do their teachers and parents, and because they prize it, they want to keep it.

This is just one aspect of the serious questions about ownership that can arise in regard to students' work. Who gets to have and keep the work students produce? For how long? If schools and districts need these records for accountability purposes, they cannot release them. Or can they? In most places, these debates are taking place on the assumption that there is only one right answer, since there is only one copy of the work. Here, again, is a place where technology (including such simple devices as copiers) can support a broader social ownership of and involvement in students' work. Without technological assistance, ownership issues must be imperfectly and often (from someone's perspective) unhappily resolved. If the performance records use computer and video technologies, it will be important to think about how they can be made accessible to all. Schools, public libraries, and community centers may all need to provide equipment and services for making student work more broadly accessible.

Providing Libraries of Examples and Interpretive Tools

The third important role for technology in making assessment a tool for reform is helping people to build and apply interpretive frameworks for viewing performance (Frederiksen, 1992). Consider for a moment the problem of interpreting a videotape of a student's exhibition of a science project. The videotape shows the student explaining the purpose of her project, the approach she took in undertaking it, how she dealt with problems that came up, and her findings and interpretations of them. The tape also shows how she made sure that her audience is following her ideas and how she answered questions from her teachers and peers. A judge evaluating the exhibition will view a continuous flow of events, activities, and remarks. Many things will be going on all at once, at many levels. There will be multiple aural and visual cues. A novice evaluator will be in essentially the same position as a novice student of botany or archaeology looking for the first time at a set of botanical specimens or a collection of fossils.

John Audubon is reported to have said that to train a naturalist, one first has "to teach him how to see." Seeing that differentiates among things seen requires an interpretive framework or conceptual model that serves as a lens to permit that differentiation between critical features of specimens or fossils or, in this case, aspects of a student's project exhibition. Moreover, the process of seeing and categorizing is knowledge based (Medin, 1989), and communication about what is seen, whether botanical specimens or performances, depends on a socially shared interpretive framework. The concepts and categories used derive their meaning from the collection of exemplars—ideal models—to which they refer (Brown, Collins, & Duguid, 1989). Thus, an interpretive framework is developed from looking at and discussing exemplars of the class of items to be interpreted, and the framework is then learned when groups of people apply it to interpret new instances of that class of items.

The challenge for technology, therefore, is to create tools to help teachers and students and other participants in the assessment system develop shared interpretive frameworks for perceiving and communicating about learning and teaching. Such tools should include multimedia databases or libraries of performance exemplars that illustrate aspects of performance against an interpretive framework and that groups of teachers, students, or community members can study to learn how to interpret and evaluate student performances (Frederiksen & Collins, 1989).

To help people learn how to apply existing frameworks, the exemplar library should include a set of interpreted or scored performances, along with rationales for why they were scored as they were. These performances should be chosen to provide clear-cut and contrasting positive and negative examples for each of the assessment concepts to be employed. Groups of teachers or students can then learn to categorize these exemplars in the same way they are classified within the library. The group approach allows the meaning of assessment concepts to emerge from conversations about performance and its interpretation.

These exemplars may be used for different purposes by teachers, expert assessors, parents, and other participants in the assessment system. Expert assessors will need to go beyond the study of the clear-cut exemplars in order to learn to score so they can achieve high levels of agreement with other experts. For purposes of classroom instruction and school-community discussions, however, teachers, students, and parents may use the library to develop an understanding of the assessment concepts and how they are manifested in performance.

The technology should also include software tools for annotating and interpreting student projects in accordance with the interpretive framework. These tools will be useful to teachers in grading students' projects and for communicating appraisals to students. Teachers may also use these tools for creating their own libraries of exemplars to document performance assessment tasks they and their students have developed and to show others their view of how important educational goals can be demonstrated. Tools for building libraries of examples should include tools for video editing and for creating multimedia databases so that teams of teachers can create alternative interpretive frameworks that they can propose to others as ways of improving the assessment system.

Expanding the Community of Participants

If the link between assessment and reform is to have large-scale impact, the community of participants involved in creating and discussing the assessments and evaluating and interpreting students' work must be very large. Networking or interactive telecommunications technologies are key elements for the expansion of this community. First, these technologies enable teachers and students to develop and share assessment activities and experiences across time and space. Second, they establish scoring comparability within the wider community. Third, they foster the enrichment and evolution of the assessment system itself.

DEVELOPING AND SHARING ASSESSMENT ACTIVITIES. It will be very important for participants, particularly teachers, to be able to discuss, share, argue about, and swap assessment ideas informally with other teachers who have similar expertise and interests and who teach students at comparable grade levels. Because these teachers will often be either physically distant or hard to reach in real time, networking technologies can play a major role in supporting these teacher conversations. Other teacher-based networks have proven very helpful in promoting teachers' development and supporting their involvement in project-based classroom activities (Riel, 1990; Ruopp, Gal, Drayton, & Pfister, 1993), and the network approach should prove successful with assessment as well. A database of libraries of performance examples and student work that teachers can access should be part of this telecommunications system.

Students as well as teachers will use the system to access and share assessment activities. The network will also serve as a browsing tool to help students choose, with the help of their teachers, appealing project ideas, courses, or research options. It can also support collaborative work among students in remote locations.

ESTABLISHING COMPARABILITY OF SCORING. The success of a large-scale and widely distributed assessment system will depend in part on the ability of groups of teachers in separate locations to provide comparable scoring of student performance. To maintain such calibrated scoring, teachers must have opportunities to evaluate previously assessed performances from each other's districts and then to discuss any differences in their independent assessments in order to reach a consensus in their scoring methods. Applying such techniques of social moderation across districts requires technology that allows teachers to share performance recordings and appraisals. It also requires network technology to support the ensuing conversations and software to support collaborative video analysis, collaborative access to a database, and video teleconferencing. The database should support graphical and statistical comparisons among different groups' scoring of multiple performances. These comparisons will alert scorers to tasks that require discussion and moderation.

FOSTERING THE ENRICHMENT AND EVOLUTION OF THE ASSESS-MENT SYSTEM. Enrichment of an existing assessment system occurs through teachers' introducing new ideas for assessment activities and new ways to interpret students' performance within an existing interpretive framework. Evolution occurs through the introduction of new values and perspectives into the system by system users. Interpretive frameworks must be considered social documents that will undergo modification over time.

Publishing Good Work on the Network

When many teachers are working together to create engaging and challenging assessment tasks for students, and students are producing increasingly impressive work, there must be more ways than there are now to recognize and disseminate what teachers and students have accomplished. For teachers, we envision a technology-based system in which they submit assessment tasks that they have designed and tried in their own classrooms, along with scoring rubrics and evidence as to the value of the tasks. These materials are reviewed by committees of colleagues, and those deemed acceptable for publication are published on the network as valuable tasks for other teachers to use in their classrooms. Teachers whose tasks are published can cite this as an accomplishment on their résumés and include it in their portfolios. Of course, teachers could share tasks informally as well.

Similarly, students should have access to the same telecommunications system for publishing work that they have produced and that committees of students have reviewed and selected. Students could create journals for presenting their research, writings, or artwork. To the extent that these publications increasingly reflect larger and more diverse populations of students, they will provide both inspiration to other students about what to aim for and an interesting barometer of how much improvement there may be in students' best work. For students, too, having work published on the system will be a citable achievement that can be included in their portfolio of accomplishments. Journals can provide a means for celebrating good work, and publications can be used as credentials for the workplace and for higher education.

Conclusion

We have argued that for assessment to be a significant tool of school reform, more is required than changing the form of the assessment and changing the standards by which students' work is assessed. Although these are critical changes, they are not likely by themselves to produce the kind of impact needed. An assessment system that can productively advance reform goals for student learning must be, in the first instance, a widely shared social system, in which large numbers of students, teachers, and community members participate. As we have described, it must be grounded in conversations about student work as evidence of learning and accomplishment; in the development of a common language for discussing learning, accomplishments, and standards; and in the development of shared values and transparent criteria for evaluating student work.

Technology can promote the linking of assessment with reform by supporting the development, functioning, and expansion of this social system. Specifically, technologies must be enlisted, designed, and developed that allow people in the system to engage in more authentic and complex learning activities, to have portable and replayable copies of student achievements, to use libraries of examples and tools for interpreting student work, to expand the assessment community by enlisting more participants, and to publish selected works.

Although many of the technologies that will be optimal to support an assessment system linked to reform are not yet available (or not widely so), simpler technologies are at hand that can fulfill some of the requirements we have described. Clearly, however, a serious development and research effort is required to create the kind of technological infrastructure we are urging.

Unfortunately, there is not yet a widespread understanding of the critical need teachers and students will have for technological support when they see an assessment system that is an agent of reform. Currently, many educators and test developers think of technology only as a tool for actually *doing* the assessment, for administering tests, scoring them, and reporting results. In the system we envision, technology will make it easier for the many participants in the system to communicate, to use and refine their judgment, to access a rich database of student work, and to have lively and productive conversations about that work as evidence of student learning. Functioning in these areas, technology can indeed help to improve teaching and learning.

REFERENCES

Alverno College Faculty. (1979/1985). *Assessment at Alverno College* (rev. ed.). Milwaukee, WI: Alverno College.

American Association for the Advancement of Science. (1989). *Science for all Americans: A Project 2061 report on literacy goals in science, mathematics, and technology.* Washington, DC: Author.

Brown, J., Collins, A., & Duguid, P. (1989). Situated cognition and the culture of learning. *Educational Researcher, 18*(1), 32–42.

California State Department of Education. (1989). *A question of thinking: A first look at students' performance on open-ended questions in mathematics.* Sacramento: Author.

Camp, R. (1992). Assessment in the context of schools and school change. In Hermine H. Marshall (Ed.), *Redefining student learning: Roots of educational change* (pp. 241–263). Norwood, NJ: Ablex.

Collins, A., Hawkins, J., & Frederiksen, J. (1990, April). *Technology-based performance assessments.* Paper presented at symposium on technology-sensitive performance assessment, annual meeting of the American Educational Research Association, Boston.

Darling-Hammond, L. (1992, April). *Reframing the school reform agenda.* Invited address given at the annual meeting of the American Educational Research Association, San Francisco.

Frederiksen, J. (1992, April). *Learning to "see": Scoring video portfolios.* Paper presented at the annual meeting of the American Educational Research Association, San Francisco.

Frederiksen, J., & Collins, A. (1989). A systems approach to educational testing. *Educational Researcher, 18*(9), 27–32.

Hawkins, J., Collins, A., & Frederiksen, J. (1990). Interactive technologies and the assessment of learning. In *Proceedings of the UCLA Conference on Technology Assessment: Estimating the future.* University of California, Los Angeles.

Lesh, R., & Lamon, S. (Eds.). (1992). *Assessment of authentic performance in school mathematics.* Washington, DC: American Association for the Advancement of Science.

McDonald, J. P. (1993). Three pictures of an exhibition: Warm, cool, and hard. *Phi Delta Kappan, 74*(6), 480–485.

Medin, D. (1989). Concepts and conceptual structure. *American Psychologist, 44,* 1469–1481.

Mitchell, R. (1992). *Testing for learning: How new approaches to evaluation can improve American schools.* New York: Free Press.

National Council of Teachers of Mathematics. (1989). *Curriculum and evaluation standards for school mathematics.* Reston, VA: Author.

National Council on Education Standards and Testing. (1992). *Raising standards for American education: A report to Congress, the Secretary of Education, the National Goals Panel, and the American people.* Washington, DC: Author.

National Governors' Association (1990). *Educating America: State strategies for achieving the National Education Goals.* Washington, DC: Author.

Resnick, L., & Resnick, D. (1992). Assessing the thinking skills curriculum: New tools for educational reform. In B. Gifford & M. O'Connor (Eds.), *Changing assessments: Alternative views of aptitude, achievement, and instruction* (pp. 37–75). Boston: Kluwer.

Riel, M. (1990). Cooperative learning across classrooms in electronic learning circles. *Instructional Science, 19,* 445–466.

Rothman, R. (1992). Auditors help Pittsburgh make sure its portfolio assessment measures up. *Education Week, 11*(40), 27–28.

Ruopp, R., Gal, S., Drayton, B., & Pfister, M. (Eds.). (1993). *LabNet: Toward a community of practice.* Hillsdale, NJ: Erlbaum.

Sheingold, K. (1991). Restructuring for learning with technology: The potential for synergy. *Phi Delta Kappan, 73*(1), 17–27.

Sheingold, K., Roberts, L. G., & Malcom, S. M. (Eds.). (1992). *This year in school science 1991: Technology for teaching and learning.* Washington, DC: American Association for the Advancement of Science.

U.S. Congress, Office of Technology Assessment. (1992). *Testing in American schools: Asking the right questions* (Summary). Washington, DC: Office of Technology Assessment.

Wolf, D. (1989). Portfolio assessment: Sampling student work. *Educational Leadership, 46*(7), 35–39.